MW00613631

A World Trading System for the Twenty-First Century

The Ohlin Lectures

See https://mitpress.mit.edu for a complete list of titles in this series.

A World Trading System for the Twenty-First Century

Robert W. Staiger

The MIT Press
Cambridge, Massachusetts
London, England

© 2022 Massachusetts Institute of Technology

This work is subject to a Creative Commons CC-BY-NC-ND license.

Subject to such license, all rights are reserved.

The MIT Press would like to thank the anonymous peer reviewers who provided comments on drafts of this book. The generous work of academic experts is essential for establishing the authority and quality of our publications. We acknowledge with gratitude the contributions of these otherwise uncredited readers.

This book was set in Palatino LT by Westchester Publishing Services. Printed and bound in the United States of America.

Library of Congress Cataloging-in-Publication Data
Names: Staiger, Robert W., author.
Title: A world trading system for the twenty-first century / Robert W. Staiger.
Description: Cambridge, Massachusetts : The MIT Press, [2022] | Series:
    Ohlin lectures | Includes bibliographical references and index.
Identifiers: LCCN 2022000723 (print) | LCCN 2022000724 (ebook) |
    ISBN 9780262047302 (hardcover) | ISBN 9780262371292 (pdf) |
    ISBN 9780262371308 (epub)
Subjects: LCSH: International economic relations. | Commercial treaties. |
    Foreign trade regulation. | Foreign trade regulation—Developing
    countries. | Globalization.
Classification: LCC HF1365 .S73 2022 (print) | LCC HF1365 (ebook) |
    DDC 337.1—dc23/eng/20220310
LC record available at https://lccn.loc.gov/2022000723
LC ebook record available at https://lccn.loc.gov/2022000724

10 9 8 7 6 5 4 3 2 1

To Sally, again

And in memory of my father, David S. Staiger,
February 2, 1928–December 10, 2019

Contents

Preface

The multilateral trading system is in trouble. Governed by the World Trade Organization (WTO), which came into existence in 1995 and builds on and extends the principles of its twentieth-century predecessor agreement, the General Agreement on Tariffs and Trade (GATT), this system of global trade rules is facing a growing list of twenty-first-century challenges that include the rise of large emerging markets led by China, efforts to address climate change, the growing importance of digital trade, the rise of offshoring and global value chains, and the push for regulatory harmonization as an end in itself. These challenges reflect changes in the global economy that have occurred in recent decades, and they raise questions about the legitimacy of the GATT/WTO as the arbiter of global trade rules. Is the WTO, an institution that has traditionally been about "shallow integration" with a focus on trade impediments imposed at the border rather than on "deep integration" that results from direct negotiations over behind-the-border measures, capable of meeting these challenges? Or do we need a new global trade order for the twenty-first century?

In this book I address these questions, arguing that the best hope for creating an effective world trading system for the twenty-first century is to build on the foundations of the world trading system of the twentieth century. I construct this argument in two steps: first, by developing an understanding of why GATT worked and the economic environment it is best suited for (part I), and second, by evaluating from the perspective of this understanding whether the changes in the global economy that have occurred in recent decades imply the need for changes in the design of the GATT/WTO (part II). Throughout I adopt the view that design should reflect purpose, and that identifying the fundamental purpose of a trade agreement in a given economic environment—that is, what problem the agreement should solve for

the member governments—is essential to understanding its appropriate design in that environment. Building on these steps, I argue that
the terms-of-trade theory of trade agreements provides a compelling
framework for understanding the purpose of a trade agreement in
the twentieth century and the success of GATT. I further argue that
according to this understanding, the logic of GATT's design features
transcend many, though not all, of the current challenges faced by the
WTO (part III).

Two overarching themes emerge from the research that I describe
in this book. A first theme is this: Trade agreements that lack deep-
integration provisions are not necessarily "weak" agreements; by the
same token, those trade agreements that contain the most developed
deep-integration provisions should not necessarily be seen as the "gold
standard." Indeed, I contend that where the terms-of-trade theory
is applicable the opposite may be closer to the truth, as shallow-
integration agreements then hold out the possibility that countries
could reach the international efficiency frontier without sacrificing
national sovereignty.

A second theme is more subtle. To a first order, when it comes to
trade agreements, it could be said that the primary task of national
governments during the GATT era was to dismantle the excessively
high trade barriers of the large industrialized countries and to move
the world from a starting point far away from the international efficiency frontier to a position on the frontier—or in the language of
the terms-of-trade theory, to escape from a terms-of-trade-driven prisoner's dilemma. By the end of the twentieth century much, though not
all, of this task had been completed. For the twenty-first century, by
contrast, it could be said that while in many ways the fundamental
problem for trade agreements to solve has not changed, the primary
task for the WTO has shifted away from helping governments traverse *to* the efficiency frontier and toward providing them with the
flexibility they need to remain *on* the frontier in the face of various
shocks to the world trading system, including the rise of China and
the large emerging economies, the digitalization of trade, and the rising threat of climate change. For this era, how well countries are able to
rebalance and renegotiate their commitments within the GATT/WTO
framework is likely to become paramount to the WTO's success. I argue
that in principle, the GATT/WTO is as well equipped for this second task as the GATT proved to be for the first task. And while the
rise of offshoring and global value chains and the push for regulatory

harmonization as an end in itself may reflect a change in the purpose of trade agreements and therefore present more fundamental challenges to the GATT/WTO approach, I argue that there is still a strong case for building on the GATT/WTO foundation to address these particular twenty-first-century problems where they arise.

In short, the message of this book can be summarized as follows: The best advice for designing a world trading system for the twenty-first century may not be Facebook founder Mark Zuckerberg's famous motto "Move fast and break things," but rather Britain's now-ubiquitous wartime slogan from World War II: Keep calm and carry on. With this advice I am not claiming that reforms to the world trading system are not needed, or that all is well at the WTO. But I am claiming that the basic architecture of the GATT/WTO—and of the GATT, in particular—is well suited to guide the design of the world trading system of the twenty-first century.

Part I and portions of part II are based largely on my 2016 Ohlin Lectures, presented September 27–28 in Stockholm. Some readers may notice that this book is larger and longer than other books in the Ohlin Lectures series. While the themes of my Ohlin Lectures are the same themes of this book, the intervening five years between those lectures and my writing of this book have allowed me to investigate various aspects of those themes in greater detail, and providing coverage of that additional research has added substantially to the book that I would have written in 2016.

Having described for readers what this book is, it is equally important to be clear about what this book is not. It is not a synthesis of the broader literature on trade agreements; instead, as it is built around my Ohlin Lectures, it is narrowly focused on my own work (mostly with coauthors). And it is not a book about US trade policy or the trade policy of any other country for the twenty-first century; rather, it is about whether the existing multilateral trade rules can provide an environment where countries with heterogeneous tastes and circumstances can best choose their trade policies to achieve their objectives in the twenty-first-century global economy.

While writing this book I have benefited from the input of many people. I thank Jim Anderson, Emily Blanchard, Davin Chor, Caroline Freund, Matthew Grant, Sally Kraft, Yotam Margalit, Fernando Parro, Dani Rodrik, Veronica Terriquez, Weihuan Zhou, and seminar participants at the WTO for many helpful comments and discussions, and the 2021 class of Fellows at Stanford's Center for Advanced Study in the Behavioral Sciences (CASBS) for helpful feedback. I am particularly grateful to Kyle Bagwell, Chad Bown, Henrik Horn, Bob Keohane, Michele Ruta, Alan Sykes, and several anonymous reviewers for detailed comments. I am also grateful to CASBS for providing a productive atmosphere, despite the COVID-19 pandemic, during the period over which this book was drafted. Winston Chen and Paul Hager provided outstanding research assistance during the preparation of this book. And of course, I extend my gratitude to those at the Stockholm School of Economics who hosted me during my Ohlin Lectures and provided the impetus for writing this book.

1 Introduction

Individuals are the ultimate drivers of globalization, but governments set the rules of the game. And the rules can be very important to the outcome. This book is about the rules that guided the global economy of the twentieth century, how those rules came about, the logic of their design, their successes and failures, and whether they are adequate for the twenty-first century.

My focus is on the World Trade Organization (WTO) and its predecessor, the General Agreement on Tariffs and Trade (GATT). The WTO is where governments come to agree on the rules of globalization, or at least the multilateral rules that apply to all 164 member countries and their preferential trade agreements. These rules solve problems that would arise under "the law of the jungle," and they define the constitution of the global trade order.

The GATT/WTO is "member-driven," accepting the sovereign right of each country to define its policy preferences and seeking mutually advantageous trade liberalization as judged by the member governments. As an institution, the GATT/WTO has traditionally been about "shallow integration," with a focus on negotiations to reduce tariffs and other trade impediments imposed at the border rather than on direct negotiations over behind-the-border measures. And it has been very successful, hosting eight rounds of multilateral negotiations beginning with the first GATT (Geneva) Round of 1947 and culminating in the Uruguay Round that created the WTO in 1995. The commitments made in these GATT rounds helped to dismantle the web of highly restrictive trade protections that had been erected in the 1920s and 1930s, and ushered in a wave of globalization over the next 60 years that transformed the world economy. By the time the results of the Uruguay Round had been fully implemented, average tariffs on industrial goods had been reduced to below 4 percent on an ad valorem basis and quantitative

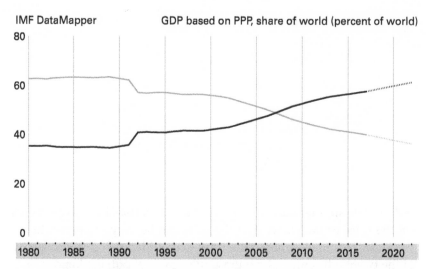

IMF DataMapper   GDP based on PPP, share of world (percent of world)

● Emerging market and developing economies   ● Advanced economies

Figure 1.1
The rise of emerging market and developing economies. Gross domestic product measured at purchasing power parity as a percent of world. *Source*: Created from IMF DataMapper with data from IMF (2017).

restrictions were largely eliminated (WTO 2007; Bown and Crowley 2016).

But during the last several decades the ground has shifted, and the WTO's Doha Round, begun in 2001 and now suspended, has disappointed. Two changes to the world economy stand out as emblematic of this shifting landscape.

First, the latest wave of globalization brought large emerging and developing countries, led by China, from the background of the world economy to its forefront. Figure 1.1 illustrates this reversal of relative importance by gross domestic product (GDP). In 1980, the emerging and developing economies accounted for 37 percent of the share of world GDP, with advanced economies making up the remaining 63 percent. By 2007, these shares were 50/50, and today the share of the world's GDP captured by emerging and developing countries is approaching 60 percent.

And second, with the rise of offshoring and global supply chains, the latest wave of globalization also changed the nature of trade itself. In the early years of GATT, international trade amounted to the international exchange of raw materials and finished or largely finished goods. Today, much of international trade consists of the movement

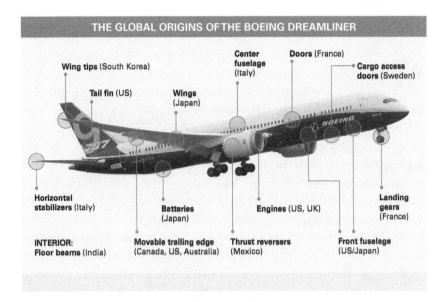

THE GLOBAL ORIGINS OF THE BOEING DREAMLINER

Wing tips (South Korea)

Center fuselage (Italy)

Doors (France)

Cargo access doors (Sweden)

Tail fin (US)

Wings (Japan)

Horizontal stabilizers (Italy)

Batteries (Japan)

Engines (US, UK)

Landing gears (France)

INTERIOR: Floor beams (India)

Movable trailing edge (Canada, US, Australia)

Thrust reversers (Mexico)

Front fuselage (US/Japan)

Figure 1.2
The rise of offshoring. *Source*: From Business Insider, https://www.businessinsider.com/. © 2017 Insider Inc.. All rights reserved. Used under license.

of parts and components and associated services from one country to another and back again for assembly, as exemplified by the sourcing decisions involved in the production of the Boeing Dreamliner illustrated in figure 1.2.

Against this backdrop, multilateralism is stumbling, and with it the WTO, whose legitimacy is being questioned as never before. Of course, the world also experienced four years of trade in the Donald Trump era, marked by the provocative and ubiquitous Trump trade tweets, of which figure 1.3 provides but one example. But the challenges faced by multilateralism in general and the WTO in particular are about something much more subtle—and far bigger—than Trump.

Recent decades have witnessed a clear evolution away from the shallow approach to integration pioneered by GATT and toward a preference for "deep" integration with a focus on the trade effects of regulations and other behind-the-border measures and increasingly with the goal of regulatory harmonization as an end in itself, as exemplified by regional and mega-regional negotiations (some ongoing, some completed, some failed) over the Transatlantic Trade and Investment Partnership (TTIP), the Comprehensive Economic and Trade Agreement

Figure 1.3

(CETA), and the Trans Pacific Partnership (TPP).[1] To a lesser extent, this evolution can also be seen in the transition from GATT to the WTO. China's entry into the world trading system, formalized with its 2001 accession to the WTO, has challenged an approach to globalization that was designed fundamentally with market economies in mind. More recently, the increasing importance of digital trade has made WTO rules, crafted in a largely pre-digital world, look out of date; and the world has witnessed a strong backlash within many countries against globalization itself, from those who have not shared in the gains and from those who feel that the sovereignty of their governments has

---

1. See Hofmann, Osnago, and Ruta (2017) for a database on the provisions contained in these kinds of agreements.

been eroded. Beyond these direct challenges, the increasing urgency of addressing climate change raises questions about the role that the WTO should play in this effort.

In the face of all these challenges, is multilateralism dead? In this book, I argue that the prognosis for multilateralism is not as dire as that, though I will suggest that the multilateralism the world has experienced over the past 75 years may be unusual and that multilateralism may now be entering a period of hibernation until more favorable conditions for its ascendancy once again return.

Do we need a new global trade order for the twenty-first century? That is difficult to say. But what seems clear is this: Meeting globalization's challenges in the twenty-first century will require a nuanced response capable of addressing multilateralism's current shortcomings, and to succeed we need a correct diagnosis of those shortcomings. For such a diagnosis, it is imperative to understand why GATT worked, the economic environment it is best suited for, and whether the changes in the economic environment in recent decades imply the need for changes in the design of the GATT/WTO or possibly a new approach to trade agreements altogether, or rather simply imply the need for better use of the agreements already in place. It is such an understanding that I attempt to provide in this book.

What's at stake? The future path of globalization is at stake. Which international institutions will set the rules of globalization is at stake. What trade-offs we will face in our globalized world is at stake. In short, the stakes of getting this right are very high.

In the rest of this chapter, I sketch in broad and intuitive terms the main themes that I will develop in greater detail in the rest of the book. While later chapters provide the technical detail necessary for the formal arguments that underpin many of the statements that I make in the book, my intent here is to provide an overview of these themes at a level that would be accessible to anyone with an undergraduate Economics 101 background.[2] As such, there are no equations in this chapter, and there is nothing beyond the bare minimum in terms of formal notation. Nor have I included in this chapter the qualifications that a careful treatment would demand or citations to the relevant literature (beyond citations for a reproduced figure or quotation): those too will come in later chapters. Instead, this chapter is composed only of words, graphs,

---

2. Indeed, the material in section 1.1 comes from a pair of public lectures I gave in Calgary (the 2018 Dr. Frank Anton Distinguished Lecture) and Turin (the 2018 Luca d'Agliano Lecture).

and a few plots of data to convey the main ideas. Readers uninterested in material developed in this way may wish to skim the rest of this chapter or skip ahead to chapter 2.

1.1 A Roadmap for the Book

I start with a key point: From the perspective of economics, the legitimacy of the WTO as an international institution is not built on the case for free trade; rather, it is built on the case for internalizing negative international policy externalities. This is an important point, because the case for free trade, while one of the most powerful insights in all of economics, relies on a set of special assumptions that are unlikely to hold in the real world across the WTO's diverse membership; and the case for internalizing negative externalities is far more general by comparison.

The Purpose of a Trade Agreement

To explain this point in simple terms, I begin here with the basics of industry-level supply and demand analysis in a closed economy. This is reproduced in figure 1.4, which with the quantity of good a

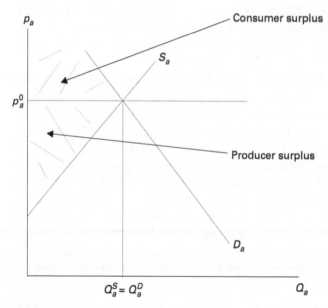

Figure 1.4
A closed economy.

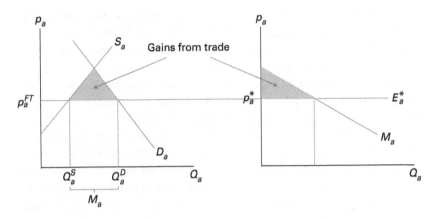

Figure 1.5
The gains from trade.

measured on the horizontal axis and its price measured on the vertical axis depicts a downward-sloping demand curve labeled D_a and an upward-sloping supply curve labeled S_a whose intersection determines the market-clearing price of good a in the closed economy, labeled p_a^0. Also depicted in figure 1.4 is the standard measure of economic welfare generated by this industry: the sum of consumer surplus (the area below the demand curve and above the market-clearing price) and producer surplus (the area above the supply curve and below the market-clearing price).

Suppose now that this country opens up to trade, and in particular that it is a small open economy trading freely with the world at a world price for good a that is below the closed-economy price p_a^0 depicted in figure 1.4. This situation is depicted in the two panels of figure 1.5.

The left panel of figure 1.5 displays the same information as figure 1.4—that is, the country's demand and supply curves for good a—but now with the lower price for good a that prevails in the country under free trade, p_a^{FT}. As the left panel depicts, at this lower free-trade price, the economy's quantity demanded for good a increases (we move down the downward-sloping demand curve) and its quantity supplied of good a decreases (we move down the upward-sloping supply curve), and the economy makes up its shortfall of supply relative to demand at the free-trade price by importing the difference, M_a, from the rest of the world. And at this lower free-trade price, the economy's consumer surplus has increased and its producer surplus has decreased relative to the closed-economy magnitudes depicted in figure 1.4, resulting in the net increase in consumer-plus-producer surplus depicted by the shaded triangle in the left panel of figure 1.5 and labeled "gains from trade." This is the classic welfare gain from free trade that is taught in every introductory economics course.

The right panel of figure 1.5 packages this information in a more compact form. This panel depicts the country's downward-sloping import demand curve (its quantity demanded minus its quantity supplied), labeled as M_a; it also depicts the foreign export supply curve that this small country faces, labeled as E_a^*, which is horizontal (infinitely elastic) at the world price p_a^* earned by foreign exporters. The gains from free trade are given in this panel by the shaded area under the country's import demand curve and above the world price. Finally, notice that the country's price of good a depicted in the left panel of figure 1.5, p_a^{FT}, is the same as the world price depicted in the right panel of figure 1.5, p_a^*, reflecting the fact that in figure 1.5 the country trades freely in good a with the world.

Now suppose that this country places a tariff τ_a on its imports of good a. This will not alter the world price of good a, p_a^*, owing to the small size of the country under consideration and the fact that it is therefore a price taker on world markets. But the tariff will raise the domestic price of good a to a price above p_a^{FT} (say p_a^1), and the implications are depicted in the three panels of figure 1.6.

The top left panel of figure 1.6 depicts the changes in welfare that are brought about by the imposition of the tariff. Because the tariff has increased the domestic price of a, consumer surplus in the economy is reduced, from the area below the demand curve and above the free-trade price p_a^{FT} to the smaller area below the demand curve and above the higher, tariff-distorted price p_a^1. By itself, this reduction in consumer surplus is unambiguously bad for the country. But there are two offsetting effects that also need to be considered.

First, producer surplus rises with the higher domestic price of a, from the area above the supply curve and below the free-trade price p_a^{FT} to the area above the supply curve and below the tariff-distorted price p_a^1: The implied redistribution of surplus from domestic consumers to domestic producers in industry a is given by the shaded trapezoid in the top left panel of figure 1.6. Depending on how the country feels about this redistribution (e.g., is it worth it to have consumers pay higher prices for good a and give up some consumer surplus so that producers of good a can earn higher incomes, assuming that a better way to help producers of good a cannot be found?), it could be either

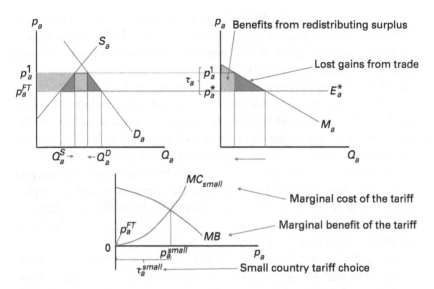

Figure 1.6
A small country's unilateral tariff choice.

a good thing for the country or a bad thing or neutral. And second, some of the lost consumer surplus is converted into tariff revenue: The implied conversion of consumer surplus into tariff revenue is given by the shaded rectangle (with dimensions $\tau_a \times M_a$) in the top left panel of figure 1.6. Depending on how the country feels about the conversion of consumer surplus into tariff revenue (e.g., is it worth it to have consumers pay higher prices for good a so that tariff revenue can be collected to fund the provision of public goods, assuming that a better way to fund government services cannot be found?), this could also be either a good thing for the country or a bad thing or neutral.

Finally, there *is* a portion of the lost consumer surplus that simply disappears, as measured by the two triangles of shaded area in figure 1.6: This is the "dead-weight" efficiency loss associated with the tariff, and it forms the crux of the economist's case for free trade. If the redistributions of surplus caused by the tariff that I have described are not valued by the country—that is, if consumer surplus, producer surplus, and tariff revenue are all valued by the country in the same way so that their distribution across these three components is irrelevant to the country's overall welfare—then all that the country has accomplished with a tariff is to create dead-weight efficiency loss and thereby hurt itself by reducing its gains from free trade. This case can be seen directly from the top right-hand panel of figure 1.6, where the shaded triangle represents the lost gains from trade associated with the imposition of the tariff, with the shaded trapezoid then representing the (smaller) gains from trade that remain. In this case, it is clear that free trade would be the best (welfare maximizing) policy for the country.

On the other hand, if the country *does* value the redistribution of surplus it has orchestrated with its tariff, then the size of the shaded trapezoid depicted in the top right panel of figure 1.6 *understates* the value of the country's gains from trade under the tariff, because it overstates the value to the country of the lost consumer surplus and understates the value to the country of the gains in producer surplus and/or tariff revenue. In this case, as a result of this redistribution the welfare that the country experiences with the tariff could then be larger than the welfare that it experiences under free trade.

The upshot is that the country may gain from a tariff because of the redistributive effects of the tariff, but there is also an efficiency cost that has to be weighed against any such gain. This trade-off is depicted in the bottom panel of figure 1.6, which displays the domestic price of good a on the horizontal axis and the marginal benefit and marginal cost to the country of a higher tariff—and therefore of a higher domestic price of good a—on the vertical axis. As depicted, the marginal cost of the tariff is increasing as the tariff rises above free trade (zero) and the domestic price p_a rises above the free-trade price $p_a^{FT} = p_a^*$, reflecting the increasing size of the dead-weight loss triangles depicted in the top panels of figure 1.6 that would occur as the tariff (and hence the domestic price of good a) is increased. And in this bottom panel, I have illustrated the case where the country does indeed value the redistribution of surplus triggered by its tariff but does so at a decreasing rate, which then implies that the marginal benefit of the tariff starts out at a strictly positive level and declines as the tariff is raised to higher levels. The optimal tariff choice for this country is determined where the marginal benefit curve crosses the marginal cost curve in the bottom panel of figure 1.6, and I have labeled this tariff choice τ_a^{small} to reflect the fact that I am considering here a country that is small in world markets.

I now come to a crucial observation: If it is accepted that each country has the sovereign right to define its own preferences over its policy choices, and if the country under consideration chooses the tariff τ_a^{small} unilaterally as I have depicted the country does in the bottom panel of figure 1.6, and if all other countries of the world are also small in world markets and make analogous unilateral tariff choices given their policy preferences, then these tariff choices will be *internationally efficient* relative to the policy preferences of each country, and there is nothing for a trade agreement to do! This is because, as figure 1.6 reflects for the country under consideration, each country will have then set its tariff at a level where the marginal benefit to the country of a slightly higher tariff would be just offset by the marginal cost to the country of a slightly higher tariff. And owing to the fact that the country is small on world markets so that its tariff choice does not impact the world price p_a^*, the tariff revenue associated with τ_a^{small} will be collected entirely from the country's own consumers, who face higher domestic prices, *not* from foreign exporters. As a consequence, there are no benefits or costs of the country's slightly higher tariff that would be borne by the rest of the world—and hence *no international externalities associated with its tariff choice*—ensuring that each country's unilaterally optimal tariff choice will then also be optimal from the point of view of the world as a whole.

Evidently, the world I have just described could be riddled with tariffs, and yet there is nothing that a trade agreement could—or should—do about this. What, then, is the purpose of the trade agreements that we observe? One possibility is that, while countries have the sovereign right to define their own policy preferences, they may have difficulty committing to policies that reflect these preferences, and they might then seek trade agreements as external commitment devices to help them avoid the temptation to choose trade protection. I will return to this possibility at several points in later chapters.

But there is another possibility that becomes apparent once an assumption that I have thus far maintained is relaxed—namely, the assumption that the country under consideration is small in world markets. To illustrate, I now revisit this country's unilateral tariff choice, but under the assumption that the country is *large* in world markets. This is illustrated in figure 1.7.

The key difference between the large-country tariff choice depicted in figure 1.7 and the small-country tariff choice in figure 1.6 can be seen by comparing the top right panels of each figure: The foreign export supply curve E_a^* is horizontal in figure 1.6 but it is upward sloping in figure 1.7, reflecting the fact that when the country under consideration is large it is not a price taker on world markets, and its tariff can therefore impact the world price p_a^*. Put differently, when the country under consideration is large, foreign exporters will accept a lower price p_a^* in

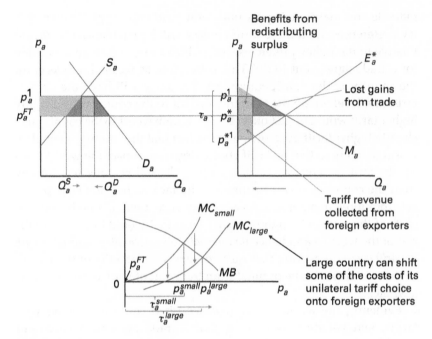

Figure 1.7
A large country's unilateral tariff choice.

the face of the country's tariff τ_a in order to continue to sell into the country's market. And this means that a portion of the tariff revenue collected by the country is collected not from its own consumers but from *foreign exporters*.[3]

The top right panel of figure 1.7 depicts the drop in the world price to p_a^{*1} that accompanies the increase in the country's domestic price to p_a^1 when the (now large) country imposes a tariff t_a on imports of good a. The tariff revenue collected from foreign exporters corresponds to the shaded rectangle between the free-trade world price p_a^* and the lower world price p_a^{*1} that prevails after the tariff has been imposed: The difference between p_a^* and p_a^{*1} is the amount of the tariff that foreign exporters "absorb" via a price drop on each unit of good a that they export to this country. This tariff revenue was not present in the small-country case depicted in figure 1.6 because in the small-country

3. While the Trump administration made a point of emphasizing the tariff revenue it collected from foreigners with its trade actions, several recent studies have cast doubt on this claim, at least if the tariffs are in place for only a short period of time. I discuss the findings of these studies in the context of the material presented in chapter 5.

case, foreign exporters are unwilling to lower their price in order to maintain sales in the small-country market, hence the infinitely elastic foreign export supply curve that the small country faces. The presence of this new source of tariff revenue has a key implication: As the bottom panel of figure 1.7 depicts, the tariff revenue collected from foreign exporters *offsets* to some degree the dead-weight efficiency costs to the country associated with its tariff, shifting down the marginal cost curve for the tariff of a large country relative to the marginal cost curve for a small country and leading to the *higher tariff choice* τ_a^{large}.

As a result, and independent of the underlying policy preferences of countries, the tariffs chosen unilaterally by large countries are *inefficiently high*, and they are inefficiently high because of the *negative international externality* that is created when a large country suppresses foreign exporter prices with its tariff increases, thereby shifting some of the costs of its tariff onto foreign exporters. The purpose of a trade agreement is, then, to internalize these negative policy externalities and thereby reduce tariffs and expand trading opportunities. By addressing these inefficiencies, it is possible for all countries to gain as judged by their own policy preferences from the mutually beneficial expansion of trade.

Clearly, the purpose of a trade agreement that I have outlined here—and the expectation that trade agreements expand trade volumes that derives from this purpose—has nothing to do with the case for free trade, since for my arguments to hold it is neither necessary nor sufficient that countries accept that the case for free trade applies to them. But to be relevant, these arguments do require that countries have market power (in the form of monopsony power to depress foreign exporter prices) and use it when making trade policy choices outside the confines of a trade agreement. Figure 1.8, reproduced from Broda, Limão, and Weinstein (2008), provides striking support for this position (I discuss in later chapters empirical evidence for this and related issues more thoroughly).

For 15 countries that were not at the time GATT/WTO members, figure 1.8 plots the country's median Harmonized System (HS) four-digit industry ad valorem tariff level (vertical axis) against the median of a measure of the country's market power across these four-digit industries (horizontal axis). The measure of market power is taken to be the inverse of the estimated industry-level foreign export supply elasticity faced by the country, with a truly small country that faces an infinitely elastic foreign export supply curve in an industry

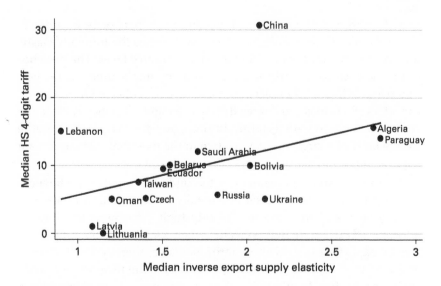

Figure 1.8
The relationship between market power and unilateral tariff choices. HS denotes Harmonized System product classification. *Source*: Broda, Limão, and Weinstein (2008, figure 3).

corresponding to a market power measure of zero. The fact that the 15 country data points are spread out along the horizontal axis in figure 1.8 over a range from 0.75 to 2.75 indicates that most countries, even seemingly "small" countries, possess significant market power in at least some industries. And the fact that figure 1.8 displays a strong positive relationship between market power and the tariff levels of the countries that wield it indicates that countries do indeed use their market power when setting tariffs outside the confines of a trade agreement.

The Architecture of the GATT/WTO
If the purpose of a trade agreement is to allow countries to internalize the negative international externalities of their trade policy choices, then the fundamental legitimacy of the GATT/WTO can be assessed with the answer to a single question: Is the GATT/WTO well-designed to serve this purpose?

Generally, designing an effective institution to address an international externality is exceedingly difficult (think climate change). But there is a particular structure to the international externality embodied in the arguments I have reviewed that makes this task more manageable in the case of a trade agreement, at least along some dimensions.

The structure that I am referring to is this: The international externality that is created when a large country suppresses foreign exporter prices with its tariff increases is a *pecuniary* externality, traveling through international prices and therefore *markets*. A pecuniary externality normally does not create an inefficiency, but it does when it is combined with market power, which the large-country condition ensures. And as this externality travels through markets, it can to some degree be shaped—and in principle mitigated—by specific features of institutional design that serve to alter the transmission mechanism of the externality, a feat that would be far more difficult if not impossible for international *nonpecuniary* externalities, such as those caused by an increase in the global carbon stock that are transmitted through the atmosphere.

What are the key features of GATT/WTO design? And can these features be seen to mitigate the international policy externality at the core of the problem for a trade agreement to solve? The two pillars of the GATT/WTO architecture are nondiscrimination and reciprocity. Nondiscrimination requires that tariffs abide by the most-favored-nation (MFN) principle, according to which imports of the same product from different countries face the same tariff in a given market. Reciprocity refers to an ideal of balanced changes in tariffs across countries whereby, as a result of these tariff changes, each country experiences a change in foreign access to its markets and implied import volume that is equivalent in value to the change in its access to foreign markets and implied export volume.

In a multicountry world, the MFN principle helps to keep the structure of the international trade policy externality as simple as in a two-country world. To see why, consider the discussion above regarding the purpose of a trade agreement. One way to interpret this discussion is from the perspective of a two-country world, where the importing country under consideration imports good a from a single foreign exporting country and imposes the tariff τ_a on imports of good a from that country. But the discussion is equally valid when there are many foreign exporting countries, provided that the country under consideration abides by MFN and imposes a single tariff τ_a on imports of good a independent of which foreign exporting country those imports come from, because in that case there is still just a single world price through which the international externality associated with the choice of τ_a will travel. This simplicity would be destroyed in a multicountry world if the MFN principle did not apply, because with the importing country imposing discriminatory tariffs, there would then be multiple world prices for good *a*—one for each foreign exporting country facing a distinct level of the tariff on its exports of good *a* to the importing country—and therefore multiple, distinct paths through which the international policy externality could travel.

With MFN preserving the simple structure of the international trade policy externality described above, can reciprocity then be seen as a way to mitigate these externalities? At a basic level the answer is "yes." This is because reciprocity defines a measured, *proportionate response* to a country's trade policy changes by its trading partners that *keeps each country facing the trade-offs of a small country* and thereby converts the logic of a large country's unilateral tariff choices depicted in figure 1.7 into that of a small country as depicted in figure 1.6. And for a member-driven institution, where what is important is not so much *what* policies are chosen by its members but rather *how* those policies are chosen, this feature goes a long way to explaining the appeal of the design of the GATT/WTO for addressing the international policy externalities of its member countries.

To see this, I return to the large-country tariff choice depicted in figure 1.7, but suppose now that the importing country under consideration understands that the foreign exporting country (or countries) will respond reciprocally to any tariff change that it initiates. Figure 1.9 illustrates the implications of this anticipated reciprocal tariff response from the foreign country.

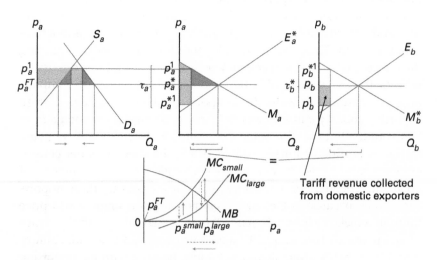

Figure 1.9
A large country's tariff choice in the presence of reciprocity.

The new element in the top panels of figure 1.9 relative to the top panels of figure 1.7 is contained in the top right-most panel of figure 1.9, which depicts a reciprocal tariff response by the foreign country on a good b that it imports from the country under consideration. This tariff response is labeled in the figure as τ_b^*. The response is *reciprocal* in that it corresponds to a measured, *proportionate response* to the tariff τ_a imposed by the importing country under consideration, and if calibrated to do so, the tariff τ_b^* can, for the foreign country, collect exactly the same amount of tariff revenue from its trading partner's exporters that its trading partner is collecting from its exporters with the tariff τ_a.[4] In figure 1.9, this equivalence is reflected by the fact that the area of the shaded rectangle in the top middle panel of figure 1.9, which represents the tariff revenue that the country under consideration collects from foreign exporters with its tariff τ_a, is equal to the area of the shaded rectangle in the top right-most panel of figure 1.9, which represents the tariff revenue that the foreign country collects from the exporters of the country under consideration with its reciprocal tariff response τ_b^*.

The implications of this tariff response for the tariff choice of the large importing country under consideration are depicted in the bottom panel of figure 1.9. As shown there, the ability of this country to collect (net) tariff revenue from foreign exporters—which caused the downward shift in the marginal cost curve of the large country's tariff relative to that of a small importing country, and which led to the inefficient unilateral tariff choices of the large country—is neutralized by the reciprocal tariff response of the foreign exporting country and the tariff revenue it collects from the exporters of this country, with the result that the large importing country under consideration faces the trade-offs of a small country and, like the small country, makes internationally efficient tariff choices.

In short, the legitimacy of the GATT/WTO as the multilateral institution that sets the rules of the global trade order can be defended on the grounds that its foundational principles of nondiscrimination and reciprocity are designed to induce large countries to make the tariff choices that they would make if they were small countries, and thereby to induce all countries to eliminate market power considerations from their tariff choices. By serving this function, it can be argued that the GATT/WTO helps its member governments solve the fundamental trade agreement problem and achieve the international efficiency frontier.

---

4. In chapter 4 (note 4), I confirm that this feature is implied by the definition of reciprocity that I introduced just above.

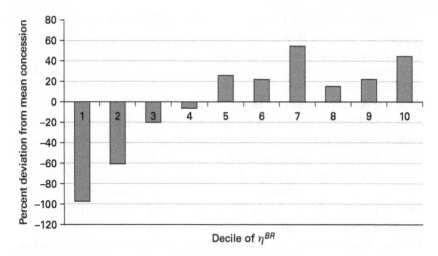

Figure 1.10
The relationship between market power and the tariff cuts that countries agree to when they join the WTO. *Source*: Bagwell and Staiger (2011, figure 2).

If the GATT/WTO serves this function, then the tariff cuts that countries agree to when they join the WTO should reflect these market power considerations, with larger tariff cuts occurring where market power is high. Figure 1.10, reproduced from Bagwell and Staiger (2011), provides support for this position, focusing on five countries that joined the WTO subsequent to its creation in 1995 (I discuss the findings of this paper in greater detail in chapter 3). In this figure, a measure of the market power wielded by each country at the six-digit HS industry level (denoted as η^{BR} in the figure) is used to distribute the products into 10 bins by decile of market power along the horizontal axis, with the lowest decile of market power on the left and the highest on the right; the tariff cuts (expressed as percent deviations from the mean tariff cut) that these countries agreed to when they joined the WTO are measured on the vertical axis. Figure 1.10 displays a strong positive relationship between market power and the tariff cuts that countries agree to when they become WTO members, consistent with the position that the GATT/WTO is indeed helping to induce large countries to make the tariff choices that they would make if they were small countries.

The implications of the GATT/WTO reciprocity principle can also be seen in the responses elicited by the tariff actions of the Trump administration on imported steel and aluminum. For example, in a March 2, 2018 article titled "Trump's Tariffs Prompt Global Threats of Retaliation," the *New York Times* described the European Union (EU) countermeasures in these terms:

The European Union detailed a three-step plan to penalize $3.5 billion of American trade—the same amount of European steel and aluminum the bloc estimates would be harmed by the planned tariffs. It proposed taxing American exports including bourbon, bluejeans, orange juice, cranberries, rice and motorcycles.... A European Union official said that the bloc had been preparing for the announcement for months and that everything was in place for a swift, proportionate response.

The reciprocal ("proportionate") tariff response of the EU is in line with the response envisioned under GATT/WTO rules to a unilateral increase in tariffs such as that initiated by the Trump administration. As figure 1.9 suggests, such a response prevents the United States from using these tariffs to increase the revenue that (on net) it collects from foreign exporters. And facing the trade-offs of a small country in the face of this reciprocal response, if the United States still wants to raise its tariffs, then according to the logic I have described, it is internationally efficient for it to be allowed to do so.

Notice too that, contrary to how it might appear, the US tariff action and the EU response described by the March 2 *New York Times* article do not, as far as they go, constitute the outbreak of a trade war. Rather, in limiting the EU's response to be in line with the reciprocity principle, this is how the GATT/WTO system works to *avoid* a trade war. The US Council of the International Chamber of Commerce (ICC) stated as much with regard to the novel role played by a fledgling GATT in 1955 when, in the context of US actions restricting trade in dairy products and European responses to those actions, it observed the following:

The Organization's control over countermeasures of this kind enables it to keep such measures within reasonable limits: to allow countermeasures commensurate with the action which occasions them; and to hold in check emotional reactions which might result in punitive measures by countries injured against the country responsible for the injury. The control over countermeasures is a check on the development of trade wars. (US Council of the ICC 1955)

From this perspective, what *does* look like the beginnings of a trade war was reported in the *New York Times* on March 3 with the headline "Escalating Trade Fight, Trump Threatens Higher Taxes on European Cars":

President Trump warned on Saturday that he would apply higher taxes on imported European cars if the European Union carried through on its threat to retaliate against his proposed stiff new tariffs on steel and aluminum. "If the E.U. wants to further increase their already massive tariffs and barriers on U.S. companies doing business there, we will simply apply a Tax on their Cars which freely pour into the U.S.," Mr. Trump wrote on Twitter from Florida, where he was spending part of the weekend. "They make it impossible for our cars (and more) to sell there. Big trade imbalance!..."

In the end, the EU did carry through on its threat to retaliate against the new US steel and aluminum tariffs with reciprocal tariff hikes of its own, and the threatened further US tariffs on imported cars from the EU were never imposed. So in this case, at least, where there was an initial unilateral trade action by the United States and a reciprocal response from its injured trading partner, that ended there, one could say that a trade war was averted—or, perhaps more accurately, especially when viewed alongside other trade actions of the Trump administration that I will return to later, that it was a "one-sided" trade war.

What about the shallow approach to integration that is the hallmark of the GATT/WTO? Can this feature of GATT/WTO design be seen as compatible with an institution whose purpose is to internalize the negative international externalities of the trade policy choices of its member countries? Could a shallow approach to integration ever hope to mitigate these externalities? Or should this approach be seen rather as a failing of the GATT/WTO, as a sign of institutional weakness, an inability to proceed sufficiently far in pursuit of globalization?

These are important questions, and their answers are complex. But there is one sense in which a clear foundation for GATT's shallow approach to integration can be seen in the arguments I have made: According to those arguments, at the dawn of the GATT, only trade policies, *not domestic policies*, would have been set inefficiently. This is because it is the tariff that most directly imposes the international externality that is responsible for the international inefficiency of unilateral policy choices, and it is therefore the tariff that bears the imprint of these motives. For this reason, an approach to integration that focuses on liberalizing tariffs and other border impediments to trade, with rules that prevent countries from introducing protective domestic measures as *substitutes* for tariffs once tariffs and other border measures have been constrained by the agreement, can in principle accomplish everything that a trade agreement needs to accomplish in order to implement internationally efficient policy outcomes. As I will describe in later chapters, this is essentially the approach that the GATT/WTO has taken. From this perspective, the underlying approach of the GATT/WTO can be seen as avoiding the sharpest conflicts between globalization and national sovereignty, and indeed as making domestic policy choices more effective, not less.

Finally, in describing the trade actions of the Trump administration with regard to imports of steel and aluminum, I noted that these actions, in combination with the reciprocal tariff response from the EU, did not constitute a trade war but were instead in line with the kinds of reciprocal tariff adjustments envisioned under the GATT/WTO design. To be clear, I was using this episode only to illustrate a specific point, not to make a blanket statement about the WTO-consistency of the Trump administration's world view of the ideal global trading system. In fact, while US dissatisfaction with the GATT/WTO has been building for some time and certainly did not start with the Trump administration, the Trump administration took US distaste for the WTO to a new level. For this reason, it is instructive at this point to compare the rules-based trading system of the GATT/WTO as I have described that system against the alternative global trade order envisioned by the Trump administration.

What was the Trump administration's vision for the global trade order? Wilbur Ross, then US secretary of commerce, in an opinion piece for the Wall Street Journal published on May 25, 2017, put it this way:

An ideal global trading system would facilitate adoption of the lowest possible level of tariffs. . . . [C]ountries with the lowest tariffs would apply reciprocal tariffs to those with the highest and then automatically lower that reciprocal tariff as the other country lowers theirs. This leveling technique could be applied product by product or across the board on an aggregated basis. Such a modification would motivate high-tariff countries to reduce their tariffs on imports.

And the vision articulated by Commerce Secretary Ross was echoed in various Trump tweets, such as the one reproduced in figure 1.11. Evidently, according to this vision, the purpose of trade agreements would be to achieve reciprocal free trade or, barring that, at least a "level playing field" across countries. And as for the means of achieving this purpose, the ideal global trading system, according to the Trump administration, would dispense with MFN and seek reciprocity in tariff *levels*, not in tariff changes as reciprocity works in the GATT/WTO and which I have illustrated in the previous figures.

When a country Taxes our products coming in at, say, 50%, and we Tax the same product coming into our country at ZERO, not fair or smart. We will soon be starting RECIPROCAL TAXES so that we will charge the same thing as they charge us. $800 Billion Trade Deficit-have no choice!

Figure 1.11

In short, the Trump administration's vision for the global trade order amounts to a "repeal and replace" strategy, as it poses an existential challenge to the pillars of the GATT/WTO architecture. It would abandon MFN. It would emphasize a form of reciprocity that is not found in the GATT/WTO. And in seeking global free trade as the ultimate goal, it would strike at the heart of what the GATT/WTO means when it says it is a "member driven" organization. At a minimum, this vision, expressed by a US administration in the early decades of the twenty-first century, illustrates the depth of the challenges that now confront the rules-based world trading system of the twentieth century.

The Role of Rules in a Rules-Based Global Trading System
I have argued so far that the key design features of the GATT/WTO are consistent with an institution whose purpose is to internalize the negative international externalities of the trade policy choices of its member countries. But what difference do these rules make anyway? While it seems clear enough that in the presence of these externalities countries can gain from negotiations over their trade policy choices, what would be lost if countries engaged in "power-based" tariff bargaining to address these issues without reference to any previously agreed-on rules?

Broadly speaking, the rules-based system of the GATT/WTO has two main potential advantages over a power-based approach to tariff bargaining. First, the rules of the GATT/WTO can *simplify* the tariff bargaining problem and make it manageable, which can help countries negotiate to efficient policies. And second, these rules can mitigate the power of the most powerful countries and, in so doing, encourage weaker countries that might otherwise be vulnerable to exploitation by the stronger countries to *participate* in the global trading system.

Regarding its simplifying role, I have noted that MFN simplifies the structure of the international policy externality that would otherwise arise in a multicountry world, ensuring that this externality continues to take the simple form that it would take in a two-country world. As for reciprocity, it can be seen to shape GATT/WTO tariff negotiations in two ways: It is a norm of negotiation when a tariff is to be reduced and bound at a lower level, and it is a rule that defines the threat point for renegotiation when a previously bound tariff is to be raised.

If countries abide rigidly by these norms and rules, reciprocity in combination with MFN affords a dramatic simplification of the tariff bargaining problem. This is because as a norm of negotiation, reciprocity fixes the terms of exchange of market access: If it has been previously agreed that the negotiations will abide by reciprocity, then the *terms of the deal are fixed*, with countries exchanging market access concessions and implied trade volumes *one for one*. And by defining the threat point for renegotiation, reciprocity indirectly determines the extent of market access that is exchanged through the implied requirement that this exchange is "voluntary"; that is, *the size of the deal is determined* by the negotiating party that wants the smallest deal at these terms, because if that party were pushed in the bargain to accept a bigger deal/lower tariffs than it wanted, it could always renegotiate subsequently to raise tariffs and—with reciprocity defining its threat point—in the end get the size of the deal it wanted anyway while preserving the reciprocal terms. And with the terms of the deal fixed and its size determined, there are no other dimensions of the deal left for countries to bargain over!

Regarding the role of GATT/WTO rules in mitigating the power of the most powerful countries, this role is obviously fulfilled if, as I have described above, countries rigidly abide by MFN and reciprocity in their tariff bargaining, since if under these rules and norms there is nothing left to bargain over, then there is clearly no room for the exercise of power in tariff negotiations. But even absent rigid adherence to these rules and norms, the ability of countries to exert their power in GATT/WTO tariff bargains is likely to be constrained. For example, even if not joined by reciprocity, the MFN requirement alone still dilutes the ability of a powerful country to enjoy the benefits of its power. This is because in exerting its power to secure for its exporters more-than-reciprocal tariff concessions from its bargaining partner, the nondiscriminatory nature of those tariff cuts will ensure that other exporting countries siphon off part of the gain.

The upshot is that the rules of the GATT/WTO tend to blunt the exercise of bargaining power. Why, then, would powerful countries accept these rules? One reason is that the efficiency gains from simplifying the bargaining may be sufficiently great that powerful countries can gain directly from the rules even as their ability to exert bargaining power is constrained. But there is also a further reason that powerful countries may see it in their interest to support a rules-based multilateral trading system: by making a commitment to adhere to these rules, powerful countries can help secure the participation of weaker countries that might otherwise fear exploitation, and *all* countries can gain as a result.

The Declining Hegemon

This last observation suggests that the most powerful countries may benefit from a rules-based multilateral trading system precisely because they *are* so powerful. This may help explain why the United States was, along with the United Kingdom, the champion of the rules-based system at its creation in 1947 with the birth of GATT.

But it is then also not hard to imagine that, if the position of the most powerful countries in the world trading system were to erode sufficiently, weaker countries might well choose to participate in trade bargaining even under a power-based system. And in that case, the powerful countries might then prefer to escape from the rules and pursue power-based trade bargaining with the weaker countries.

This raises the possibility that, with the rise of the large emerging and developing economies and the decline in hegemonic status that the United States has experienced in recent decades, support for the rules-based system could wane. Being far less dominant in the global economy than it was in 1947, the United States no longer needs international rules to help it commit not to exploit other countries in trade bargaining in order to convince those countries to engage in the global economy. And if the declining hegemonic position of the United States is indeed a primary cause of the challenges now faced by the rules-based multilateral trading system, to repair that system the world may have to wait for the rise of another hegemon. Along these lines and in the broader context of security and trade, historian/commentator Robert Kagan sees the rules-based international order as a historical anomaly made possible by US leadership, which is now collapsing and, as Erlanger (2018) puts it in his review of Kagan (2018), "returning the world to its natural state—a dark jungle of competing interests, clashing nationalism, tribalism and self-interest."

If this is the correct diagnosis, it is full of irony. According to this diagnosis, the design of the rules-based multilateral trading system has proved effective in solving an important and still-relevant problem, yet the system will inevitably collapse. And while China is seen by many as a source of some of the greatest challenges for the rules-based trading system of the twenty-first century, if this diagnosis is correct it may be that the rise of China is the world's best hope for the return of a viable rules-based multilateral trading system.

In any case, to the extent that this diagnosis does capture the main cause of the rules-based trading system's ills, there is great value in attempting to support, preserve, and improve the existing global trade order until such time as it can again thrive on its own. As noted previously, the fundamental design of the rules-based multilateral trading system has proved effective in solving an important and, by this diagnosis, still-relevant problem, and it should not be allowed to wither away. By this diagnosis, the shallow-integration approach of the GATT/WTO is well designed to solve the fundamental trade agreement problem. As such, a stark trade-off between sovereignty and globalization may be avoidable, but only if the WTO is supported and its approach strengthened. Could China be the next hegemon that the WTO is looking for? Currently, this may seem unlikely to many, but as its dominance grows, China may see that it is in its interest to more fully commit to these rules; until that time, according to this diagnosis, the WTO deserves broad support as the legitimate constitution of the global trade order.

The Implications of Offshoring

The rise of offshoring could provide an alternative diagnosis for the current challenges faced by the rules-based trading system, and one that is in some sense more dire than that implied by a declining hegemon. This is because in altering the nature of trade, offshoring may also have changed the nature of international price determination and the international policy externalities that are the source of the problem that the rules of the GATT/WTO are well designed to solve. And if this is the case, then in a world economy dominated by offshoring and global value chains, new and different rules may be needed to help countries address the novel international policy externalities that arise.

This can be seen most clearly with regard to the potential implications of offshoring for the efficacy of shallow integration. According to the arguments I have reviewed thus far, at the dawn of the GATT only trade policies, not domestic policies, would have been set inefficiently, because it is the tariff that most directly imposes the international externality that is responsible for the international inefficiency of unilateral policy choices. This statement holds for the nature of trade that dominated most of the twentieth century—that is, the international exchange of finished or largely finished goods and raw materials, where international prices are determined by the kinds of supply-equals-demand market clearing conditions that are featured in the figures described above. But when trade is dominated by specialized components, such as is the case with the production and assembly of the Boeing Dreamliner illustrated in figure 1.2, exchanged between sellers and buyers that have limited outside market options at the time that the exchanges occur, the prices at which these trades occur may be determined by bargaining, and novel impacts of trade and domestic policies on international prices can then arise. And as a result, even when they are not yet constrained by a trade agreement, all policies, both trade *and* domestic, may be set inefficiently. When this is the case, the foundation for the GATT/WTO shallow approach to integration no longer holds, and a deeper approach to integration may be needed to address the policy inefficiencies of the global economy.

It is therefore possible that the rise of offshoring has changed the nature of international policy externalities, and in doing so, it has made the shallow-integration approach of the GATT/WTO no longer suitable for solving the fundamental trade agreement problem. If this is so, then deeper forms of integration will be required to achieve internationally efficient policies, and a stark trade-off between sovereignty and globalization may now be unavoidable (and as I will discuss, something similar may be behind the push toward regulatory harmonization as an end in itself). But it is also possible that the rise of offshoring has *not* fundamentally changed the nature of international policy externalities, or has changed the nature of the policy externalities only temporarily, as offshoring itself may be a transitory phenomenon. Either way, it is difficult to see how "repeal and replace" could be the right strategy for arriving at an effective world trading system for the twenty-first century, as that strategy risks throwing the baby out with the bathwater and, by undercutting the WTO, undermining the best hope for a balance between globalization and national sovereignty. Instead, building on the GATT/WTO foundation to address these twenty-first-century problems where they exist seems like a sensible approach, even if the world trading system of the twentieth century is ultimately in need of a more fundamental overhaul.

The Stakes of Getting It Right

There would also be another implication of the demise of the WTO: the loss of an international institution that has built-in procedures for rethinking levels of market access commitments in an orderly, rules-based fashion. Through its reciprocity principle, GATT/WTO market access commitments are structured as "liability rules" that permit legal buyouts of previously agreed-on market access commitments whenever a country believes that its previous commitments to levels of market access are no longer serving its interests. As I will argue in later chapters, these and other built-in flexibilities may help the logic of GATT's design to transcend many of the current challenges faced by the WTO, including the challenges posed by China's economic model, the rise of large emerging and developing economies in the world trading system more generally, digital trade, and efforts to address climate change.

In short, in light of what has come before and what is at stake, the best advice for creating a world trading system for the twenty-first century may not be "Move fast and break things," but rather "Keep calm and carry on."

I   The World Trading System of the Twentieth Century

Over the next five chapters, I delve into the economic logic of the broad design features of the General Agreement on Tariffs and Trade (GATT), reviewing a body of research that seeks to understand the success of GATT in serving as the constitution of the world trading system of the twentieth century. In light of the changes in the economic environment that globalization has brought about over the past three decades, understanding the logic of GATT's design, and in what environments that logic makes economic sense, is a precursor to evaluating whether changes are warranted to the constitution of the world trading system for the twenty-first century and, if so, what changes are needed.

Chapter 2 begins with an overview of GATT and the World Trade Organization (WTO), and there I also introduce the basic features of a modeling framework that has been used to interpret the design of these institutions. In chapters 3, 4, and 5, I discuss research that evaluates this design as it relates specifically to tariff bargaining, the foundational activity of the GATT/WTO. Part I concludes with chapter 6, where I shift focus and describe research that emphasizes the incompleteness of the GATT/WTO contract and interprets some of its more puzzling design features from that perspective.

2 The GATT/WTO

In this chapter I provide a broad overview of the General Agreement on Tariffs and Trade (GATT) as well as its successor the World Trade Organization (WTO), and of the basic modeling framework that will provide my foundation for an economic interpretation of GATT's design features, its successes, and ultimately its shortcomings. I begin by describing GATT's design and a brief history of how it came to be, and I then present the modeling framework.

2.1 The Design of the GATT/WTO

Origins
The direct historical antecedents of what would eventually serve as the de facto constitution of the world trading system of the twentieth century arose at a time of crisis.[1] Trade barriers had become increasingly restrictive in the decade following World War I and reached a climax when the United States enacted the Smoot-Hawley Tariff Act of 1930, increasing average US tariffs from 38 to 52 percent. US trading partners responded, and soon tariff rates among all the major powers were generally on the order of 50 percent. As Hudec (1990, 5) explains, "The postwar design for international trade policy was animated by a single-minded concern to avoid repeating the disastrous errors of the 1920's and 1930's."

In 1934, the US Congress passed the Reciprocal Trade Agreements Act (RTAA). Under the RTAA, the United States for the first time engaged in bilateral reciprocal tariff bargaining with a sequence of trading partners, and it combined this bilateral bargaining approach

---

1. The material in this section builds from chapter 3 of Bagwell and Staiger (2002) and section 4 of Bagwell and Staiger (2010a).

with unconditional most-favored-nation (MFN) treatment, according to which exports from each country with whom the United States had an agreement under the RTAA would automatically receive the lowest ("most favored nation") tariff rate that the United States offered to any exporting country. It is widely acknowledged that much of the GATT architecture was inspired by prior US experience with the RTAA.

What is less well appreciated is the way in which the RTAA was itself influenced by the successes and failures of the many international attempts that came before it to address the problem of high and rising trade barriers. During the decade following World War I, the United States took part in a number of multilateral bargaining efforts to address this issue, each largely unsuccessful. In describing the evolution away from multilateral bargaining and toward the bilateral bargaining approach that would eventually be embodied in the RTAA, Tasca (1938, 7) attributes the lack of success of these earlier multilateral attempts to the complexity of multicountry bargaining:

> The adoption of a policy of bilateral actions does not preclude the use of multilateral conventions to liquidate trade barriers. During the post-war period various attempts to proceed upon this basis have met with little success. It is the method itself which possesses weaknesses in certain respects.... The complexities involved in such a program of concerted action arise in part out of the fundamental variations in national tariff systems. This means that practically only horizontal reductions in tariffs can be considered feasible. But the differences in the economies concerned and their varying positions in the world economy demand reductions in trade barriers according to the circumstances in each case. Moreover, the diffusion of responsibility grows with the number of prospective contractants. Nations became less concerned with the failure of a projected plurilateral pact and more with the possibility of yielding more in the way of concessions than other nations.

As Tasca observes, these repeated failures of multilateral bargaining led to a conscious decision on the part of the United States to experiment with bilateral bargaining under the RTAA.

The RTAA was remarkable not only because it adopted a bilateral bargaining approach to the problem, but because it marked the first time that the United States combined bilateral tariff bargaining with unconditional MFN.[2] Yet while the approach embodied in the RTAA was novel from the US perspective, from the perspective of Europeans it was not. As Tasca (1938, 135) observes, for decades before, the

---

2. The United States had, since 1922, adopted an unconditional MFN approach, but it maintained an "autonomous" (i.e., unilateral) tariff up until the RTAA (see Tasca 1938, 116–121).

approach of combining bilateral tariff bargaining with MFN treatment "formed the essential basis of the commercial policies of numerous European countries." In fact, it appears that the design and implementation of the RTAA built on lessons learned from the European experience in at least two important ways.

First, the European experience with bilateral tariff bargaining established the practical necessity of granting unconditional MFN. As Wallace (1933, 629) writes

After the World War, France experimented with the idea of abandoning the most-favored-nation clause ... By 1927 France was again driven back to the granting of most-favored-nation treatment, either de jure or de facto. The reason is not far to seek. When a country, by exclusive tariff bargains, institutes discriminations against third countries, then the greater these discriminations the greater will be the pressure against that country for their removal. In each successive negotiation it finds that the firmest demand of the other country is for equality of treatment, present and future, guarded by a most-favored-nation clause or its equivalent.

In effect, the European experience with bilateral tariff bargaining taught the important lesson that a country's current bargaining partners would require the assurance that any future bilateral deals that it struck with other countries would not substantially erode the value of the concessions being granted, and that the most practical way to provide assurance against such "concession erosion" was with a promise of unconditional MFN. The promise of unconditional MFN was included in the RTAA in part to address the concession erosion issue.[3]

Second, the European experience provided an object lesson in the power of the perverse incentive to raise tariffs and adopt so-called bargaining tariffs to better position oneself for future negotiations. According to Wallace (1938, 630):

This padding of tariff rates in anticipation of negotiations is a chief reason why half a century of bargaining has meant on the whole higher and higher tariff rates in Europe instead of lower and lower rates.

This also informed the design of the RTAA. As Tasca (1938, 179) observes:

The United States Tariff Commission in submitting recommendations on tariff bargaining declared, "The Congress should formulate restrictions designed to

---

3. Other arguments articulated at the time for adopting a policy of unconditional MFN included the perceived "multilateralization" benefits that this inclusion was expected to engender and a reduction in the risk of war (see, for example, Culbert 1987 and Rhodes 1993).

prevent the inclusion in reciprocity agreements of illusory concessions; that is, the removal of trade barriers or the reduction of tariff rates when such barriers and rates had been raised in anticipation of tariff bargaining, the amount of the concessions being smaller than or not greater than the previous increases in barriers and rates. Specifically, it is suggested that the Congress prescribe that all concessions included in the reciprocity agreements, on both sides, be made from the rates and relating to the barriers in effect at a date which shall be fixed by the Congress."

The lessons learned from the European experience with bilateral tariff bargaining may therefore have contributed to the success of bilateral tariff bargaining under the RTAA by helping the United States avoid the twin problems associated with concession erosion and bargaining tariffs that plagued the European efforts before it. But, as it happened, the adoption of unconditional MFN would itself introduce a different potential issue for the RTAA, one that was related to the earlier problem of bargaining tariffs that the Europeans had experienced but took a slightly different form: While in the European experience this issue had taken the form of the unilateral positioning of pre-negotiation tariffs, under the RTAA the analogous issue became how to design bilateral agreements with early negotiating partners to best preserve bargaining power for later agreements with other negotiating partners. This task was made difficult by the unconditional MFN requirement, which automatically granted "for free" to other potential bargaining partners any tariff concessions granted to early negotiating partners.

The preservation of bargaining power for later negotiations became a major preoccupation of the United States under the RTAA. Describing the tactics used by the United States in this regard, Tasca (1938, 146–147) notes:

There are, then, five methods being utilized by the United States to assure the compatibility of the unconditional most-favored-nation clause with a conventional tariff bargaining program. By far the most basic is the chief supplier formula. This is reenforced by the reclassification of commodities in the tariff schedules of the Act of 1930. The use of partial reductions in successive agreements, the simultaneous negotiations with groups of countries and the withdrawal clause are subsidiary to the first two. They play the part of supporting beams in those instances in which the chief supplier is not entirely applicable to existing conditions.

In effect, by granting tariff concessions to a negotiating partner only on those products for which the partner was the principal ("chief") supplier, possibly combined with product reclassification for tariff purposes to heighten the dominance of the partner in these products, it was thought that much of the free-rider potential created by unconditional MFN could be eliminated. And where free-riding remained a substantial possibility, three additional tactics were available: splitting the concession into a sequence of partial tariff reductions negotiated with different countries in successive agreements; attempting to engage groups of countries in simultaneous negotiations; and threatening to withdraw or modify the earlier agreement if free-riding continued.

Beckett (1941) reviews the US experience under the RTAA and emphasizes the difficulties involved in preserving bargaining power in the presence of unconditional MFN, even when the chief supplier rule is applied. As she describes, split concessions often became the preferred method to prevent undue loss of bargaining power in an early negotiation:

It is important to notice that the use of the chief supplier rule involves certain special difficulties. A problem arises, for instance, when, during the process of negotiation with small countries, it is impossible to isolate any commodities in which the other country is our chief supplier...A further difficulty appears when two or more countries supply almost exactly the same quantity of a given commodity or when two countries are the chief suppliers of the commodity in alternative years. If a substantial reduction in duty is granted in the trade agreement with one country, bargaining power with the other country is lost. To avoid such embarrassment, simultaneous negotiations of two agreements can be attempted. More often a split concession is granted: that is, a small reduction in duty is made in the agreement with the first country and an additional reduction in the agreement with the second country. By this procedure bargaining power with the second country is preserved. (Beckett 1941, 23)

Tasca (1938, 146) also emphasizes the importance in this regard of the various withdrawal clauses that were included in the RTAA:

If the major benefits of a duty concession fall to a third country and "in consequence thereof an unduly large increase in importation" takes place, the contractants may withdraw the concession or impose a quantitative restriction upon imports of that item. Concessions are granted by the United States only after careful study in order to gauge the effects upon the whole economy; if these calculations should fail, then there exists a remedy in resort to this clause. But what is more significant, this withdrawal clause forestalls any third country from reaping any considerable benefit from a concession which might in any manner lessen its incentive to promulgate a pact with the United States.

The practice of granting split concessions became the most frequently observed manifestation of bargaining tariffs under the RTAA, while the threat to withdraw or modify a concession was typically kept in the background but seen as providing an important means of maintaining bargaining leverage for later negotiations.

In short, tariff bargaining under the RTAA exhibited a number of central features. The approach was decidedly bilateral, chosen only after the United States had considered, attempted, and ultimately rejected multilateral tariff bargaining. Prior European experience with concession erosion and bargaining tariffs influenced the design and implementation of the RTAA along important dimensions. And unconditional MFN, the chief supplier rule, split concessions, and withdrawal/modification clauses were understood to be central to the operation of reciprocal tariff bargaining under the RTAA.

Between 1934 and 1947, the United States successfully concluded separate bilateral agreements with 29 countries. Encouraged by its success in the bilateral arena with the RTAA, the United States sought to build on the key components and establish a multilateral institution. In 1946, negotiations began for the creation of an International Trade Organization (ITO). As with the RTAA, under the ITO it was expected that negotiations between governments would result in reciprocal and mutually advantageous reductions in tariffs, and the principle of nondiscrimination would then ensure that the reduced tariffs would be extended to all member countries. In 1947, GATT was negotiated and was intended to serve as an interim agreement, but the ITO was never ratified by the US Congress.

Stated Purpose
What is the stated purpose of GATT? According to its preamble, the objectives of the contracting parties include "raising standards of living, ensuring full employment and a large and steadily growing volume of real income and effective demand, developing the full use of the resources of the world and expanding the production and exchange of goods."

As for the means to achieve this purpose, the preamble of GATT states that "reciprocal and mutually advantageous arrangements directed to the substantial reduction in tariffs and other barriers to trade and to the elimination of discriminatory treatment in international commerce" would contribute toward these goals. The objectives stated in the preamble to the WTO are broadened to include the exchange of not only goods but also of services, and to acknowledge the additional objectives of sustainable development, the protection and preservation of the environment, and the greater inclusion of developing countries to share in the gains from the growth of trade. But the means to achieve this purpose as stated in the WTO preamble are identical to those in the GATT preamble (with the phrase "international trade relations" in the WTO preamble replacing "international commerce" from the GATT preamble).

Perhaps surprisingly to economists, free trade is not a stated objective of GATT or the WTO. This reflects the fact that, as a "member-driven organization" that serves as a trade policy negotiating forum for member governments with diverse interests, priorities, and needs, the GATT/WTO is designed with the aim of securing mutually beneficial agreements among these governments, and free trade is not necessarily something to which all member governments will aspire.

In total, there were eight rounds of GATT negotiations that together spanned almost 50 years. The primary focus of the earlier rounds was the reduction of import tariffs on goods. In the final GATT round, known as the Uruguay Round, governments took on several new issue areas (e.g., investment, services, and intellectual property) and formed the WTO. The WTO has sponsored a ninth round, the Doha Round, launched in 2001 and as yet uncompleted. The WTO embraces the rules and agreements made in GATT negotiations, but it is also a full-fledged international organization with an explicit organizational charter and a unified dispute-settlement system. In effect, with the creation of the WTO, participating governments fulfilled their original quest with the ITO for an official international organization that would set and administer the rules of the world trading system.

Architecture

GATT/WTO member governments are obliged to abide by a set of rules. In GATT, these rules were laid out in a series of 39 articles. The WTO has incorporated these GATT articles and extended the principles embodied in them to a number of new issue areas. I now provide an overview of the GATT/WTO legal structure by focusing on the principles embodied in these articles.

It is helpful to distinguish between three broad elements: substantive obligations, exceptions to those obligations, and dispute settlement procedures. The substantive obligations of a GATT/WTO member relate to tariff commitments, MFN treatment, and a general "code of conduct" in the international-trade arena. Broadly speaking, these provisions oblige the member governments to concentrate national protective measures into the form of tariffs, to apply them on a nondiscriminatory basis to other members, and to honor any tariff "bindings" made in a GATT/WTO negotiation, where the tariff binding refers to a legal maximum level above which a country agrees not to raise its tariff.

As mentioned, the GATT/WTO also provides for certain exceptions to these obligations. One class of exceptions is for "original" actions, such as when a member seeks to suspend an obligation temporarily, or to permanently withdraw a previous concession through renegotiation. The rationale for including exceptions of this nature is that a government is more likely to make a substantial tariff commitment if it knows that the legal system has "safeguards" allowing its concessions to be modified or withdrawn under appropriate conditions. Of course, a tariff commitment would lose its meaning if exceptions for original actions were not subject to some disciplining structure. In part for this reason, and in part to maintain a balance between the rights and obligations of the members, GATT/WTO rules permit as well a second class of exceptions for "retaliatory" actions. Specifically, if a government modifies or withdraws a previous concession, then GATT/WTO rules recognize that a cost may be borne by a trading partner. This partner may then seek "compensation" from the government for the harm done (e.g., a tariff reduction from the government on some other good), and if this fails the partner is allowed to achieve "self-help compensation" through retaliation. The meaning of retaliation is that the trading partner can reciprocate by withdrawing a concession of a "substantially equivalent" nature.

The third element mentioned above is GATT/WTO dispute settlement procedures. Here, a central issue is the determination whether the actions by one country serve to "nullify or impair" the benefits expected under the agreement by another country. Nullification or impairment includes actions taken by one country "which harmed the trade of another, and which 'could not reasonably have been anticipated' by the other at the time it negotiated for a concession" (Jackson 1997, 115). In the typical "violation complaint," a country is alleged to have failed to comply with one or more of its GATT/WTO obligations, leading to a prima facie case of nullification or impairment.

An important distinction arises between the procedures associated with safeguard exceptions and those that are associated with nullification or impairment. The safeguard procedures provide explicitly for the *lawful* suspension of obligations or withdrawal of negotiated concessions, and these procedures specify as well the permissible retaliatory responses of trading partners. By contrast, the dispute settlement procedures govern retaliation against a country that takes a harmful action that its trading partners could not have anticipated under GATT/WTO rules. In the typical complaint, at issue is whether the offending country has violated GATT/WTO rules, and retaliation here may then be more directly concerned with the enforcement of rules.

The procedure for settling disputes consists of three stages: First, there is a consultation phase among the involved parties; second, a GATT/WTO panel (and, after appeal, the appellate body) conducts an investigation and issues a ruling and recommendation; and as a last resort, authorization of retaliation occurs. Resolution is often achieved in the first stage, or it may follow the panel ruling. If the panel finds that nullification or impairment has occurred, then it recommends that the offending country correct any illegal measures. The offending country may be unwilling to do so, however. In this case, it may seek a negotiated resolution by offering the harmed country compensation through MFN tariff reductions on some other goods. If compensation is not offered, or if it is offered but rejected, then the harmed country may follow through with the last-resort response: an authorized and discriminatory suspension of tariff concessions. In practice, the number of authorized retaliations has been small, though this number has grown in the WTO era. As Rhodes (1993, 109) observes, however, the threat of authorized retaliation is often the catalyst for a resolution of the dispute in the earlier stages.

It is notable that, while authorized retaliation in the context of dispute resolution is allowed to be discriminatory, it is nevertheless generally limited to the suspension of concessions of a substantially equivalent nature. One might have thought that the GATT/WTO would authorize and coordinate maximal retaliation against a member government found to be in violation of the rules by the GATT/WTO's own dispute settlement body. But in fact, as the early report of the US International Chamber of Commerce (quoted in chapter 1) observed, the GATT dispute settlement procedures keep a *lid* on permissible retaliation levels, and this is how the GATT/WTO dispute settlement system works to avoid a trade war. This point was reflected in a statement made by one of the drafters of the original GATT articles governing retaliation in the context of dispute settlement, as found in Petersmann (1997, 82–83):

The drafting history of Article XXIII:2 confirms that it was designed to limit the customary law right of unilateral reprisals, whose exercise had contributed so much to the "law of the jungle" in international economic affairs during the 1930's, and to introduce, as stated by one of the drafters, "a new principle in international economic relations. We have asked the nations of the world to confer upon an international organization the right to limit their power to retaliate. We have sought to tame retaliation, to discipline it, to keep it within bounds. By subjecting it to the restraints of international control, we have endeavored to check its spread and growth, to convert it from a weapon of economic warfare to an instrument of international order."

Indeed, Schwartz and Sykes (2002) argue that the major innovation in the dispute settlement procedures of the WTO relative to GATT was the addition of a mechanism for arbitrating the magnitude of authorized retaliation so that an effective lid on retaliation could be maintained.

Finally, it is often observed that, along with MFN, reciprocity is a pil-lar of the GATT/WTO architecture. In the GATT/WTO, the principle of reciprocity refers to the ideal of mutual changes in trade policy that bring about changes in the volume of each country's imports that are of equal value to changes in the volume of its exports. The preceding dis-cussion contains two instances in which the notion of reciprocity arises. First, as I have observed, when governments negotiate in GATT/WTO rounds, they do so with the stated goal of obtaining mutually advan-tageous arrangements through reciprocal reductions in tariff bindings: In this context, it is often observed that governments approach negoti-ations seeking a "balance of concessions," whereby the market access value of the tariff cut offered by one government is balanced against an "equivalent" concession from its trading partner. This first instance of reciprocity therefore refers to changes in tariffs in a liberalizing direction. Second, when a government seeks to renegotiate its tariff commitments and modifies or withdraws a previous concession as an original action, and more generally whenever a government takes an action that nullifies or impairs the benefits expected under the agree-ment by another government, GATT/WTO rules permit substantially affected trading partners to retaliate in a reciprocal manner, by with-drawing "substantially equivalent concessions." This second instance of reciprocity refers to changes in tariffs in an upward direction.

The balance achieved through reciprocity in tariff negotiations and the role of retaliation in preserving this balance is reflected in the remark by a drafter of the GATT articles governing retaliation as quoted in Jackson (1969, 170–171):

What we have really provided, in the last analysis, is not that retaliation shall be invited or sanctions invoked, but that a balance of interests once established, shall be maintained.

And the unique role of retaliation in the GATT legal system as a means of preserving reciprocity is pointed out by Dam (1970, 80–81):

> The best guarantee that a commitment of any kind will be kept (particularly in an international setting where courts are of limited importance and, even more important, marshals and jails are nonexistent) is that the parties continue to view adherence to their agreement as in their mutual interest. . . . Thus, the GATT system, unlike most legal systems . . . is not designed to exclude self-help in the form of retaliation. Rather, retaliation, subjected to established procedures and kept within prescribed bounds, is made the heart of the GATT system.

2.2 The Purpose of Trade Agreements

I now present the outlines of a basic modeling framework that will provide my foundation for an economic interpretation of GATT's design features, its successes, and ultimately its shortcomings.[4] In this section, I develop the model to answer one simple but fundamental question: What problems would governments want a trade agreement to help them solve? The answer to this question clarifies the purpose of a trade agreement and can help guide its design to serve that purpose.

To provide an answer, I abstract from possible domestic commitment problems that a government might face that could lead to *domestic* inefficiencies in its unilaterally chosen policies and that it might seek to solve with help from a trade agreement as an external commitment device.[5] I focus instead on characterizing the possible *international* inefficiencies that might arise under unilaterally chosen policies and that a trade agreement could address. A useful starting point for this purpose is the standard two-country, two-good general equilibrium model of trade familiar from any undergraduate international trade course.

The General Equilibrium Trade Model

The standard general equilibrium model of trade has two countries, home (no *) and foreign (*), who trade two goods that are normal goods in consumption and produced in perfectly competitive markets under conditions of increasing opportunity costs. I denote by x the natural import good of the home country and by y the natural import good of the foreign country, and I define $p \equiv p_x / p_y$ and $p^* \equiv p_x^* / p_y^*$ to

---

4. The material in this section builds from Bagwell and Staiger (2002, chap. 2).
5. On the possibility that trade agreements might help solve domestic commitment problems, see the literature reviewed in Bagwell and Staiger (2002, 32–34).

be, respectively, the local relative price in the home and foreign market. With τ the home-country import tariff and τ^* the foreign-country import tariff, each expressed in ad valorem terms and assumed to be set at nonprohibitive levels, it then follows that $p = (1 + \tau)p^w \equiv p(\tau, p^w)$ and $p^* = p^w / (1 + \tau^*) \equiv p^*(\tau^*, p^w)$, where $p^w \equiv p_x^* / p_y$ is the "world" (i.e., untaxed) relative price. The foreign terms of trade is then given by p^w while the home terms of trade is given by $(1/p^w)$. I am assuming for now that governments possess tariffs as their only tax/subsidy instrument. This ensures that both producers and consumers face the same local relative price in the market within which they reside. In later chapters, I will introduce into the model a richer array of government policies that include the possibility of regulatory standards as well as production and/or consumption taxes/subsidies; in the presence of the additional tax/subsidy policies, consumers and producers residing in the same market may face different local prices.

Production possibilities in each country are defined by a production possibilities frontier, which with Q denoting production, I represent by the decreasing and concave function $Q_y(Q_x)$ in the home country and $Q_y^*(Q_x^*)$ in the foreign country, defined over the feasible values of production of x in each country. Production in a country occurs at the point on the production possibilities frontier where the marginal rate of transformation between x and y is equal to the local relative price, allowing home and foreign production functions to be represented as $Q_i = Q_i(p)$ and $Q_i^* = Q_i^*(p^*)$ for $i = \{x, y\}$. Consumption depends on both the local relative price—which defines the trade-off faced by consumers and, in determining the point on the production possibilities frontier at which the economy operates, also implies the level and distribution of factor income in the economy measured at local prices—and on tariff revenue, which is distributed lump-sum back to consumers in the country where it is collected. I denote by R the tariff revenue collected in the home country and by R^* the tariff revenue collected in the foreign country, each measured in units of the country's export good at local prices. National consumption in the home and foreign country can then be written as $D_i = D_i(p, R)$ and $D_i^* = D_i^*(p^*, R^*)$ for $i = \{x, y\}$, where tariff revenue is defined implicitly by $R = [D_x(p, R) - Q_x(p)][p - p^w]$ or $R = R(p, p^w)$ for the home country and by $R^* = [D_y^*(p^*, R^*) - Q_y^*(p^*)][1/p^* - 1/p^w]$ or $R^* = R^*(p^*, p^w)$ for the foreign country, and where each country's tariff revenue is an increasing function of its terms of trade under the normal-goods assumption. This allows national consumption to be written as $C_i(p, p^w) \equiv D_i(p, R(p, p^w))$ and $C_i^*(p^*, p^w) \equiv D_i^*(p^*, R^*(p^*, p^w))$ for $i = \{x, y\}$, with C_i decreasing in p^w and C_i^* increasing in p^w.

To express the trade balance and equilibrium conditions of the model, I define home-country imports of x and exports of y by $M_x(p, p^w) \equiv C_x(p, p^w) - Q_x(p)$ and $E_y(p, p^w) \equiv Q_y(p) - C_y(p, p^w)$, respectively. Similarly, foreign-country imports of y and exports of x are defined by $M_y^*(p^*, p^w) \equiv C_y(p^*, p^w) - Q_y^*(p^*)$ and $E_x^*(p^*, p^w) \equiv Q_x^*(p^*) - C_x^*(p^*, p^w)$, respectively. For any world price, we also have

$$p^w M_x(p(\tau, p^w), p^w) = E_y(p(\tau, p^w), p^w) \text{ and} \tag{2.1}$$

$$M_y^*(p^*(\tau^*, p^w), p^w) = p^w E_x^*(p^*(\tau^*, p^w), p^w), \tag{2.2}$$

which are the balanced trade conditions, where I now make explicit the dependence of the local price on the tariff and the world price. The equilibrium world price, $\tilde{p}^w(\tau, \tau^*)$, is then determined by the requirement of market clearing for good y:

$$E_y(p(\tau, \tilde{p}^w), \tilde{p}^w) = M_y^*(p^*(\tau^*, \tilde{p}^w), \tilde{p}^w), \tag{2.3}$$

with market clearing for good x implied by (2.1), (2.2), and (2.3).

Thus, given any pair of tariffs, the equilibrium world price is determined by (2.3), and the equilibrium world price and the given tariffs then determine in turn the local prices and thereby the production, consumption, import, export, and tariff revenue levels. I focus on the standard case and therefore assume that the Lerner and Metzler paradoxes[6] are ruled out so that

$$\frac{\partial \tilde{p}^w(\tau, \tau^*)}{\partial \tau} < 0 < \frac{\partial \tilde{p}^w(\tau, \tau^*)}{\partial \tau^*} \text{ and}$$

$$\frac{dp(\tau, \tilde{p}^w(\tau, \tau^*))}{d\tau} > 0 > \frac{dp^*(\tau^*, \tilde{p}^w(\tau, \tau^*))}{d\tau^*}. \tag{2.4}$$

For future reference, I note that the first set of inequalities in (2.4) implies that, if the home tariff τ were reduced by a small amount, there exists a small reduction in the foreign tariff τ^* that would hold the equilibrium world price $\tilde{p}^w$ constant.

Government Objectives

I now turn to the specification of government objectives. The trade policy objectives of real-world governments are diverse, and it is

---

6. Bagwell and Staiger (2016, 499–501) consider the implications for the purpose of trade agreements when the Metzler and/or Lerner paradoxical cases arise.

important to allow for this diversity when considering the purpose of a trade agreement, lest the purpose ascribed to the agreement is unduly limited by the trade policy objectives ascribed to governments. Even in the simple model of a world economy presented here, there are many possible motives for government trade policy intervention that could be entertained.

For example, a government might care only about the level of national consumption and hence the level of real national income when choosing its tariffs, either because it is unconcerned about the distribution of income and consumption among its citizens or because it has lump-sum redistributive instruments to handle these concerns. The preferences of such a government in the home country could be represented in the model with the objective function $G(C_x, C_y)$, with G increasing in both arguments. Notice that, as $C_i(p, p^w)$ is decreasing in p^w for $i \in \{x, y\}$ as indicated above, I can also write this objective function as

$$G(C_x(p, p^w), C_y(p, p^w)) \equiv W(p, p^w), \tag{2.5}$$

where W is decreasing in p^w; similarly, for the foreign government, I can write

$$G^*(C_x^*(p^*, p^w), C_y^*(p^*, p^w)) \equiv W^*(p^*, p^w), \tag{2.6}$$

where W^* is increasing in p^w given that $C_i^*(p^*, p^w)$ is increasing in p^w.

But real-world governments often view tariffs as a tool to address distributional concerns.[7] Why would these governments use tariffs for this purpose when it is well known that there are other policy interventions that are, in principle, better suited for this task? One reason could be that in practice, these governments lack not only the policy ideal of lump-sum taxes but also any of the other policy instruments that, if available, would typically dominate tariffs as tools for influencing the distribution of income and preserve the economist's case for free trade. In the context of this limited set of policy options, tariffs might then be the best available policy response to address these concerns.[8]

---

7. These concerns likely reflect a combination of a desire of governments to serve some notion of social welfare, such as that embodied in the "conservative social welfare function" introduced by Corden (1974), and political economy motives that serve politically favored groups (as in Grossman and Helpman 1994).
8. There are a variety of reasons why, as a practical matter, such nontariff instruments may not be available to governments. They include administrative costs and funding

Or it could be that, even though some of these policy instruments are technically available to governments, the welfare of their citizens is determined by more than simply the material standard of living that can be attained with a given level of consumption; it might depend as well on the *manner* in which the income to support this level of consumption is attained, with the receipt of lump-sum transfers or direct subsidy payments diminishing personal dignity in a way that earning income at market prices—even if not the prices that would prevail under free trade—would not.

In any event, the fact is that many governments use tariffs to address distributional concerns and, more broadly, as tools of industrial policy, and therefore they choose tariffs to affect the sectoral pattern of production in their economies for reasons that go beyond how that production translates into real national income and thereby national consumption levels. In terms of the model, these governments would appear to have preferences over where on the production possibilities frontier their economy operates, independent of the national consumption levels that are attained. Such government preferences for the home country could be represented in the model by the objective function $G(C_x, C_y, Q_x, Q_y(Q_x))$. The distribution and level of factor income measured in local prices would be pinned down for a given choice of Q_x and therefore $Q_y(Q_x)$ on the production possibilities frontier. Conditional on the aggregate level of national consumption C_x and C_y, the home government would then have its own preference ranking over the choice of Q_x and $Q_y(Q_x)$ as reflected in the function G. For given Q_x and $Q_y(Q_x)$ and the factor incomes that are implied, it is again natural that G is increasing in C_x and C_y, because when factor incomes are fixed, increasing C_x and C_y amounts to increases in tariff revenue according to the national budget constraint. Notice again that I can write this objective function as

$$G(C_x(p, p^w), C_y(p, p^w), Q_x(p), Q_y(Q_x(p))) \equiv W(p, p^w), \tag{2.7}$$

where W is decreasing in p^w. And similarly for the foreign government, I can write

---

requirements that, when taken into account, could make these instruments impractical or at least less attractive than tariffs. See also Rodrik (1987), Drazen and Limão (2008), and Limão and Tovar (2011) on additional reasons why governments may choose to use tariffs for purposes of redistribution. I discuss the possible role of tariffs as a tool of industrial policy more generally in chapter 7.

$$G^*(C_x^*(p^*, p^w), C_y^*(p^*, p^w), Q_x^*(p^*), Q_y^*(Q_x^*(p^*))) \equiv W^*(p^*, p^w), \quad (2.8)$$

where W^* is increasing in p^w.

More generally, a government's preferences over the sectoral pattern of production in its economy could arise for reasons of national security, or from the societal benefits of maintaining a robust middle class with access to stable and good-paying jobs that are more prevalent in one sector than they are in another, or from the desire to preserve employment in a region that is dependent on a particular sector, or from the avoidance of sector-specific negative externalities of an "eyesore" variety. Any of these nonpecuniary features could be embedded in the model without changing the formal structure that I have outlined above, as long as they do not invalidate the competitive equilibrium conditions that the model assumes or lead to transborder nonpecuniary externalities. And, for each of these cases, I can once again write the associated home-government objective function as in (2.7), with W decreasing in p^w, and similarly I can again write the associated foreign-government objective function as in (2.8) with W^* increasing in p^w.

Evidently, in all of the cases I have described, government preferences can be represented in the model with the home-country and foreign-country objective functions expressed in the form $W(p, p^w)$ and $W^*(p^*, p^w)$, respectively, where W is decreasing in p^w and W^* is increasing in p^w and where the difference across these various government objectives translates into differences in how W varies with p and how W^* varies with p^*.[9] To capture all these possibilities in a unified framework, I will therefore follow Bagwell and Staiger (1999, 2002) and represent the trade policy objectives of the home and foreign government with the general functions $W(p, p^w)$ and $W^*(p^*, p^w)$, with the only structure placed on W and W^* that, holding its local price fixed, each government is assumed to achieve higher welfare when its terms of trade improve:[10]

$$\frac{\partial W(p, \tilde{p}^w)}{\partial \tilde{p}^w} < 0 \text{ and } \frac{\partial W^*(p^*, \tilde{p}^w)}{\partial \tilde{p}^w} > 0. \quad (2.9)$$

---

9. See also Bagwell and Staiger (1999; 2002, 18–21) for an inventory of the formal models of trade policy determination in the economics literature that are captured by this structure.

10. See Bagwell and Staiger (2002, 19–20) for a description of the change in the home and foreign tariff that would increase $\tilde{p}^w$ while holding fixed an economy's local price. Throughout, I also impose standard regularity conditions so that all second-order conditions are globally satisfied and all partial derivatives of W and W^* are finite.

The Purpose of a Trade Agreement

I now turn to the central question of this chapter: What problems would governments want a trade agreement to help them solve? In the absence of a trade agreement, I assume that each government would set its trade policy to maximize its objective function, taking as given the tariff choice of its trading partner. This yields the following home and foreign reaction functions:

$$\text{Home Reaction Function}: W_p \frac{dp}{d\tau} + W_{p^w} \frac{\partial \tilde{p}^w}{\partial \tau} = 0 \tag{2.10}$$

$$\text{Foreign Reaction Function}: W_{p^*}^* \frac{dp^*}{d\tau^*} + W_{p^w}^* \frac{\partial \tilde{p}^w}{\partial \tau^*} = 0, \tag{2.11}$$

where subscripts denote partial derivatives. The joint solution to (2.10) and (2.11) defines the noncooperative (Nash) tariff pair (τ^N, τ^{*N}). Notice that under (2.4) and (2.9), the home-country reaction function (2.10) implies $W_p < 0$ while the foreign-country reaction function (2.11) implies $W_{p^*}^* > 0$. I will return to this feature of noncooperative tariffs below.

Under a trade agreement, by contrast, I assume that the two governments negotiate to a position on the efficiency frontier, where this frontier is defined by

$$\max_{\tau, \tau^*} W(p(\tau, \tilde{p}^w), \tilde{p}^w) \tag{2.12}$$

$$s.t. \ W^*(p^*(\tau^*, \tilde{p}^w), \tilde{p}^w) \geq \overline{W}^*,$$

with $\overline{W}^*$ denoting any feasible level of foreign welfare. The efficiency frontier is characterized by solving (2.12) for each value of $\overline{W}^*$, and it traces out the locus of Pareto efficient tariff pairs (τ^E, τ^{*E}). The associated first-order conditions are

$$W_p \frac{dp}{d\tau} + W_{p^w} \frac{\partial \tilde{p}^w}{\partial \tau} + \lambda \left[\left(W_{p^*}^* \frac{\partial p^*}{\partial p^w} + W_{p^w}^* \right) \frac{\partial \tilde{p}^w}{\partial \tau} \right] = 0 \tag{2.13}$$

$$\left[W_p \frac{\partial p}{\partial p^w} + W_{p^w} \right] \frac{\partial \tilde{p}^w}{\partial \tau^*} + \lambda \left[W_{p^*}^* \frac{dp^*}{d\tau^*} + W_{p^w}^* \frac{\partial \tilde{p}^w}{\partial \tau^*} \right] = 0, \tag{2.14}$$

where λ is the Lagrange multiplier on the constraint in (2.12). Solving (2.13) for λ and substituting the result into (2.14), together with the price definitions, yields the condition that defines the locus of efficient tariffs:

$$[\tau W_p + W_{p^w}] \frac{\partial \widetilde{p}^w}{\partial \tau^*} - \left[\frac{\left[W_p \frac{dp}{d\tau} + W_{p^w} \frac{\partial \widetilde{p}^w}{\partial \tau} \right] \times \left[W_{p^*}^* \frac{dp^*}{d\tau^*} + W_{p^w}^* \frac{\partial \widetilde{p}^w}{\partial \tau^*} \right]}{\left[\frac{1}{\tau^*} W_{p^*}^* + W_{p^w}^* \right] \frac{\partial \widetilde{p}^w}{\partial \tau}} \right] = 0.$$

(2.15)

A familiar special case of the efficiency locus defined by (2.15) arises when governments care only about the level of national consumption and hence the level of real national income when choosing their tariffs. In this case, as I have noted above, we then have that the home and foreign welfare functions $W(p, p^w)$ and $W^*(p^*, p^w)$ can be written in the particular form given in (2.5) and (2.6), respectively, and it is straightforward to show that (2.15) then simplifies to the Mayer (1981) locus of efficient tariffs defined by $(1 + \tau) = 1/(1 + \tau^*)$. The Mayer locus includes the point of reciprocal free trade $\tau = 0 = \tau^*$, but it also includes a locus of other efficient pairs of tariffs in which an import tariff in one country is exactly offset by an import subsidy of the same magnitude in the other country. To understand the conditions for efficiency along the Mayer locus, notice that at any point on the locus we have

$$p = (1 + \tau)\widetilde{p}^w(\tau, \tau^*) = \frac{1}{(1 + \tau^*)} \widetilde{p}^w(\tau, \tau^*) = p^*.$$

Hence, along the Mayer locus, tariffs are adjusted to maintain equality in relative local prices between the home and foreign countries, with different tariff pairs resulting in different world prices and therefore different distributions of income across trading partners through shifts in the (positive or negative) tariff revenue collected by each country. When $W(p, p^w)$ and $W^*(p^*, p^w)$ are not assumed to conform to the particular structure in (2.5) and (2.6), equation (2.15) still determines the efficient relationship between home and foreign tariffs, but it need not be the case that this relationship equates relative local prices across trading partners, and it need not be the case that this relationship is satisfied by reciprocal free trade.

Continuing now with the general government preferences $W(p, p^w)$ and $W^*(p^*, p^w)$ as described above, a first question is whether the noncooperative tariff choices are efficient. If they are, then assuming that the two governments have entered into negotiations voluntarily, there is nothing for a trade agreement to do since it cannot offer a Pareto improvement over the noncooperative outcome. Using (2.10) and (2.11) together with (2.4) and (2.9), and also using the fact that the noncooperative tariffs imply $W_p < 0$ and $W_{p^*}^* > 0$, it is straightforward to confirm that the first-order condition for efficiency given in (2.15) is violated when evaluated at the noncooperative tariff pair (τ^N, τ^{*N}) defined by (2.10) and (2.11); more specifically, the left-hand side of (2.15) is strictly negative. This implies that, regardless of which of the underlying motives for tariff intervention included in the general government objective functions $W(p, p^w)$ and $W^*(p^*, p^w)$ is operative, noncooperative tariffs are *too high* relative to the efficiency locus.[11] And as Bagwell and Staiger (1999; 2002, chap. 2) demonstrate, starting at the Nash equilibrium, mutual gains for governments are therefore possible only if they both cut their tariffs. Clearly, this case for tariff liberalization in a trade agreement has nothing to do with the economist's case for free trade, since it arises regardless of the underlying motives for trade protection captured in the general government objective functions $W(p, p^w)$ and $W^*(p^*, p^w)$, and as discussed above, many of those motives would violate the assumptions that underlie the case for free trade as an efficient outcome.

We may now ask, Why are noncooperative tariffs inefficiently high? If we can identify the reason, then we can say that addressing this reason is the problem that governments want a trade agreement to help them solve. We can say this because by solving this problem, a trade agreement would bring countries to the efficiency frontier, and at that point there is no possibility of further Pareto gains for the governments.

To proceed formally, we need to characterize the difference between the Nash first-order conditions in (2.10) and (2.11) and the first-order conditions for efficiency given in (2.15). To aid in this characterization, it is useful to pick a specific point on the efficiency locus and compare the conditions that define that pair of efficient tariffs to the conditions that define the pair of Nash tariffs.

A point on the efficiency locus that is particularly illuminating for this purpose is the point that Bagwell and Staiger (1999) call the "political optimum," defined as the tariff pair (τ^{PO}, τ^{*PO}) that satisfies

$$\text{Home Political Optimum}: W_p \frac{dp}{d\tau} = 0 \Leftrightarrow W_p = 0 \qquad (2.16)$$

$$\text{Foreign Political Optimum}: W^*_{p^*} \frac{dp^*}{d\tau^*} = 0 \Leftrightarrow W^*_{p^*} = 0, \qquad (2.17)$$

---

11. In particular, the fact that the left-hand side of (2.15) is strictly negative when evaluated at the noncooperative tariff pair (τ^N, τ^{*N}) means that τ^N is too high relative to the level of τ^* that would be efficient in combination with τ^N. Analogously, τ^N is too high relative to the level of τ that would be efficient in combination with τ^{*N}. It is in this sense that noncooperative tariffs (τ^N, τ^{*N}) are too high relative to the efficiency locus.

where the second equality in (2.16) and in (2.17) follows from the second set of inequalities in (2.4). In the special case where governments care only about the level of national consumption and hence the level of real national income when choosing their tariffs, and where the government objectives therefore take the particular form in (2.5) and (2.6), the politically optimal tariffs correspond to reciprocal free trade, a point on the Mayer locus. That politically optimal tariffs are efficient as well under the general government objective functions $W(p, p^w)$ and $W^*(p^*, p^w)$ described above can be immediately confirmed using (2.16) and (2.17) by noting that, when evaluated at the tariff pair (τ^{PO}, τ^{*PO}), the condition for efficiency (2.15) is satisfied:

$$
\left[\tau W_p + W_{p^w}\right] \frac{\partial \widetilde{p}^w}{\partial \tau^*} - \left[\frac{\left[W_p \frac{dp}{d\tau} + W_{p^w} \frac{\partial \widetilde{p}^w}{\partial \tau} \right] \times \left[W_{p^*}^* \frac{dp^*}{d\tau^*} + W_{p^w}^* \frac{\partial \widetilde{p}^w}{\partial \tau^*} \right]}{\left[\frac{1}{\tau^*} W_{p^*}^* + W_{p^w}^* \right] \frac{\partial \widetilde{p}^w}{\partial \tau}} \right]
$$

$$
= W_{p^w} \frac{\partial \widetilde{p}^w}{\partial \tau^*} - W_{p^w} \frac{\partial \widetilde{p}^w}{\partial \tau^*} = 0.
$$

But comparing (2.16) and (2.17) to (2.10) and (2.11), it is now also apparent that the noncooperative tariffs fail to reach the political optimum because of the presence of a single term, $W_{p^w} \frac{\partial \widetilde{p}^w}{\partial \tau}$, in the home-country reaction curve and a single term, $W_{p^w}^* \frac{\partial \widetilde{p}^w}{\partial \tau^*}$, in the foreign-country reaction curve. These terms represent the incentive each country has when choosing its tariff noncooperatively to manipulate the terms of trade in its favor and thereby to shift a portion of the costs of its tariff intervention onto its trading partner.

For the home government, this term is the product of two negative terms: the term $\frac{\partial \widetilde{p}^w}{\partial \tau}$, which is strictly negative as long as the home country is large and therefore has market power on world markets; and the term W_{p^w}, which is also negative and reflects the negative income effect of a terms-of-trade deterioration holding local prices in the home economy fixed. And as this product is itself positive, its presence in (2.10) drives the home noncooperative tariff choice higher than the tariff that would imply $W_p = 0$, ensuring that at the noncooperative tariff, we in fact have $W_p < 0$ (as I have observed).

For the foreign government, this term is the product of two positive terms: the term $\frac{\partial \widetilde{p}^w}{\partial \tau^*}$, which is strictly positive as long as the foreign country is large and therefore has market power on world markets; and the term $W_{p^w}^*$, which is also positive and reflects the positive income effect of a terms-of-trade improvement holding local prices in the foreign economy fixed. And as this product is itself also positive, its presence in (2.11) drives the foreign noncooperative tariff choice higher than the tariff that would imply $W_{p^*}^* = 0$, ensuring that at the noncooperative tariff, we in fact have $W_{p^*}^* > 0$ (as I have observed).

The fact that these terms lead the home and foreign government to choose tariffs in the noncooperative equilibrium that imply $W_p < 0$ and $W_{p^*}^* > 0$ is also revealing. As Bagwell and Staiger (1999; 2002, chap. 4) show, if each government were offered the opportunity to alter its tariff from the noncooperative level without impacting its terms of trade, it would choose to *cut* its tariff: The home tariff cut would decrease the local relative price p in the home economy according to the second inequality in (2.4), leading to a rise in home welfare in the amount $\Delta W = W_p[-\frac{\partial p}{\partial \tau}] > 0$; and the foreign tariff cut would increase the local relative price p^* in the foreign economy according to the second inequality in (2.4), leading to a rise in foreign welfare in the amount $\Delta W^* = W_{p^*}^*[-\frac{\partial p^*}{\partial \tau^*}] > 0$. Viewed in this light, it is then clear that it is the ability of each government to shift some of the costs of its tariff onto its trading partner through terms-of-trade movements that drives each government to choose the overly high tariffs that obtain in the noncooperative equilibrium.

Hence, regardless of which of the underlying motives for tariff intervention included in the general government objective functions $W(p, p^w)$ and $W^*(p^*, p^w)$ is operative, the purpose of a trade agreement is the same: to eliminate the unilateral incentive that governments have to manipulate their terms of trade and thereby help governments escape from a terms-of-trade-driven prisoner's dilemma.

Bagwell and Staiger (1999, 2002) make this same point, but from the other direction. They observe that the Nash first-order conditions (2.10) and (2.11) would be converted to the conditions (2.16) and (2.17) if the terms-of-trade manipulation terms $W_{p^w}\frac{\partial \bar{p}^w}{\partial \tau}$ and $W_{p^w}^*\frac{\partial \bar{p}^w}{\partial \tau^*}$ were dropped from (2.10) and (2.11), respectively. Further, they demonstrate that the conditions (2.16) and (2.17) define a point on the efficiency frontier, which they refer to as the political optimum. They then observe that the politically optimal tariffs can be interpreted as the tariffs that would arise under unilateral choices in a hypothetical world in which governments are not motivated by the terms-of-trade implications of their trade policy choices, in the sense that the home government acted as if $W_{p^w} \equiv 0$ and the foreign government acted as if $W_{p^w}^* \equiv 0$. And by showing that the tariffs selected unilaterally by governments with these hypothetical preferences would satisfy (2.16) and (2.17) and thus be efficient, where the evaluation of efficiency is undertaken with respect to the actual government preferences, they conclude that when governments have objectives that can be represented by the general form $W(p, p^w)$ and $W^*(p^*, p^w)$ subject to (2.9), the only rationale for a trade agreement is to eliminate the unilateral incentive that governments have to manipulate their terms of trade.

Whether politically optimal tariffs are seen as a particular point on the efficiency frontier that can be usefully compared to the first-order conditions defining the noncooperative tariffs, as I have emphasized here, or as a useful hypothetical thought experiment for noncooperative tariff choices, as in the original Bagwell and Staiger (1999, 2002) presentation, is immaterial. As long as politically optimal tariffs as defined by (2.16) and (2.17) are efficient in a given environment, we can conclude from the Nash first-order conditions (2.10) and (2.11) that the purpose of a trade agreement in that environment is to eliminate the unilateral incentive that governments have to manipulate their terms of trade.[12]

Positive but Also Normative?

Now is a good time to pause and consider a question that has been lurking behind the approach that I have adopted for identifying the purpose of a trade agreement. I have accepted the sovereign right of each national government to define its own policy preferences. I have then characterized the task that a trade agreement must accomplish if it is to eliminate the international inefficiencies associated with unilateral policy choices as judged by the preferences of the member governments. I have called this task the purpose of a trade agreement. Because the GATT/WTO is a member-driven organization and the members are national governments, this seems a reasonable approach from which to draw positive conclusions about the purpose of a trade agreement. But does this approach also have normative implications? Is it enough for the world trading system to serve the interests of its member *governments*? Can a case for the legitimacy of the GATT/WTO be built around a demonstration that it is well designed to serve these interests, where by "legitimacy" I have in mind a "right to rule" concept along the lines articulated by Buchanan and Keohane (2006)?[13]

---

12. Notice that I have said nothing here about whether a trade agreement would actually implement the political optimum, only that the politically optimal tariffs are useful as a comparator to noncooperative tariffs when evaluating the purpose of a trade agreement.
13. Buchanan and Keohane (2006, 411) define legitimacy in the case of global governance institutions as "the right to rule, understood to mean both that institutional agents are

If national governments were always and everywhere the faithful servants of their citizens, where the desires of their citizens were aggregated into policy directives for the governments through political processes that their citizens saw as legitimate, then the answers to these questions would clearly be "yes." But most real-world governments operate far from this ideal. And so, in the real world, the answers are not so clear.

Looking to the international political economy literature for guidance on these questions provides a mixed view. On the specific question of what determines the legitimacy of an international institution, Peter (2017) notes that there are two approaches in the literature: a "state-centered" approach and a "people-centered" approach. Beitz (1979, 408) describes the state-centered approach as one in which "international society is understood as domestic society writ large, with states playing the roles occupied by persons in domestic society." In the people-centered approach, it is instead the welfare of individuals that is taken as the basis for the determination of an international institution's legitimacy (Buchanan 2003). If the purpose of a trade agreement that I have identified above can be interpreted as having normative relevance, then establishing a claim of legitimacy for the GATT/WTO based on a demonstration that it is well designed to serve this purpose falls squarely on the state-centered approach. Under this interpretation, like the preferences of consumers in a domestic context, the preferences of national governments are taken as sovereign in the international context, and the legitimacy of a trade agreement is judged on its ability to deliver efficient outcomes where efficiency is assessed using the preferences of the member governments.[14] This interpretation seems tenuous, but what are the viable alternatives?

One possibility would be to dispense completely with the nation-state as the unit of observation for normative purposes and to evaluate the legitimacy of the GATT/WTO based on how close the agreement comes to maximizing a global social welfare function defined over the welfare of individuals. This would amount to a people-centered approach. For example, the GATT/WTO's design might be judged with

morally justified in making rules and attempting to secure compliance with them and that people subject to those rules have moral, content-independent reasons to follow them and/or to not interfere with others' compliance with them." See also Franck (1990).

14. To be clear, while this approach can be described as state-centered, it is otherwise distinct from the approaches to evaluating legitimacy featured in the international political economy literature and reviewed in Peter (2017), as it uses a different set of (state-centered) criteria.

a criterion based on a utilitarian ideal, where global welfare is measured by the sum of the utilities across all individuals in the world
and where each individual's utility enters that sum with an equal
weight.[15] Or a Rawlsian criterion, under which global social welfare
is only as high as the utility of the least-well-off individual on the
planet, might be used to judge the design of the agreement. As a general
matter, it is of course important to know how an agreement performs
according to these normative benchmarks. But as a means to evaluate
the legitimacy of the GATT/WTO, these benchmarks seem unwork-
able, because to proceed with such an evaluation would require that a
consensus emerge regarding the correct normative benchmark, and it
seems unlikely that such a consensus could ever exist.[16]

Another possibility for assessing legitimacy would be a hybrid approach somewhere in between the state-centered and people-centered
approaches, maintaining the nation-state as the unit of observation but
including more interests from each nation in the global social welfare
function than simply the interests of each member government. Such
an approach might, for example, mirror the "tripartite" structure of
national representation in the International Labor Organization (ILO),
where each member country is represented by three national interests:
its government, its workers, and its employers. The analogue for assessing the legitimacy of the GATT/WTO might be to include in the global
social welfare function used in that assessment representatives of government, exporter, and importer interests in each member country (or
possibly government, producer, and consumer interests). But again, a
consensus on the appropriate representation would be needed to make
this approach workable.[17]

---

15. See Maggi and Ossa (2020) for an approach to evaluating the normative properties of
a trade agreement along these lines.
16. Partly the difficulty in reaching a consensus on this matter rests with the fact that it
involves value judgments over which there will always be disagreements. And partly the
difficulty can be traced to disagreements over factual matters, such as the importance of
market failures and the array of policy instruments that real-world governments have to
pursue their objectives.
17. There is also another issue raised by moving away from a state-centered approach to
evaluating the legitimacy of a trade agreement: If interests beyond those of the member
governments are to be represented in a trade agreement, how are commitments that serve
those interests but not also the interests of the member governments to be enforced? This
issue seems germane for the GATT/WTO, where enforcement ultimately comes down
to tariff retaliation and governments hold the levers of this enforcement mechanism,
and it may explain why under the ILO's tripartite representation (unique among United
Nations agencies) no member state is under any obligation to ratify any ILO convention
or recommendation (see Johnston 1970, 90).

In light of these consideration, it is useful to think of the question of the legitimacy of the world trading system as applying at two levels. First, at the international level there is the question of whether the GATT/WTO can be seen as legitimate from the perspective of the member governments. And second, at the national level there is the question of whether the member governments can be seen as legitimate from the perspective of their own citizens. If both questions can be answered in the affirmative, then the GATT/WTO can be said to be legitimate from both the state-centered and the people-centered perspective. But as trade agreements are fundamentally government-to-government contracts, the key question of legitimacy for the GATT/WTO as an international institution—and the only question whose answer it has any meaningful control over—relates to the first question, not the second.

My approach in this book is to therefore focus on the answer to the first question—Does the GATT/WTO have the moral authority to make rules and attempt to secure compliance with those rules from its member governments—and to acknowledge that an answer to this question can provide only part of the answer to the larger question of the legitimacy of the world trading system. But it is an important part of the answer. If this first question *cannot* be answered in the affirmative, then it is hard to see how the GATT/WTO could remain viable, since it would presumably lack support from the governments that are its members. And if this question can be answered in the affirmative, then the central *international* task in designing a constitution for the world trading system has been accomplished with the design of the GATT/WTO. And with this state-centered task accomplished, attention could then be focused on the task of establishing that each national government satisfies agreed criteria for legitimacy, thereby ensuring that the world trading system, so designed, could be said to be legitimate from a people-centered perspective as well.

Generality

Thus far I have emphasized the wide array of government objectives that are consistent with the conclusion that the purpose of a trade agreement is to eliminate the unilateral incentive that governments have to manipulate their terms of trade. But I have maintained a very particular and simple economic environment within which to derive these results. How dependent is this conclusion on the economic environment within which governments operate? An immediate implication of the discussion above is that this conclusion does depend on governments having a complete set of trade taxes at their disposal. This can be seen from the definition of politically optimal tariffs, which in general requires the use of both τ and τ^* to satisfy the two conditions in (2.16) and (2.17).[18] As has been emphasized by Ossa (2011) and Bagwell and Staiger (2012, 2015, 2016), when limitations are placed on the trade taxes that governments possess, different roles for a trade agreement can arise. That said, some of the most salient restrictions on trade tax/subsidy instruments are associated with commitments made as a *result* of trade agreements (e.g., to restrict the use of export subsidies), and it is not clear that such restrictions should be taken as given when attempting to identify the underlying purpose of trade agreements, as is my intent here.

Beyond the assumption that governments have a complete set of trade taxes, however, the conclusion that the purpose of a trade agreement is to eliminate the unilateral incentive that governments have to manipulate their terms of trade is surprisingly robust to alternative economic environments. It holds in a many-country version of the model that I have outlined, provided that tariffs are imposed on a nondiscriminatory (MFN) basis (Bagwell and Staiger 1999, 2002), and it holds in partial equilibrium versions of these models (Bagwell and Staiger 2001a). It holds in competitive environments for trade in goods or trade in services when governments have access to regulatory standards and/or additional domestic tax/subsidy policies (see Bagwell and Staiger 2001b; Staiger and Sykes 2011, for trade in goods; Staiger and Sykes 2021, for trade in services). And it holds in models of Cournot or monopolistic competition with homogeneous firms (Bagwell and Staiger 2002, chap. 9; 2012a; 2012b; 2015) and in models of monopolistic competition with heterogeneous firms (Bagwell and Lee 2020; Campolmi, Fadinger, and Forlati 2020; Costinot, Rodriguez-Clare, and Werning 2016, 2020). For this reason, it is useful to adopt a common shorthand for referring to models that share this prediction

---

18. An exception is when the government objective functions take the particular form in (2.5) and (2.6) and the politically optimal tariffs correspond to reciprocal free trade, a point on the Mayer locus. In this case, if only one of the two governments had access to a tariff, it could still be concluded that the purpose of a trade agreement is to eliminate the unilateral incentive that this government has to manipulate its terms of trade, because at the political optimum neither government imposes a tariff, so it is immaterial that one of them does not have access to a tariff. And Staiger and Sykes (2021) show that the lack of available trade taxes that can arise with certain types of services trade does not change the purpose of a trade agreement; I review their findings in chapter 9. Also, to be clear, notice that for the arguments in the text to remain valid, there is no requirement that governments have a complete set of *tax* instruments, only that they have a complete set of *trade* taxes.

about the purpose of a trade agreement, and I will follow Bagwell and Staiger's (2002) terminology and sometimes make use of the phrase "terms-of-trade theory of trade agreements" as a catchall for models of this kind.[19]

This is not to say that preventing terms-of-trade manipulation is the only possible purpose for a trade agreement. Indeed, as I noted at the outset of this chapter, I am intentionally abstracting from the possibility that a trade agreement could serve as a policy commitment device for its member governments when those governments struggle to make policy commitments to their private sectors on their own. And as I will review in later chapters, the arguments I have made here do not extend to all economic environments; as I alluded to in chapter 1, some of the environments where these arguments do not extend may be more important in the twenty-first century than they were in the twentieth century, raising the possibility of an evolution of the purpose of trade agreements over time. But as I have illustrated here, these arguments do apply in a remarkably broad set of circumstances, suggesting that a trade agreement that is designed well to solve the terms-of-trade manipulation problem will be a very useful trade agreement to its member governments. From this perspective, it is therefore meaningful when assessing the reasons for GATT's success and determining the basis for its legitimacy to evaluate the degree to which its design features are well equipped to serve this function. It is to this evaluation that I now turn.

---

19. But see Grossman (2016) for a different perspective on this terminology.

3   What Do Trade Negotiators Negotiate About?

In chapter 2, I presented formal arguments that point to the elimination of terms-of-trade manipulation as the central purpose of a trade agreement, and I suggested that this provides a natural dimension on which to evaluate the design features of GATT. How well-designed is GATT to help its member governments solve the terms-of-trade manipulation problem and thereby escape from a terms-of-trade-driven prisoner's dilemma? In this and the next two chapters I evaluate GATT's design as it relates to tariff bargaining, the foundational activity in the GATT/WTO. After some preliminaries, I begin this evaluation by asking what negotiators negotiate about in the GATT/WTO. If there is no evidence that these negotiations serve to remove the imprint of market power from unilateral tariff choices, then there is little point in asking whether the design features of the GATT/WTO can be interpreted as helping to serve this purpose.

3.1   Preliminaries

Three of the most basic features of GATT tariff negotiations raise questions about the wisdom of GATT's design (and the negotiating behavior it induces), and pose an immediate challenge to the terms-of-trade theory if these features are to be interpreted through the lens of that theory. Why do governments adopt a mercantilist approach in GATT/WTO negotiations, viewing their own tariff cuts as "concessions" to be granted only in return for foreign tariff cuts from their trading partners? What accounts for the emphasis on market access that permeates the language of GATT/WTO tariff negotiations? And how can governments hope to achieve meaningful benefits from GATT/WTO negotiations anyway if their negotiations are focused narrowly on tariffs to the exclusion of the myriad other government interventions that can also have trade effects? Since any model of trade agreements that purports to capture the underlying logic of the GATT/WTO must be able to account for these basic features of GATT tariff negotiations, I begin this chapter by considering how these three questions can be answered within the modeling framework of chapter 2.

If tariff negotiations begin from the noncooperative tariff choices characterized by equations (2.10) and (2.11), the first question has an immediate answer: Beginning from their tariff reaction curves, governments should view *any* change in their own tariffs as a concession, to be granted only in return for something that they would value from their negotiating partner; and as Bagwell and Staiger (1999; 2002, chap. 4) show, and as I described in chapter 2, from this starting point each government would indeed gain from at least a small *cut* in its own tariff if its trading partner agreed to *reciprocate* with a tariff cut of its own that was calibrated to preserve the terms of trade between them—recall from the first inequality in equation (2.4) that it is indeed a downward movement in the trading partner's tariff that would achieve this. Hence, while the government behavior singled out by this first question might seem surprising and somehow mercantilist if one took the view that the logic of trade negotiations should be based on the case for free trade, from the perspective of the terms-of-trade theory of trade agreements embodied in the modeling framework of chapter 2, this behavior is not surprising at all: there is no other way that governments *could* behave.[1]

The answers to the second and third questions are related to each other and more nuanced. A first observation is that GATT tariff negotiations are indeed considered negotiations over *market access*, with tariff commitments treated as commitments to *conditions of competition* in the domestic market between domestic producers and foreign suppliers.[2] I have developed the modeling framework of chapter 2 without reference to the phrase "market access restrictions," making use instead of the phrase "terms-of-trade improvement." But as Bagwell and Staiger

---

1. Bagwell and Staiger (2002, 191–192) provide the proof in this setting that a trade agreement must entail tariff cuts by each country if it is to improve upon the noncooperative welfare levels for each country.

2. As a GATT/WTO legal matter, market access is defined by the competitive relationship between imported and domestically produced products, and a negotiated tariff commitment is treated as a policy commitment to a particular competitive relationship between imported and domestic products and hence a market-access commitment.

(2002, 28–30) have shown, a direct link between these two phrases is easily forged: When the home government raises its import tariff and thereby shifts in its import demand curve, the consequent "price effect" (i.e., the home country's terms-of-trade improvement) has a corresponding "volume effect" (i.e., the foreign country's reduction in access to the home market). Viewed from this perspective, the terms-of-trade theory has no difficulty accounting for the fact that real-world negotiators emphasize the market access implications of trade policy.[3]

To illustrate the point more formally, I follow Bagwell and Staiger (2002, 28–30) and, for a given world price p^w and home tariff τ, define the market access that the home country affords to the foreign country by the home-country import demand function evaluated at that world price and home tariff level, $M_x(p(\tau, p^w), p^w)$; similarly, given a world price p^w and a foreign tariff τ^*, I define the market access that the foreign country affords to the home country by $M_y^*(p^*(\tau^*, p^w), p^w)$. Let us now say that a government secures additional market access from its trading partner through negotiations if the trading partner's negotiated policy changes shift out its import demand curve for at least *some* world price. According to this definition, if the home government were to *fail* to secure additional market access as a result of the foreign government's agreed policy changes, then the foreign import demand curve would shift in (weakly) at all world price levels and lead to a (weakly) higher equilibrium world price $\tilde{p}^w$ and therefore a terms-of-trade loss (weakly) for the home country, assuming that the Marshall-Lerner stability conditions are met. With the link between changes in market access and changes in the terms of trade established, the findings of the terms-of-trade theory can be translated into the language of market access. For instance, it may be confirmed (Bagwell and Staiger 2001b) that the essential inefficiency arising in the noncooperative tariff choices characterized by (2.10) and (2.11) can be described as one of insufficient market access. Hence, the modeling framework of chapter 2 provides a rationale for why governments would emphasize the market access implications of trade policy and seek to expand market access in their tariff negotiations. This answers the second question posed above.

---

3. This emphasis can be seen, for example, in the following excerpt from a GATT dispute panel report (as quoted in Petersmann 1997, 168): "The main value of a tariff concession is that it provides assurance of better market access through improved price competition. Contracting parties negotiate tariff concessions primarily to obtain that advantage."

In answer to the third question, a starting point is to observe that, while governments do focus narrowly on tariffs in their market access negotiations, it is not true that this focus is to the exclusion of the myriad other government interventions that can also have trade effects through their impacts on the conditions of competition. Indeed, the very purpose of many of the GATT articles that lay down the code of conduct described in chapter 2 is to ensure that nontariff policy interventions do not unilaterally alter the market access implications of a negotiated tariff commitment, and thereby to secure the property rights over negotiated market access that a tariff commitment implies.[4]

The real issue raised by this third question, then, is whether governments can negotiate to the efficiency frontier under the *shallow* approach to liberalization that GATT embodies, whereby governments negotiate only over tariffs and where the tariff commitments they make translate into market-access commitments as a result of the accompanying GATT articles. Is it possible to reach the efficiency frontier with respect to *all* government policies when governments negotiate directly only over tariffs in this way? As I next demonstrate, the answer according to the terms-of-trade theory is, at least in principle, "yes."

To this end, I now extend the modeling framework from chapter 2 to allow governments to also choose regulatory standards. To keep things simple, I will focus on a production standard, such as a minimum legal working age or a maximum legal emissions level per unit of output, which might be applied to a particular sector or on an economy-wide basis and which could potentially alter the shape of the country's production possibilities frontier and hence, for given local prices, its production choices. Below I sketch arguments that can be found in more detail in Bagwell and Staiger (2001b).[5]

By letting σ denote the standard in the home country and σ^* the standard in the foreign country, it is direct to show that introducing these standards into the modeling framework of chapter 2 will result in two

---

4. As Petersmann (1997, 136) observes, "the function of most GATT rules (such as Articles I–III and XI) is to establish conditions of competition and to protect trading opportunities"

5. These arguments have been extended to the case of domestic production subsidies and to the case of competition policy by Bagwell and Staiger (2006) and Bagwell and Staiger (2002, chap. 9), respectively, and to the case of product standards and domestic production and consumption taxes/subsidies by Staiger and Sykes (2011) for trade in goods and by Staiger and Sykes (2021) for trade in services. I will discuss environments where these arguments do not hold, as pointed out by Antràs and Staiger (2012a, 2012b) and Grossman, McCalman, and Staiger (2021), in chapters 10 and 11, respectively.

changes to the model. First, the equilibrium world price determined by the market clearing condition now takes the form $\widetilde{p}^w = \widetilde{p}^w(\sigma, \sigma^*, \tau, \tau^*)$: That is, in addition to its tariff, a country's standard also impacts the equilibrium world price through its impact on the country's production possibilities frontier. And second, as each government may have its own reasons to set its standard, the home and foreign government objectives are now represented, respectively, by $W(\sigma, p(\tau, \widetilde{p}^w), \widetilde{p}^w)$ and $W^*(\sigma^*, p^*(\tau^*, \widetilde{p}^w), \widetilde{p}^w)$, with

$$\frac{\partial W(\sigma, p, \widetilde{p}^w)}{\partial \widetilde{p}^w} < 0 \text{ and } \frac{\partial W^*(\sigma^*, p^*, \widetilde{p}^w)}{\partial \widetilde{p}^w} > 0,$$

but otherwise left unrestricted as before. Importantly, as the government objectives reflect, I am assuming the absence of cross-border nonpecuniary externalities associated with standards choices so that neither government cares *directly* about the standard chosen by the other government but only indirectly through the possible *trade effects* of that choice. I am therefore excluding the possibility that the government of one country might care about how weak labor standards in its trading partner would impact the welfare of the trading partner's workforce, but I am including the possibility that this government might care about the trade effects of the trading partner's weak labor standards and be concerned that these trade effects could fuel "race-to-the-bottom" pressures that might lead to the adoption of weak labor standards also in its own country.

It is straightforward to show that equation (2.15) continues to provide the condition for efficient tariffs in this extended setting. And when combined with this condition, the first-order conditions that the efficient standards must satisfy can be written as

$$W_\sigma + W_p \frac{dp}{d\tau} \frac{d\tau}{d\sigma}\Big|_{d\widetilde{p}^w=0} = 0 \tag{3.1}$$

$$W^*_{\sigma^*} + W^*_{p^*} \frac{dp^*}{d\tau^*} \frac{d\tau^*}{d\sigma^*}\Big|_{d\widetilde{p}^w=0} = 0. \tag{3.2}$$

The efficiency frontier is therefore attained when tariffs satisfy (2.15) and standards satisfy (3.1) and (3.2). The interpretation of (3.1) and (3.2) is central to understanding why a shallow approach to integration can work in this setting.

Consider the first-order condition for the efficient choice of the home-country standard σ. According to (3.1), σ should be chosen to maximize the welfare of the home government when the home government also adjusts its tariff τ so as to ensure that the equilibrium world price $\widetilde{p}^w$ does not change. The reason this standards choice is efficient is that, provided that $\widetilde{p}^w$ is not altered, the foreign government is indifferent to both the level of τ and the level of σ that the home government chooses, as can be confirmed by inspection of the foreign government's welfare function $W^*(\sigma^*, p^*(\tau^*, \widetilde{p}^w), \widetilde{p}^w)$; therefore, efficiency demands that the home government should also be indifferent to small changes in σ that, with the accompanying changes in τ defined in (3.1), preserve $\widetilde{p}^w$. But recalling now the definition of market access introduced previously, it is clear that the changes in σ and τ that preserve $\widetilde{p}^w$ are simply those changes that hold fixed the position of the home import demand curve evaluated at the initial equilibrium world price $\widetilde{p}^w$, and hence they amount to changes in σ and τ that preserve the market access evaluated at the initial equilibrium world price $\widetilde{p}^w$ that the home government has granted to the foreign government through tariff negotiations.

In this light, it can now be seen that tariff negotiations to achieve efficient levels of market access, in combination with a code of conduct spelled out in a set of GATT articles to ensure that nontariff policy interventions cannot unilaterally alter the market access implied of a tariff commitment, contain all the ingredients to allow governments, at least in principle, to reach the efficiency frontier in their settings of both tariffs *and* standards. In particular, as Bagwell and Staiger (2001b) demonstrate, if governments were to negotiate over tariffs alone, and if they were then permitted to make unilateral standards choices while also compelled by GATT's "market-access preservation rules" to accompany these standards choices with tariff adjustments that preserve the market access implied by their negotiated tariff selections, then they would negotiate tariffs that satisfy (2.15) and make standards choices that satisfy (3.1) and (3.2). Evidently, with these "shallow" negotiations, the governments would reach the efficiency frontier, and the terms-of-trade theory thereby provides a strong foundation for a shallow approach to negotiated trade liberalization.[6]

---

6. What is not provided by the arguments I have reviewed here is a formal explanation for why governments would prefer this method of liberalization to the alternative of deep integration, where the governments negotiate directly over all policies—both tariffs and nontariff instruments. In chapter 12, I will suggest one possible explanation. Also, while there is a basic affinity between the theoretical arguments I have presented here and the shallow approach to trade liberalization embodied in GATT/WTO rules, Bagwell and

Notice also that the terms-of-trade theory provides an interpretation, with a twist, of the common observation that GATT began with the "low-hanging fruit" of tariff liberalization and only later had to confront the more difficult task of dealing with behind-the-border measures. The twist is that, according to the terms-of-trade theory, the fundamental problem for a trade agreement to address has not changed; it is simply that as tariffs were negotiated downward, the pressure to distort behind-the-border policies for inefficient terms-of-trade manipulation reasons grew, and the initial GATT rules that were supposed to ensure a code of conduct in the international-trade arena to prevent such behavior proved inadequate for the task. The result has been a growing focus over time on addressing the trade-distorting aspects of nontariff barriers. Importantly, what is revealed under this interpretation is that there are two plausible ways to respond to this challenge. One response is to give up on GATT's shallow approach to integration and the rules applying to behind-the-border measures that were meant to facilitate that approach and to pursue instead deep integration. But an alternative response, and one which as a matter of principle the terms-of-trade theory puts on equal footing, is to maintain GATT's basic approach and work to strengthen the rules that could facilitate shallow integration.

Finally, it should be acknowledged that I have abstracted from a number of challenges that a shallow approach to integration must overcome in practice, and these abstractions have allowed me to draw a sharper line between shallow and deep integration than exists in reality. At a more practical level, therefore, the message of the terms-of-trade theory is not so much that *no* degree of deep integration is necessary to reach the efficiency frontier, but rather that the market-access orientation of the GATT/WTO can provide a potentially useful *guardrail* to delineate the "depth" of integration that trade agreements should be willing to contemplate in order to reach the efficiency frontier: According to the terms-of-trade theory, there is no reason for a trade agreement to go deeper than what is required to ensure that property rights over negotiated market access are reasonably secure. Such a guardrail can help governments avoid conflicts between globalization and national sovereignty that, according to the terms-of-trade theory, would be unnecessary.

Staiger (2001b) propose modifications to GATT/WTO rules that would more closely align those rules with these theoretical arguments.

This answers the third question posed at the outset of this chapter. With these most basic questions addressed, I now turn to the central question of the chapter: What do trade negotiators negotiate about?

3.2 Evidence from WTO Accession Negotiations

If the GATT/WTO is well designed to help its member governments escape from a terms-of-trade-driven prisoner's dilemma, there should be evidence of this in the pattern of tariff cuts that the member governments agree to in a GATT/WTO negotiation. Looking for such evidence would be simple if all governments sought to maximize the real national income of their citizens with their tariff choices and negotiations were assumed to take governments to the political optimum: One might simply look to see how close governments got to reciprocal free trade as a result of their negotiations. But when governments have diverse preferences over trade policy, such as is reflected in the objective functions that I have adopted in the modeling framework of chapter 2, things are not as straightforward. According to the terms-of-trade theory, if governments are able to negotiate to the political optimum, what should remain after the GATT/WTO negotiations are completed is the portion of each government's noncooperative tariff choices that are not driven by the international cost shifting that is associated with terms-of-trade manipulation. The challenge in evaluating the performance of GATT/WTO negotiations is, then, to disentangle these two components of noncooperative tariffs so that the magnitude of the cost-shifting component reflected in the noncooperative tariff levels can be compared to the magnitude of the negotiated tariff cuts.

Of course, this all presupposes that governments would be caught in a terms-of-trade-driven prisoner's dilemma in the absence of tariff negotiations, which in turn requires that countries possess significant and widespread market power in world markets and that the unilateral tariff choices of governments reflect the market power that they possess. Broda, Limão, and Weinstein (2008) provided the first systematic evidence on these prior questions, and as I noted in chapter 1, they find strong evidence that countries routinely have market power in their import markets and use it in setting noncooperative trade policy.[7] Here I focus on the pattern of tariff liberalization in GATT/WTO

---

7. For a review of the broader empirical literature on these questions, see Bagwell, Bown, and Staiger (2016). A number of papers have exploited the aggressive use of tariffs by the Trump administration and the tariff responses of its trading partners to investigate

negotiations. I describe the findings of Bagwell and Staiger (2011), who explore whether the observed tariff cuts in WTO accession negotiations conform with the tariff cuts that, according to the terms-of-trade theory, would deliver governments to the political optimum.[8]

To identify the portion of a government's noncooperatively chosen tariff level that is driven by international cost shifting, I now return to the expressions for the noncooperative tariffs and the politically optimal tariffs presented in chapter 2. Focusing on the home government, the expression for the noncooperative tariff in (2.10) can be rewritten as

$$Home\ Reaction\ Function : W_p = -W_{p^w} \left[\frac{\partial \tilde{p}^w / \partial \tau}{dp / d\tau} \right],$$

and recall that the politically optimal tariff for the home government is defined in (2.16) by the condition

$$Home\ Political\ Optimum : W_p = 0.$$

I impose the assumption that $W_{pp} < 0$ holds globally over nonprohibitive tariffs. This condition must hold as long as W is globally concave over nonprohibitive tariffs even if the home country is small on world markets, so that there exists a unique solution to the home government's unilateral welfare-maximizing tariff choice. And I assume for the moment that if the home government were to cut its tariff from its reaction-curve level to its politically optimal level, the foreign government would respond with a tariff cut that was calibrated to hold the equilibrium world price $\tilde{p}^w$ constant. I can then write the difference between the home government's noncooperative tariff and its politically optimal tariff as

$$\tau^{BR} - \tau^{PO} = H \left(-W_{p^w} \left[\frac{\partial \tilde{p}^w / \partial \tau}{dp / d\tau} \right] \right),$$ (3.3)

where I now denote by τ^{BR} the home government's "best response" tariff that solves (2.10) for any foreign tariff, where $H(0) = 0$ and H is a decreasing function and where all the magnitudes on the right-hand

---

how local and world prices respond to the imposition of tariffs (see, for example, Amiti, Redding, and Weinstein 2019 2020; Fajgelbaum et al. 2020; and Cavallo et al. 2021). I discuss the findings of these papers in the context of material presented in chapter 5.

8. See Bagwell and Staiger (2016, 488–492) for a discussion of why the political optimum, among all possible points on the efficiency frontier, might be viewed as a natural focal outcome of GATT/WTO negotiations.

side of (3.3) are evaluated at the noncooperative tariff level τ^{BR}. Finally, rearranging (3.3) delivers an expression for the home government's politically optimal tariff, expressed in terms of magnitudes evaluated at its noncooperative tariff level:

$$\tau^{PO} = \tau^{BR} - H\left(-W_{p^w}\left[\frac{\partial \widetilde{p}^w / \partial \tau}{dp/d\tau}\right]\right). \tag{3.4}$$

In effect, (3.4) points to the term $-W_{p^w}\left[\frac{\partial \widetilde{p}^w / \partial \tau}{dp/d\tau}\right]$, evaluated at the home government's noncooperative tariff choice, as the determinant of the component of the home government's noncooperative tariff that is attributable to terms-of-trade manipulation and the international cost shifting that it represents, and therefore as the determinant of the magnitude of the tariff cut which according to (3.3) is required to move the home government from its noncooperative tariff choice to its politically optimal level. This term, which is weakly negative under (2.4) and (2.9), is composed of three sub-terms, each with a ready interpretation. The home country's market power on world import markets is reflected in $\partial \widetilde{p}^w / \partial \tau$, with (3.4) implying that $\tau^{PO} = \tau^{BR}$ when the home country is small on world markets and $\partial \widetilde{p}^w / \partial \tau = 0$, and with τ^{PO} falling further below τ^{BR} as the market power of the home country rises and $\partial \widetilde{p}^w / \partial \tau$ becomes increasingly negative. This market power effect is tempered by the magnitude of $dp/d\tau$, which reflects the size of the domestic distortion introduced by the home tariff and keeps τ^{PO} closer to τ^{BR} when this distortion and hence $dp/d\tau$ is higher. Finally, $-W_{p^w}$ reflects the value that the home government places on a small improvement in its terms of trade; with its local prices held fixed when evaluating $-W_{p^w}$, this amounts to the degree to which the home government values the extra tariff revenue that is generated by the fall in p^w and the implied rise in $\tau = \frac{p}{p^w} - 1$, all evaluated at τ^{BR}. Notice that as τ^{BR} approaches the prohibitive level and home imports shrink toward zero, $-W_{p^w}$ approaches zero (because the import volume on which tariff revenue is earned approaches zero) and τ^{PO} approaches τ^{BR} from below.

In order to take relationships like (3.3) and (3.4) to the data, Bagwell and Staiger (2011) work with a partial equilibrium many-good, many-country version of the model of chapter 2 where income effects are absent. Under MFN tariffs, there continues to be a common world price $\widetilde{p}_g^w$ faced by all countries for each good g. For simplicity, I continue for now to couch the discussion in terms of a two-country home-and-foreign world and only introduce notation for the many-country version of the model when that notation is needed.

In the partial equilibrium version of the model where all tariff revenue is spent on the numeraire good, the relationships in (3.3) and (3.4) hold for each non-numeraire good g, imports of good g (denoted by M_g) depend only on the local price of good g (denoted by p_g), and $W_{p_g^w} = -M_g(p_g(\tau_g, \tilde{p}_g^w))$, reflecting the fact that the magnitude of the (negative) income effect of a small deterioration in the home country's terms of trade for good g, holding its local price of good g fixed, is given by the volume of its imports of good g. Bagwell and Staiger then show that for home import good g, the term $W_{p^w}\left[\frac{\partial \tilde{p}^w/\partial \tau}{dp/d\tau}\right]$ that enters (3.3) and (3.4) can be written equivalently as $\frac{M_g^{BR}}{p_g^{BR}}\left[\frac{\omega_g^{BR}}{\eta_g^{*BR}}\right]$, where ω_g^{BR} is the elasticity of home import demand (defined positively) for good g and η_g^{*BR} is the elasticity of foreign export supply of good g, and where the superscript BR indicates that the variable is evaluated at the best-response home tariff τ_g^{BR} for import good g. A particularly simple form of these relationships arises when demand and supply curves are linear. In this case, and focusing on (3.3), the difference $\tau_g^{BR} - \tau_g^{PO}$ is proportional to $\frac{M_g^{BR}}{\tilde{p}_g^{wBR}}$: That is, according to the terms-of-trade theory, if governments use their GATT/WTO negotiations to move from non-cooperative tariffs to the point on the efficiency frontier at which they each adopt politically optimal tariffs, then when demands and supplies are linear their negotiated tariff cuts should rise proportionately with the ratio of pre-negotiation (noncooperative) import volume to world price.

A challenge in taking these predictions to the data is that they are developed in a static model where tariff negotiations are conceived as a one-off event that carries countries from their noncooperative tariff choices to the politically optimal tariffs. In fact, there have been eight completed rounds of GATT negotiations spanning many decades and culminating in 1995 with the completion of the Uruguay Round and the creation of the WTO. This gradual liberalization process complicates the possibility of a straightforward application of the predictions embodied in (3.3) and (3.4) to the observed negotiated tariff cuts of the GATT/WTO membership.

To overcome this challenge, Bagwell and Staiger focus on a set of non-GATT-member countries who joined the WTO in separate accession negotiations occurring after the Uruguay Round was completed.

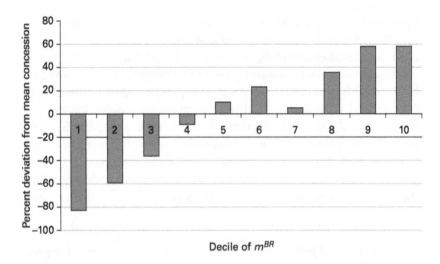

Decile of m^{BR}

Figure 3.1
Percent deviation from mean concession by m^{BR} decile. *Source*: Reproduced from Bagwell and Staiger (2011, fig. 1).

These accession negotiations come close to the one-off negotiating events that the model envisions. The maintained hypothesis is that, at the time of these negotiations, existing GATT/WTO members had largely completed the process of negotiating their tariffs to politically optimal levels, and new members were therefore asked to agree to once-and-for-all tariff cuts from best-response to politically optimal levels in exchange for the rights of WTO membership. A limitation of this focus is that it excludes from the evaluation of GATT/WTO tariff liberalization the major industrialized countries that were all original or early GATT members and historically have been the dominant actors in GATT/WTO tariff negotiations. I will return to this point below. Figures 3.1 and 3.2 confirm that the patterns of tariff liberalization predicted by (3.3) are present in the data.

For a sample of 16 countries that negotiated membership in the WTO subsequent to its creation in 1995, figure 3.1 plots the percent deviation from mean negotiated tariff cut against the decile of pre-negotiation import volume to world price, $m^{BR} \equiv \frac{M_{gc}^{BR}}{\tilde{p}_g^{wBR}}$, where the subscript c now indexes these acceding countries and the subscript g refers to a six-digit Harmonized System (HS) product. Evidently, negotiated tariff cuts rise in a roughly proportional way with normalized pre-negotiation import volume $\frac{M_{gc}^{BR}}{\tilde{p}_g^{wBR}}$, as is predicted by the version of (3.3) that applies to

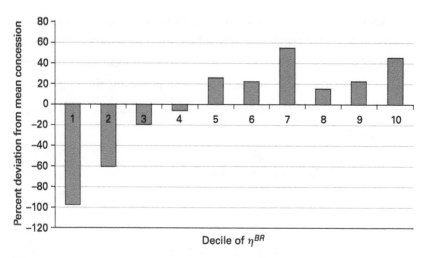

Figure 3.2
Percent deviations from mean concessions by η^{BR} decile. *Source*: Reproduced from Bagwell and Staiger (2011, fig. 2).

a partial equilibrium model where demands and supplies are linear. And, for a sample of five of these countries where estimates of ω_{gc}^{BR} and η_{gc}^{*BR} from Broda, Limão, and Weinstein (2008) are available, figure 3.2 plots the percent deviation from mean negotiated tariff cut by decile of $\eta^{BR} \equiv \frac{M_{gc}^{BR}}{p_{gc}^{BR}}\left[\frac{\omega_{gc}^{BR}}{\eta_{gc}^{*BR}}\right]$, revealing a strong positive relationship as the terms-of-trade theory predicts.

Bagwell and Staiger also present regression results based on the relationship in (3.4), both for their partial equilibrium model with general demands and supplies and for the special case of that model in which demands and supplies are linear. Recall that in deriving (3.3) and (3.4), I assumed that if the home government were to cut its tariff from its reaction-curve level to its politically optimal level, the foreign government would respond with a tariff cut that was calibrated to hold the equilibrium world price $\tilde{p}^w$ constant. To derive relationships that form the basis of their estimated regressions, Bagwell and Staiger relax this assumption and allow for more general tariff responses from trading partners (or no response at all). As they demonstrate, this influences the interpretation of some of the estimated coefficients in their regressions but does not change the essential predictions of the terms-of-trade theory with regard to the pattern of tariff liberalization that should be observed: If WTO negotiations implement the efficient political optimum, then controlling for the level of the pre-negotiation tariff τ_{gc}^{BR}, the tariff level on imports of good g to which the government of country c agrees in a WTO negotiation should be lower the larger is the magnitude of the pre-negotiation normalized import volume $\frac{M_{gc}^{BR}}{\widetilde{p}_g^{wBR}}$ (in the case of linear demands and supplies) or, more generally, the larger is the pre-negotiation cost-shifting term $\frac{M_{gc}^{BR}}{p_{gc}^{BR}} \left[\frac{\omega_{gc}^{BR}}{\eta_{gc}^{*BR}} \right]$. Estimating regressions of the form

$$\tau_{gc}^{WTO} = \beta_0 + \beta_1 \tau_{gc}^{BR} + \beta_2 \frac{M_{gc}^{BR}}{\widetilde{p}_{gc}^{wBR}} + \epsilon_{gc} \tag{3.5}$$

and

$$\tau_{gc}^{WTO} = \phi_0 + \phi_1 \tau_{gc}^{BR} + \phi_2 \frac{M_{gc}^{BR}}{p_{gc}^{BR}} \left[\frac{\omega_{gc}^{BR}}{\eta_{gc}^{*BR}} \right] + \upsilon_{gc}, \tag{3.6}$$

where τ_{gc}^{WTO} is the ad valorem tariff level bound by acceding country c on HS six-digit product g in its GATT/WTO negotiation and ϵ_{gc} and υ_{gc} are error terms, Bagwell and Staiger find robust evidence that $\hat{\beta}_1 > 0$ and $\hat{\beta}_2 < 0$ and that $\hat{\phi}_1 > 0$ and $\hat{\phi}_2 < 0$, as the terms-of-trade theory predicts.

I noted earlier that a limitation of the 2011 Bagwell and Staiger paper is that, in focusing on non-GATT-member countries that joined the WTO in accession negotiations after the Uruguay Round was completed, the paper excludes from the evaluation of GATT/WTO tariff liberalization the major industrialized countries that were all original or early GATT members and historically dominanted GATT/WTO tariff negotiations. This limitation is addressed by Ludema and Mayda (2013), who extend the search for tariff-bargaining evidence consistent with the terms-of-trade theory to a broader and more representative cross-section of the GATT/WTO membership.

To develop the prediction that they take to the data, Ludema and Mayda (2013) work within a partial equilibrium, perfectly competitive many-good many-country model along the lines employed by Bagwell and Staiger (2011). In this model, as I have observed above, the purpose of a trade agreement is to eliminate the implications of market power from the unilateral tariff choices that governments would otherwise make. But while Bagwell and Staiger assess the extent to which the observed tariff cuts in WTO accession negotiations conform to the tariff cuts that would implement the political optimum and hence can be understood from the perspective of the terms-of-trade theory as allowing governments to reach the efficiency frontier, Ludema and Mayda assess the extent to which free-riding by nonparticipants in the negotiations—and the consequent *failure* of GATT/WTO tariff bargaining to reach the efficiency frontier—can be understood from the perspective of the terms-of-trade theory.

In particular, to capture key features of the GATT/WTO tariff-bargaining process, Ludema and Mayda (2013) posit an extensive form tariff negotiation game in which countries negotiate bilaterally over MFN tariffs and participation is endogenous.[9] They exploit the fact that, when importing country c cuts an MFN tariff on product g, all exporting countries facing that tariff enjoy the same terms-of-trade improvement, $\partial \tilde{p}_g^w / \partial \tau_{gc}$, the magnitude of which depends on country c's market power. But recall that in this partial equilibrium setting, the magnitude of the (negative) income effect of a small deterioration in country c's terms of trade for good g, holding fixed its local price of good g, is given simply by the volume of its imports of good g, $W_{p_g^w}^c = -M_{gc}(p_{gc}(\tau_{gc}, \tilde{p}_g^w))$. The flip side is that the (positive) income effect of the implied terms-of-trade improvement that is enjoyed by each exporting country c^* varies in proportion to its *share* of country c's total imports of product g: $W_{p_g^w}^{c^*} = \theta_{gc}^{c^*} \times M_{gc}(p_{gc}(\tau_{gc}, \tilde{p}_g^w))$, where $\theta_{gc}^{c^*}$ is the share of country c's imports of good g that is supplied by exporting country c^*.

Ludema and Mayda (2013) show that in the model of MFN tariff bargaining with endogenous participation that they propose, if inefficiency occurs in equilibrium in the negotiation over τ_{gc}, it occurs because exporters of good g to country c below a critical export-share threshold—who by the above logic have less to gain from a reduction in τ_{gc}—choose not to participate in the negotiation with country c over τ_{gc} and choose instead to free-ride on the MFN tariff cut that country c agrees to in its negotiation over τ_{gc} with those exporters of good g *above* the critical export-share threshold who, having the most to gain from a reduction in τ_{gc}, choose to participate in the negotiations. And Ludema and Mayda show that an implication of this finding is that where exporters of a good g into country c are less concentrated as

---

9. I discuss the tariff negotiation game posited by Ludema and Mayda (2013) again at various points in chapters 4 and 5, when I compare their approach to modeling GATT tariff negotiations with the approaches adopted by Bagwell, Staiger, and Yurukoglu (2020a, 2020b, 2021).

measured by the Herfindahl index, free-riding in GATT/WTO tariff negotiations will be more of a problem, and the negotiated level of τ_{gc} will continue to bear more of the imprint of country c's market power than in the case where exporters are highly concentrated.

It is this relationship between exporter concentration and the degree to which negotiated tariff levels continue to reflect importer market power, derived in a setting that appends a particular model of tariff bargaining to an underlying model conforming to the terms-of-trade theory of trade agreements, that Ludema and Mayda (2013) study and take to the data. Focusing on 36 GATT members that include all the major industrialized countries as well as a number of developing and emerging economies, they find that as a result of the free-rider effects created by MFN, between one-tenth and one-quarter of the tariff liberalization that would have been required in the Uruguay Round, to completely eliminate the imprint of market power from these tariff schedules and to bring these countries all the way to the efficiency frontier, did not occur. As I noted previously, Ludema and Mayda therefore provide an important quantification of the failure of GATT/WTO tariff bargaining to reach the efficiency frontier as a result of the MFN free-rider effect in the Uruguay Round. But along the way they also provide strong confirmation of the predictions of the terms-of-trade theory itself for a wide cross-section of the GATT/WTO membership, concluding that the terms-of-trade-manipulation motive drives unilateral tariff choices and that GATT tariff negotiating rounds were intended to neutralize this motive.

Like Ludema and Mayda (2013), other researchers have also found evidence consistent with the predictions of the terms-of-trade theory in the negotiated tariff outcomes of a wide cross-section of the GATT/WTO membership. For example, Nicita, Olarreaga, and Silva (2018) focus on the nature of the tariff commitments made by WTO member countries—commitments that, as I have noted, take the form of bindings defining the maximum allowable level for the tariff—and exploit the fact that countries differ in the degree to which their negotiated WTO tariff commitments constrain their applied tariffs (i.e., the tariff levels that they actually set). Developing a prediction of the terms-of-trade theory that relates both the tariffs that are applied at the level of the binding and those that are applied below the binding to measures of a country's market power, and examining the tariffs of 101 WTO member countries, Nicita, Olarreaga, and Silva find evidence broadly consistent with this prediction.[10] Beshkar and Bond (2017) similarly use the terms-of-trade theory to develop a relationship between the market power that a country wields, on the one hand, and on the other hand, the levels at which it binds its tariffs in GATT/WTO negotiations and the tariffs that it actually applies. In this case, exploiting the fact that, as described in chapter 2, a country can under certain conditions escape from its tariff bindings and set applied tariffs above the binding, they find support for the relationship predicted by the terms-of-trade theory in this regard in the tariffs of 109 WTO members.[11]

Together, these papers provide reinforcing evidence that the observed pattern of negotiated tariff cuts in the GATT/WTO corresponds with the pattern of observed market power in the way that the terms-of-trade theory suggests that it should.

10. See also Beshkar, Bond, and Rho (2015) for related findings that focus on the relationship predicted by the terms-of-trade theory between market power and the *difference* between the bound and applied level of the tariff ("tariff overhang"); they find empirical support for this relationship in tariff data for 108 WTO member countries.
11. See also Bown and Crowley (2013) who, using data on the antidumping and safeguard actions of the United States over the period 1997–2006, find empirical support for predictions of the terms-of-trade theory when that theory is developed in a repeated-tariff-game setting subject to stochastic trade volume shocks and where self-enforcement constraints are binding.

4 Tariff Bargaining in the GATT/WTO

In chapter 3, I presented evidence that countries use GATT negotiations to help them remove the imprint of market power from their unilateral tariff choices. In this chapter, I move on to the next logical question: How well designed is GATT to help its member governments achieve this purpose? A unique feature of the GATT and its successor, the WTO is that detailed bargaining records for many of its negotiation rounds are available to researchers and can be used to help answer this question. With these bargaining records, it is possible to probe beyond the outcomes of GATT/WTO negotiations and examine the bargaining behavior that led to those outcomes. In this chapter, I describe research that makes use of these records.[1]

Each GATT/WTO round proceeds under a specific tariff bargaining protocol. The first five GATT rounds involved selective product-by-product MFN tariff negotiations on a bilateral "request-offer" basis—each government requests tariff cuts from its bargaining partner in the bilateral and offers the tariff cuts that it is prepared to make in the bilateral if its requests are granted—and this was also true to varying degrees of the eighth (Uruguay) round and the currently suspended WTO (Doha) round.[2] Principal supplier status shapes the bargaining pairs that form in a round, and a double coincidence of wants must

---

1. The GATT bargaining records for the first seven of the eight GATT rounds are available in PDF form at https://www.wto.org/english/docs_e/gattbilaterals_e/indexbyround_e.htm.
2. The sixth (Kennedy) and seventh (Tokyo) rounds of GATT negotiations took a linear-cut and formula-cut approach to tariff negotiations, respectively, but even in these rounds bilateral product-by-product negotiations played an important complementary role. As Hoda (2001, 47) notes, "A linear or formula approach did not obviate the need for bilateral negotiations: they only gave the participants an additional tool to employ in the bargaining process."

exist between any viable pair of bargaining partners: Each country in the bargaining pair must be a principal supplier of at least one good to the other country in the pair so that each has something of value to offer the other. In essence, GATT's reliance on the principal supplier rule has the effect of reducing the number of viable bilateral bargains in the round to a manageable level while at the same time allowing countries to focus on those bilaterals where the mutual stakes of the bargaining parties are likely to be highest. The object of negotiation is the tariff binding, the legal maximum level above which a country agrees not to raise its tariff. As Hoda (2001, 44–45) explains, the protocols for the first five rounds were similar:

Each round began with the adoption of a decision convening a tariff conference on a fixed future date. The decision required the contracting parties to exchange request lists and furnish the latest edition of their customs tariffs and their foreign trade statistics for a recent period well in advance of the first day of the conference and the offers had to be made on the first day. The negotiations were concluded generally over a period of six to seven months after the offers had been made.... These negotiations were essentially bilateral between pairs of delegations.

Bagwell, Staiger, and Yurukoglu (2020a) is the first paper to analyze the GATT bargaining records. They focus on the Torquay Round (1950–1951) of GATT negotiations, identify stylized facts from this round that emerge from an analysis of the bargaining data, and suggest that these stylized facts reflect a pragmatic approach to tariff bargaining that was induced by the pillars of the GATT architecture and the bargaining forum that these pillars helped to create. To begin, in this chapter I describe how, through the lens of the terms-of-trade theory, the GATT pillars of reciprocity and MFN can simplify the tariff bargaining problem, but at a potential cost, and thereby can be seen to facilitate a pragmatic approach to tariff bargaining. I then describe the findings of Bagwell, Staiger, and Yurukoglu.

4.1   Theory

As I noted in chapter 2, MFN and reciprocity are two pillars of the GATT architecture. Do these pillars create a bargaining forum that is well designed to address the terms-of-trade manipulation problem? To provide an answer to this question from the perspective of the terms-of-trade theory, I first return to the two-country model presented in chapter 2 and focus on the implications of GATT's reciprocity rules and norms in that setting. I then consider MFN in a multicountry extension of this model and describe how MFN and reciprocity work in tandem to shape the tariff bargaining forum within which GATT/WTO members negotiate. Throughout I keep technical details to a minimum and refer interested readers to Bagwell, Staiger, and Yurukoglu (2020a) for more detail and to Bagwell and Staiger (1999, 2002, 2005, 2010b, 2018a) where these theoretical findings were originally derived and presented.

Recall from chapter 2 that the GATT/WTO principle of reciprocity refers to the ideal of mutual changes in trade policy that bring about changes in the volume of each country's imports that are equal in magnitude to the changes in the volume of its exports. As I noted previously, there are two instances in GATT where this principle is applied: first, when governments seek reciprocity through a "balance of concessions" in their GATT Article XXVIII bis negotiations to liberalize tariffs, and second, when one government reverses its negotiated tariff liberalization, perhaps in a formal GATT Article XXVIII renegotiation but more generally whether it does so de facto or de jure, its trading partners are permitted to maintain reciprocity through retaliation by withdrawing "substantially equivalent concessions" of their own. Hence, the first instance of reciprocity applies when tariffs are moving in the downward direction, while the second applies when tariffs are moving in the upward direction. The first instance is a negotiating norm rather than a requirement that must be satisfied by negotiated tariff movements in the downward direction, but it is a norm that was strongly embedded in the culture of GATT (see, for example, Curzon 1965, 74). The second instance is a rule that specifies the maximum permissible retaliatory response and therefore is a requirement that governs the movements of previously negotiated and bound tariffs in the upward direction. In what follows, I describe the implications that arise according to the terms-of-trade theory from a strict application of reciprocity in both directions.

I begin by defining reciprocity within the model of chapter 2, following Bagwell and Staiger (1999).[3] Consider a tariff negotiation that, starting from an initial pair of tariffs, (τ^0, τ^{*0}), results in a new pair of tariffs, (τ^1, τ^{*1}). Denoting the initial world and home-country local

---

3. The concept of reciprocity has a long history in many literatures but, when used, has not always been unambiguously defined, and as Keohane (1986) notes, this has often led to confusion. The definition of reciprocity that I adopt here, which follows Bagwell and Staiger (1999), formalizes the notion of "substantially equivalent concessions" that is at the heart of the GATT/WTO concept of reciprocity.

prices as $\widetilde{p}^{w0} \equiv \widetilde{p}^{w}(\tau^0, \tau^{*0})$ and $p^0 \equiv p(\tau^0, \widetilde{p}^{w0})$ and the new prices as $\widetilde{p}^{w1} \equiv \widetilde{p}^{w}(\tau^1, \tau^{*1})$ and $p^1 \equiv p(\tau^1, \widetilde{p}^{w1})$, I will say that the tariff changes conform to *the principle of reciprocity* when

$$\widetilde{p}^{w0}[M_x(p^1, \widetilde{p}^{w1}) - M_x(p^0, \widetilde{p}^{w0})] = [E_y(p^1, \widetilde{p}^{w1}) - E_y(p^0, \widetilde{p}^{w0})], \qquad (4.1)$$

where, as (4.1) reflects, changes in trade volumes are valued at the existing world price. The key point is to notice that, by using the home-country balanced trade condition recorded in equation (2.1), the reciprocity condition in (4.1) may be rewritten as

$$[\widetilde{p}^{w1} - \widetilde{p}^{w0}]M_x(p^1, \widetilde{p}^{w1}) = 0, \qquad (4.2)$$

which implies $\widetilde{p}^{w1} = \widetilde{p}^{w0}$, provided only that $M_x(p^1, \widetilde{p}^{w1}) > 0$. An analogous definition of reciprocity holds from the perspective of the foreign country, with an analogous implication. According to (4.2), reciprocity can therefore be given a simple characterization in the two-country two-good model of chapter 2: Mutual changes in trade policy conform to the principle of reciprocity if and only if they leave $\widetilde{p}^{w}$—the terms of trade between the home and foreign country—unchanged.[4] With this characterization in hand, I next consider how strict adherence to reciprocity simplifies the tariff bargaining problem in this two-country setting.

Consider, first, the implication when governments adhere strictly to reciprocity in the downward direction. With reciprocity in the downward direction fixing the *balance* of market access concessions to be exchanged at one-for-one and therefore fixing the terms of trade at $\widetilde{p}^{w0}$

---

4. Bagwell and Staiger (1999, n16) extends this result to a many-good version of the model of chapter 2, while Bagwell and Staiger (2016, online app.) provides a generalization of a number of additional features of reciprocity to the many-good general equilibrium setting. These properties of reciprocity are also shown to hold in a two-sector partial equilibrium setting where the non-numeraire sector is a monopolistically competitive industry with many varieties (Bagwell and Staiger 2015) or a homogeneous-good industry with a monopoly or (Cournot) oligopoly structure (Bagwell and Staiger 2012a), and in a three-good partial equilibrium setting where each of the two non-numeraire goods is a competitive homogeneous-good industry (Bagwell and Staiger 2001a). Notice too that, by fixing relative exporter prices (the terms of trade), reciprocity also ensures that any changes in the tariff revenue collected by one country from the exporters of its trading partner must be matched by changes in the tariff revenue that its trading partner collects from its exporters (Bagwell and Staiger 1999, n16); this confirms the equivalence between reciprocity and the matching of changes in tariff revenue collected by each country from the exporters of its trading partner that I asserted in the intuitive discussion of chapter 1.

according to (4.2), the two governments are then only bargaining over the *depth* of the reciprocal tariff cuts to which they will agree. The depth of these cuts determines the home tariff τ^1, and hence the home local price according to $p(\tau^1, \tilde{p}^{w0})$ and its import volume according to $M_x(p(\tau^1, \tilde{p}^{w0}), \tilde{p}^{w0})$; and it determines the foreign tariff τ^{*1}, and hence the foreign local price according to $p^*(\tau^{*1}, \tilde{p}^{w0})$ and its import volume according to $M_y^*(p^*(\tau^{*1}, \tilde{p}^{w0}), \tilde{p}^{w0})$. This means that the preferred depth of the reciprocal tariff cuts for the home government would be associated with the home tariff level $\hat{\tau}^1$ defined by $W_p(p(\hat{\tau}^1, \tilde{p}^{w0}), \tilde{p}^{w0}) = 0$, and the home government would propose that the foreign government reciprocate with the tariff $\tau^{*R}(\hat{\tau}^1)$ defined by $\tilde{p}^w(\hat{\tau}^1, \tau^*) = \tilde{p}^{w0}$ that leaves $\tilde{p}^w$ unchanged. Likewise, the preferred depth of the reciprocal tariff cuts for the foreign government would be associated with the foreign tariff level $\hat{\tau}^{*1}$ defined by $W_{p*}^*(p^*(\hat{\tau}^{*1}, \tilde{p}^{w0}), \tilde{p}^{w0}) = 0$, and the foreign government would propose that the home government reciprocate with the tariff $\tau^R(\hat{\tau}^{*1})$ defined by $\tilde{p}^w(\tau, \hat{\tau}^{*1}) = \tilde{p}^{w0}$ that leaves $\tilde{p}^w$ unchanged.

If the two governments *agree* on the preferred depth of reciprocal tariff cuts in the sense that $\hat{\tau}^1 = \tau^R(\hat{\tau}^{*1})$ and $\hat{\tau}^{*1} = \tau^{*R}(\hat{\tau}^1)$, then their preferred proposals will agree, and there will be no haggling: By holding themselves strictly to the GATT norm of reciprocity in the downward direction and thereby eliminating strategic considerations over the implications of their agreed tariffs for the terms of trade, governments succeed in eliminating strategic considerations *completely* from their tariff bargaining. And in this case, the agreed tariffs satisfy $W_p(p(\hat{\tau}^1, \tilde{p}^{w0}), \tilde{p}^{w0}) = 0$ and $W_{p*}^*(p^*(\hat{\tau}^{*1}, \tilde{p}^{w0}), \tilde{p}^{w0}) = 0$, implying that governments implement the political optimum point on the efficiency frontier.

On the other hand, if the two governments *disagree* over the preferred depth of reciprocal tariff cuts, in the sense that $\hat{\tau}^1 \neq \tau^R(\hat{\tau}^{*1})$ and $\hat{\tau}^{*1} \neq \tau^{*R}(\hat{\tau}^1)$, with one government wanting deeper reciprocal tariff cuts than the other government, then their preferred proposals will disagree. It is in this case that the application of reciprocity in the upward direction becomes important: In effect, because of this second application of reciprocity, strategic considerations will still be absent from the negotiations, and there will still be no haggling, and the government wanting the *less* ambitious agreement will get its way. This is because if this government were pushed in the negotiations to liberalize its tariff below the level that it prefers, it could always—subsequent to the negotiations—unilaterally raise its tariff back up to this level, and the most that the other government would be allowed to do under this second application of reciprocity is to retaliate with a tariff hike of its own that keeps the terms of trade at the level $\tilde{p}^{w0}$, thereby allowing the first government to achieve its preferred tariff after all. Knowing this, the two governments are aware when they make their initial tariff proposals that the government wanting the less ambitious agreement will ultimately get its way.[5]

In a tariff bargaining model meant to reflect the two applications of reciprocity in GATT, Bagwell and Staiger (1999) capture this implication of reciprocity in the upward direction in a shorthand way by assuming that when the two governments make tariff proposals that disagree, the proposal with the highest tariff pair and implying the lowest trade volume is ultimately implemented. They show that, even in the case where the two governments disagree over the preferred depth of reciprocal tariff cuts, it will still be the case that *all* strategic considerations in tariff bargaining are eliminated if the governments abide by strict reciprocity in the two instances where reciprocity arises in GATT. Intuitively, reciprocity in the downward direction fixes the "price" at which market access is to be exchanged between the two governments; reciprocity in the upward direction then amounts to an assurance of "voluntary exchange" whereby no government can be forced as a result of the negotiations to accept more trade volume than it desires at this price, determining the depth of the tariff cuts to which the two governments will agree.[6] At this point, there is no room left in the negotiations for strategic behavior.

More formally, as Bagwell and Staiger (1999) demonstrate in their model of tariff bargaining, in the two-country model presented in chapter 2, it is a dominant strategy for the home government to propose the tariff pair $(\hat{\tau}^1, \tau^{*R}(\hat{\tau}^1))$ and for the foreign government to propose the tariff pair $(\hat{\tau}^{*1}, \tau^R(\hat{\tau}^{*1}))$, and the implemented tariff pair is then determined by the least ambitious tariff proposal (i.e., the proposal that implies the smallest amount of reciprocal liberalization). Notice that,

---

5. This point is related to Tasca's (1938, 146) discussion, from which I quote in chapter 2, of the importance of various "withdrawal clauses" in the Reciprocal Trade Agreements Act (RTAA).

6. The "voluntary exchange" aspect induced by reciprocity in the upward direction and its impact on the bargaining outcome as modeled in Bagwell and Staiger (1999) echoes the logic of reciprocity described by Dam (1970) in the passage I quoted from in chapter 2, that governments understood that "the best guarantee that a commitment of any kind will be kept ... is that the parties continue to view adherence to their agreement as in their mutual interest ...."

unless the proposals happen to agree and the political optimum is implemented, only one of the two governments will achieve its preferred tariff and hence preferred local price and import volume, and it is easily checked that in this case the condition for efficiency in equation (2.15) will be violated at the agreed tariffs.

Therefore, according to the terms-of-trade theory of trade agreements, as a general matter, strict adherence to GATT's reciprocity rules will introduce a trade-off. On the one hand, strict adherence to these rules can eliminate strategic considerations from bargaining and in this way help governments avoid the attendant bargaining costs (e.g., in the form of bargaining delay) that they might otherwise incur. On the other hand, the constraints that reciprocity imposes on the possible tariff bargaining outcomes may prevent the two governments from ever reaching the efficiency frontier.

If we think of the initial tariff pair from which negotiations begin as corresponding to the Nash tariffs defined by the joint solution to (2.10) and (2.11), then this trade-off becomes less favorable the greater are the asymmetries in the market power wielded by the two governments. This is because such asymmetries translate into an initial terms of trade, $\widetilde{p}^{w0} \equiv \widetilde{p}^{w}(\tau^{N}, \tau^{*N})$, which is then further away from the terms of trade $\widetilde{p}^{w}(\tau^{PO}, \tau^{*PO})$ necessary to implement a point on the efficiency frontier in this bargaining game (i.e., the political optimum). It is only in the special case where the distribution of market power wielded by governments happens to be symmetric across countries, so that $\widetilde{p}^{w0} \equiv \widetilde{p}^{w}(\tau^{N}, \tau^{*N}) = \widetilde{p}^{w}(\tau^{PO}, \tau^{*PO})$, that the efficiency frontier is reached under strict adherence to GATT's reciprocity rules and the trade-off vanishes. Viewed through the lens of the terms-of-trade theory, the applications of reciprocity found in the GATT/WTO can thus be seen as facilitating a pragmatic approach to tariff bargaining in an environment where bargaining frictions might otherwise be substantial, and one that is most likely to lead to good tariff bargaining outcomes when the world does not exhibit large asymmetries along the relevant dimensions.

It is interesting to note that the absence of strategic bargaining behavior is seen by GATT practitioners and legal scholars as a hallmark of the tariff bargaining that occurred in the early GATT rounds and as distinguishing GATT tariff bargaining from the tariff bargaining that preceded it. Describing the bargaining techniques in use during the first five GATT rounds of request-offer tariff negotiations, Curzon (1966) emphasizes the role of reciprocity in dictating the balance that each country struck between its requests for and offers of market access and the lack of strategic behavior that this balance induced:

> Their requests cannot be higher than their offers and negotiations start from this maximum position: if all requests are granted all the offers will be fulfilled. Similarly all other contracting parties are likely to make offers which match the requests they have made. As some of the requests are rejected, some of the offers are withdrawn. This procedure has been raised to a Gatt principle and is not laid down by any rule. It is a convention but one which creates a much better negotiating climate than the opposite trend which was a feature of the classical bilateral negotiations. Then, everyone put forward very low offers with the intention of increasing gradually if the bargaining proved profitable. A country never knew, however, when it had reached the maximum its partner was willing to concede. (Curzon 1965, 74)

Curzon further clarifies this feature in his description of the behavior of GATT newcomers that tried unsuccessfully to pursue classical bargaining strategies:

> Several newcomers to GATT unaware of this new technique and starting with low offers found that in the course of negotiations they were unable to reach the level of requests they aimed for. Their initially low offers were taken as proof of their intentions and they either had to go home with a tariff higher than expected or had to increase their offers in the course of the negotiations. (Curzon, 1965, 74)

Here, Curzon describes a tariff bargaining forum in which there is no point in making lowball initial offers because governments expect nonstrategic behavior from their bargaining partners, and such offers would be taken at face value.

I next consider the role played by MFN in a multicountry extension of the two-country model and how MFN and reciprocity can, in principle, work together to simplify the multilateral tariff bargaining problem. To this end, I consider an extension of the model to three countries, where the home country now exports good y to two foreign countries, "$*1$" and "$*2$," and imports good x from each of them (the two foreign countries do not trade with each other). Each foreign country can impose a tariff τ^{*i} for $i \in \{1, 2\}$ on its imports of good y from the home country, and the home country can set tariffs on its imports of good x from the two foreign countries.

If the home country were to apply the *discriminatory* tariffs τ^1 to imports from foreign-country 1 and $\tau^2 \neq \tau^1$ to imports from foreign-country 2, then separate world prices would apply to its trade with each partner, p^{w1} for its trade with foreign-country 1 and p^{w2} for its trade with foreign-country 2. This follows because there is a single local price p in the home economy, and the pricing relationships $p = (1 + \tau^1)p^{w1}$ and $p = (1 + \tau^2)p^{w2}$ then imply $p^{w1} \neq p^{w2}$ whenever $\tau^1 \neq \tau^2$.

The MFN rule imposes the nondiscrimination requirement $\tau^1 = \tau^2 \equiv \tau$. A first and immediate implication of the MFN rule can now be appreciated: Under MFN, a single equilibrium world price, $\widetilde{p}^w(\tau, \tau^{*1}, \tau^{*2})$, must prevail, as was noted in previous chapters. This is important because it means that when the MFN rule applies, the representation of government preferences introduced in the two-country model of chapter 2 extends without qualification to the three-country setting, with these government preferences given by $W(p, \widetilde{p}^w)$, $W^{*1}(p^{*1}, \widetilde{p}^w)$, and $W^{*2}(p^{*2}, \widetilde{p}^w)$, where $p = (1 + \tau)p^w \equiv p(\tau, p^w)$ and $p^{*i} = p^w/(1 + \tau^{*i}) \equiv p^{*i}(\tau^{*i}, p^w)$, $i = \{1, 2\}$, and where (in line with the two-country model) I assume that the function $\widetilde{p}^w$ as defined here is decreasing in τ and increasing in τ^{*1} and τ^{*2}. And with government preferences of this form, it is straightforward to show that the political optimum—defined by the three tariffs that satisfy the three conditions $W_p(p, \widetilde{p}^w) = 0$, $W^{*1}_{p^{*1}}(p^{*1}, \widetilde{p}^w) = 0$, and $W^{*2}_{p^{*2}}(p^{*2}, \widetilde{p}^w) = 0$ continues to be efficient.

Evidently, in a multilateral world, the MFN principle ensures that the international externality at the root of the problem to be solved by a trade agreement is still the same terms-of-trade externality, driven by movements in $\widetilde{p}^w$, that arises in the simpler two-country setting. Notice, though, that according to the equilibrium world price function $\widetilde{p}^w(\tau, \tau^{*1}, \tau^{*2})$, each country's welfare will be affected by the tariff choices of the remaining two countries if these tariff choices affect the world price. This implies, in turn, that in a multilateral world, bilateral MFN tariff bargains will in general impose terms-of-trade externalities on third countries, indicating a potentially important multilateral dimension associated with such bargains that further complicates the bargaining problem.[7] This is where reciprocity, now in combination with MFN, can again simplify things.

To see the simplification that is afforded when MFN is combined with reciprocity in this setting, consider a tariff bargain between the home country and foreign-country 1, and suppose for the moment that foreign-country 2 refuses to join the negotiations and keeps its tariff

---

7. In the absence of MFN, there would also be multilateral dimensions associated with any bilateral (discriminatory) tariff bargain, but the nature of the spillovers would be different (Bagwell and Staiger 2005; Bagwell, Staiger, and Yurukoglu 2021).

held fixed at the level τ_0^{*2}. How will foreign-country 2 be impacted by the bilateral tariff bargain between the home country and foreign-country 1? When the home country lowers its MFN tariff τ on imports of x, $\widetilde{p}^w(\tau, \tau^{*1}, \tau_0^{*2})$ rises and foreign-country 2 therefore enjoys a terms-of-trade improvement, because foreign-country 2's exporters enjoy a higher price for their exports of x into the home-country market and because foreign-country 2 also pays a lower price for imports of y from the home country, owing to the stimulus to home-country export supply of y that is created by the home country's tariff cut. On the other hand, when foreign-country 1 lowers its tariff τ^{*1} on imports of y, $\widetilde{p}^w(\tau, \tau^{*1}, \tau_0^{*2})$ falls; foreign-country 2 therefore suffers a terms-of-trade decline because foreign-country 2's exporters receive a lower price for their exports of x into the home-country market owing to the increased competition that they face from the stimulated export supply of x coming from foreign-country 1 as a result of foreign-country 1's tariff cut, and because foreign-country 2 also pays a higher price for imports of y from the home country owing to foreign-country 1's increased demand for imports of y from the home country as a result of foreign-country 1's tariff cut.

Hence, when the home country and foreign-country 1 *both* lower their tariffs as part of a bilateral tariff negotiation, the sign of the impact on $\widetilde{p}^w(\tau, \tau^{*1}, \tau_0^{*2})$ and therefore on foreign-country 2 is in general *ambiguous* and depends on the relative size of the home and foreign-country-1 tariff cuts. And it is straightforward to show that the cuts in τ and τ^{*1} that exactly balance these opposing forces and leave $\widetilde{p}^w(\tau, \tau^{*1}, \tau_0^{*2})$ unchanged are precisely the tariff cuts that conform to reciprocity as I have defined reciprocity in (4.1). But now recall that foreign-country 2 has, by assumption, kept its tariff held fixed at the level τ_0^{*2}. So if $\widetilde{p}^w(\tau, \tau^{*1}, \tau_0^{*2})$ is held fixed by the reciprocal tariff cuts that the home country and foreign-country 1 negotiate, it follows that $p^{*2}(\tau_0^{*2}, \widetilde{p}^w(\tau, \tau^{*1}, \tau_0^{*2}))$ is then also held fixed, and therefore neither the trade volumes of foreign-country 2, $M_y^{*2}(p^{*2}(\tau_0^{*2}, \widetilde{p}^w), \widetilde{p}^w)$ and $E_x^{*2}(p^{*2}(\tau_0^{*2}, \widetilde{p}^w), \widetilde{p}^w)$, nor its welfare $W^{*2}(p^{*2}(\tau_0^{*2}, \widetilde{p}^w), \widetilde{p}^w)$, will be impacted by the bilateral tariff negotiation between the home country and foreign-country 1: There will be no third-party spillovers to foreign-country 2 from the bargain. Evidently, under the GATT pillars of MFN and reciprocity, if foreign-country 2 refuses to bargain it will get nothing, and the bargain between the home country and foreign-country 1 can proceed without strategic considerations, exactly as in the two-country setting discussed previously.

These and related points are developed more fully in Bagwell and Staiger (2005, 2010b).[8]

Now suppose that foreign-country 2 decides to join the negotiations. In this case it is easy to see how the home country could engage in a *sequence* of bilateral bargains, first with foreign-country 1 and then with foreign-country 2, where each bargain abides by MFN and reciprocity and where there are then no strategic considerations and no third-party spillovers associated with either bilateral. If the home country's negotiations with foreign-country 1 do not exhaust the home country's desire for reciprocal tariff cuts, it could then continue to engage in further reciprocal tariff liberalization with foreign-country 2.

The process I have just described looks much like the "split concessions" technique for preserving bargaining power, as described by Beckett (1941, 23) in the context of the RTAA discussed in chapter 2, whereby "a small reduction in duty is made in the agreement with the first country and an additional reduction in the agreement with the second country," all the while achieving reciprocity in each bilateral and maintaining MFN.[9] But a key difference between the RTAA and GATT is that in a GATT round, these bilateral negotiations occur *simultaneously* rather than sequentially. It was thought that this would speed up the bilateral negotiating process in GATT relative to the RTAA and that it would allow the properties of MFN and bilateral reciprocity (described above) to be extended to *multilateral* reciprocity, relaxing the need for strict bilateral balance between concessions granted and concessions obtained and allowing countries to focus instead on achieving

8. I have described this result in a simple two-goods model. See Bagwell and Staiger (2002, app. B) for a discussion of this result in the many-goods setting. See also Ossa (2014) and the discussion of Ossa in Bagwell and Staiger (2016, 512–513) for a qualification to this result that arises in a monopolistic competition setting. The modeling framework considered by Ludema and Mayda (2013) that I discussed in chapter 3 does not allow for the possibility that tariff cuts in a bilateral could be balanced in such a way as to reduce or eliminate movements in world prices and thereby reduce or eliminate third-party spillovers, because that framework is partial equilibrium and abstracts from export taxes; see Bagwell and Staiger (2001a) for an analysis of reciprocity that establishes that its key properties are preserved in a partial equilibrium setting where both import taxes and export taxes are available.

9. Bagwell and Staiger (2010b) investigate the properties of sequential tariff liberalization under MFN and reciprocity and relate their results to the entry of new and economically significant countries into the world trading system. I will return to this work in chapter 7, when I discuss the "latecomers problem" that the WTO's Doha Round may be grappling with.

the desired balance on a multilateral basis. As one early GATT report put it (see also Curzon 1965, 75–77):

Multilateral tariff bargaining, as devised at the London Session of the Preparatory Committee in October 1946 and as worked out in practice at Geneva and Annecy, is one of the most remarkable developments in economic relations between nations that has occurred in our time. It has produced a technique whereby governments, in determining the concessions they are prepared to offer, are able to take into account the indirect benefits they may expect to gain as a result of simultaneous negotiations between other countries, and whereby world tariffs may be scaled down within a remarkably short time.... The multilateral character of the Agreement enabled the negotiators to offer more extensive concessions than they might have been prepared to grant if the concessions were to be incorporated in separate bilateral agreements. Before the Geneva negotiations a country would have aimed at striking a balance between the concessions granted to another country and the direct concessions obtained from it without taking into account indirect benefits which might accrue from other prospective trade agreements; it might even have been unwilling to grant an important concession if it had been obliged to extend that concession to third countries without compensation. (Interim Commission for the ITO 1949, 5)

In effect, the report from the Interim Commission for the ITO observed that GATT rounds made it possible for governments to exchange in a balanced way the spillovers across bilaterals that might arise from a lack of bilateral reciprocity, and thereby still achieve overall—multilateral—reciprocity so that this feature enabled a more extensive agreement.

To see how the implications of MFN and bilateral reciprocity described above extend also to multilateral reciprocity, it is helpful to consider a four-country setting, where the home country now trades with three foreign countries indexed by $i \in \{1, 2, 3\}$, and where the equilibrium world price function is now given by $\tilde{p}^w(\tau, \tau^{*1}, \tau^{*2}, \tau^{*3})$, with $\tilde{p}^w$ decreasing in τ and increasing in τ^{*1}, τ^{*2}, and τ^{*3}. To fix ideas, suppose that foreign-country 3 refuses to join the negotiations and keeps its tariff held fixed at the level τ_0^{*3}. And suppose that the home country negotiates bilaterally, and also now simultaneously, with foreign-country 1 and foreign-country 2 in a negotiating "round." And finally, suppose for simplicity that the home country's desire for reciprocal tariff cuts is at least as great as the sum of the desire for such tariff cuts from foreign-country 1 and foreign-country 2.

Consider first the possibility that the bilateral MFN negotiations proceed along the lines of bilateral reciprocity described above. In its bilateral with foreign-country 1, the home country could offer to cut its

MFN tariff τ in exchange for a reciprocal tariff cut from foreign-country 1 to the level that foreign-country 1 prefers, $\hat{\tau}^{*1}$, implying the home tariff level $\tilde{\tau} = \tau^R(\hat{\tau}^{*1}, \tau_0^{*2}, \tau_0^{*3})$ defined by

$$\tilde{p}^w(\tilde{\tau}, \hat{\tau}^{*1}, \tau_0^{*2}, \tau_0^{*3}) = \tilde{p}_0^w$$

and therefore implying the exchange of reciprocal tariff cuts $\Delta\tau = \tilde{\tau} - \tau_0$ and $\Delta\tau^{*1} = \hat{\tau}^{*1} - \tau_0^{*1}$ in this bilateral. And the home country could engage in further reciprocal tariff cuts with foreign-country 2, offering a further tariff cut in exchange for a reciprocal tariff cut from foreign-country 2 to the level that foreign-country 2 prefers, $\hat{\tau}^{*2}$, implying the home tariff level $\bar{\tau} = \tau^R(\hat{\tau}^{*1}, \hat{\tau}^{*2}, \tau_0^{*3})$ defined by

$$\tilde{p}^w(\bar{\tau}, \hat{\tau}^{*1}, \hat{\tau}^{*2}, \tau_0^{*3}) = \tilde{p}_0^w \tag{4.3}$$

and the exchange of reciprocal tariff cuts $\Delta\tau = \bar{\tau} - \tilde{\tau}$ and $\Delta\tau^{*2} = \hat{\tau}^{*2} - \tau_0^{*2}$ in this bilateral. Under this first possibility, the home country negotiates two tariff bindings, one with foreign-country 1 and a second, lower one with foreign-country 2; and when these two bilaterals occur simultaneously, it is the lower binding that summarizes the implications of the round for the "applied" home-country tariff that enters the world price function in (4.3).

With these agreed tariff changes satisfying reciprocity in each bilateral, the overall changes in tariffs negotiated in the round as a result of the two bilaterals will of course, by construction, satisfy reciprocity as well and therefore leave the terms of trade unaltered, as is reflected in (4.3). Hence, as I described above in the context of the three-country model, in the four-country setting it is also true that when each of the bilateral MFN negotiations adheres to reciprocity, there are no strategic considerations and no third-party spillovers from the bilaterals, and in this case the nonparticipating foreign-country 3 receives nothing.

But now consider an alternative possibility for the outcomes of each of the bilaterals. Suppose that in its bilateral with foreign-country 1 the home country offers the tariff cut $\Delta\tau = \tilde{\tau} - \tau_0$ in exchange for the tariff cut $\Delta\tau^{*1} = \hat{\tau}^{*1} - \tau_0^{*1}$ from foreign-country 1; and suppose in its bilateral with foreign-country 2 the home country demands the tariff cut $\Delta\tau^{*2} = \hat{\tau}^{*2} - \tau_0^{*2}$ while offering nothing in return. Now reciprocity is violated in each bilateral, with the home country granting greater-than-reciprocal tariff cuts in its bilateral with foreign-country 1 and receiving greater-than-reciprocal tariff cuts in its bilateral with foreign-country 2. Viewed in isolation, each bilateral would alter the terms of trade $\tilde{p}^w$, with foreign-country 3 enjoying a terms-of-trade improvement as a result of the tariff cuts exchanged in the home country's bilateral with foreign-country 1 and suffering a terms-of-trade deterioration as a result of the tariff cuts exchanged in the home country's bilateral with foreign-country 2. Nevertheless, this alternative possibility still delivers the same overall outcome of the negotiating round, as embodied in the tariffs $\tilde{\tau}$, $\hat{\tau}^{*1}$, and $\hat{\tau}^{*2}$, with τ^{*3} held fixed at τ_0^{*3}. And so, as (4.3) indicates, once the outcomes of the bilaterals are viewed in their totality, it is clear that the various violations of bilateral reciprocity that I have just described offset each other, so that *multilateral reciprocity* is still maintained, the terms of trade are still preserved, and strategic considerations and third-party spillovers are still eliminated.

It is in this general way, as the quoted passage from the Interim Commission for the ITO report suggests, that the innovation introduced by GATT rounds of simultaneous bilateral MFN tariff bargains, over the earlier sequential bilateral MFN tariff bargains of the RTAA, may have relaxed the constraint of bilateral reciprocity and allowed governments—by "exchanging" spillovers across bilaterals in a balanced way—to continue to enjoy the benefits of MFN and reciprocity under the less stringent requirement of multilateral reciprocity.[10]

Bagwell and Staiger (2018a) provide the dominant-strategy arguments that formalize these insights in the context of a three-country model. In the tariff bargaining game that they consider, the three countries take as given the initial tariff vector and the accompanying world price and then make simultaneous tariff proposals. Mimicking the request-offer structure of GATT tariff negotiations, a strategy for each country is a proposal for its own tariff and that of its trading partner(s), where a proposal must satisfy MFN and multilateral reciprocity. Each country's proposal, if accepted, would imply an import volume for itself. Bagwell and Staiger then construct a simple mechanism that takes the proposals made by the three countries and assigns a vector of tariffs. If the proposals agree, the tariff vector comprised of each country's own tariff proposal is assigned. If the proposals do not agree, the mechanism assigns a vector of tariffs that maximizes the trade volume subject to maintaining the initial world price (reciprocity

---

10. What is not answered here is what exactly the countries gain from the relaxation of the bilateral reciprocity constraint to a multilateral reciprocity constraint. But it is not hard to imagine trading patterns—for example, such as those featured in the triangular trade model of Maggi (1999)—where the relaxation of this constraint would make a difference to the bargaining outcomes.

in the downward direction) and subject to a "voluntary exchange" constraint under which no country is forced to import a volume in excess of its implied import volume (reciprocity in the upward direction). When the proposals do not agree, with one side wanting deeper reciprocal tariff cuts than the other, a "rebalancing" of offers is required because the depth of the offer(s) on the "long" side of the market must be reduced to match the depth on the "short" side. For the constructed mechanism, Bagwell and Staiger show that if countries use dominant strategies, each country's proposal must specify a tariff for itself that delivers its preferred local price and trade volume, given the initial world price; and under dominant-strategy proposals, the implemented tariff vector is efficient if and only if the initial world price corresponds to the world price that would also prevail at the politically optimal tariffs, just as I described above in the context of reciprocity in the two-country setting.

The upshot is that, when negotiations must satisfy MFN and multilateral reciprocity, a strategically complex multilateral bargaining problem is converted into a comparatively straightforward collection of bilateral bargains, because under MFN and multilateral reciprocity, it is a dominant strategy for each participating government to propose for a given import product the tariff that generates its preferred local price and trade volume for the fixed terms of trade. Hence, when governments adhere strictly to MFN and multilateral reciprocity in their GATT tariff bargains, there should be an absence of strategic behavior among the participating governments. A further implication of Bagwell and Staiger's (2018a) analysis is that, under MFN and multilateral reciprocity, a government anticipates that any subsequent rebalancing of offers necessary for multilateral reciprocity would arise later in the round after all offers had been recorded and that this might lead to a reduction in the depth of its overall (multilateral) offer. This implies that there will be an important multilateral element to the bilateral bargains. And finally, at a more specific level, these features imply that when tariff bargaining takes place under the constraints of MFN and multilateral reciprocity, offers (as opposed to requests) play a central role and are not often modified, lowball initial offers are absent, and linkages across bilaterals are present.[11] This summarizes the bargaining behavior that would be expected in a tariff bargaining forum shaped

---

11. Outcomes consistent with either zero or one modification to the initial offer can arise under the mechanism characterized by Bagwell and Staiger (2018a). If shocks (e.g., a given bilateral randomly fails) were introduced, additional offer modifications could naturally arise.

by the requirements of MFN and multilateral reciprocity when viewed through the lens of the terms-of-trade theory.

4.2 Torquay Round Bargaining Records

With the theoretical considerations developed above as a guide, I now describe the findings of Bagwell, Staiger, and Yurukoglu (2020a) with regard to the bargaining records of the Torquay Round, which cover negotiations that spanned a 10-month period over 1950 and 1951. There were 37 negotiating parties at Torquay, representing 39 countries and accounting for well over 80 percent of world trade as of 1949.[12] Of the 666 possible bargaining pairs, 298 formed, reflecting the bargaining structure implied by the principal supplier rule: Bagwell, Staiger, and Yurukoglu report that, on average, 1.25 exporting countries bargained with an importing country over a given tariff, with the requirement of a double coincidence of wants then determining the list of viable bilaterals. The GATT Torquay bargaining records cover 292 of the 298 bilaterals that were formed, 148 of which were successfully completed and led to agreed tariff commitments on thousands of tariff-line products. The United States engaged in bilateral negotiations with 24 of its 36 potential negotiating partners and reached final agreement with 15 of them.

Bagwell, Staiger, and Yurukoglu document three stylized facts of the tariff bargaining at Torquay that conform broadly to the predictions of the terms-of-trade theory outlined above. First, initial offers were not often modified in the negotiations. On products where a country made at least one offer in the bilateral, it made an average of 1.36 offers in a bilateral on that product; on products where a country made at least one request in the bilateral, modification was even more rare, with an average of 1.02 requests in a bilateral on that product. Moreover, offers played a central role in the bargaining, because when proposals were modified, it was the offers, not the requests, that were adjusted: 82 percent of the counterproposals made in a bilateral involved a modification of an own-tariff-cut offer, not a modification of the request for a tariff cut from the bargaining partner. In this sense, it appears that offers were taken at face value—if my bargaining partner's initial offer did not meet my initial request, then I reduced the depth of my offer

---

12. Belgium, Luxembourg, and the Netherlands belonged to the Benelux customs union, which negotiated its common external tariffs as a single entity.

to match the depth of my partner's offer rather than request that my partner increase their offer to match my initial request—much as Curzon (1965, p. 74) suggests in the passage than I quoted earlier in this chapter and as the terms-of-trade theory predicts.

Second, there was a notable absence of initial lowball offers, with the initial offers cutting tariffs on average to 82.2 percent of their existing levels and with the final offers cutting tariffs to 80.9 percent of their existing levels, corresponding to an average downward movement in offers made within a bilateral over the 10 months of negotiations that amounted to less than 2 percent of the initial offers. Moreover, even this amount of downward movement hides an interesting fact: As Curzon (1965, 74) has observed, the lack of lowball initial offers was particularly striking for countries that had previous negotiating experience in earlier GATT rounds. This is documented in tables 4.1 and 4.2.

Table 4.1, which is excerpted from table A3 of the online appendix to Bagwell, Staiger and Yurukoglu (2020a), reports negotiating statistics for the subset of countries at Torquay that had also been present at the previous GATT (Annecy) round. Table 4.2, excerpted from table A2 of the same online appendix, reports the same statistics for the six countries (Austria, Germany, Korea, Peru, Philippines, and Turkey) that were negotiating their accession to GATT during the Torquay Round and hence were GATT newcomers. "Sales" refer to requests of and offers on a country's own tariffs, while "Purchases" refer to requests of and offers on the tariffs of the country's bargaining partner. Each table presents country-specific numbers that refer to a given Seller-Purchaser-HS6.[13]

As the Sales columns of table 4.1 reflect, when the focus is limited to experienced GATT negotiators, on average the initial offers reduced tariffs to 80.8 percent of their existing levels and the final offers reduced tariffs to 80.6 percent of their existing levels, corresponding to an average downward movement in offers made within a bilateral for these countries that amounted to 0.2 percent. By contrast, for the GATT newcomers, the Sales columns of table 4.2 reveals that the analogous numbers were 85.5 percent and 81.9 percent, amounting to an average downward movement in offers made within a bilateral for the

---

13. In their online appendix, Bagwell, Staiger, and Yurukoglu (2020a) also report cross-country numbers for a given Seller-HS6 across all its bargaining partners that reflect similar patterns.

Table 4.1
GATT old-timers.

		Sales			Purchases		
		Ad Val	Specific	All	Ad Val	Specific	All
		Country-Specific					
Initial request	Mean	0.543	0.577	0.554	0.512	0.582	0.539
over existing	SD	0.235	0.306	0.260	0.257	0.321	0.286
tariff	Min	0	0	0	0	0	0
	Max	1	1	1	1	1	1
	N	17681	7971	25652	15621	9911	25532
Initial offer over	Mean	0.804	0.817	0.808	0.796	0.845	0.817
existing tariff	SD	0.195	0.233	0.208	0.213	0.218	0.216
	Min	0	0	0	0	0	0
	Max	1	1	1	1	1	1
	N	8387	3577	11964	6578	5008	11586
Final agreed	Mean	0.797	0.827	0.806	0.773	0.831	0.802
concession over	SD	0.200	0.235	0.212	0.211	0.240	0.228
existing tariff	Min	0	0	0	0	0	0
	Max	1	1	1	1	1	1
	N	5603	2394	7997	3384	3341	6725

Source: Reproduced from Bagwell, Staiger, and Yurukoglu (2020a, online app., table A3).

newcomer countries that amounted to 4.2 percent. And a comparison of the Purchases columns across the two tables indicates that bargaining partners did not alter their behavior when confronted with the bargaining behavior of newcomers: on average, the downward movement in the offers made to experienced and first-time GATT negotiators was 0.015 percent and 0.013 percent, respectively.

Third, there is evidence that multilateral linkages gave rise to issues of sequencing across the bilaterals. Initial offers on the table would sometimes sit dormant for long periods of time, only to be finalized with a single modification at the time that other bargains were also being concluded. Specifically, Bagwell, Staiger, and Yurukoglu report that for bilaterals that ended in a final agreement, an average of 11.8 weeks passed between the last offer or modified offer made in the bilateral and the announcement of an agreement. And some agreements were themselves also modified at the conclusion of the round. Bagwell, Staiger, and Yurukoglu report that, for the average agreement,

Table 4.2
GATT newcomers.

		Sales			Purchases		
		Ad Val	Specific	All	Ad Val	Specific	All
				Country-Specific			
Initial request	Mean	0.471	0.611	0.544	0.571	0.617	0.585
over existing	SD	0.294	0.327	0.319	0.223	0.290	0.246
tariff	Min	0	0	0	0	0	0
	Max	1	1	1	1	1	1
	N	4306	4696	9002	6366	2756	9122
Initial offer over	Mean	0.827	0.870	0.855	0.829	0.840	0.833
existing tariff	SD	0.229	0.203	0.213	0.179	0.225	0.197
	Min	0	0	0	0	0	0
	Max	1	1	1	1	1	1
	N	1798	3445	5243	3607	2014	5621
Final agreed	Mean	0.725	0.846	0.819	0.807	0.849	0.820
concession over	SD	0.170	0.241	0.234	0.183	0.232	0.201
existing tariff	Min	0	0	0	0	0	0
	Max	1	1	1	1	1	1
	N	668	2271	2939	2887	1324	4211

Source: Reproduced Bagwell, Staiger, and Yurukoglu (2020a, online app., table A2).

modifications applied to 3.5 percent of the total number of products on which initial agreement was reached.[14]

Bagwell, Staiger, and Yurukoglu also provide evidence that these multilateral linkages were driven by a desire of governments to maintain multilateral reciprocity in their bargains. They do this by exploiting the unexpected collapse of a number of bilaterals that occurred in the middle of the Torquay Round, where these bilaterals involved the United States, on one side, and the United Kingdom and several of its Commonwealth partners, on the other side. As Bagwell, Staiger, and Yurukoglu observe, if third parties were counting on indirect trade benefits from the MFN tariff cuts negotiated in the US–UK/

14. As Bagwell, Staiger, and Yurukoglu (2020a) note, a feature of the Torquay Round bargaining data that is not accounted for by the theoretical framework I have outlined is the fact that when a country chose to reduce the depth of its offers, it did so by removing products from its offers, not by reducing the magnitude of the tariff cut offered on a given product.

Commonwealth country bilaterals to help them achieve multilateral reciprocity in the Torquay Round, then there should have been an observable reaction in the bilateral bargaining records of these third countries and their bargaining partners when the US–UK/Commonwealth country bilaterals unexpectedly collapsed, as these third countries would have sought to rebalance their outstanding offers in light of this development and re-establish multilateral reciprocity, whereas no such reaction would be expected if strictly bilateral reciprocity had been demanded and achieved by all countries all along. Analyzing the bargaining records, Bagwell, Staiger, and Yurukoglu find that, subsequent to the collapse of the US–UK/Commonwealth country bilaterals, third countries did indeed scale back their outstanding offers to the United States and its Commonwealth bargaining partners at the same time that the United States and its Commonwealth bargaining partners reoriented their offers toward these third countries, consistent with the view that important rebalancing with third countries occurred after the collapse of the US–UK/Commonwealth country bilaterals and therefore with the view that the attainment of multilateral as opposed to bilateral reciprocity was an important feature of the Torquay Round.

Overall, the evidence from the bargaining records of the Torquay Round supports two important claims. First, this evidence confirms that the bargaining behavior in the Torquay Round can be usefully interpreted through the lens of the terms-of-trade theory, suggesting in turn that this theoretical framework captures an important component of what governments were trying to achieve when they created GATT. And second, it confirms that there is an economic logic to the pillars of GATT's architecture when it comes to the bargaining forum that these pillars helped to create, and that the apparently nonstrategic nature of the bargaining behavior induced by these pillars arguably contributed importantly to the success of GATT tariff bargaining relative to what had come before.

Of course, as I alluded to earlier, it is not self-evident that the terms-of-trade-driven prisoner's dilemma that seems to lie at the heart of the problem that the GATT was created to address 75 years ago is still the central problem that a trade agreement should be designed to address today. And even if the goal *is* to help governments escape from their terms-of-trade-driven prisoner's dilemma, the evidence I have reviewed here does not imply that GATT's architecture is perfect or that it cannot be improved upon. But at a minimum, this evidence suggests that the GATT architecture warrants respect—not because it seems to produce "good outcomes," but because it seems well designed to address an important problem and can therefore claim a deeper legitimacy—and that the GATT/WTO should not be discarded in favor of a new institutional approach without an understanding of what would be lost. In their discussion of the meaning of legitimacy in the context of global governance institutions more generally, Buchanan and Keohane (2006, 407) put the point this way:

Judgments about institutional legitimacy have distinctive practical implications. Generally speaking, if an institution is legitimate, then this legitimacy should shape the character of both our responses to the claims it makes on us and the form that our criticisms of it take. We should support or at least refrain from interfering with legitimate institutions. Further, agents of legitimate institutions deserve a kind of impersonal respect, even when we voice serious criticisms of them. Judging an institution to be legitimate, if flawed, focuses critical discourse by signaling that the appropriate objective is to reform it, rather than to reject it outright.

5   Tariff Bargaining without GATT/WTO Rules

In chapters 3 and 4, I have argued that the terms-of-trade theory can be helpful in interpreting what countries achieve (Bagwell and Staiger 2011) as well as what they do not achieve (Ludema and Mayda 2013) in GATT negotiations, and I have argued that the impacts of the GATT bargaining forum on observed bargaining behavior can be understood and interpreted through the lens of this theory (Bagwell, Staiger, and Yurukoglu 2020a). From this perspective, the design features of GATT and the WTO appear to be aimed at helping member governments escape from a terms-of-trade-driven prisoner's dilemma, and these design features display an underlying logic that arguably contributed to the efficacy of GATT/WTO tariff bargaining relative to the attempts at tariff bargaining that came before it.

But what does the terms-of-trade theory say about the efficacy of tariff bargaining in the *absence* of these rules? And can the theory be used to evaluate the case for changes in the rules that govern tariff bargaining in the GATT/WTO? In this chapter, I discuss recent research that begins to address these questions. I first consider what theory alone can tell us, focusing on the findings of Bagwell and Staiger (2005) and Bagwell, Staiger, and Yurukoglu (2018, 2020b). I then turn to Bagwell, Staiger, and Yurukoglu (2021), who combine a model of tariff bargaining with a quantitative trade model to assess the impacts of changes in the GATT/WTO tariff bargaining protocol, focusing on the role of MFN treatment.

5.1   Theory

Recall from the theoretical discussion in chapter 4 that, in the presence of the GATT/WTO pillars of MFN and reciprocity, countries wanting a less ambitious tariff agreement will get their way and there will be insufficient tariff liberalization relative to what is needed to reach the efficiency frontier; the only exception to this is when the distribution of market power wielded by governments happens to be symmetric across countries so that their negotiations reach the political optimum. And as I noted in chapter 3, insufficient tariff liberalization is also a property of the MFN tariff bargaining in Ludema and Mayda (2013) even when reciprocity is not imposed, as the free-riding under MFN in that setting prevents countries from liberalizing enough to eliminate all the imprints of market power from their tariff choices and reach the efficiency frontier. These findings raise the natural question of whether governments might be able to negotiate to outcomes closer to the efficiency frontier within the GATT/WTO if the MFN restriction were removed.

Any claim that the removal of MFN is the magic bullet for achieving efficiency in a multicountry tariff bargaining setting is put in doubt by the results of Bagwell and Staiger (2005). Bagwell and Staiger work with a three-country, two-good general equilibrium trade model along the lines of the model I described in chapter 4, and they focus on the following question: If countries were somehow able to find their way to a point on the efficiency frontier, what rules for bilateral negotiations would be sufficient to keep them there? Bagwell and Staiger restrict attention to points on the efficiency frontier where each government would prefer to unilaterally raise its tariff, and where each government would experience a welfare reduction when its export good is confronted with a higher tariff from a trading partner. Noting that these restrictions guide attention to points on the efficiency frontier that are consistent with the nature of GATT tariff bindings, and considering initially a tariff bargaining setting in which the reciprocity principle is not operative, they show that in the absence of MFN, even if countries were positioned at a point on the efficiency frontier they are not likely to stay there, as the home country and either of its trading partners could increase their joint welfare by engaging in discriminatory tariff liberalization together at the expense of the third country.

This is made clear in figure 5.1. With the home country's discriminatory tariff on imports from foreign-country i denoted by τ^i and foreign-country i's tariff on imports from the home country denoted by τ^{*i} for $i \in \{1, 2\}$, and with τ^i on the vertical axis and τ^{*i} on the horizontal axis, figure 5.1 depicts the position of the iso-welfare contours of the home country and foreign countries i and $j \neq i$ that must prevail at

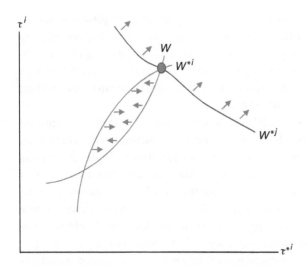

Figure 5.1
Efficient tariffs. *Source*: Adapted from Bagwell and Staiger (2005, fig. 1).

any point on the efficiency frontier consistent with the nature of GATT tariff bindings.

The key point is that, as figure 5.1 displays, emanating from any such efficient set of tariffs there must be a downward lens described by the iso-welfare contours of the home country and foreign-country i into which these two countries could jointly liberalize in a discriminatory fashion and enjoy mutual gains at the expense of foreign-country j. In this sense, Bagwell and Staiger argue that in the absence of MFN (and reciprocity), *all* points on the efficiency frontier that are consistent with the nature of GATT bindings are susceptible to "bilateral opportunism."[1]

To understand why this must be the case, recall that when the home country imposes discriminatory tariffs, there will be separate world prices that apply to its trade with each partner, p^{wi} for its trade with foreign-country i and p^{wj} for its trade with foreign-country j; and with foreign-country j's welfare then given by $W^{*j}(p^{*j}(\tau^{*j}, \widetilde{p}^{wj}), \widetilde{p}^{wj})$, its iso-welfare contour in figure 5.1 is simply the iso-$\widetilde{p}^{wj}$ locus (because τ^{*j} is fixed in figure 5.1), which is negatively sloped under standard

---

1. Bagwell and Staiger (2005) also demonstrate that in the absence of MFN, the bilateral opportunism problem persists for a significant set of points on the efficiency frontier even when the reciprocity principle is introduced as a constraint on tariff bargaining.

assumptions. The downward lens then implies that, by jointly reducing their tariffs on each other's imports slightly from an efficient starting point, the home country and foreign-country i can, through the resulting trade diversion from foreign-country j, worsen foreign-country j's terms of trade (reduce $\widetilde{p}^{wj}$) and thereby take surplus from it and convert its loss into their own mutual gain.

For example, in the special case where all three governments are concerned only about the level of real national income and where they began from the efficient point of mutual free trade, figure 5.1 would simply reflect the fact that the home country and foreign-country i would suffer only a second-order loss from exchanging small discriminatory import subsidies with each other and would together enjoy a first-order gain from the improvement in the terms-of-trade that the home country would then experience with foreign-country j.[2] An analogous statement applies equally well when the government objectives take the more general form introduced in chapter 2. And it can also be seen that an efficient point cannot look any other way than as depicted in figure 5.1: If the lens were in the upward direction, then all three countries could gain from a small increase in both τ^i and τ^{*i}, contradicting the efficiency of the initial point; the same is true if the iso-welfare contours of the home country and foreign-country i were tangent.

The bilateral opportunism problem that arises in the absence of MFN suggests that countries would not be able to sustain an efficient tariff agreement in the absence of MFN and would instead be induced to over-liberalize to tariff levels that lie below the efficiency frontier. Bagwell and Staiger (2005) also show that MFN alone is not enough to eliminate the possibility of bilateral opportunism, though they show that it does change the nature of the problem: under MFN, there can be a bilateral incentive to either liberalize tariffs below or raise tariffs above the efficiency frontier, depending on the characteristics of the particular point on the efficiency frontier at which countries are initially positioned.

In fact, Bagwell and Staiger (2005) show that MFN can eliminate the possibility of bilateral opportunism only when it is joined with reciprocity. This provides further theoretical support for the proposition

---

2. As Bagwell and Staiger (2005) demonstrate, while it is the home country that enjoys the direct benefit of the terms-of-trade improvement with foreign-country j from this maneuver, the downward adjustments in τ^i and τ^{*i} can always be made in such a way as to ensure that foreign–country i shares in these gains.

that these two principles together represent a solid foundation for the GATT/WTO architecture. Recall though, that, as noted above, when MFN and reciprocity are applied rigidly in tariff negotiations, there will typically be insufficient tariff liberalization relative to what is needed to reach the efficiency frontier; so while the rules of MFN and reciprocity would secure a position on the efficiency frontier once reached, it is unlikely that such a position can be reached under those rules.

This brings back into focus the specific question that Bagwell and Staiger (2005) are asking in their paper—namely, which rules for bilateral negotiations would be sufficient to keep countries on the efficiency frontier if they were initially positioned there. Bagwell and Staiger do not study a specific extensive-form game of tariff bargaining, and therefore they cannot say where the equilibrium bargaining outcome would actually end up, given a specific set of rules. And this means in turn that they cannot provide an answer to the question whether the bargaining outcome absent MFN is better or worse for the world than the outcome in the presence of MFN, especially since according to their findings *both* bargaining outcomes are unlikely to be efficient.

An answer to this question is provided by Bagwell, Staiger, and Yurukoglu (2018, 2020b). These papers extend the results of Bagwell and Staiger (2005) to a specific tariff bargaining game where equilibrium bargaining outcomes with and without MFN can be derived. In particular, Bagwell, Staiger, and Yurukoglu consider an environment where the home country is engaged in tariff bargaining bilaterally and simultaneously with each of its two foreign trading partners, along the lines of the simultaneous bilateral bargains that occurred under the bargaining protocols of many of the GATT rounds. And to derive where the equilibrium bargaining outcome would actually end up, Bagwell, Staiger, and Yurukoglu adopt the "Nash-in-Nash" equilibrium solution concept of Horn and Wolinsky (1988), wherein the outcome of simultaneous bilateral bargaining is characterized by a Nash equilibrium between separate bilateral Nash bargaining problems. According to the Nash-in-Nash solution, any given bilateral negotiation results in the Nash bargaining solution taking as given the outcomes of the other negotiations.

As Bagwell, Staiger, and Yurukoglu (2020b) discuss, the Nash-in-Nash solution concept has pluses and minuses when used to represent simultaneous bilateral tariff bargaining in the GATT/WTO. On the plus side, it is a tractable solution concept that has been widely applied in the Industrial Organization literature to provide quantitative assessments of situations that involve bilateral bargaining with externalities. In other work that I will describe below, Bagwell, Staiger, and Yurukoglu (2021) employ this solution concept in combination with a quantitative trade model to assess the efficacy of alternative tariff bargaining protocols. On the minus side, the Nash-in-Nash solution concept requires only that the solution be immune to bilateral deviations. It does not, for example, allow the possibility that a country involved in multiple bilateral tariff bargains might consider pulling out of all of its bilaterals together, and it implies that the participation constraint must hold at the bilateral level but need not hold at the multilateral level.[3] In adopting the Nash-in-Nash approach, the view expressed by Bagwell, Staiger, and Yurukoglu (2020b), and the view that I take here, is a pragmatic one: GATT/WTO tariff negotiations are complex, with no one currently available bargaining model able to adequately reflect all these complexities. In this light, the Nash-in-Nash equilibrium solution provides a potentially valuable approach, albeit only one such approach, for exploring the efficiency properties of bilateral tariff negotiations in various settings.[4]

When the Nash-in-Nash approach is applied to an analysis of bilateral discriminatory tariff bargaining (and in the absence of the reciprocity principle) in the three-country two-good model, Bagwell, Staiger, and Yurukoglu (2020b) are able to demonstrate a formal sense in which this bargaining does in fact result in excessive liberalization and lead to a point below the efficiency frontier, much as is suggested by the findings of Bagwell and Staiger (2005). To formalize this result, Bagwell, Staiger, and Yurukoglu focus on Nash-in-Nash equilibria of

---

3. That is, under the Nash-in-Nash solution concept, a country must prefer its equilibrium tariff agreement in a bilateral relative to disagreement in that bilateral, but it need not prefer the overall multilateral tariff agreement to an alternative in which the round fails and all countries return to their status quo tariffs.

4. As I discussed in chapter 4, if countries are assumed to stick rigidly to MFN and (multilateral) reciprocity in their bilateral bargains, then strategic considerations are completely eliminated, and Bagwell, Staiger, and Yurukoglu (2020a) offer support for this interpretation of the GATT tariff bargaining protocol in the context of the Torquay Round. The paper by Ludema and Mayda (2013) that I discussed in chapter 3 attempts to capture elements of the GATT tariff bargaining setting with a bargaining protocol that features a different set of simplifications, most notably the existence of side payments in the form of lump sum transfers that allow the choice of tariffs to be separated from the division of surplus within each bilateral. In addition, the economic model that Ludema and Mayda adopt does not feature the possibility that the third-party spillovers from MFN could be mitigated by a balance of tariff cuts in the bilateral, a feature that can arise (though is not imposed by a reciprocity rule) in the model employed by Bagwell, Staiger, and Yurukoglu (2020b).

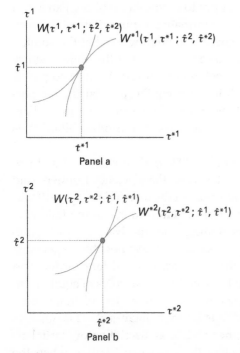

Figure 5.2
Nash-in-Nash equilibrium tariffs.

the bilateral discriminatory tariff bargaining game that yield tariffs that are interior (i.e., equilibria where tariffs/import subsidies do not reach their lower bounds and drive local prices to zero) and that, as with the efficient tariffs studied in Bagwell and Staiger (2005), are consistent with the nature of GATT tariff bindings (i.e., equilibria where each government would prefer to unilaterally raise its tariff and would experience a welfare reduction when its export good is confronted with a higher tariff from a trading partner). According to the Nash-in-Nash solution concept, such tariffs must imply the tangency conditions in each bilateral that are illustrated in the two panels of figure 5.2.

Panel a of figure 5.2 is associated with the bilateral between the home country and foreign-country 1. In it, the home country's discriminatory tariff imposed on imports from foreign-country 1, τ^1, is depicted on the vertical axis and foreign-country 1's tariff on imports from the home country, τ^{*1}, is depicted on the horizontal axis. Panel a holds fixed at the equilibrium Nash-in-Nash level the tariffs $\hat{t}^2$ and $\hat{t}^{*2}$ that the home country and foreign-country 2 apply to each other's trade. Panel b of figure 5.2 provides the analogous information for the bilateral between the home country and foreign-country 2, holding fixed at the equilibrium Nash-in-Nash level the tariffs $\hat{t}^1$ and $\hat{t}^{*1}$ that the home country and foreign-country 1 apply to each other's trade. As the two panels of figure 5.2 show, at the Nash-in-Nash equilibrium tariffs, the parties in each bilateral are at a tangency of their respective iso-welfare contours, taking the equilibrium outcomes in the other bilateral as given.

Bagwell, Staiger, and Yurukoglu (2020b) demonstrate that these Nash-in-Nash equilibrium tariffs lie below the efficiency frontier—and thus that the Nash-in-Nash equilibrium of the discriminatory tariff bargaining game exhibits excessive tariff liberalization—in the following sense. First, they show that, beginning from the Nash-in-Nash equilibrium point illustrated in figure 5.2, it is always possible to generate Pareto gains for all three countries by *increasing* all four tariffs. And second, they show that, beginning from the Nash-in-Nash equilibrium point, it is not possible to generate Pareto gains for all three countries unless at least one of the four tariffs is increased. This answers the question whether the outcome of bilateral discriminatory tariff bargaining will indeed end up below the efficiency frontier: when the Nash-in-Nash solution concepts is applied, the answer is "yes."

The remaining question is whether this outcome is better or worse than the outcome of bilateral MFN tariff bargaining. In their working paper, Bagwell, Staiger, and Yurukoglu (2018) include an analysis of bilateral MFN tariff bargaining. Because their analysis is couched in a three-country two-good general equilibrium setting, the Nash-in-Nash solution concept is difficult to apply in a meaningful way when the home country is restricted to an MFN tariff, because this means that in its two bilaterals, the home country is making offers on a single (MFN) tariff, a bargaining protocol that is on its face incompatible with the Nash-in-Nash approach. As Bagwell, Staiger, and Yurukoglu discuss, this issue reflects in part the low-dimensionality of the model they work with: If each country were importing multiple goods and each country were to negotiate its tariff on any given import good only with the single principal supplier of that good, the Nash-in-Nash solution concept would extend in a straightforward way to the consideration of MFN tariffs. And in part the issue also reflects the choice to abstract from the intricacies of the tariff binding—which as noted, defines the legal maximum level above which a country agrees not to raise its tariff—in the modeling of tariff negotiations. In reality, multiple exporting countries sometimes do negotiate and reach agreement over bindings on the same MFN tariff, because the negotiating right itself can have value in a later dispute over the binding. A model that captured this feature of tariff bindings might more naturally accommodate the Nash-in-Nash solution in the presence of MFN tariffs.[5]

Be that as it may, Bagwell, Staiger, and Yurukoglu (2018) proceed with the assumption that under bilateral MFN tariff bargaining, each country negotiates its tariff on any given import good only with the single principal supplier of that good. In their three-country two-good model, this means that there is in fact only one bilateral bargain in the case of MFN tariff bargaining, between the home country and the principal supplier of exports of x into its market, say, foreign-country 1. So the "Nash-in-Nash" analysis of MFN bilateral tariff bargaining then focuses on the single Nash bargain between the home country and foreign-country 1 over the tariffs τ and τ^{*1}. Given this focus, Bagwell, Staiger, and Yurukoglu find that the bilateral MFN tariff negotiation leads to tariffs that are typically inefficient and that can exhibit either over- or under-liberalization to varying degrees. These findings mirror those under MFN in Bagwell and Staiger (2005), where, as I noted previously, it is shown that MFN alone cannot eliminate the bilateral opportunism problem but does change the nature of the problem, which can in the presence of MFN generate bilateral incentives to either liberalize tariffs below or raise tariffs above the efficiency frontier depending on the characteristics of the particular point on the efficiency frontier from which countries are initially positioned.

In any case, with Nash-in-Nash solutions under both MFN and discriminatory tariff bargaining leading to inefficient outcomes, there is no obvious a priori ranking across these two protocols. This provides an answer to the question of whether the outcome achieved absent MFN is better or worse than the outcome achieved in the presence of MFN. According to the Nash-in-Nash solution concept adopted in Bagwell, Staiger, and Yurukoglu (2018, 2020b), the answer is: "It depends."

---

5. That said, in their analysis of Torquay Round bargaining data Bagwell, Staiger, and Yurukoglu (2020a) report that, on average, 1.25 exporting countries bargain with an importing country over a given tariff; so the assumption of negotiating on a given tariff only with a single principal supplier—which Bagwell, Staiger, and Yurukoglu (2018), adopt—is close to what is observed in the GATT bargaining data, at least for the Torquay Round.

Evidently, theory alone cannot say whether tariff bargaining outcomes in the GATT/WTO would be improved upon or hindered if the MFN principle were abandoned, so turning to quantitative methods ("theory with numbers") to answer this question seems warranted. This is the approach of the paper by Bagwell, Staiger, and Yurukoglu (2021), to which I now turn.

5.2 Quantitative Trade Modeling of Uruguay Round Tariff Bargaining

As a way to model situations characterized by bilateral bargaining with externalities, a key advantage of the Nash-in-Nash solution concept is its tractability. My focus here is on the approach and main findings of Bagwell, Staiger, and Yurukoglu (2021), who exploit this tractability and employ the Nash-in-Nash approach to study simultaneous bilateral tariff bargaining under alternative bargaining protocols with and without MFN in a quantitative trade model based on Caliendo and Parro (2015).

The Caliendo and Parro (2015) model is a version of the many-country, multisector, continuum-of-goods Ricardian model in which markets are perfectly competitive (Eaton and Kortum 2002; Costinot, Donaldson, and Komunjer 2011), extended to include an input-output structure whereby intermediate goods are used as inputs into final goods. Bagwell, Staiger, and Yurukoglu (2021) estimate the parameters of this trade model with 1990 data on trade, production, input-output flows, tariffs, and "gravity" variables (e.g., distance between trading partners) aggregated to 67 sectors (49 traded, 18 non-traded) for six key industrialized countries (the United States, the European Union, Japan, Canada, South Korea, and Australia) and with the rest of the world aggregated into five regional entities. They then use the predicted trade patterns from the model to identify a set of viable tariff-negotiating country pairs, and they use the negotiated tariff outcomes of the Uruguay Round to estimate the parameters of a tariff bargaining model layered on top of the trade model, where these country pairs bargain bilaterally and simultaneously.

More specifically, to model tariff bargaining in the Uruguay Round, Bagwell, Staiger, and Yurukoglu assume that countries abide by a bargaining protocol with three features: Countries negotiate only over MFN tariffs and cannot engage in bilateral bargaining over discriminatory tariffs; they respect their existing tariff bindings and cannot raise tariffs above bound levels in their bilaterals;[6] and their bilaterals are structured according to the principal supplier rule. Bagwell, Staiger, and Yurukoglu do not impose reciprocity on the bargaining outcomes, though they do assess the degree to which the predicted bargaining outcomes from the model conform to a reciprocity norm. Finally, they abstract from political economy and other distributional motivations and assume instead that countries seek to maximize their real national income—an assumption that, as they observe, is at odds with important features of reality but is closest to the spirit of the Ricardian trade model within which they work.

Treating 1990 as the benchmark year for the Uruguay Round (1986–1994) of GATT negotiations, the model's predicted trade flows can be used to identify principal supplier status at the country-sector level, from which Bagwell, Staiger, and Yurukoglu then construct viable bilateral bargaining pairs for the round according to the model. These are the pairs of countries that, in 1990 and according to the model, are each principal suppliers of at least one product into the other country's market. According to the model's predictions, Bagwell, Staiger, and Yurukoglu identify seven viable bargaining pairs that involve five of the six industrial countries negotiating over 151 tariffs covering 55 percent of 1990 world trade in industrialized goods: For comparison, according to the data at this level of aggregation there are 12 viable pairs that involve all six industrial countries and would negotiate over 214 tariffs covering 61 percent of 1990 world trade in industrialized goods.[7] The difference between model predictions and data in this regard reflects the fact that the estimated model does not predict the trade flows in the data with perfect accuracy. To be consistent with the model, Bagwell, Staiger, and Yurukoglu use the model-predicted trade flows to identify the viable bargaining pairs.

---

6. The multilateral rounds that are the focus of Bagwell, Staiger, and Yurukoglu (2021), occur under GATT Article XXVIII bis, and the purpose of such negotiations is to achieve reductions in the levels of tariff bindings. Tariff offers that violate existing bindings would instead have to occur in the context of an Article XXVIII renegotiation and include the bargaining partner with which the original tariff concession was negotiated.

7. Of the six industrial countries included as separate entities in the trade model, Canada is the one that, according to model estimates, fails to meet the "mutual principal supplier" criterion necessary for a viable bilateral bargain. As Bagwell, Staiger, and Yurukoglu (2021) note, this reflects in part the fact that US–Canada trade is excluded from the principal supplier calculations because, as a consequence of the US–Canada Free Trade Agreement in place in 1990, the United States and Canada did not negotiate over each other's MFN tariffs in a bilateral in the Uruguay Round.

Armed with the model-consistent structure of the bilateral bargaining country pairs in the Uruguay Round and focusing only on tariff bargaining (and therefore abstracting from the set of broader non-market-access issues covered in the round), Bagwell, Staiger, and Yurukoglu then adopt the Nash-in-Nash solution concept, wherein the outcome of the simultaneous bilateral bargaining of these country pairs is characterized by a Nash equilibrium between separate bilateral Nash bargaining problems. And they select as their estimates of the bargaining powers across countries in each bilateral those bargaining power parameters that allow the model predictions of Nash-in-Nash tariff bargaining outcomes to most closely match the actual tariff bargaining outcomes of the Uruguay Round. According to these estimates, Bagwell, Staiger, and Yurukoglu find that Japan was the strongest bargainer in the Uruguay Round while the United States and Australia were the weakest, although they caution that these bargaining power estimates have large standard errors and should be taken with a similarly large grain of salt.

Importantly, Bagwell, Staiger, and Yurukoglu find that under MFN, there was insufficient tariff liberalization, in the sense that the bargaining pairs did not achieve free trade or the outcome that would have maximized world real income according to the model.[8] According to their estimates, the Uruguay Round tariff negotiations under MFN achieved roughly one-third of the world real income gains that could have been achieved relative to the 1990 status quo if countries had found a way to negotiate all the way to free trade on the tariffs they were negotiating in the round. This "unfinished business" suggests that the free-rider force associated with MFN is at work, and it provides a possible opening for an alternative bargaining protocol that abandons MFN and allows countries to negotiate instead over discriminatory tariffs. And that is the counterfactual that Bagwell, Staiger, and Yurukoglu consider.

In particular, to evaluate the impact of the abandonment of MFN on tariff bargaining, Bagwell, Staiger, and Yurukoglu re-solve their model for the Nash-in-Nash bargaining equilibrium under the assumption that the same bargaining pairs that, according to the model, bargained

---

8. As Bagwell, Staiger, and Yurukoglu (2021) note, given that there exist tariffs in the world that were not under negotiation in the Uruguay Round, according to their model-consistent bargaining pairs, free trade in the tariffs that were under negotiation would not necessarily maximize world real income. In fact, they find in light of these preexisting distortions that some import subsidies would be required to maximize world real income.

over MFN tariffs in the Uruguay Round continue to bargain with each other under the same bargaining powers when MFN is abandoned. Further, in a given bilateral, each pair is assumed to bargain over all tariffs that either party in that pair had bargained over in the presence of MFN, but now does so with discriminatory tariff cuts offered only to the bargaining partner in the bilateral. The discriminatory counter-factual analyzed by Bagwell, Staiger, and Yurukoglu therefore focuses on the intensive margin (i.e., depth of tariff-cutting activity) impacts of abandoning MFN, abstracting from any extensive margin (i.e., breadth of tariff-cutting activity) impacts that this might have.

Bagwell, Staiger, and Yurukoglu report two main findings. First, they find that abandoning MFN would result in inefficient over-liberalization of tariffs, and that this over-liberalization is sufficiently pronounced that it would lead to a deterioration in worldwide welfare relative to the negotiated outcomes in the presence of MFN. In fact, according to their results, if tariff bargaining in the Uruguay Round had proceeded without the MFN requirement, the resulting tariff agreement would have wiped out the world real income gains that MFN tariff bargaining in the Uruguay Round produced and would have instead led to a small *reduction* in world real income relative to the 1990 sta-tus quo level—a result that is possible under Nash-in-Nash bargaining because, as noted, the participation constraint need only hold at the bilateral level. And second, they find that MFN has a dampening effect on the expression of bargaining power that would be lost in the absence of MFN, with the weaker bargainers (the United States and Australia according to their estimates) losing the most from the abandonment of MFN and the strongest bargainers (Japan according to their estimates) actually gaining when the MFN restriction is removed.

It is interesting to reflect on these quantitative findings in light of the theoretical results of Bagwell, Staiger, and Yurukoglu (2018, 2020b). While the theory indicates that Nash-in-Nash bargaining in the presence of MFN could result in either inefficient under- or over-liberalization, the quantitative findings of Bagwell, Staiger, and Yurukoglu (2021) indicate that for the Uruguay Round it was under-liberalization in the presence of MFN that was the problem. And while the theory indicates that Nash-in-Nash bargaining in the absence of MFN must result in inefficient over-liberalization, the quantitative findings indicate that this bargaining would have led to inefficient over-liberalization in the Uruguay Round of such a magnitude that it would have resulted in an actual *decline* in world real income relative to the

1990 status quo. The MFN finding reflects the dominance of positive third-party externalities associated with reductions in the MFN tariffs negotiated in each bilateral of the Uruguay Round, and Bagwell, Staiger, and Yurukoglu quantify these externalities and confirm that they are indeed positive.[9] The discriminatory tariff findings reflect the power of the negative externalities that are unleashed when countries compete to reduce tariffs on a discriminatory basis across bilaterals, and Bagwell, Staiger, and Yurukoglu also quantify these externalities and confirm that they are indeed negative. In this regard, it is also interesting to note that according to Bagwell, Staiger, and Yurukoglu's findings, discriminatory tariff bargaining would look like a winning proposition to each bargaining country relative to MFN tariff bargaining if those countries viewed each of their bilaterals in isolation. It is only when the equilibrium implications of the competitive tariff-cutting across bilaterals that arises in the absence of MFN is taken into account that the true cost of the abandonment of MFN is revealed.

Finally, I mentioned previously that, while Bagwell, Staiger, and Yurukoglu do not impose reciprocity on the bargaining outcomes of the Uruguay Round in their model, they do assess the degree to which the predicted bargaining outcomes from the model conform to a reciprocity norm. Their findings indicate that among bargaining countries there are only modest departures from multilateral reciprocity, with these departures bearing little relationship to estimated bargaining powers, reinforcing the conclusion that MFN has a dampening effect on the expression of bargaining power in tariff negotiations. And among non-bargaining countries, they find that departures from reciprocity were more significant and always in a direction that was favorable to these countries, reflecting the ability of these countries to free-ride on the MFN tariff cuts of others.

5.3   Interpreting Trump's (One-Sided) Trade War

I close this chapter with a brief discussion of the tariff actions taken by the Trump administration, or what I referred to in passing in chapter 1 as Trump's "one-sided" trade war. It might seem strange to include such a discussion in a chapter on tariff bargaining, but as I now argue,

---

9. As the MFN results of Bagwell and Staiger (2005) and Bagwell, Staiger, and Yurukoglu (2018) confirm, in theory these third-party externalities could be either positive or negative.

following Mattoo and Staiger (2020), these trade actions can be interpreted as the Trump administration's attempt to implement *power-based*
tariff bargaining, the antithesis of the rules-based tariff bargaining
facilitated by the GATT/WTO. As such, this episode provides an illuminating window into how power-based tariff bargaining works (or
does not work).

A broad caricature of these trade actions is as follows. The Trump
administration took unilateral actions to raise tariffs. Its injured trading
partners responded with countermeasures that amounted to reciprocal tariff hikes of their own. In some cases, the Trump administration
responded to these countermeasures with further punitive unilateral
tariffs, which led to further countermeasures from its trading partners,
some of which were reciprocal and some of which were less than reciprocal. In the end, several bilateral deals were struck, some involving
the reciprocal removal of tariffs and others the avoidance of threatened
further tariff increases by the Trump administration but with most of
the already-imposed tariffs remaining in place pending possible further
deals.[10]

Two observations are in order. First, I refer to this as a one-sided trade
war because it is clear that the Trump administration was initiating a
trade war and that its trading partners were not engaging. In response
to the initial Trump tariffs, US trading partners responded with countermeasures that were in line with the GATT/WTO reciprocity principle.
And as the Trump administration then reacted with further punitive
tariff escalations, at each escalation US trading partners responded with
either reciprocal or, in some cases, less-than-reciprocal tariff increases
of their own. In abiding by the reciprocity principle, these responses
amounted to textbook "countermeasures commensurate with the action
which occasions them" of the sort described by the US Council of the
International Chamber of Commerce (ICC) report on GATT that I quoted
from in chapter 1. And despite the escalations by the Trump administration, with their reciprocal responses US trading partners were able
to "hold in check emotional reactions which might result in punitive
measures by countries injured against the country responsible for the
injury," as the ICC report suggested that GATT's reciprocity principle

---

10. The definitive timeline of the events associated with the Trump administration's
trade actions is provided on Chad Bown's blog; see Chad P. Brown and Melina
Kolb, "Trump's Trade War Timeline: An Up-to-Date Guide," Peterson Institute for
International Economics, last updated October 31, 2021, https://www.piie.com/blogs/
trade-investment-policy-watch/trump-trade-war-china-date-guide.

was intended to do.[11] In short, this was a one-sided trade war, with the United States playing the role of the aggressor and US trading partners attempting to tailor their responses to stay within the bounds of the rules-based trading system.[12]

A second observation is this: It seems fairly clear that the Trump tariffs were viewed by the Trump administration not as an end in themselves but as *bargaining tariffs*—that is, as tariffs that were raised above the levels to which the United States had committed in existing trade agreements in order to bring US trading partners back to the bargaining table and adjust the terms of existing trade agreements in favor of the United States. In this light, Mattoo and Staiger (2020) argue that the Trump tariffs can be interpreted as a crude attempt to implement the vision of the global trading system articulated by Trump's commerce secretary, Wilbur Ross in the passage I quoted in chapter 1:

> An ideal global trading system would facilitate adoption of the lowest possible level of tariffs. . . . [C]ountries with the lowest tariffs would apply reciprocal tariffs to those with the highest and then automatically lower that reciprocal tariff as the other country lowers theirs. This leveling technique could be applied product by product or across the board on an aggregated basis. Such a modification would motivate high-tariff countries to reduce their tariffs on imports. (*Wall Street Journal*, May 25, 2017)

More specifically, Mattoo and Staiger argue that these actions amount to a US-led effort to repeal the rules-based trading system and replace it with a power-based system where countries are free to bargain in a way that is not constrained by a particular set of agreed-on rules of behavior.[13] I will return to this interpretation in chapter 12. But for now,

---

11. Of course, the reciprocity principle does give the injured country some leeway over which products to place on its retaliation list, and countries often place on these lists their trading partner's most politically sensitive products so as to increase the cost of the trading partner's actions within the bounds of reciprocity. See, for example, the account of the EU retaliation for the US steel safeguard actions of 2002 in Rosegrant (2006); see also Fajgelbaum et al. (2020), and Kim and Margalit (2021) for evidence that China's response to US tariffs was consistent with this behavior. But reciprocity still constrains the overall volume of trade that can be subject to retaliation.

12. That said, there were also some interesting responses from US trading partners that would be difficult to interpret from a straightforward application of reciprocity within the context of the terms-of-trade theory of trade agreements. For example, as Bown (2021) documents, at the same time that China was reciprocally retaliating bilaterally against the United States during this period, it was unilaterally lowering its applied MFN tariffs toward the rest of the world.

13. An interesting and open question is what formal role the adoption of bargaining tariffs actually plays; that is, why couldn't bargaining tariffs remain as off-equilibrium

the important point is that the world may have just experienced what power-based tariff bargaining looks like, and the initial indications are that it is not pretty.[14]

Finally, while I am not aware of academic papers that have examined the efficacy of the Trump administration's specific approach to tariff bargaining as compared to a rules-based approach, a number of recent papers have exploited the aggressive use of tariffs by the Trump administration and the tariff responses of its trading partners to investigate how local and world prices respond to the imposition of tariffs. These include papers by Amiti, Redding, and Weinstein (2019); Fajgelbaum et al. (2020); and Cavallo et al. (2021).[15] Interestingly, each of these papers finds very little response of foreign exporter prices to the imposition of the Trump tariffs.

The findings of these papers are surprising, as they would seem to suggest that the United States is a small open economy, a finding that would go against a large body of existing evidence to the contrary; see, for example, Bagwell, Bown, and Staiger (2016) for a literature review. This suggestion is not quite correct: The estimation employed by Fajgelbaum et al. (2020) controls for country-time and product-time effects and, as a consequence, is unable to pick up foreign exporter price effects of tariffs that operate through relative wage or other factor-price changes at the country or sector level. Hence, as these authors emphasize, their results do not imply that the United States is a small open economy unable to affect world prices.[16] But the estimation methodologies employed by Amiti, Redding, and Weinstein (2019)

---

threats? One possibility is that, by applying these high tariffs, the Trump administration was establishing the credibility of its threat to follow through with high tariffs if its bargaining partners did not acquiesce. And likewise, by responding with reciprocal countermeasures, its bargaining partners were signaling their commitment to avoid bargaining with the US in a power-based setting and instead to stay within the rules-based system.

14. See, for example, the early evaluations of the bilateral deals that have resulted from the Trump administration's trade actions, available on Chad Bown's blog at https://www.piie.com/blogs/trade-investment-policy-watch/trump-trade-war-china -date-guide. Notice also that, under the bargaining tariff interpretation of Mattoo and Staiger (2020), the power-based tariff bargaining attempted by the Trump administration has similarities to the European experience with bilateral tariff bargaining of the early twentieth century as described by Wallace (1933) and discussed in chapter 2.

15. See also Flaaen, Hortacsu, and Tintelnot (2020) for the particular case of washing machines.

16. Indeed, in their quantification of the welfare impacts of the Trump tariffs and the response from US trading partners, Fajgelbaum et al. (2020) adopt sector-level parameter assumptions for their general equilibrium model that imply that the United States is *not* a small open economy.

and Cavallo et al. (2021) should in principle pick up all foreign exporter price effects of tariffs, so the findings of these two papers do carry this implication.

However, on closer examination the findings of these two papers may not be so surprising in relation to the existing evidence either, for at least two reasons. First, as these papers note, they are (by necessity) estimating only short-term responses of prices to tariffs. Amiti, Redding, and Weinstein (2019) use monthly data from January 2017 to December 2018 to estimate the price effects of the Trump tariffs and the tariff responses of US trading partners; but the bulk of these tariffs were not imposed until the spring and summer of 2018 (Trump safeguard tariffs on washing machines and solar panels are the exception—they were imposed in January 2018), so these estimates reflect the impacts of tariffs on prices over just a few months. As Amiti, Redding, and Weinstein observe, if prices are sticky within this few-months horizon, then their estimation would miss price adjustments to the tariffs that occur at longer time horizons, and it is typically at longer time horizons that the evidence against the United States as fitting the characteristics of a small open economy has been offered. Cavallo, et al. (2021) extend the data analysis by eight months to August 2019, but (as they also note) a similar observation applies.[17]

A second and related reason that these findings may not be so surprising relates to an observation I made earlier: If the Trump tariffs were viewed as bargaining tariffs, they were then likely seen as temporary but with a highly uncertain duration. And as Amiti, Redding, and Weinstein (2019) observe, in the face of this uncertainty it is possible that foreign exporters would simply choose to "ride out the storm" rather than make price adjustments—a strategy that could make sense over a short time horizon but would not be viable in the longer term.

So there is nothing *necessarily* contradictory between the finding shared by Amiti, Redding, and Weinstein (2019) and Cavallo et al. (2021)—namely, that foreign exporter prices did not fall in response to imposition of the Trump tariffs and therefore that the United States appeared to behave as a small country during this episode—and the findings of the earlier literature that suggests the United States is a

---

17. Amiti, Redding, and Weinstein (2020) extend their earlier analysis to cover data through October 2019, thereby covering a similar time horizon to Cavallo et al. (2021), and they find broadly similar results to their earlier analysis (with the notable exception of the foreign exporter price responses in the steel sector).

large country with considerable market power in world markets. Simply put, the resolution of these seemingly contradictory findings may be that the finding shared by these two papers reflects the short time horizon over which evidence of price effects was collected, combined with the temporary and uncertain status of the tariffs themselves. Still, there is at least one remaining puzzle: When Cavallo et al. examine how US exporter prices respond to the foreign retaliatory tariffs, they *do* find that US exporters reduced their prices in response to the retaliatory tariffs from US trading partners, and especially so in response to China's tariffs. It is not clear how the short-time-horizon account suggested just above could hold for foreign exporters to the United States but not equally apply to US exporters into China. Cavallo et al. (2021) suggest some potential alternative explanations, but it is likely that additional work will be needed to provide a complete accounting of these effects and a fully satisfactory resolution of the implications of these two papers with the existing literature.

6　The GATT/WTO as an Incomplete Contract

Despite filling 24,000 pages, the WTO agreement, like all real-world contracts, is far from anything resembling a complete contract where the rights and obligations of each WTO member are specified for every possible future state of the world. And there are many features of GATT and the WTO that seem hard to square with a complete contracts perspective. This is true in the design of GATT/WTO rules, which display an interesting mix of rigidity and discretion: The tariff binding is an obvious example of this mixture of rigidity (at the binding) and discretion (below the binding), but there are also many other examples, relating to the GATT/WTO treatment of nontariff policies, its nondiscrimination provisions, its various escape clauses, and its provisions for renegotiation. And it is true in the role of the GATT/WTO court, which is often called on to play an interpretive or possibly gap-filling role regarding the provisions of the GATT/WTO contract.

There is evidence that the designers of GATT were well aware of the inevitable incompleteness of the contract they were drafting and the importance of the design choices they were making. For example, in his proposal for a liberal postwar trading system, which many regard as a "first draft" of what would ultimately become the GATT (Culbert 1987), James Meade emphasized the trade-off between writing a more detailed and precise contract (which Meade referred to as the "Charter for a Commercial Union") versus relying on the dispute settlement system (embodied in a proposed International Commerce Commission) to interpret the contract when disputes inevitably arise:

If an attempt were made to draft a Charter for a Commercial Union of this type, one of the most important questions would be how precisely worded should be the definition of the discriminations and degrees of protection that would be disallowed to members of the Union and of the actions which would be permitted or disallowed to state trading organisations. It is in this connection that the major dilemma is to be faced. If an attempt is made to define very rigidly and precisely exactly what any member may or may not do in all possible circumstances, it is probable that as circumstances change and as states introduce new methods of trading certain state measures may be precluded which it is not in the general intention of the Charter to disallow and certain other measures may be allowed which it is in the intention of the Charter to forbid. On the other hand, if the Charter is drawn up in much less precise terms and expresses only in the most general terms the types of protective device which it is intended to forbid and the general maximum degree of protection which it is intended to allow, then very great responsibility will rest upon the International Commerce Commission or similar body whose duty it was to interpret the Charter. The success of the Union will depend upon the formulation of the Charter in terms, which, on the one hand, do not attempt to put international trade into an impossible strait jacket and, on the other hand, do not impose upon the International Commerce Commission such a burden of semi-legislative duties that it could not bear. (Meade 1942, reproduced in Culbert 1987, 399–408)

The papers that I have discussed thus far do not emphasize contractual incompleteness as a feature of the GATT/WTO contract. Even when the set of policies covered by a trade agreement is assumed to be incomplete, as when governments possess multiple policy instruments but only tariffs are the subject of negotiation, these papers focus on whether such a shallow-integration approach can nevertheless replicate a complete contract and reach the efficiency frontier when accompanied by GATT articles that help to secure property rights over the negotiated market access implied by a tariff commitment.

In this chapter, I shift focus and describe research that emphasizes the incompleteness of the GATT/WTO contract. I begin by evaluating the design of a number of GATT/WTO rules from an incomplete-contracts perspective, describing the results of Horn, Maggi, and Staiger (2010). I then turn to the role of the court in resolving disputes, focusing on the paper by Maggi and Staiger (2011). And finally, I describe the results of Staiger and Sykes (2017), who evaluate the role of what is perhaps exhibit A for the proposition that the GATT/WTO is an incomplete contract—namely, the so-called non-violation clause. Throughout the chapter my intent is not to argue that specific features of the GATT/WTO correspond to the optimal incomplete contracts that these papers characterize, but instead to illustrate how a number of the broad features of GATT/WTO design can be seen to resonate with the contracting trade-offs that are emphasized in these papers.

6.1 Rules

The passage from James Meade quoted above suggests that the nature of incompleteness of the GATT/WTO contract resulted from the purposeful design choices of its drafters. Can these design choices be illuminated by considering the optimal choices that governments would make given the key features of the contracting environment that they faced when designing the GATT/WTO?

Horn, Maggi, and Staiger (2010) address this question, emphasizing two fundamental challenges that governments face when designing a trade agreement: First, the agreement must keep in check the incentive of governments to act opportunistically on a *wide array of policy instruments*, both border policies and especially "domestic" measures; second, there is *substantial uncertainty* about the circumstances that will prevail during the lifetime of the agreement. These challenges mean that a complete contract would have to be comprehensive in its policy coverage, and it would have to be highly state contingent.

But such a contract would be prohibitively costly to write, a view that is shared by many trade-law scholars. For example, on the impracticality of achieving comprehensive policy coverage in a trade agreement, Hudec (1990, 24) writes:

> The standard trade policy rules could deal with the common type of trade policy measure governments usually employ to control trade. But trade can also be affected by other "domestic" measures, such as product safety standards, having nothing to do with trade policy. It would have been next to impossible to catalogue all such possibilities in advance.

And regarding state contingencies, Schwartz and Sykes (2002, 181–184) write:

> Many contracts are negotiated under conditions of considerable complexity and uncertainty, and it is not economical for the parties to specify in advance how they ought to behave under every conceivable contingency.... The parties to trade agreements, like the parties to private contracts, enter the bargain under conditions of uncertainty. Economic conditions may change, the strength of interest group organization may change, and so on.

To model these features, Horn, Maggi, and Staiger follow an approach along the lines of Battigalli and Maggi (2002) and assume that contracting costs are increasing in the number of policies and state variables included in the agreement.

In such a contracting environment, the choices to be made are how many and which policies to cover in the agreement and what kind of policy contingencies, if any, to include. The first choice determines how much *policy discretion* governments will have under the agreement; the second choice determines how *rigid* the agreement will be. In general, the more rigid (fewer state contingencies) the agreement is and the greater the policy discretion allowed (fewer policies covered), the less costly the agreement will be to write, but at the same time, the further its performance will be from the "first-best" complete contingent contract. The question, then, is deciding which features of the complete contingent contract are the most cost-effective to include in the agreement and which are best to leave out. The answer to this question will determine the design of the agreement, and presumably, the answer will depend on the features of the contracting environment. To investigate this basic question, Horn, Maggi, and Staiger (2010) adopt a terms-of-trade perspective on the purpose of trade agreements and allow that governments have both border and domestic instruments and face uncertainty about the conditions that will prevail when their agreement is implemented.

Their analysis of policy discretion points to conditions under which the GATT's shallow approach to integration (described in chapter 3) could be optimal, even if the accompanying GATT articles that are there to secure the property rights over the negotiated market access implied by a tariff commitment fail to achieve their intended purpose. Of course, when there is a cost of including additional policies in the contract as is assumed, it is not surprising that focusing the agreement on a subset of policies might be optimal once the contracting costs are taken into account. But Horn, Maggi, and Staiger's result goes further: They show that if only a subset of policy instruments is to be contracted over, and when the purpose of the trade agreement is to aid governments in their efforts to escape from a terms-of-trade-driven prisoner's dilemma, the resulting agreement must take as its primary focus the *tariff, not* domestic policies.[1]

---

1. The assumption that the purpose of the trade agreement is to aid governments in their efforts to escape from a terms-of-trade-driven prisoner's dilemma is important for this result: As a general matter, there is no guarantee that the result would hold. For example, if the purpose of the agreement is to help a government make commitments to its private sector, contracting over a domestic policy (e.g., production subsidy) can be better than contracting over a tariff, an implication of the findings of Staiger and Tabellini (1987); see in particular their proposition III and especially note 11.

To see the intuition for this finding, it is useful to consider first the finding of Copeland (1990), who showed that when governments look to a trade agreement as a means of escape from a terms-of-trade-driven prisoner's dilemma, contracting on tariffs can always improve over the noncooperative equilibrium, even if other domestic policies are non-negotiable and left to be chosen unilaterally by governments after the negotiations have concluded.[2] As Copeland explains, this is because beginning from the noncooperative policy choices, when the home government agrees to reduce its tariff by a small amount, it is constraining the *first-best instrument* for reducing its import volume and manipulating the terms of trade, and it then attempts to compensate for the loss of unfettered use of its tariff by using its domestic instruments as *second-best* tools for restricting import volume; but as these are second-best instruments for this purpose, in the end the home government will not restrict its import volume as much as it did under its unconstrained noncooperative policy choices. For the home government's welfare, none of this matters, because the first-order conditions that are satisfied at its noncooperative choices ensure that it suffers no first-order welfare impact by slightly constraining its own tariff. But its trading partner enjoys a first-order gain from the expansion of the home-country import volume. A completely analogous description holds when the foreign government also agrees to reduce its tariff by a small amount beginning from its noncooperative policy choices. Hence, both governments are ensured a higher level of welfare if, beginning from their noncooperative policy choices, they each agree to reduce their tariff by a small amount and then make their own unilateral choices over their domestic, nontariff policies.[3]

From this perspective, it can now be understood why governments could *not* improve upon the noncooperative outcome if, beginning from their noncooperative policy choices, they agreed to a small change in their *domestic* policies but were allowed to choose their *tariffs* unilaterally. The reason is that, given that the tariff is the first-best instrument

---

2. Domestic policies are assumed non-negotiable for exogenous reasons in Copeland (1990) because his analysis does not include contracting costs or other frictions that could give rise endogenously to contract incompleteness.

3. That each government can benefit from the constraint placed on the other government's tariff when they both abide by these constraints can be confirmed by recalling from chapter 3 that the fundamental inefficiency associated with noncooperative policies in this setting can be described as one of insufficient market access. And the implications of the constraints on tariffs that I have described in the text amount to a small expansion of each country's market access.

for reducing import volumes, any agreement to change slightly the domestic policies from their noncooperative levels will induce compensating changes in the tariff that *fully offset* the impact of these changes on import volumes. This shuts down the one channel—an expansion of import volume—through which, as Copeland (1990) shows, welfare improvements are generated when instead tariffs are constrained, leaving only the second-order losses that each government suffers from the constraints placed on its own domestic policies.

Hence, when the problem to address is terms-of-trade manipulation, it is necessary that tariffs are among the set of policies over which governments negotiate: That is, shallow integration *must* take as its primary focus the tariff, not domestic policies. It is sometimes argued that GATT's emphasis on contracting over tariffs reflects the fact that border measures are more transparent than domestic policies and are therefore less costly to contract over. While this may well be true, the result of Horn, Maggi, and Staiger indicates that there is also a more fundamental explanation for this basic feature of GATT/WTO design: it reflects the nature of the problem that the agreement is designed to solve.

Horn, Maggi, and Staiger (2010) also present findings on when discretion over domestic policies should be allowed in a trade agreement. To understand these findings, it is helpful to consider in more detail the modeling setup that they adopt. The setting is a multisector partial equilibrium trade model, similar to that described in chapter 3. Governments are assumed to choose their policies to maximize their real national income, and government objective functions are therefore specified along the lines of (a partial equilibrium analogue of) the particular form given in (2.5) and (2.6). Further, Horn, Maggi, and Staiger consider a trade agreement that would maximize the joint surplus of the two governments, $W^G \equiv W + W^*$, sector by sector. Focusing on a sector for which the home country is an importer and the foreign country is an exporter, they ask whether the benefits of adding a home-country domestic policy κ (in addition to the tariff τ) to the agreement is worth the contracting costs of doing so, and thereby whether moving from shallow to deep integration would increase the joint surplus of the two governments once contracting costs are accounted for.[4]

To develop an expression that can be used to bound the benefits of adding κ to the agreement, Horn, Maggi, and Staiger note that, for a

---

4. Horn, Maggi, and Staiger (2010) derive results in the context of a domestic subsidy, but the results are more general, and here I describe them in terms of any home-country domestic policy κ.

given level of τ, the joint surplus gained by deepening the agreement to include κ is given by

$$\Delta_{deep}^{WG}(\tau) \equiv W^G(\kappa_{deep}(\tau), \tau) - W^G(\kappa_{shallow}(\tau), \tau)$$

$$= \int_{\kappa_{deep}(\tau)}^{\kappa_{shallow}(\tau)} [-W_\kappa^G(\kappa, \tau)] d\kappa, \tag{6.1}$$

where $\kappa_{deep}(\tau)$ is the level of κ that maximizes joint surplus W^G given τ and $\kappa_{shallow}(\tau)$ is the level of κ that maximizes home-country welfare W given τ. In writing (6.1) I have assumed that an increase in κ improves the home country's terms of trade so that $\partial p^w / \partial \kappa < 0$, and it is straightforward to show that this ensures that $\kappa_{shallow}(\tau) > \kappa_{deep}(\tau)$.[5] Note that by the definition of $\kappa_{deep}(\tau)$ we must have $W_\kappa^G(\kappa_{deep}(\tau), \tau) = 0$, and under the assumption that W^G is concave in κ, we also have that $[-W_\kappa^G(\kappa, \tau)]$ rises from zero as κ rises from $\kappa_{deep}(\tau)$ to $\kappa_{shallow}(\tau)$. Hence, it follows from (6.1) that if the maximum value of $[-W_\kappa^G(\kappa, \tau)]$ over this interval of κ, $[-W_\kappa^G(\kappa_{shallow}(\tau), \tau)]$, is small, then $\Delta_{deep}^{WG}(\tau)$ is small.[6] Finally, by the definition of $\kappa_{shallow}(\tau)$, we have $W_\kappa(\kappa_{shallow}(\tau), \tau) = 0$ and hence

$$[-W_\kappa^G(\kappa_{shallow}(\tau), \tau)] = [-W_\kappa(\kappa_{shallow}(\tau), \tau)] + [-W_\kappa^*(\kappa_{shallow}(\tau), \tau)]$$

$$= -[W_\kappa^*(\kappa_{shallow}(\tau), \tau)].$$

Therefore, for any level of contracting costs that would be incurred if κ were added to the agreement, shallow integration is guaranteed to be preferred to deep integration if $[-W_\kappa^*(\kappa_{shallow}(\tau), \tau)]$ is sufficiently small for the relevant range of τ (i.e., for the best tariff under deep integration, the best tariff under shallow integration, and all tariffs in between).

What, then, can be said about the magnitude of $[-W_\kappa^*(\kappa_{shallow}(\tau), \tau)]$, that is, the impact (taken positively) on foreign-country welfare of a small increase in the home-country's domestic policy κ? Horn, Maggi, and Staiger allow for the possibility of production and consumption externalities in any of a country's import sectors, and they arm the

---

5. This assumption is without loss of generality; if instead $\kappa_{deep}(\tau) > \kappa_{shallow}(\tau)$, then the limits of integration in (6.1) would be switched, but everything else would be the same.

6. As $[-W_\kappa^G(\kappa_{shallow}(\tau), \tau)]$ becomes small, the range of integration in (6.1), $\kappa_{shallow}(\tau) - \kappa_{deep}(\tau)$ must not increase "too fast." See Horn, Maggi, and Staiger (2010, n18) for the technical conditions under which this is ensured.

importing-country government with domestic policies that can address
these externalities in a first-best way. But they assume that the exporting country experiences no externalities in its export sectors, and that
it has no trade or domestic policies that apply to those sectors. This
implies that the exporting government's objective in each of its export
sectors amounts to the sum of consumer and producer surplus in that
sector. In this setting, and recalling the focus on an import sector for
the home country, the impact a small increase in the home country's
domestic policy κ has on a foreign country's welfare is then given simply by the magnitude of the income effect of the induced terms-of-trade
deterioration suffered by the foreign country, which is in turn proportional to the volume of home-country imports of this good from the
foreign country; that is, we have

$$[-W_\kappa^*(\kappa_{shallow}(\tau), \tau)] = M \times \left(-\frac{\partial p^w}{\partial \kappa}\right),\tag{6.2}$$

where M is the volume of home-country imports and all magnitudes on
the right-hand side of (6.2) are evaluated at τ and $\kappa_{shallow}(\tau)$. Evidently,
when $M \times \left(-\frac{\partial p^w}{\partial \kappa}\right)$ is small for the relevant range of τ, the cost to joint
surplus of leaving κ to discretion is small.

As Horn, Maggi, and Staiger observe, (6.2) points to three conditions under which the cost of leaving κ to discretion will be small,
so that omitting κ from the agreement will be an attractive way to
save on contracting costs. The first two conditions relate to the deter-
minants of the magnitude of $(-\partial p^w/\partial \kappa)$. If the importing country
faces a highly elastic foreign export supply curve so that it has little
market power on world markets, then $(-\partial p^w/\partial \kappa)$ will be small; and
if, as an instrument for manipulating the terms of trade, κ is a poor
substitute for τ, the first-best instrument for terms-of-trade manipulation, then again $(-\partial p^w/\partial \kappa)$ will be small, regardless of how much
market power the home country has on world markets. With the mag-
nitude of $(-\partial p^w/\partial \kappa)$ sufficiently small when either of these conditions
is met, it will not be worth incurring the contracting costs to deepen
the agreement to cover κ, no matter what the magnitude of the trade
volume under a shallow agreement (M) is. The third condition relates
to the magnitude of the trade volume: If M is sufficiently small for
the relevant range of τ, it will not be worth the contracting costs to
deepen the agreement to cover κ no matter what the magnitude of
$(-\partial p^w/\partial \kappa)$ is.

The upshot is that, according to these findings, leaving a country's domestic policy out of the trade agreement is likely to be an attractive way to save on contracting costs if the country has *little monopoly power in trade*, or if it *trades little*, or if the domestic policy is a *poor substitute* for import tariffs as a tool to manipulate terms of trade. The first two conditions vary naturally across countries, and they may also vary over time. As Horn, Maggi, and Staiger note, such variation could help illuminate the general evolution that has occurred over time in the GATT/WTO toward tighter constraints on subsidies and other domestic policies as trade volumes have increased and the importance of trade in the world economy has grown, and in this light it could also contribute to an explanation of the increasing tension between the forces of globalization and the preservation of national sovereignty. And this variation could help illuminate as well the exemptions from some of these commitments that the WTO provides to developing and especially the least-developed country members, whose trade volumes and extent of market power remain small. The combined increase in China's market power and trade volume since its 2001 accession to the WTO may also help explain the growing attention that has been paid by WTO members to China's subsidy and domestic policies in particular. The last condition varies naturally across instruments and suggests an approach to determining which domestic policies to focus the negotiations on if a decision is made to deepen the agreement.

There is also a further possible benefit of leaving a domestic policy out of the agreement, even when the cost of describing the *policy* in the contract is small. As Horn, Maggi, and Staiger demonstrate, if in the complete contract the policy is state contingent, and if the cost of describing all the relevant *state variables* in the contract is prohibitively high, then it may be better to leave the policy to discretion—where the unilaterally chosen level of the policy will be susceptible to terms-of-trade manipulation but can at least be chosen by the government in a state-contingent way—than the alternative of rigidly constraining the policy in the agreement. This finding resonates with the statement of Meade (1942), quoted above, describing the futility of attempts to "define very rigidly and precisely exactly what any member may or may not do in all possible circumstances. . . ."

Horn, Maggi, and Staiger then turn to consider whether the agreement should be state contingent and, if so, what state variables should be included. A notable finding here is that the incomplete-contracts perspective provides a novel rationale for the inclusion of escape-clause type provisions in a trade agreement: A clause that makes the tariff contingent on positive shocks to the import demand level—broadly analogous to the GATT Article XIX escape clause—can be attractive not because the complete state-contingent contract would include such a clause, but because in a shallow agreement the inclusion of this clause provides an indirect means of managing the distortions that arise when domestic policies are left to discretion. The potential attractiveness of such a clause can be understood once it is recalled from (6.2) that the joint-surplus cost of leaving a domestic policy to discretion rises with the import volume M. What Horn, Maggi, and Staiger show is that it can be optimal from the point of view of the joint surplus of the two countries to allow the domestic government to respond to an underlying surge in import volume by raising its tariff to tamp down the rise in M and thereby keep a lid on the distortions to its unilaterally chosen domestic policies that would otherwise follow.

Finally, Horn, Maggi, and Staiger offer an incomplete-contracts interpretation of the GATT/WTO's reliance on the tariff binding as the legal commitment that governments make to each other in their tariff negotiations and of the so-called national treatment (NT) clause, which prohibits the use of internal tax and regulatory policies that discriminate against imported products. Recalling that a tariff binding defines a legal maximum level for the tariff to which it applies, it is intuitive that permitting a government to set a tariff below this level whenever it desires to do so will be attractive if (a) the purpose of the agreement is to address terms-of-trade manipulation and (b) to save on contracting costs, the binding is not state contingent. Given (a), the joint surplus of the two governments must increase strictly if a government is permitted to lower its tariff below its binding whenever conditions are such that it would wish to do so (i.e., conditions such that its binding is set above its reaction curve level for the tariff), because this would generate a Pareto improvement for the two governments. And given (b), with the binding not state contingent, a realized state could indeed arise under which the (rigid) binding is set above a government's reaction curve tariff level for that state, and if the binding were not defined as a legal maximum so that the government in question could lower its tariff below the binding, then it could not take advantage of this opportunity for a Pareto improving reduction in its tariff. As for the NT clause, Horn, Maggi, and Staiger demonstrate that the nature of discretion that a contract can allow under the NT clause is *broader* than what the contract can allow in the absence of the NT clause, and they argue that under certain conditions the new opportunities for discretion afforded under the NT clause will be desirable to governments.[7]

It should be noted that Horn, Maggi, and Staiger's 2010 paper adopts the view that in designing their contracts, governments deal with uncertainty about the conditions that will obtain over the life of the contract by either paying the cost to specify state-contingent commitments in their agreement or by allowing for some policy discretion to achieve state-contingency "for free." An alternative possibility, one that I have described in chapter 2 and that is also prominently featured in the GATT/WTO, is to design rules for ex post *renegotiation* of the commitments made in the contract should circumstances change. I close this section with a brief mention of the paper by Maggi and Staiger (2015), who adopt an incomplete-contracts perspective to focus on rules for ex post renegotiation, and in particular on whether commitments in a trade agreement should be designed as *property rules* or rather *liability rules*.

In the law-and-economics literature, property rules and liability rules refer to two fundamental ways that a right can be protected under the law (Calabresi and Melamed 1972). More specifically, these rules govern the way that a right can be exchanged between parties once ownership of the right has been initially assigned to one of the parties. To illustrate the difference between these rules in the context of a trade agreement, let us suppose that the home government has agreed to a policy of free trade and has thereby granted the foreign government the right to expect that its exporters will not have to pay a tariff to sell in the home-country market. If the home government subsequently wishes to impose a tariff, how will the foreign government's right to expect free trade for its exporters be protected under the law? If the right is protected by a property rule, the home government must buy back its right to impose a tariff in a voluntary transaction in which the value of the right is agreed on by the two governments: This means that if the home government cannot get the foreign government to agree to its terms, it cannot impose a tariff. But if the right is protected by

---

7. Focusing on the implications of NT for internal taxation, Horn, Maggi, and Staiger (2010) demonstrate this by comparing the pricing relationships that must hold when internal taxation conforms to NT and when it does not. Throughout, they restrict attention to simple instrument-based contacts that pin down specific policy instruments (possibly in a state-contingent way). As they note, more sophisticated contracts that pinned down functions of multiple policy instruments could expand the contracting possibilities. A possible example of such a contract is the non-violation clause of GATT, which I discuss later in this chapter.

a liability rule, the home government must simply pay an objectively valued sum (typically determined by the court) to the foreign government: once that sum is paid, the home government can impose a tariff whether or not the foreign government objects.

Property rules and liability rules therefore define different *disagreement points* for renegotiation, and the choice between them is considered by many legal scholars and trade policy practitioners to be a central issue for the design of a trade agreement.[8] Of course, with renegotiation opportunities, if there were no transaction costs the Coase theorem would apply, and the disagreement point, these rules, and indeed the trade agreement itself would be irrelevant for the policy outcome. But in settings where transaction costs are an important feature of the renegotiation environment, the choice between these rules can make a difference to the policy outcome, and legal scholars (Pauwelyn 2008) have pointed to interesting variation in the choice between property and liability rules across GATT/WTO articles as well as evolution in these choices through time.

In their formal analysis Maggi and Staiger (2015) highlight a key transaction cost that is prominent in the specific setting of trade agreements—namely, that compensation between governments is typically highly inefficient, often taking the form of "self-help" through court-authorized tariff retaliation. In the presence of these costly ex post government-to-government transfers, Maggi and Staiger show that the choice between property rules and liability rules is consequential, and that efficiency may be better served by property rules in some environments and by liability rules in other environments. And from this perspective, they illustrate how the broad logic of GATT/WTO choices over these rules, too, can be illuminated from an incomplete-contracts perspective.

6.2 Disputes

In the previous section I described the findings of Horn, Maggi, and Staiger (2010) regarding two kinds of contractual incompleteness, rigidity and discretion, that find representation in the GATT/WTO agreement. Their formal analysis does not identify an explicit role for a dispute settlement body, but their findings are suggestive of a trade-off

---

8. See, for example, Jackson (1997), Schwartz and Sykes (2002), Lawrence (2003), and Pauwelyn (2008).

between writing a more complete and precise contract ex ante and relying on a court to sort things out ex post, much as in the trade-off described by Meade (1942). And it is often observed informally that the Dispute Settlement Body of the WTO plays an important role in helping to "complete" the incomplete WTO contract.

In this section I describe the findings of Maggi and Staiger (2011), who focus on the role of the court in a setting where trade agreements are incomplete contracts. To the two kinds of contractual incompleteness considered by Horn, Maggi, and Staiger (2010), Maggi and Staiger add a third: the use of off-the-shelf language in the contract that is essentially costless to write but is also imprecise or *vague*. Maggi and Staiger consider the design of an *optimal institution* that maximizes the ex ante joint payoff of the governments, where the institution is composed of a contract that can feature rigidity, discretion, or vagueness, and a court whose mandate when invoked can be to modify, fill gaps in, or interpret the contract, or simply enforce contractual obligations that are unambiguous. In addition to the introduction of vagueness as a form of contractual incompleteness, a novel feature of the formal setup introduced by Maggi and Staiger is the potential for an "activist" role for the court in settling disputes along the equilibrium path.

To develop their findings, Maggi and Staiger work within a partial equilibrium two-country model and focus on a sector where the home country plays the role of the importer and the foreign country plays the role of the exporter. The home government chooses a binary import policy $\tau \in \{FT, P\}$ (Free Trade or Protection) in this sector, and its payoff is $W(\tau; \varphi)$, where $\varphi \equiv (\varphi_1, \varphi_2, \ldots, \varphi_N)$ is a vector of state variables, each corresponding to a binary event (e.g., $\varphi_1 \equiv$ "there is/is not an import surge," $\varphi_2 \equiv$ "the domestic industry does/does not shut down"). The home government gains from protection in this sector in every state—that is, $\gamma(\varphi) \equiv W(P; \varphi) - W(FT; \varphi) > 0$ for all φ, though the magnitude of these gains varies with the state φ, reflecting some combination of terms-of-trade and political/distributional considerations. The foreign (exporting) government is passive in this sector, and its payoff is given by $W^*(\tau; \varphi)$. The foreign government always prefers that the home country adopt free trade—that is, $\gamma^*(\varphi) \equiv W^*(P; \varphi) - W^*(FT; \varphi) < 0$ for all φ, with the magnitude of its loss from home-country protection also varying with φ. Finally, by assumption, transfers are not possible between governments at the ex post stage (once the state φ is realized). Therefore, absent an ex ante agreement between the two governments, the home government always chooses protection.

At the ex ante stage (i.e., before the state φ is realized), the two governments can create an institution consisting of a contract and a mandate for the court. Maggi and Staiger look for the institution that maximizes the expected joint surplus of the two governments, under the assumption that at this ex ante stage, governments can find a way to make costless transfers so as to distribute the surplus between them.[9] Letting $\Gamma(\varphi) \equiv \gamma(\varphi) + \gamma^*(\varphi)$ denote the joint gain for the two governments from protection in state φ and following Maggi and Staiger, I will say that the first-best policy in state φ is protection when $\Gamma(\varphi) > 0$ and is free trade when $\Gamma(\varphi) \leq 0$, and I let ω^{FT} and ω^P denote the sets of states for which the first-best policy is free trade and protection, respectively. Hence, for the two governments, the first-best/expected-joint-surplus-maximizing outcome would have the home government choosing $\tau = FT$ for $\varphi \in \omega^{FT}$ and choosing $\tau = P$ for $\varphi \in \omega^P$. The question, then, is what combination of contract and court mandate can come closest to achieving the first-best payoff once the costs of writing the contract and litigating disputes are taken into account.

What are the contracting possibilities open to the governments? Assuming that the payoff levels of the governments are not verifiable by the court but that the realized state φ is observed by both the governments and the court, the first-best outcome could be implemented by a complete state-contingent contract that specified in detail all of the relevant state variables $(\varphi_1, \varphi_2, \ldots, \varphi_N)$. Such a contract, however, would be very costly to write. Appealing to these contracting costs, Maggi and Staiger assume that the complete contract is unavailable, and they allow governments to choose instead among three contracting possibilities.

A first possibility is that the governments do not write a contract at all, and thereby they avoid contracting costs completely by leaving the policy to discretion. The possibility of a *discretionary contract* of this kind can be interpreted as leaving a "gap" in the coverage of a broader contract when it comes to the policy τ. A second possibility is that the governments write a *rigid contract* that specifies $\tau = FT$ in all states;

---

9. As Maggi and Staiger (2011) note, the assumption that government-to-government transfers are available at the ex ante stage when the trade agreement is being negotiated but unavailable at the ex post stage when disputes arise can be justified on the grounds that GATT/WTO negotiating rounds typically extend beyond tariff negotiations to include other issue areas as well, and that at this ex ante stage, care can be taken to include issue areas that can serve as indirect transfers; see, for example, Hoekman and Kostecki, (1995, 61–62).

this is a contract without contingencies that Maggi and Staiger assume has a small cost to write. And the third possibility is that governments use off-the-shelf language to write a *vague contract*, which Maggi and Staiger also assume has small writing costs and which pins down the first-best policy unambiguously in some states of the world but whose interpretation is *ambiguous* in other states. For example, a clause in the contract stating that protection is allowed if the home-country's import-competing industry suffers "serious injury due to increased imports" might be unambiguously met (or not met) in some states of the world, but in other states it might be open to interpretation.

What about the mandate for the court? Here, Maggi and Staiger consider four possibilities. Three of these are "activist" in nature and paired with the three contract types described above: The court could be asked to *fill gaps* in a discretionary contract, it could be asked to *interpret* a vague contract when the meaning of the contract is not clear, or it could be asked to *modify* a rigid contract and provide an escape from commitments that were specified unambiguously in the contract. A fourth court mandate is "nonactivist" and consists of simply enforcing obligations that are stated crisply and unambiguously in the contract (unless modified under the modification mandate). In Maggi and Staiger's model, it is always optimal for the court to be asked to serve at least this nonactivist role, regardless of the contracting option chosen by the governments; in their formal analysis, this role never leads to disputes in equilibrium, so it is kept in the background. The focus, then, is on which contracting option should be pursued and whether or not it should be paired with an activist court mandate.

Finally, regarding the settlement of disputes, Maggi and Staiger assume that invoking the court is costly, with the exporter government (complainant) incurring cost $c^* > 0$ and the importer government (defendant) incurring cost $c > 0$. If invoked, the court is assumed to always follow its mandate, and if it is given one of the three activist mandates, the court attempts to complete the contract for the realized state as the governments would have done ex ante had they paid the cost to do so.[10] Specifically, the court observes a noisy signal of Γ and issues the ruling that maximizes the expected joint payoff of the governments given the signal. The ruling is a policy determination that is automatically enforced—in essence the contract is modeled as

10. As Maggi and Staiger (2011) note, this assumption about court behavior is broadly in line with the rules set out by the Vienna Convention (and adhered to by the WTO).

a property rule, as the home government must implement the policy ruling of the court and has no possibility of buyout—and the court gets the ruling "wrong" with probability $qk(\varphi)$ where $k(\varphi) \in [0, 1/2]$ and $q \in [0, 1]$ parameterizes the overall (inverse) quality of the court.

With this setup, the optimal institution will correspond to one of six possibilities. The governments can write a vague, rigid, or discretionary contract (no contract at all) and endow the court with a nonactivist enforcement-only mandate. Or they can write one of these contracts and endow the court with an activist mandate to interpret (for the vague contract), modify (for the rigid contract), or gap-fill (for the discretionary contract), in addition to its enforcement role.

Not surprisingly, the quality of the court is a key factor in determining the optimal institution, but the precise manner in which court quality enters the determination is somewhat subtle. To illustrate this, recall that a dispute can occur along the equilibrium path in this model only if the court is invoked under one of its activist mandates; notice that court behavior as modeled is the same regardless of which activist mandate is invoked.

Suppose, then, that a state is realized for which an activist mandate for the court applies. The foreign government will file a complaint with the court in this state if and only if the home government chooses $\tau = P$ and the foreign government expects a benefit from filing that exceeds the filing cost, or

$$\Pr(\text{court ruling is } FT \mid \varphi) \times |\gamma^*(\varphi)| > c^*. \tag{6.3}$$

And anticipating this filing behavior, the home government will choose $\tau = P$ in this state if it can do so without triggering a dispute—that is, if (6.3) fails to hold—or if (6.3) holds and the home government expects a benefit from choosing to protect that exceeds its court costs in the dispute that undoubtedly will follow:

$$\Pr(\text{court ruling is } P \mid \varphi) \times \gamma(\varphi) > c. \tag{6.4}$$

Notice that embedded in this discussion is the assumption that the two governments will forgo "vigilante justice" and instead operate within the rule of law they have created, submitting to the court's will in the event of a dispute. This was the essence of what governments hoped to achieve with GATT dispute settlement procedures that were "designed to limit the customary law right of unilateral reprisals, whose exercise had contributed so much to the 'law of the jungle' in international economic affairs during the 1930's, and to introduce, as stated by one of the drafters, 'a new principle in international economic relations,' " as noted by Petersmann (1997, 82–83) and discussed also in chapter 2.[11]

Using (6.3) and (6.4), Maggi and Staiger demonstrate that equilibrium disputes will arise in this setting under two circumstances: Either the importer government is acting opportunistically and chooses $\tau = P$ when $\varphi \in \omega^{FT}$, hoping to exploit the inaccuracy of the court and get away with protection when free trade would maximize the joint surplus of the governments, or the exporter government is acting opportunistically and files against protection when $\varphi \in \omega^P$, hoping to exploit the inaccuracy of the court and force free trade when protection would maximize the joint surplus of the governments. And in either case, when a dispute arises there are two costs to the expected joint surplus of the governments: the cost associated with an erroneous court ruling, and the court costs borne by each government. In fact, Maggi and Staiger show that the beneficial impacts of an activist court all occur *off equilibrium* in the "shadow" of the court, when there is no dispute: as long as c and c^* are not above a threshold level, the first-best outcome is achieved for a given state φ *if and only if the court is not invoked*.[12]

Hence, if the quality of the court is high, there will be little room for opportunistic behavior as long as the court is given an activist mandate, and the optimal institution will simply minimize contract writing costs. As Maggi and Staiger explain, this argues for leaving gaps in the contract when the quality of the court is sufficiently high and giving the court a mandate to fill them if a dispute should arise. It is interesting to note that the optimality of an extreme reliance on the court in these circumstances runs counter to the more balanced approach suggested by Meade (1942), who, as quoted earlier, argued that "the success of the Union will depend upon the formulation of the Charter in terms, which, on the one hand, do not attempt to put international trade into an impossible strait jacket and, on the other hand, do not

---

11. Maggi and Staiger's (2011) model does not offer a formal explanation of why governments would wish to submit to a court in this way, but in their conclusion they offer some thoughts on a multi country extension of their model that could provide a formal explanation.

12. The threshold limits on c and c^* are needed for the "if" part of this statement, because these limits ensure that the foreign government will always file against $\tau = P$ for $\varphi \in \omega^{FT}$ and the home government will always choose $\tau = P$ for $\varphi \in \omega^P$, even if that triggers a court filing. See Maggi and Staiger (2011, n21) for details.

impose upon the International Commerce Commission such a burden of semi-legislative duties that it could not bear." The reason for this prescriptive difference is that Maggi and Staiger's analysis highlights the *off-equilibrium* effects of the court: as they note, when the quality of the court is sufficiently high, its impacts are *all* off equilibrium, so that in fact it has no duties to actually bear.

For levels of court quality in an intermediate range, Maggi and Staiger find that writing a vague contract and giving the court a mandate to interpret is optimal. The fact that the off-the-shelf language of the vague contract pins down the first-best policy unambiguously in some states of the world makes its low writing cost worthwhile relative to simply leaving a gap in the contract, and an activist court of intermediate quality can still on net be worthwhile through its beneficial off-equilibrium effects on government behavior. Finally, if court quality is below a threshold level, the opportunistic government behavior that an activist court mandate invites will be too costly and the beneficial off-equilibrium effects too weak, and it is better not to grant the court an activist mandate. In this case, it is optimal to have either a vague or a rigid contract in combination with a nonactivist court that simply enforces obligations that are stated crisply and unambiguously in the contract.

It is interesting to reflect on the message of Maggi and Staiger's analysis with regard to the desirability of an activist court. According to their analysis, if a dispute has occurred, in some sense the dispute settlement procedures have already failed because court costs will be borne and the court may make an incorrect ruling. But the key question is how accurate the court is in resolving disputes overall. If it is reasonably accurate, then its beneficial impact lies not in the disputes that *do* occur and that it resolves correctly, but rather in all the disputes that *did not* occur in its shadow.

Finally, some empirical evidence that suggests at least at a broad level the relevance of these findings is provided in the related paper by Maggi and Staiger (2018). That paper begins from the modeling approach of Maggi and Staiger (2015) that I described briefly in the previous section, where governments can renegotiate the contract ex post using costly transfers and where the optimal ex ante contract can take the form of a property rule or a liability rule, but where no signal is observed by the court and where there are no disputes. And it extends that setting to one where the court, if invoked under an activist mandate, can observe a noisy signal of the joint benefits from protection for the two governments and where disputes occur in equilibrium, as in Maggi and Staiger (2011).

In this extended setting, Maggi and Staiger (2018) demonstrate that, depending on the accuracy of the signal observed by the court, the optimal contract can be a property rule (possibly with escapes triggered by the signal received by the court) if court accuracy is sufficiently high, or it can be a liability rule (again possibly with escapes triggered by the signal received by the court) if court accuracy is sufficiently low. And they show that according to the model, the early settlement of disputes should be less frequent when the disputes are over optimally designed property rules than when the disputes are over optimally designed liability rules. With data on the outcomes of 109 GATT-era disputes and 348 WTO-era disputes, Maggi and Staiger find support for this prediction, and hence they provide support for the position that the basic structure of GATT/WTO rules reflects an underlying logic that, if not optimal, is at least broadly interpretable from an incomplete-contracts perspective.

6.3 The Non-Violation Clause

The non-violation clause is one of the more unique features of dispute settlement in the GATT/WTO. This provision, which was an important focus of the drafters of GATT in 1947 (Hudec 1990) and whose relevance was reaffirmed with the creation of the WTO in 1995 (Petersmann 1997), allows one GATT/WTO member government to seek compensation from another for adverse trade effects of the other's policies, even though those policies do not violate specific obligation under the GATT/WTO agreement.

That a GATT/WTO dispute could feature a non-violation complaint is itself explicit acknowledgment that the GATT/WTO contract is incomplete and does not expressly address all the potential policy measures that might undermine the GATT/WTO bargain. Moreover, according to the terms-of-trade theory of trade agreements, the non-violation clause is not a mere theoretical curiosum: It plays a central role in facilitating the shallow-integration approach of the GATT/WTO (Bagwell and Staiger 2001b, 2006; Staiger and Sykes 2011, 2021). But the prominence given to the non-violation clause by its drafters and legal scholars and suggested by economic theory is not matched by the role it plays in observed GATT/WTO disputes, where non-violation complaints have at best been of minor importance (Staiger and Sykes

2013). In particular, GATT/WTO disputes that feature non-violation complaints have been both rare and mostly unsuccessful relative to disputes that feature more traditional "violation" complaints (alleging a breach of GATT/WTO obligations), raising the question of whether the non-violation clause really plays any important role at all in the GATT/WTO.

Of course, observed disputes reflect only on-equilibrium impacts, and it is possible that the relatively minor on-equilibrium role of non-violation complaints belies an important role for the non-violation clause that occurs off equilibrium. Indeed, in the theoretical treatments of Bagwell and Staiger (2001b, 2006) and Staiger and Sykes (2011, 2021), the impacts of the non-violation clause are essentially *all* off equilibrium, because the formal frameworks developed in those papers do not predict disputes along the equilibrium path. What is needed to provide a formal answer to this question is a framework that generates equilibrium disputes and incorporates the possibility of a non-violation complaint along with the violation complaint, so that an assessment can be made as to whether important off-equilibrium impacts of the non-violation clause can coexist according to the framework with the relatively minor on-equilibrium role of the non-violation clause that has been observed in actual GATT/WTO disputes.

In this section I describe the findings of Staiger and Sykes (2017) who, building on Maggi and Staiger (2011), have developed such a framework to evaluate the potential importance of the non-violation clause. Staiger and Sykes begin with the binary tariff choice of the home government $\tau \in \{FT, P\}$ considered by Maggi and Staiger (2011) and extend the home government's choices to include as well a binary choice over a domestic regulation $r \in \{FT, R\}$. With this extended setting as their starting point, Staiger and Sykes then introduce into the model differences in both the contracting possibilities and the possibilities for litigation across the two kinds of policy instruments, with the goal of incorporating the key features that distinguish violation from non-violation complaints into a model that generates trade disputes along the equilibrium path.

To this end, Staiger and Sykes assume that the tariff is covered by an ex ante contract that takes the vague form introduced in the Maggi and Staiger (2011) analysis. Moreover, Staiger and Sykes assume that when invoked with a "violation" claim (i.e., a claim by the foreign government that the choice of $\tau = P$ in state φ violates the commitment that the home government made under the contract), the court is given a mandate to interpret the vague contract over τ. And, as in the Maggi and Staiger analysis, this claim is treated as a property rule: if the court rules for free trade, the home government must remove its tariff.

However, consistent with a shallow-integration approach, Staiger and Sykes assume that the domestic regulation is left outside the contract or, in the terminology of Maggi and Staiger (2011), that it is covered by a discretionary contract. Staiger and Sykes further assume that the court is *not* given a mandate to fill gaps. Rather, if the foreign government wishes to dispute the choice of $r = R$ by the home government, it must file a non-violation complaint which, consistent with GATT/WTO rules, is modeled by Staiger and Sykes as a liability rule as in Bagwell and Staiger (2001b, 2006). If the court rules for free trade, the home government is under no obligation to remove the regulation, but if it does not remove the regulation, then the foreign government is owed compensation, the level of which is determined by the court.[13]

Finally, and again consistent with GATT/WTO rules, Staiger and Sykes assume that a non-violation complaint can also be filed against the choice of $\tau = P$, either by itself or together with a violation complaint; and again, and in contrast to the violation complaint, a non-violation complaint against $\tau = P$ is treated as a liability rule. Staiger and Sykes assume that the foreign government pays a court cost c^* for each claim that it files against a home-government policy choice, and the home government pays a court cost c for each claim that it defends against. Importantly, if the non-violation complaint is filed together with a violation complaint, the non-violation complaint will only be ruled on by the court if the court first rules *against* the violation complaint. This sequencing of court decisions follows GATT/WTO practice and is in line with the principle of judicial economy, because the property rule/liability rule distinction across violation and non-violation claims implies that a ruling against the home government on the violation claim would render meaningless to the foreign government a subsequent ruling on the non-violation claim.

In this setting, as in the original setting of Maggi and Staiger (2011), equilibrium disputes arise when one of the governments or the other is acting opportunistically within the leeway offered by the incomplete

---

13. Staiger and Sykes, interpret their modeling of the treatment of domestic regulation as analogous to Maggi and Staiger's (2011) discretionary contract with a court mandate to fill gaps, with the proviso that the court ruling is in this case treated as a liability rule. In describing the Staiger and Sykes model here, I find it convenient to provide a slightly different interpretation, but the two interpretations are substantively equivalent.

contract and the potential errors of the court. But the extensions introduced by Staiger and Sykes allow the role of non-violation complaints in these disputes to be gauged at the same time that the implied off-equilibrium importance of the non-violation clause can be assessed. Specifically, Staiger and Sykes identify parameter ranges for their model under which the model can match qualitatively two stylized facts exhibited by non-violation and violation claims in observed GATT/WTO disputes. First, there are substantial numbers of non-violation claims, but most of these claims are not ruled on; second, conditional on a ruling, the success rate of non-violation claims is low, both in absolute terms and relative to the success rate of violation claims. For model parameters within the implied range and therefore consistent with a relatively minor on-equilibrium role for the non-violation clause, Staiger and Sykes demonstrate that the off-equilibrium impacts of the non-violation clause on the joint surplus of governments can be positive and substantial.

To understand the intuition for these findings, it is helpful to consider how the foreign-government filing decisions and the home-government policy decisions from Maggi and Staiger (2011), as described by (6.3) and (6.4), are altered in this extended setting. To avoid a taxonomy of cases, Staiger and Sykes assume that there is no state in which the "first best" involves both tariff and regulatory intervention, and the same goes for the unilateral optimum policy choice of the home government. To characterize government decisions, Staiger and Sykes then partition the states of the world into three sets: the sets $\omega^{\mathcal{FT}}$ and $\omega^{\mathcal{P}}$, denoting the sets of states for which the first-best policy is, respectively, free trade $\mathcal{FT} \equiv (\tau = FT, r = FT)$ and protection $\mathcal{P} \equiv (\tau = P, r = FT)$; and a new set $\omega^{\mathcal{R}}$, where the first-best policy is regulation $\mathcal{R} \equiv (\tau = FT, r = R)$. The trade effects of protection and regulation are normalized to be the same, so that the foreign government is hurt equally by either home-government policy intervention, with its loss given by $\gamma^*(\varphi) \equiv W^*(\mathcal{P}; \varphi) - W^*(\mathcal{FT}; \varphi) = W^*(\mathcal{R}; \varphi) - W^*(\mathcal{FT}; \varphi)$. And the ranking of policy choices from the perspective of the joint surplus of the two governments is assumed to be given by $\mathcal{P} \succ \mathcal{FT} \succ \mathcal{R}$ for $\varphi \in \omega^{\mathcal{P}}$, $\mathcal{R} \succ \mathcal{FT} \succ \mathcal{P}$ for $\varphi \in \omega^{\mathcal{R}}$, and $\mathcal{FT} \succ \mathcal{P} \succ \mathcal{R}$ for $\varphi \in \omega^{\mathcal{FT}}$. In words, when protection is first best, the alternative of free trade is better for joint surplus than regulation; when regulation is first best the alternative of free trade is better for joint surplus than protection; and when free trade is first best the alternative of protection is better for joint surplus than regulation.

What filing behavior must the model predict if it is to be consistent with the stylized facts in the data? In order for there to be substantial numbers of non-violation claims, most of which are not ruled on, the model must predict substantial numbers of disputes in which the foreign government files both a violation and a non-violation claim and where the court rules in favor of the violation claim and therefore does not proceed to rule on the non-violation claim.[14] Moreover, given that a violation complaint is involved, these disputes must be over the home government's choice of protection $\mathcal{P}$; and given that the accuracy of court rulings is assumed to be better than a coin flip ($qk(\varphi) < \frac{1}{2}$ for all φ), the quality of the court must be high (low q) and these disputes must occur in substantial numbers in $\omega^{\mathcal{FT}}$ and/or $\omega^{\mathcal{R}}$ rather than in $\omega^{\mathcal{P}}$ (because if they occurred in substantial numbers in $\omega^{\mathcal{P}}$, a high-quality court would rule against the violation claim with high probability and would then proceed to rule on the non-violation claim). Finally, there must be very few disputes that erupt over the home government's choice of $\mathcal{R}$ for $\varphi \in \omega^{\mathcal{R}}$, because each of those disputes would involve only a non-violation claim, and each such dispute would lead to a ruling on that claim.

Turning to the second stylized fact, to ensure that the success rate of those non-violation claims that are ruled on is low both in absolute terms and relative to the success rate of violation claims, and given that it has already been established that the quality of the court must be high to account for the first stylized fact, the model must predict either a small number of disputes that involve a non-violation claim against the home government's choice of $\mathcal{R}$ for $\varphi \in \omega^{\mathcal{R}}$, or a small number of disputes that involve both a violation and a non-violation claim against the home government's choice of $\mathcal{P}$ for $\varphi \in \omega^{\mathcal{P}}$, or small numbers of both of these kinds of disputes. In the former case, the court rules on the non-violation claim, and rules against it with high probability. In the latter case, the court rules on the violation claim and rules against it with high probability, and then rules on the non-violation claim and rules against that claim with high probability as well.

The remaining question is this: What parameter ranges of the model, beyond the low q identified above, would be needed to deliver this

---

14. Settlement is another way in which claims made in a GATT/WTO dispute are not ruled on, and the model of Staiger and Sykes abstracts from this possibility. But as they observe (Staiger and Sykes 2017, n31), the available evidence on settlement of violation versus non-violation claims in the GATT/WTO is not biased in the direction that would be needed to account for the relative paucity of rulings on non-violation claims.

filing behavior? To identify these ranges, Staiger and Sykes adopt the small-litigation-cost (small c and c^*) focus of Maggi and Staiger (2011). To account for the stylized facts exhibited by non-violation and violation claims in observed GATT/WTO disputes, they then turn their primary attention elsewhere, highlighting the cost of government-to-government transfers and the degree to which nontariff policies are good substitutes for the tariff for purposes of terms-of-trade manipulation.

To reflect these new features, Staiger and Sykes introduce two additional parameters into the model. First, they assume that in the event of a successful non-violation claim against either $\mathcal{P}$ or $\mathcal{R}$, the court sets the compensation level to be paid by the home government, $b(\varphi)$, at the level of harm suffered by the foreign government, $\gamma^*(\varphi)$, so that $b(\varphi) = |\gamma^*(\varphi)|$; but an "iceberg" transfer cost $\delta \in (0,1)$ diminishes the amount of the transfer actually received by the foreign government, $b^*(\varphi)$, so that $b^*(\varphi) = \delta \times b(\varphi)$. The parameter δ therefore captures the degree to which government-to-government transfers are costly in the context of a trade dispute, with a low value for δ corresponding broadly to the GATT/WTO "self-help reciprocity" approach to compensation. And second, Staiger and Sykes parameterize the degree to which regulation $\mathcal{R}$ is a good substitute for protection $\mathcal{P}$ for the purpose of terms-of-trade manipulation with the parameter $\theta \in (0,1)$ and the assumption that $\gamma^{\mathcal{R}}(\varphi) = \theta \times \gamma^{\mathcal{P}}(\varphi)$ for $\varphi \in \omega^{\mathcal{FT}}$, where $\gamma^{\mathcal{R}}(\varphi) \equiv W(\mathcal{R}; \varphi) - W(\mathcal{FT}; \varphi)$ and $\gamma^{\mathcal{P}}(\varphi) \equiv W(\mathcal{P}; \varphi) - W(\mathcal{FT}; \varphi)$. In words, a low θ signifies that $\mathcal{R}$ is a poor substitute for $\mathcal{P}$ for the purpose of terms-of-trade manipulation, and therefore in $\omega^{\mathcal{FT}}$ the home government gains little in deviating from $\mathcal{FT}$ to $\mathcal{R}$ as compared to what it would gain if it deviated from $\mathcal{FT}$ to $\mathcal{P}$ (i.e., $\gamma^{\mathcal{R}}(\varphi)$ is small compared to $\gamma^{\mathcal{P}}(\varphi)$ for $\varphi \in \omega^{\mathcal{FT}}$).

The upshot is that, once it is recalled that in the Staiger and Sykes model disputes arise only when one government or the other is behaving opportunistically, the relatively minor role of non-violation complaints in observed GATT/WTO disputes can be understood through the lens of this model as primarily attributable to two underlying forces: one that reflects a feature of the GATT/WTO institutional environment (the inefficiency of government-to-government transfers) and a second that reflects a feature of the policy environment (the low degree of substitutability between tariffs and domestic policies as a means of terms-of-trade manipulation). The foreign government's incentive to use the non-violation claim opportunistically against efficient policy choices of the home government is kept in check by the level of compensation specified under GATT/WTO rules and the inefficiency of GATT/WTO compensation mechanisms (a low δ reflecting self-help reciprocity). And the home government's incentive to make opportunistic choices over nontariff policy instruments for inefficient terms-of-trade manipulation—choices that could trigger a non-violation claim—is kept in check by the low degree of substitutability between tariffs and such policies for this purpose (low θ). Together, these features help to keep the frequency of non-violation rulings low. And given these features, the relatively common occurrence of non-violation claims filed as opposed to ruled on then reflects the low dispute costs (low c and low c^*) and high court accuracy (low q), which together ensure that there are substantial numbers of GATT/WTO disputes that involve opportunistic policy intervention (the choice of $\mathcal{P}$ for $\varphi \in \omega^{\mathcal{FT}}$) and elicit the filing of both violation and non-violation claims that usually result in a (correct) court ruling in favor of the violation claim and no ruling on the non-violation claim. The high success rate of violation claims and low success rate of non-violation claims then reflects the high accuracy of the court (low q) and a dispute selection effect caused by relatively high court costs for the complainant (high $\frac{c^*}{c}$).[15]

Under these parameter restrictions, what does the model imply about the potential importance of the non-violation clause? To answer this question, Staiger and Sykes examine the equilibrium behavior of the home and foreign government according to the model under these parameter restrictions when the non-violation clause is removed. In this counterfactual, the foreign government can only file a violation complaint, and it can only file it against $\mathcal{P}$. This implies that the home government can always choose $\mathcal{R}$ with impunity. The question

---

15. Staiger and Sykes (2017) show that the model requires a relatively high court cost for the foreign (complainant) government as compared to the home (respondent) government (high $\frac{c^*}{c}$), in order to ensure that the predictions are consistent with the second stylized fact. As they explain, this delivers a dispute selection effect, whereby most disputes arise because of opportunistic behavior on the part of the home government rather than the foreign government, and this accounts for the high success rate of violation complaints; see also Maggi and Staiger (2011), for a similar observation. And the high quality of the court ensures that this effect does not extend to the success rate of non-violation complaints, owing to the censoring of court rulings on these complaints that is attributable to the sequencing of court decisions.

is, under these parameter restrictions, where the presence of the non-violation clause has only a minor on-equilibrium effect on the expected joint surplus of the two governments, could the presence of this clause nevertheless be having a large impact *off* equilibrium? The answer, according to the model of Staiger and Sykes, is "yes," if and only if a large drop in expected joint surplus is implied by the model when the non-violation clause is counterfactually removed.

Staiger and Sykes are indeed able to find ranges of parameters within these parameter restrictions where this is implied, and hence parameter ranges that describe a world consistent with the observed features of non-violation claims in GATT/WTO disputes and in which the non-violation clause nevertheless has important impacts. As they explain, these impacts stem from off-equilibrium effects of the non-violation clause that operate for $\varphi \in \omega^{\mathcal{P}}$ and for $\varphi \in \omega^{\mathcal{FT}}$, where the presence of the non-violation clause has four positive effects. For $\varphi \in \omega^{\mathcal{P}}$, the presence of the non-violation clause can convert an undisputed choice of $\mathcal{R}$ into a choice of $\mathcal{P}$ that leads to a violation complaint, which is good for joint surplus provided that q, c, and c^* are sufficiently small. And for $\varphi \in \omega^{\mathcal{FT}}$, the presence of the non-violation clause can convert an undisputed choice of $\mathcal{R}$ into a first-best choice of $\mathcal{FT}$; it can convert an undisputed choice of $\mathcal{R}$ into a choice of $\mathcal{P}$ that leads to a violation complaint that is good for joint surplus provided that q, c, and c^* are sufficiently small; and it can convert a choice of $\mathcal{P}$ that would have been met with a violation complaint into a first-best choice of $\mathcal{FT}$.

The off-equilibrium effects of the non-violation clause in the model world identified by Staiger and Sykes resonate with the way legal scholars describe the workings of the non-violation clause in the GATT/WTO. For example, in describing how the non-violation clause fits within the broader context of GATT/WTO flexibilities, such as those provided by the renegotiation provisions of GATT Article XXVIII, Petersmann (1997, 172) observes that the function of non-violation complaints in the WTO is to provide a check on the domestic policy autonomy of member countries "and to prevent the circumvention of the provisions in GATT Article XXVIII ... if a member, rather than withdrawing a concession de jure in exchange for compensation or equivalent withdrawals of concessions by affected contracting parties, withdraws a concession de facto."

More broadly, in this model world, governments make efficient market access commitments with contracts over border measures while preserving policy autonomy over domestic taxes and regulations, and the non-violation clause functions mostly off equilibrium to reroute policy interventions into forms that are explicitly addressed by the GATT/WTO contract and to thereby prevent the circumvention of these market access commitments, a function that is in line with the role emphasized by economists and legal scholars and envisioned by the drafters of GATT.

II Meeting the Challenges of the Twenty-First Century

A number of key challenges have arisen in recent decades as a result of changes in the world economy, and the WTO must contend with them if it is to remain an effective constitution of the world trading system for the twenty-first century. My goal in these next five chapters is to distinguish between challenges that would require fundamental departures from the GATT and WTO approach and those that could plausibly be addressed by making more modest adjustments to, or better use of, existing GATT/WTO principles and rules. Throughout I emphasize broad themes that can help guide the thinking on possible WTO reforms rather than the details of specific reforms.

First, there is a set of interrelated challenges for the WTO associated with the rise of the large emerging economies, including China. I discuss these challenges and research that relates to them in chapter 7. Next, chapter 8 takes up the challenges faced by the WTO in accommodating efforts to address global climate change and the positive role that the WTO might play in addressing this issue. In chapter 9, I consider the implications of digital trade for the design of the WTO, considering trade in both goods and services. In chapter 10, I describe research that speaks to the rise of offshoring and its implications for the efficacy of the design of the GATT/WTO, including its shallow-integration approach. Part II concludes with chapter 11 and my examination of specific challenges to a shallow-integration approach that are raised in the context of the growing calls for regulatory harmonization as an end in itself.

7   The Rise of Large Emerging Markets

The rise in economic importance of the large emerging and developing economies has brought these countries to the forefront of the world economy, with China playing a leading role. This has created three interrelated challenges for the world trading system. I argue in this chapter that the WTO, with some possible adjustments, is in principle well designed to address these challenges.

First, there appears to have emerged a substantial departure from reciprocity between China and its major industrialized trading partners. I suggest that the implied need for *rebalancing market access commitments* can be addressed with non-violation claims. Second, even once reciprocity between China and its major industrialized trading partners is established, there is a possibility that the Uruguay Round tariff commitments made by industrialized countries now imply the grant of a greater level of market access than these countries are comfortable with. I suggest that the implied need for *reconsideration of the level of market access commitments*, where necessary, can be addressed with GATT Article XXVIII renegotiations. And third, an asymmetry in the level of market access commitments between the developing/emerging economies and industrialized countries has emerged that is now hindering the ability of the former to gain from WTO membership. I suggest that this *"latecomers problem"* can be addressed with Article XXVIII renegotiations between industrialized countries, followed by Article XXVIII bis negotiations between industrialized and developing/emerging countries.

7.1   Rebalancing Market Access Commitments

Industrialized countries have grown increasingly frustrated with the inability of WTO rules to effectively discipline China's economic policies, owing to the nonmarket features of China's economy. For example, in its 2020 *Report to Congress on China's WTO Compliance*, the United States Trade Representative (USTR) stated:

China's non-market approach has imposed, and continues to impose, substantial costs on WTO members. In our prior reports, we identified and explained the numerous policies and practices pursued by China that harm and disadvantage U.S. companies and workers, often severely. It is clear that the costs associated with China's unfair and distortive policies and practices have been substantial. For example, China's non-market economic system and the industrial policies that flow from it have systematically distorted critical sectors of the global economy such as steel, aluminum, solar and fisheries, devastating markets in the United States and other countries. China also continues to block valuable sectors of its economy from foreign competition, particularly services sectors. At the same time, China's industrial policies are increasingly responsible for displacing companies in new, emerging sectors of the global economy, as the Chinese government and the Chinese Communist Party powerfully intervene on behalf of China's domestic industries. Companies in economies disciplined by the market cannot effectively compete with both Chinese companies and the Chinese state. (USTR 2021, 2)

Similar frustrations about China's economic policies have been voiced by the European Union (European Commission 2016).

Wu (2016, 284) attributes this frustration not so much to any one specific China policy or even a handful of specific policies, but rather to China's "complex web of overlapping networks and relationships— some formal and others informal—between the state, Party, SOEs [state-owned enterprises], private enterprises, financial institutions, investment vehicles, trade associations, and so on." Adding to this frustration is the fact that many of the distinct elements of China's unique economic model were put in place after its 2001 accession to the WTO. But rather than reflecting frustration with a bad-faith effort on the part of China to escape from its WTO commitments, it is more accurate to say that the growing frustration among industrialized countries reflects their unmet expectations that China would have by now evolved further in the direction of a market-oriented economy than it, in fact, has. Summarizing the nexus of nonmarket forces operating in China with the moniker "China, Inc.," Wu puts the point this way:

This is not to suggest that the Chinese concealed their true intentions. Throughout the 1990s, Chinese leaders openly and repeatedly stated that they sought to forge their own unique economic system. Moreover, economic developments in China's reform era have proceeded largely through incremental rather than through radical, abrupt policy shifts. Thus, the development of China, Inc. should not be understood as a deliberate ex post act to circumvent WTO rules. (Wu 2016, 292, footnotes omitted)

As Wu (2016) describes it, China, Inc. poses a particularly subtle challenge for the WTO. This is because the pursuit of complaints against China's policies through the WTO dispute settlement system has not been altogether unsuccessful in helping China's trading partners address these concerns. As Wu documents, for certain kinds of issues, such as state-coordinated economic actions, local content requirements, and state trading enterprises, the GATT/WTO legal framework has proved to be effective against those countries that have used such policies in the past, and it continues to be effective against China's use of these policies. The real challenge lies in other issues raised by China's policies—the definition of a "public body" in the context of defining the reach of WTO disciplines on subsidies, or whether China's trading partners can treat it as a nonmarket economy for purposes of administering their antidumping laws—which involve technical legal and factual questions that the WTO dispute settlement body has little prior experience resolving, with trade stakes that are potentially enormous. Left unaddressed and in light of China's sheer size, these issues have the potential to upset the fundamental balance between market access rights and obligations that lies at the core of the GATT/WTO bargain. They are the kinds of thorny issues on which, Wu argues, the WTO could founder.

So how should the WTO confront the China, Inc. challenge? To answer this question it is clarifying first to pause and revisit a fundamental question that I considered in chapter 2: What is the purpose of a trade agreement? I argued there that the purpose of a trade agreement in a wide range of settings can be seen as expanding market access to internationally efficient levels. But in all of the settings I considered, market forces—subject to the kinds of government policy interventions that typify those found in market economies—were assumed to shape the decisions of firms and consumers everywhere. Does the purpose of a trade agreement change when one of the countries adopts an economic system like China, Inc.? Reassuringly, it is straightforward to see that the answer to this question is "no," as long as world prices continue to be determined by the international market-clearing conditions that equate quantities demanded to quantities supplied on world markets.[1]

---

1. A different form of international price determination may be associated with the rise of offshoring and global value chains, and this can alter the purpose of a trade agreement from that which I have emphasized in chapter 2. The path for addressing the current impasse with China that I propose in this chapter may therefore be complicated by China's important role in global value chains. But that is a potential issue associated

This is because when one country chooses to organize the economic activity within its borders under a policy regime that features important nonmarket elements, it does not alter the fundamental international externality—namely, the world price or terms-of-trade externality— that is generated by the unilateral policy choices of this country and the unilateral policy choices of its trading partners, and that underpins the essential "insufficient market access" problem for a trade agreement to solve.

A simple way to see this is to think of noncooperative Nash policies as being determined in two steps: First, facing the constraints imposed by international market-clearing conditions, a national social planner in each country determines the economic magnitudes (the "allocation") within its national borders; and second, in each country the national social planner then chooses whether to decentralize the implementation of the desired within-country allocation using a market system and appropriate tax/subsidy/regulatory policies or instead impose this allocation directly on its citizens by fiat. The choice made in this second step could be interpreted as determining whether a country is market-oriented or not. Choosing the first option amounts to the familiar "primal" approach to solving the optimal policy problem, whereby the fictional planner decides on the allocation and then implements the desired allocation in a market economy with the appropriate policy instruments. Choosing the second option simply omits the use of markets to implement the desired allocation. But these choices will not impact the nature of the problem for a trade agreement to solve.[2]

---

with offshoring, not China per se, and I discuss the challenges to the WTO associated with the rise of offshoring and global value chains in chapter 10.

2. In chapter 2, I made use of the politically optimal point on the efficiency frontier (Bagwell and Staiger 1999, 2002) to conclude that the purpose of a trade agreement is to eliminate the unilateral incentive that governments have to manipulate their terms of trade. As long as the underlying objectives of each government can be represented as a function of the within-country allocation—and the local and world prices that would be needed to implement that allocation in a market economy—as stipulated in equations (2.7) through (2.9), it is immaterial for those arguments whether governments actually choose to implement their desired within-country allocations through the decentralized mechanism of the market or rather through a command economy. This also helps to clarify what *would* cause a problem for my argument: If, for example, China sought to use its policies to maximize its share of world trade, then its objectives would depend on more than simply its within-country allocations—its objectives would depend also on the trade volumes of other countries and therefore directly on their local prices—and the purpose of a trade agreement would no longer conform to the purpose described in chapter 2. But notice that such an objective function would imply a different purpose to trade agreements independent of whether this description fits the government of a command or a market economy. So this has nothing to do with China as China, Inc. per se.

Confirming that the purpose of a trade agreement is unchanged from that identified in chapter 2 when a country adopts an economic system like China, Inc. is clarifying, because it indicates that the challenge for the WTO posed by China's entry into the world trading system is not to find the capacity to evolve beyond its essential market access focus in order to successfully accommodate China. Rather, the challenge, succinctly put, is this: The WTO must find a way for China to make additional policy commitments, tailored to compensate for the nonmarket elements of its economy, that can serve the role of preserving the market access implied by its tariff bindings, much as the role that GATT articles play for market-oriented economies (see, for example, note 4 in chapter 3). Evidently, there is no reason to think that China's entry into the world trading system raises issues that are fundamentally inconsistent with the WTO's underlying mandate. To the contrary, the market access orientation of the GATT/WTO provides a useful guardrail for what China should be willing to contemplate—and what other WTO members have a right to expect—in the context of its WTO commitments.

In essence, then, the current circumstances that the WTO finds itself in with regard to China's economic policies can be summarized as follows. Upon China's 2001 accession to the WTO, its major industrialized trading partners believed that existing WTO rules, in combination with (a) the very substantial tariff bindings and additional specific market access commitments they had secured from China as part of its accession negotiations and (b) their expectation that China would evolve strongly in the direction of a more market-oriented economy, were sufficient to ensure that China's tariff bindings represented market access commitments that would deliver the appropriate balance between rights and obligations. But the initial set of specific commitments that China agreed to as a condition for accession to the WTO has turned out to be unsatisfactory for this purpose. This is not because China has failed to live up to its specific commitments or to comply with WTO rulings against it when it has not.[3] Rather, it is because China has not evolved toward a market economy as quickly as these trading

That said, it is an interesting question whether or not China's most recent 10-year plan announced in 2015, *China 2025* (or for that matter, *Industrie 4.0*, the 10- to 15-year strategy announced by the German government in 2011), should be interpreted as an objective function driven by just such an explicit global-market-share target.

3. As Wu (2016) notes, many of the specific commitments agreed to by China as part of its WTO Protocol of Accession (WTO 2001) can be litigated successfully in the WTO (and have been, where violation claims against it have been brought), so they are not the

partners expected, and it does not now appear that China is likely to evolve toward a market-oriented economy as strongly as these trading partners once hoped.

If this is an accurate summary of the China, Inc. challenge faced by the WTO, then the non-violation clause provides a promising path for WTO members to address the current impasse. This point is made forcefully by Jennifer Hillman (2018) who, in describing the role of a non-violation claim in the context of her congressional testimony about the best way for the United States to address the challenges created by China's economic policies, observes:[4]

It is exactly for this type of situation that the non-violation nullification and impairment clause was drafted. The United States and all other WTO members had legitimate expectations that China would increasingly behave as a market economy—that it would achieve a discernible separation between its government and its private sector, that private property rights and an understanding of who controls and makes decisions in major enterprises would be clear, that subsidies would be curtailed, that theft of IP [intellectual property] rights would be punished and diminished in amount, that SOEs would make purchases based on commercial considerations, that the Communist Party would not, by fiat, occupy critical seats within major "private" enterprises and that standards and regulations would be published for all to see. It is this collective failure by China, rather than any specific violation of individual provisions, that should form the core of a big, bold WTO case. Because addressing these cross-cutting, systemic problems is the only way to correct for the collective failures of both the rules-based trading system and China. (Hillman 2018, 10–11)

Importantly, by focusing on the departure from reciprocity in market access commitments and the implied imbalance itself, rather than specific policies that may have violated WTO legal obligations and led to this imbalance, the non-violation complaint can sidestep the kinds of thorny legal and factual issues noted above and described by Wu (2016). This feature of non-violation complaints is highlighted by Sykes (2005) in the context of disciplines on domestic subsidies:

---

source of the challenge posed by China, Inc.. And on China's record of compliance with WTO rulings against it, see Webster (2014) and Zhou (2019).

4. The non-violation clause in the original GATT 1947 was incorporated into the WTO Agreements in GATT 1994, in the General Agreement on Trade in Services (GATS), and in the Agreement on Trade-Related Aspects of Intellectual Property Rights (TRIPS). However, WTO members agreed to an extendable five-year moratorium on the use of the non-violation clause in TRIPS, and this moratorium is still in place today. Hence, it is not clear that the non-violation clause could be used to address concerns about China's intellectual property rights regime.

A nice feature of the nonviolation doctrine is the fact that it does not require subsidies to be carefully defined or measured. A complaining member need simply demonstrate that an unanticipated government program has improved the competitive position of domestic firms at the expense of their foreign competition. (Sykes 2005, 98)

Moreover, recall from chapter 6 that under a successful non-violation claim the defendant government is under no obligation to remove the measures at issue, but if it does not remove them, then the claimant government is owed compensation, the level of which is subject to arbitration by the WTO Dispute Settlement Body. Hence, a non-violation claim would provide China with the freedom to decide whether and, if so, how best to offer secure market access commitments to its trading partners that can reestablish reciprocity, with the knowledge that if its offer of market access commitments is not sufficient for this purpose, then its trading partners have the right to restore reciprocity by withdrawing market access concessions of their own as part of the resolution of a successful non-violation claim. In this way, the non-violation clause would be serving the role it was designed to serve—namely, as Petersmann (1977, 172) observes, to provide a check on the domestic policy autonomy of member countries "and to prevent the circumvention of the provisions in GATT Article XXVIII ... if a member, rather than withdrawing a concession de jure in exchange for compensation or equivalent withdrawals of concessions by affected contracting parties, withdraws a concession de facto." And crucially, any disagreements over the magnitude of the policy adjustments required to restore reciprocity between China and its trading partners would be referred to the relevant WTO dispute settlement bodies for a ruling, thereby keeping the resolution of these issues within the rules-based multilateral system.[5]

---

5. What kinds of commitments might China offer as a way to reestablish reciprocity? It is possible that China might be able to find certain policy commitments that would have clear market access implications without undermining core features of its chosen economic system. And it is possible that transparency issues would warrant the use of certain quantity commitments rather than tariff commitments as a second-best tool for generating market access commitments, as were used in the GATT accession agreements for Poland and Romania (Douglass 1972; Kostecki 1974; Haus 1991). More generally, it is likely that a combination of measures might be needed to secure market access commitments from China, but it is also likely that China is in the best position to know what combination of measures would be most effective while minimizing inconsistencies with its desired economic system.

This perspective also yields an important insight into the nature of the challenge that China, Inc. poses for the world trading system and the choices that are available to the WTO membership to address this challenge. Recall that there were two elements to China's accession negotiations: (a) a list of agreed specific market access commitments and (b) an expectation that China would evolve strongly toward a market economy. And recall that the imbalance between China's market access rights and obligations has emerged as a result of the failure of (b): China has not evolved toward a market economy to the extent that its trading partners expected. Does this imply that the only solution is for China to now promise to evolve to a market economy at the speed and to the degree that fulfills those expectations? Not at all, because it is clear that there is an alternative solution, and one that is more targeted to the underlying source of the trade tension. The alternative is for China to agree to additional specific market access commitments of its own choosing and thereby to compensate for the unanticipated nonmarket features of its economy—and hence for the shortfall in part (b)—by augmenting its specific commitments in part (a). This is what the non-violation clause can facilitate. Looked at in this way, there is no reason to think that, unless China chooses to relinquish China, Inc., "decoupling" China from the world trading system is the inevitable endgame.[6]

Clarifying the challenge for the WTO posed by China, Inc. also has a potential side benefit. As is well known, bringing successful non-violation claims in the GATT/WTO is exceptionally difficult, and

6. Here my position diverges somewhat from Hillman (2018, 13), who describes the choice facing China as one of reforming its economic system or exiting the WTO. There is still the important question of whether China can, in fact, find ways to make the needed additional market access commitments, given the unique features of its economic system. And this would no doubt be a difficult task. But as observed previously in this chapter (see note 5), several of the nonmarket economies of Eastern Europe found creative ways to do this when they joined the GATT in the 1960s and 1970s, suggesting that China might find similarly unorthodox ways to make market access commitments that can respond to those nonmarket features of its economic system that were not anticipated by WTO members at the time of China's WTO accession but that China wishes to preserve. And while finding effective disciplines on China's subsidies will be particularly important and may ultimately entail reforms of the WTO's Agreement on Subsidies and Countervailing Measures in the wider context of WTO multilateral or plurilateral negotiations (Bown and Hillman 2019), Zhou and Fang (2021) argue that these reforms are not necessary to address the China-specific issues that arise in the context of subsidy disciplines and that such reforms would be better approached outside the context of China-specific trade tensions.

indeed this is so by design. As one WTO panel report put it, "The non-violation nullification or impairment remedy should be approached with caution and treated as an exceptional concept. The reason for this caution is straightforward. Members negotiate the rules that they agree to follow and only exceptionally would expect to be challenged for actions not in contravention of those rules" (WTO 1998a). But once it is understood that the goal of a non-violation claim is to find a way to allow China to make meaningful market access commitments, and not to confront China with a choice between reforming its economy or decoupling from the world trading system, it becomes more likely that China might see it in its own interests to facilitate a successful rebalancing within the context of such a claim. As such, enlisting China's support in bringing such a claim might even be feasible. This is because it is in China's own interests, just as it is in each WTO member's own interests, to be part of a world trading system that is effective in permitting the voluntary exchange of secure, negotiated market access commitments between its members. And this is especially so if the current imbalances in the world trading system attributable to China's accession to the WTO are putting the WTO at serious risk of foundering. So, while enlisting China's support in bringing such claims against it would be unprecedented, it is not unreasonable to attempt to do so, given the unique challenge that China poses for the WTO and the world trading system.

This is not to say that the more traditional WTO violation claims against China, where viable, should not also be brought, just as with viable violation claims against any WTO member. Indeed, in her congressional testimony about the WTO case that the US should bring against China, Hillman (2018) lists 11 specific issue areas where violation claims against China might be viable (and as Hillman notes, her list is not meant to be exhaustive). But as both Hillman and also Wu (2016) make clear, even if such violation claims were all successful, they are not likely to address the fundamental sources of the imbalances that have emerged in China's market access rights and obligations and that have led to the growing frustrations of industrialized countries with China, Inc. By channeling these frustrations into non-violation claims, where such claims might perhaps be aided by China itself and where the process of filing and resolving these claims might also serve as a mechanism for resolving among the parties any pending or imminent violation claims, the existing GATT/WTO procedures for dispute settlement can be most effectively put to use.

Finally, an added benefit of addressing this issue with non-violation claims is that it helps to draw a clean distinction between concerns over non-reciprocity with China, on the one hand, and the possibility that even with reciprocity established a WTO member might wish to rethink its *own* level of market access commitments, on the other. With this distinction cleanly drawn, these two separable issues could then be addressed on separate tracks. As I describe next, the second issue is best addressed within the context of Article XXVIII renegotiations. And the separation of these two issues is crucial, because while the maintenance of reciprocity should be a central concern of attempts to address the second issue (and would be under Article XXVIII renegotiations), by design it *cannot* be a feature of the solution to the first issue (and would not be under a non-violation claim, where the whole point is to address an *im*balance and thereby *restore* reciprocity).

7.2 Reconsideration of the Level of Market Access Commitments

Suppose that the imbalance between China's market access rights and obligations in the WTO can be addressed and that reciprocity is restored in the world trading system. Does this mean that all of the major challenges to the world trading system presented by the rise of the large emerging markets will have been met? I suggest that the answer to this question is "no," because there are two additional challenges that would still remain. A first challenge relates to the impact on industrialized country income inequality that the rise of large emerging markets has had. Whether this impact would be mitigated or rather exacerbated by the restoration of reciprocity with China depends in part on how reciprocity is restored, and in particular this depends on whether reciprocity with China is restored by an expansion of access to the markets of China or rather by a reduction in access to the markets of the industrialized world. I discuss this challenge in this subsection. A second challenge relates to the history of reciprocal tariff negotiations in GATT, the historical lack of participation by nonindustrialized countries in these negotiations, and how that history has positioned the world trading system going forward in the presence of the large emerging markets today. I discuss this challenge in the next subsection.

Concerns about the possible adverse effects of trade on income inequality are not new, and indeed such effects are central predictions of the standard neoclassical models of trade. But as of the mid-1990s, the general view among economists was that, as an empirical matter, the distributional impacts of trade were relatively modest. Today that view is markedly less sanguine, thanks in part to changes in the nature and scale of trade over the past three decades—including a dramatic rise in the manufacturing exports of developing and emerging economies—and thanks in part also to changes in the focus of the economics research investigating these effects (a shift in focus from economy-wide impacts to local labor market effects).[7] This observation is especially illuminating for the current discussion, because the WTO tariff commitments in place today are the product of multilateral market access negotiations in the Uruguay Round that were completed in 1994 with the signing of the Marrakesh Agreement that created the WTO on January 1, 1995. In this light, there is a possibility that the Uruguay Round tariff commitments made by some industrialized countries now imply the grant of a greater level of market access than these countries are comfortable with, given the level of income inequality that they are now grappling with.[8]

In short, it would not be unreasonable if those industrialized countries that have experienced a significant increase in income inequality over the past several decades now wanted to pause and reconsider some of their existing tariff commitments, given that these commitments were made before the rise of the large emerging markets at a time when it was thought that the potential for trade to generate significant income inequality issues within industrialized countries was small. Of course, several important hurdles would have to be cleared before one can convincingly argue that the reimposition of tariffs is an appropriate response to a country's concerns about income inequality.

A first hurdle is to demonstrate that there are not alternative policy responses that are available to the government to address its concerns about income inequality at lower overall cost to the economy. At a general level, the targeting principle (Bhagwati and Ramaswami 1963) implies that tariffs will almost never be the first-best policy choice for achieving any particular goal (the exception, as noted in chapter 6, being for purposes of terms-of-trade manipulation, a consideration that should play no role in clearing this first hurdle). For example,

---

7. See Krugman (2019) for a nice summary of the evolution of economists' thinking on the link between trade and income inequality. The local labor market impacts of trade competition were first considered by Borjas and Ramey (1995). Autor, Dorn, and Hanson (2013) were the first to investigate the regional/local labor market impacts of trade with China.

8. Not all countries experienced rising income inequality over this period. See Bourguignon (2019) on the cross-country diversity of trends in income inequality over the past 30 years.

at least for those countries that have the means to finance them, the use of production subsidies would typically dominate tariffs as a policy tool for addressing concerns about income inequality.[9] But as I noted in chapter 2, in the real world such policies may not, in fact, be widely available to all countries. Indeed, this may be true even for rich countries: For example, after describing the labor market policies and programs that are available in the United States, Kletzer (2019, 171) concludes that "despite the array of US programs, there is considerable evidence that these labor market interventions are inadequate."[10]

A second hurdle is to demonstrate that the proposed tariff increases would actually have the intended effect on income inequality. This demonstration is complicated by the fact that technology as well as factor endowments within the industrialized countries have changed dramatically over the period that income inequality has risen, and it is therefore almost certainly true that "turning back the clock" with tariffs to achieve the trade patterns and volumes that a country experienced in an earlier time would not bring back the income distribution that the country had experienced at that time. Notice, though, that the effectiveness of tariffs as a response to rising income inequality in a country does not hinge on whether trade has *caused* the rise in inequality; rather it is simply a question of whether the use of tariffs—and the price effects that their use would generate in the country—might be part of the optimal response to addressing inequality, whatever its causes, given the technologies and factor endowments that exist today.[11]

---

9. In this regard, the WTO's Agreement on Subsidies and Countervailing Measures (SCM Agreement), which regulates the use of subsidies relating to trade in goods, includes a provision (Article 8.2(b)) that identifies assistance to disadvantaged regions as "non-actionable," granting WTO member governments wide latitude to implement the kinds of subsidies that might be called for in addressing income inequality related to the local labor market effects of trade. However, this provision was temporary, and it was allowed to lapse at the end of 1999. Reforming the SCM Agreement to reinstate Article 8 in some form would help to remove WTO legal barriers that could have the effect of precluding the use of subsidies over tariffs for purposes of addressing income inequality concerns and on these general grounds would be supported by the targeting-principle logic. See, for example, Charnovitz (2014), who makes similar arguments for the reinstatement of Article 8 in some form as that article relates to environmental subsidies.

10. That said, it should be noted that Kletzer (2019) advocates for implementing a program of wage insurance in the United States, not the use of tariffs.

11. I am abstracting from the dynamic effects of tariffs on technologies and factor supplies. There is also the deeper question of whether income inequality as typically measured, or rather broader measures of economic inequality such as inequality in job tenure prospects and the prospects for one's children, should be the target of policy interventions and how trade policy interventions would measure up to other available policy responses

Where does this discussion leave us? The reimposition of tariffs surely cannot be the centerpiece of an appropriate response to concerns about income inequality. But in light of the complexity of the issues involved and the evident lack of first-best policy instruments to address these issues, neither does there appear to be a compelling reason that tariff responses—above all other possible second-best policy responses—should be taken off the table. In the abstract, a sensible position might therefore be that industrialized countries that have experienced rising income inequality and have concerns about this development should be able to reconsider some of their Uruguay Round tariff commitments as part of a broader package of policy interventions to address these concerns.

How would the restoration of reciprocity between China and its industrialized trading partners impact these considerations? As I mentioned above, that would depend in part on how reciprocity is restored. If reciprocity with China is restored as a result of a reduction in access to the markets of the industrialized world, then this implies that some industrialized-country tariffs would rise, and these tariff increases might be structured so as to mitigate income inequality concerns in industrialized countries. On the other hand, if reciprocity with China is restored as a result of an expansion of access to the markets of China, then this implies that China would be liberalizing its import regime, which, if this does not impact China's overall trade imbalance, implies in turn that China will also be exporting more—a scenario that is likely to exacerbate the existing income inequality concerns of industrialized countries.[12] The upshot is that restoring reciprocity between China and its industrialized trading partners is unlikely to address existing concerns over income inequality and might even exacerbate these concerns.

This brings me to the possibility of GATT Article XXVIII renegotiations. Specifically, while I argued earlier that the non-violation clause is well designed to deal with concerns over nonreciprocity with China,

---

with such targets in mind. See Bourguignon (2019) for an illuminating discussion of these issues.

12. Absent any impact on its overall trade imbalance and holding its terms of trade fixed, China's unilateral import liberalization would lead to equivalent increases in its exports. And if China is large in the import markets where it liberalizes, then its terms of trade should deteriorate, implying an even larger increase in its exports to maintain its existing trade balance. Of course, if China were to make policy changes that altered its overall trade balance, additional considerations would come into play. Krugman (2019) provides a discussion of the potentially important impact of trade imbalances on US income inequality in the short run.

I now argue that Article XXVIII is well designed to deal with the possibility that, even with reciprocity established, a WTO member might wish to rethink its own level of market access commitments.

Hoda (2001) describes the mechanics of Article XXVIII renegotiations in detail and provides a comprehensive history of the hundreds of renegotiations that have occurred over the GATT and early WTO years. In brief, countries do not need to provide a rationale to initiate renegotiations under Article XXVIII; they simply need to follow the procedures for renegotiation laid out in Article XXVIII.

As Hoda (2001) explains, the key features of Article XXVIII renegotiations are that a country is allowed to modify or withdraw the tariff commitments that are the subject of its renegotiations, even if it cannot (within defined time limits) reach agreement in those negotiations with its impacted trading partners, and that its impacted trading partners are then allowed to respond—at most—in a reciprocal manner by withdrawing "substantially equivalent" tariff commitments of their own, where any disagreements over what constitutes substantially equivalent tariff commitments are subject to rulings of the relevant GATT/WTO dispute settlement bodies. In this way, with reciprocal actions defining the disagreement or "threat" point to the negotiations, Article XXVIII renegotiations avoid the possibility that a threatened or actual breakdown in those negotiations could hold up the modifications that a country desires to make to its tariff commitments. At the same time, these renegotiations imply that the original balance of negotiated reciprocal tariff commitments between the country and its trading partners is preserved; this last feature is important because as discussed in chapter 4, the application of reciprocity that delivers it ensures that inefficient terms-of-trade motives are removed from the country's incentives to initiate the renegotiation.[13]

These features of Article XXVIII are the reason that legal scholars claim that GATT/WTO tariff commitments are designed to operate as "liability rules." For example, as I noted in chapter 6, Pauwelyn (2008) distinguishes between GATT articles that are designed as liability rules and others that are designed as property rules, and he designates tariff commitments as liability rules on the basis of the renegotiation opportunities provided by Article XXVIII (as well as other similar but temporary escapes such as the GATT safeguard clause Article XIX). In explaining the logic of this design, Pauwelyn (2008, 137) writes:

---

13. Bagwell and Staiger (1999, 2002) emphasize these incentive effects of reciprocity.

Trade negotiators cannot foresee all possible situations, nor can they predict future economic and political developments, both at home and internationally. As a result of this uncertainty, they wanted the flexibility of a liability rule.

An important benefit of a liability rule is that it can allow for "efficient breach." Schwartz and Sykes (2002, S181) put the point this way:

Economic theory teaches that a key objective of an enforcement system is to induce a party to comply with its obligations whenever compliance will yield greater benefits to the promisee than costs to the promisor, while allowing the promisor to depart from its obligations whenever the costs of compliance to the promisor exceed the benefits to the promisee. In the parlance of contract theory, the objective is to deter inefficient breaches but to encourage efficient ones.

It is exactly in the spirit of efficient breach that limited use of Article XXVIII renegotiations might be made by those industrialized countries that are concerned about rising inequality and wish to reconsider some of their Uruguay Round tariff commitments as part of a broader package of policy interventions to address these concerns. Importantly, under the rules of Article XXVIII, those countries would not be making this choice "for free." Rather, they would be making this choice with the knowledge that any modification or withdrawal of tariff commitments would be met with reciprocal withdrawals of market access by their affected trading partners. If a country still prefers to raise its tariffs under these conditions, then that is how the GATT renegotiation process approximates efficient breach.[14]

It is also instructive to consider what can happen in a renegotiation of trade commitments that are not designed to operate as liability rules. Although it is not directly comparable to the Article XXVIII renegotiation of a GATT tariff commitment, the Brexit negotiations for the withdrawal of the United Kingdom from the European Union provide something of a cautionary tale. These negotiations, which had no meaningful equivalent to the reciprocity "buyout" provision of GATT's Article XXVIII that could have acted as a threat point for the outcome of the negotiations, officially began on March 29, 2017, when the United Kingdom activated its withdrawal notice under Article 50 of the Treaty on European Union, and the negotiations were concluded in October 2019. As is well known, the initial two-year negotiation period had to be extended in order that an agreement on the terms of withdrawal could be reached, and the negotiations were fraught with

---

14. Maggi and Staiger (2015) provide a formal rationale for the efficient-breach role that the reciprocity rule can play in a model where international transfers are costly.

seemingly ample room for strategic behavior.[15] The liability-rule structure of GATT Article XXVIII renegotiations acts as an insurance policy against the possibility that such renegotiations would devolve into a Brexit-like situation.[16]

7.3 The Latecomers Problem

I began this chapter by noting that there are three interrelated challenges for the world trading system created by the rise in economic importance of the large emerging and developing economies. The first of these challenges centers on China. And owing to its sheer size in world trade, China undoubtedly plays a leading role in the second challenge.

The third challenge arises from an asymmetry in the level of market access commitments between the developing/emerging economies and the industrialized countries. This asymmetry is a result of the historical lack of participation of nonindustrialized countries in 50 years of GATT reciprocal tariff negotiations, and it has led to what Bagwell and Staiger (2014) call a "latecomers problem" for the WTO that may be hindering the ability of many developing and emerging economies to gain from GATT/WTO membership. Because China made more significant (though, as it turned out, apparently still not reciprocal) market access concessions as part of its 2001 protocol for accession to the WTO than have any other emerging and developing economy WTO members to date, this third challenge is less about China than about other emerging and developing economies.[17] Following Bagwell and Staiger, I now briefly describe the latecomers problem and how it might be addressed with GATT Article XXVIII renegotiations between industrialized countries followed by Article XXVIII bis negotiations between industrialized and developing/emerging countries.[18]

---

15. See, for example, Martill and Staiger (2018) on the bargaining strategy pursued by the United Kingdom in its Brexit negotiations.

16. If flexibility in market access commitments is valued, this comparison also illustrates an advantage of GATT's shallow-integration approach. It is difficult to see how a liability-rule approach to market access commitments could be possible with a deep-integration agreement such as the European Union. On the other hand, if flexibility is not valued, as would be the case under the commitment theory of trade agreements that I mentioned briefly in chapter 2, then the fact that this possibility arises under shallow integration is not an attractive feature of the GATT/WTO approach.

17. On the unusually far-reaching market access commitments that China agreed to in its protocol of accession to the WTO relative to other developing and emerging economy GATT/WTO members, see, for example, Lardy (2001).

18. In chapter 8, I will consider an additional, possibly complementary way of addressing the latecomers problem within the context of climate policy.

Recall from chapter 4 that, according to the terms-of-trade theory, negotiations that abide by MFN treatment and reciprocity can eliminate third-party spillovers from bilateral tariff bargaining. This feature underpins the efficiency properties of a tariff negotiating forum such as GATT that relies heavily on bilateral tariff bargaining and is built on the pillars of MFN and reciprocity.

But historically GATT has extended to its developing country members an exception to the reciprocity norm, codified under "special and differential treatment" (SDT) clauses. These SDT clauses were intended to provide developing countries with a "free pass" on the MFN tariff cuts that the developed countries negotiated with one another and in this way allow developing country exporters to then share with exporters from developed countries in the benefits of greater MFN access to developed country markets.

As Bagwell and Staiger (2014) point out, however, in the presence of SDT, the fact that third-party spillovers from bilateral tariff bargaining are neutralized when those bargains abide by MFN and reciprocity now carries with it a more negative connotation: It implies that, by their very design, these SDT clauses *cannot* succeed at their intended purpose. This is because, as I described in the context of the three-country, two-good general equilibrium model of chapter 4, when two (developed) countries engage in a bilateral tariff negotiation that abides by MFN and reciprocity while the third (developing) country sits it out, the third country gets nothing from their negotiations.

Indeed, a wide range of anecdotal and empirical evidence suggests that developing countries have gained little from more than half a century of GATT/WTO-sponsored tariff negotiations. For example, based on interviews with WTO delegates and secretariat staff members, Jawara and Kwa (2003, 269) conclude:

Developed countries are benefitting from the WTO, as are a handful of (mostly upper) middle-income countries. The rest, including the great majority of developing countries, are not. It is as simple as that.

In an implicit acknowledgment of this fact, the WTO's Doha Round is semi-officially known as the Doha Development Agenda, because a fundamental objective of the round is to improve the trading prospects of developing countries. But as the declaration from the WTO Ministerial Conference in Doha, Qatar, November 14, 2001, states in part:

We agree that special and differential treatment for developing countries shall be an integral part of all elements of the negotiations.

Ironically, as Bagwell and Staiger (2014) observe, according to the terms-of-trade theory, it is the GATT/WTO's embrace of SDT that explains the disappointing developing country experience with GATT/WTO membership to begin with. This suggests that the Doha Round cannot succeed in one of its fundamental objectives under the current bargaining protocol that it has adopted.

Even if one accepts the diagnosis of the problem offered by the terms-of-trade theory, simply abandoning SDT at this point and bringing the developing and emerging market countries to the tariff bargaining table is unlikely to be sufficient to address the issue, and this is where the latecomers problem becomes relevant for the Doha Round: Because they are "latecomers" to the bargaining table relative to the industrialized countries, developing and emerging market countries are unlikely to find industrialized-country bargaining partners that can reciprocate the substantial tariff cuts that they might have to offer.[19] This kind of asymmetry is at the heart of various diagnoses of the central sticking points at Doha, such as this one:

> The real bone of contention is the aim of proposed cuts in tariffs on manufactured goods. America sees the Doha talks as its final opportunity to get fast-growing emerging economies like China and India to slash their duties on imports of such goods, which have been reduced in previous rounds but remain much higher than those in the rich world. It wants something approaching parity, at least in some sectors, because it reckons its own low tariffs leave it with few concessions to offer in future talks. But emerging markets insist that the Doha round was never intended to result in such harmonization. These positions are fundamentally at odds. (*The Economist*, 2011)

In some sense, then, the industrialized countries find themselves in a position in the Doha Round not unlike the position that the United States tried very hard to avoid in the context of sequential bilateral tariff bargaining under the 1934 Reciprocal Trade Agreements Act (RTAA) as described in chapter 2: New potential bargaining partners have arrived, but because of previous MFN tariff bargains with each other, the industrialized countries have not preserved sufficient bargaining power to engage in a substantial way with these new potential partners. Mattoo and Staiger (2020) argue that the latecomers problem and

---

19. If the arrival of the developing and emerging economies had been anticipated by the industrialized countries at the time that the latter were engaged in tariff negotiations, then the findings of Bagwell and Staiger (2010b) on bilateral sequential tariff bargaining in a GATT/WTO-like bargaining forum as an efficient means of accommodating new countries into the world trading system might apply. But it is the unanticipated arrival of the "latecomers" that makes achieving efficient tariff bargaining outcomes in the GATT/WTO framework more difficult.

its implications for the preservation of tariff bargaining power in the WTO system may be helpful for interpreting recent United States trade actions as signifying a switch from "rules-based" to "power-based" tariff bargaining. I discussed some of these points at the end of chapter 5, and I discuss Mattoo and Staiger further in chapter 12. Here I argue that existing GATT/WTO flexibilities can be used to address the latecomers problem within the rules-based system.

The essential idea is to find a way to implement the set of tariff commitments that the current WTO membership would choose to negotiate if countries were not constrained in their negotiations by their preexisting tariff bindings. This means providing countries with the flexibility to first escape from their existing GATT/WTO tariff bindings in an orderly way when necessary so that they can then engage in reciprocal MFN tariff bargaining with all willing WTO-member bargaining partners. As Bagwell and Staiger (2014) note, there are obvious dangers in encouraging such flexibility for this first step, and sufficient care would need to be taken to prevent uncontrolled unraveling of existing tariff commitments. That said, the flexibility needed for the first step is already provided in GATT by the Article XXVIII renegotiation provisions that I discussed in this chapter (i.e., industrialized countries could renegotiate in an upward direction some of the bindings to which they had previously agreed in negotiations with other industrialized countries), while the flexibility for the second step is provided by the standard bilateral tariff bargaining protocols that have been employed in the various GATT rounds under Article XXVIII bis, which I described in chapter 4 (i.e., these industrialized countries could then engage in a round of reciprocal tariff bargaining with the "latecomer" emerging and developing countries). So, at least in principle, the WTO has the design features that would allow its member governments to address the latecomers problem. But a necessary ingredient for success would be to revisit the commitment to SDT.[20]

---

20. As I observed earlier in this chapter (see note 16), an advantage of shallow integration is that it can facilitate a liability-rule approach to market access commitments that allows for flexibilities that would be difficult under deep integration. A related observation can be made here—namely, that it would be easier to address the latecomers problem and associated challenges created by a rising WTO membership and growing importance of developing and emerging economies within the membership when a shallow approach to integration is adopted than when deep integration is attempted. With shallow integration, what is at issue are tariff renegotiations and further negotiations to adjust market access commitments for member governments in the face of a changing membership. With deep integration, the task would likely be far more complicated, as the increasing membership would have to agree on which deep commitments are acceptable.

8   Climate Change

There is little doubt that crafting an effective policy response to the changes in global climate that are resulting from rising levels of atmospheric carbon will be a defining challenge for the twenty-first century. The existential threats to the planet from a failure to rise to this challenge are by now well documented.[1] The WTO and the world trading system that it governs will by necessity play a role in meeting this challenge. The only question is whether the WTO's role will be seen as obstructionist or whether it can be accommodating to the world's attempts to solve the problem of climate change, or even serve as an active contributor to the solution. For example, Mattoo and Subramanian (2013, 91) describe the relationship between climate policy and trade policy in these terms:

If countries cut emissions by different amounts, or impose carbon taxes at different levels, then carbon prices are likely to differ across countries. Countries with higher carbon prices may seek to impose additional border taxes on imports from countries with lower carbon prices in order to offset the competitive disadvantage to their firms and to prevent "leakage," an increase of carbon emissions in the form of increased production in countries with lower carbon prices.... A key issue, therefore, is the scope for trade policy actions in any climate change agreement.

In effect, the kinds of carbon policies required to address global climate change are likely to have important trade effects and lead to policy disputes that the WTO may be called on to adjudicate. And more recently, Nordhaus (2015) has called for the creation of a "Climate Club" in which member countries agree to reduce their carbon emissions and

---

1. See, for example, Wallace-Wells (2019) or any of the recent Assessment Reports of the Intergovernmental Panel on Climate Change available at https://www.ipcc.ch /reports/.

nonparticipants are penalized with tariffs imposed on them by the club members.

In this chapter I discuss some of the key issues faced by the WTO in accommodating efforts to address climate change and the constructive role that the WTO might play in addressing this challenge.[2] To aid in this discussion, I develop a simple two-country partial equilibrium model of trade that features both a "trade problem" (associated with the terms-of-trade externality) and a "climate problem" (associated with a global nonpecuniary externality from carbon emissions) for the world to solve. The model is intentionally simplistic, as my emphasis is on broad themes rather than specific details.

I begin by considering how the architecture of GATT and the WTO can continue to work to address the trade problem in this setting. I then turn to the issue of carbon border adjustments and ask what role such adjustments might play in maintaining the solution to the trade problem under the GATT/WTO architecture while accommodating implementation of the carbon taxes that would result from the successful negotiation of a global climate accord. Finally, I discuss a more active role that the WTO might play in addressing the challenge of climate change through a form of linkage between the WTO and the negotiated policy commitments of a climate accord.

8.1 Climate Policy and Trade Agreements

How does the GATT/WTO architecture work when there is both a trade problem and a climate problem to solve? A simple model can provide answers that illuminate a number of the dimensions to this question.

A Benchmark Trade-and-Carbon Model
I consider a partial equilibrium two-country model of trade in a carbon-intensive good, which for purposes here might be thought of as aluminum. I denote by c the reduction in per-capita welfare everywhere in the world from the carbon emitted by another unit of aluminum production in the home country; similarly, I denote by c^* the reduction in per-capita welfare everywhere in the world from the carbon emitted by another unit of aluminum production in the foreign country. The

---

2. This chapter draws on material from my 2018 Frank D. Graham Memorial Lecture.

parameters $c > 0$ and $c^* > 0$ can be thought of as the carbon content of production in the home and the foreign country, measured in welfare (numeraire) units. If $c \neq c^*$, then the carbon content of production differs across home and foreign producers.[3]

The home (importing) country is populated by L citizens, and the home government can impose a production tax t on its producers and an import tariff τ; similarly, the foreign (exporting) country is populated by L^* citizens, and the foreign government can impose a production tax t^* on its producers and an export tariff τ^*. All taxes/tariffs are expressed in specific terms, and negative taxes/tariffs correspond to subsidies. Notice that, given my assumptions, the home-country production tax t could equivalently be implemented as a carbon tax $\frac{t}{c}$ on home-country producers, while the foreign-country production tax t^* could equivalently be implemented as a carbon tax $\frac{t^*}{c^*}$ on foreign-country producers. It could then be said that the home country "has a higher carbon price" than the foreign country when $\frac{t}{c} > \frac{t^*}{c^*}$. In the discussion that follows, I will for convenience characterize policies in terms of tariffs and production taxes, but I will sometimes also make reference to the carbon taxes implied by the production taxes.

Home producers face producer prices q and the upward-sloping home supply curve is $S(q)$, while home consumers face the consumer price p with $p = q + t$ and have downward-sloping demand $D(p)$. The analogous prices and magnitudes in the foreign country are q^*, p^*, $S^*(q^*)$, and $D^*(p^*)$, with $p^* = q^* + t^*$. With strictly positive imports (which I assume is always the case), the arbitrage condition implies $p^* = p - \tau - \tau^*$, and the world price can be defined in standard fashion as $p^w \equiv p - \tau$ or, equivalently, by the arbitrage condition, $p^w \equiv p^* + \tau^*$. Finally, with home imports defined by $M \equiv D - S$ and foreign exports defined by $E^* \equiv S^* - D^*$, the market-clearing condition equating home imports to foreign exports,

$$D(p^w + \tau) - S(p^w + \tau - t) = S^*(p^w - \tau^* - t^*) - D^*(p^w - \tau^*),$$

defines the equilibrium world price as a function of policies, $\tilde{p}^w(\tau, t, \tau^*, t^*)$, from which each of the other equilibrium prices may

---

3. The assumption that carbon emissions impact the welfare of both countries uniformly is made for simplicity so that I can focus on differences across countries in the carbon content of their production. But at the cost of more notation, it is straightforward to show that the results I emphasize below do not depend on this assumption.

then also be derived using the pricing relationships above:

$$\tilde{p}(\tau+\tau^*,t,t^*) \equiv \tilde{p}^w(\tau,t,\tau^*,t^*)+\tau$$
$$\tilde{q}(\tau+\tau^*,t,t^*) \equiv \tilde{p}^w(\tau,t,\tau^*,t^*)+\tau-t \qquad (8.1)$$
$$\tilde{p}^*(\tau+\tau^*,t,t^*) \equiv \tilde{p}^w(\tau,t,\tau^*,t^*)-\tau^*$$
$$\tilde{q}^*(\tau+\tau^*,t,t^*) \equiv \tilde{p}^w(\tau,t,\tau^*,t^*)-\tau^*-t^*.$$

As is standard, the world price depends on the levels of each of the tariffs τ and τ^* (as well as each of the production taxes t and t^*), but reflected in (8.1) is the property that only the sum of the tariffs $\tau+\tau^*$ enters into the home and foreign consumer and producer prices (in addition to t and t^*).

I define welfare in the home country W as a weighted sum of consumer surplus (CS), producer surplus (PS), and net tax revenue ($REV \equiv \tau M + tS$) minus the welfare cost of world carbon emissions on home citizens ($L \times [cS+c^*S^*]$), with a weight $\zeta \geq 1$ placed on home producer surplus,

$$W = W(\tilde{p}(\tau+\tau^*,t,t^*),\tilde{q}(\tau+\tau^*,t,t^*),\tilde{q}^*(\tau+\tau^*,t,t^*),\tilde{p}^w(\tau,t,\tau^*,t^*))$$
$$\equiv CS(\tilde{p}(\tau+\tau^*,t,t^*))+\zeta \times PS(\tilde{q}(\tau+\tau^*,t,t^*))$$
$$+ REV(\tilde{p}(\tau+\tau^*,t,t^*),\tilde{q}(\tau+\tau^*,t,t^*),\tilde{p}^w(\tau,t,\tau^*,t^*))$$
$$- L \times [cS(\tilde{q}(\tau+\tau^*,t,t^*))+c^*S^*(\tilde{q}^*(\tau+\tau^*,t,t^*))], \qquad (8.2)$$

and with an analogous definition of foreign-country welfare W^*,

$$W^* = W^*(\tilde{p}^*(\tau+\tau^*,t,t^*),\tilde{q}^*(\tau+\tau^*,t,t^*),\tilde{q}(\tau+\tau^*,t,t^*),\tilde{p}^w(\tau,t,\tau^*,t^*))$$
$$\equiv CS^*(\tilde{p}^*(\tau+\tau^*,t,t^*))+\zeta^* \times PS^*(\tilde{q}^*(\tau+\tau^*,t,t^*))$$
$$+ REV^*(\tilde{p}^*(\tau+\tau^*,t,t^*),\tilde{q}^*(\tau+\tau^*,t,t^*),\tilde{p}^w(\tau,t,\tau^*,t^*))$$
$$- L^* \times [cS(\tilde{q}(\tau+\tau^*,t,t^*))+c^*S^*(\tilde{q}^*(\tau+\tau^*,t,t^*))]. \qquad (8.3)$$

The producer price of each country's trading partner enters the country's welfare function as a result of the world wide carbon (nonpecuniary) externality reflected in $c > 0$ and $c^* > 0$. The weights on producer surplus ζ and ζ^* are meant to capture both distributional/political economy concerns associated with the production of carbon-intensive goods, as well as possible development opportunities not captured by the model that relate to the use of carbon-intensive technologies and may differ across countries in light of different stages of development (Mattoo and Subramanian 2013). As will become clear just below, it is these considerations that account for the possibility that efficient carbon taxes in this setting need not be uniform across countries as they would be under the classic Samuelson (1954) public goods optimality condition (see, e.g., Weizman 2014).

Nash Inefficiencies in a World of Trade and Climate Problems

I define efficient policies as those that maximize the sum of home and foreign ("world") welfare.[4] Straightforward calculations confirm that the efficient tariffs τ^e and τ^{*e} and production taxes t^e and t^{*e} in this setting are characterized by

$$\tau^e + \tau^{*e} = 0 \tag{8.4}$$

$$t^e = -(\zeta - 1)\frac{q^e}{\eta^{S^e}} + (L + L^*)c; \quad t^{*e} = -(\zeta^* - 1)\frac{q^{*e}}{\eta^{S^{*e}}} + (L + L^*)c^*,$$

where η^S is the producer-price elasticity of supply in the home country and η^{S^*} is the producer-price elasticity of supply in the foreign country, and where a superscript e denotes evaluation of the magnitude at efficient policies. As expected, the first line of (8.4) confirms that there is no efficiency role for tariffs and that only their sum is relevant for determining efficiency. The second line shows that, when the weights ζ and ζ^* on producer surplus are both equal to one, the efficient carbon taxes ($\frac{t^e}{c}$ for the home country, $\frac{t^{*e}}{c^*}$ for the foreign country) will be uniform across countries and set at the Pigouvian level $(L + L^*)$ that internalizes the world wide carbon externality; but if there are distributional/development concerns associated with carbon-intensive production so that these weights are greater than one, then there is an offsetting force that pushes toward subsidizing production and that is inversely related to the elasticity of supply.

Turning to noncooperative policies, the first-order conditions that define the best-response tariff and production tax policies for the home and foreign governments can be manipulated to yield the following characterization of Nash policies:

$$\tau^N = \left[\frac{S^{*N} \times \frac{\eta^{S^{*N}}}{q^{*N}}}{E^{*N} \times \frac{\eta^{E^{*N}}}{\tilde{p}^{wN}}}\right] \times Lc^* + \frac{\tilde{p}^{wN}}{\eta^{E^{*N}}}; \quad \tau^{*N} = -\left[\frac{S^N \times \frac{\eta^{SN}}{q^N}}{M^N \times \frac{\eta^{MN}}{\tilde{p}^{wN}}}\right] \times L^*c + \frac{\tilde{p}^{wN}}{\eta^{MN}} \tag{8.5}$$

4. I am thereby implicitly assuming here that lump-sum transfers are available to distribute surplus across the two countries as desired. In the present setting, lump-sum transfers can be effected by altering τ and τ^* while leaving their sum unchanged.

$$t^N = -(\zeta - 1)\frac{q^N}{\eta^{SN}} + Lc; \qquad t^{*N} = -(\zeta^* - 1)\frac{q^{*N}}{\eta^{S*N}} + L^*c^*,$$

where η^M is the world-price elasticity of home-country import demand (defined positively) and η^{E*} is the world-price elasticity of foreign-country export supply, and where a superscript N denotes evaluation of the magnitude at Nash policies. As the second line of (8.5) implies, in the Nash equilibrium each country ignores the impact of its carbon emissions on the welfare of the other country's citizens when choosing its production tax (that is, the home country ignores L^*c when choosing its production tax and the foreign country ignores Lc^*). And as a comparison with the second line of (8.4) reveals, this tends to make each country's Nash production taxes too low and its carbon emissions too high relative to efficient levels. The expressions in the first lines of (8.5) then reveal that the Nash tariffs deviate from zero for two reasons: The first term in each expression compensates for the fact that the trading partner's production tax is too low, and the tariff is therefore employed as an instrument to reduce the trading partner's production and hence carbon emissions, modulated by the relevant elasticities; and the second term in each expression corresponds to the familiar Johnson (1953–1954) terms-of-trade-manipulation motive.

To understand further the nature of the tariff inefficiencies in the Nash equilibrium, it is illuminating to consider the tariffs that would be efficient conditional on the level of the Nash production taxes, t^N and t^{*N}, characterized in (8.5). Recalling that only the sum of tariffs is relevant for efficiency (i.e., world welfare) considerations, the tariffs that maximize world welfare conditional on the level of the Nash production taxes characterized in (8.5) satisfy the expression

$$\tau^e(t^N, t^{*N}) + \tau^{*e}(t^N, t^{*N}) = \left[\frac{S^* \times \frac{\eta^{S*}}{q^*}}{E^* \times \frac{\eta^{E*}}{\bar{p}^w}}\right] \times Lc^* - \left[\frac{S \times \frac{\eta^S}{q}}{M \times \frac{\eta^M}{\bar{p}^w}}\right] \times L^*c,$$

$$(8.6)$$

where all magnitudes on the right-hand side of (8.6) are evaluated at the Nash production taxes t^N and t^{*N} and the tariffs $\tau^e(t^N, t^{*N})$ and $\tau^{*e}(t^N, t^{*N})$. Notice that, according to (8.6), $\tau^e(t^N, t^{*N}) + \tau^{*e}(t^N, t^{*N})$ could be either positive (a net tax on trade) or negative (a net subsidy to trade).

Comparing (8.6) to the sum of the Nash tariffs characterized in the first line of (8.5), what is missing from $\tau^e(t^N, t^{*N}) + \tau^{*e}(t^N, t^{*N})$ is the second term in each Nash tariff expression—namely, the terms-of-trade-manipulation motive that makes each country's Nash tariff higher than it would otherwise be. Evidently, the first term in each of the Nash tariff expressions, which reflects the attempt by each country to use its tariff to compensate for the inefficiently low production tax of its trading partner, remains present for the efficient use of tariffs conditional on Nash production taxes. Intuitively, as the expression on the right-hand side of (8.6) reflects, controlling for the relevant elasticity considerations, it is efficient to use tariffs to shift carbon-intensive production to the country whose Nash production taxes are closest to the efficient level, which according to the second lines in (8.4) and (8.5) will be the home country when $L^*c < Lc^*$ (and therefore a net tax on trade) and the foreign country (and therefore a net subsidy to trade) otherwise.

The upshot is that the nature of the Nash inefficiencies in the absence of trade and climate agreements can be described in simple terms. Carbon taxes are too low, reflecting the presence of an international nonpecuniary externality (a climate problem). And conditional on Nash carbon taxes, tariffs are too high, reflecting the presence of an international pecuniary externality (a trade problem).

A Shallow-Integration Approach to the Trade Problem

To see whether GATT's shallow-integration approach could still solve the trade problem in a world where, as depicted above, the trade problem coexists with the climate problem, I begin from the Nash tariffs and production taxes characterized in (8.5) and suppose that countries negotiate over tariffs, with the understanding that (i) if either country subsequently makes a unilateral policy adjustment that has the effect of withdrawing market access, then its trading partner will withdraw equivalent market access in a reciprocal fashion, but that (ii) unilateral policy adjustments that leave market access unchanged will trigger no response from the trading partner. Recalling from chapter 4 that a reciprocal withdrawal of market access will hold fixed the terms of trade $\tilde{p}^w$ between the home and foreign country and that unilateral policy adjustments that leave market access unchanged will hold fixed $\tilde{p}^w$ as well, the unilateral policy options open to each country subsequent to their tariff negotiations amount to policy adjustments that may or may not decrease the level of market access implied by their tariff commitments but that in any case do not alter the terms of trade $\tilde{p}^w$.[5] In effect,

---

5. On the formal relationship between reciprocity and terms-of-trade movements in a partial equilibrium setting, such as the one I describe here, see Bagwell and Staiger (2001a, n19).

the understanding in (i) can be thought of as reflecting in a shorthand way the reciprocity provisions of GATT Article XXVIII discussed in previous chapters, while the understanding in (ii) can be thought of as reflecting GATT's "market access preservation rules."

Can tariff negotiations solve the trade problem under this representation of GATT's shallow-integration approach? As I now demonstrate, the answer is "yes." To see this, suppose that in their tariff negotiations the home and foreign countries agree to the tariff levels $\bar{\tau}$ and $\bar{\tau}^*$, respectively, defined by

$$
\bar{\tau} = \left[\frac{S^* \times \frac{\eta^{S^*}}{q^*}}{E^* \times \frac{\eta^{E^*}}{\bar{p}^w}} \right] \times Lc^*; \quad \bar{\tau}^* = - \left[\frac{S \times \frac{\eta^S}{q}}{M \times \frac{\eta^M}{\bar{p}^w}} \right] \times L^*c, \tag{8.7}
$$

where all magnitudes on the right-hand side of (8.7) are evaluated at the Nash carbon taxes t^N and t^{*N} and the tariffs $\bar{\tau}$ and $\bar{\tau}^*$. Notice from (8.7) that the home country is agreeing to an import tariff while the foreign country is agreeing to an export subsidy. And notice from (8.6) and the definitions of $\bar{\tau}$ and $\bar{\tau}^*$ in (8.7) that $\bar{\tau} + \bar{\tau}^* = \tau^e(t^N, t^{*N}) + \tau^{*e}(t^N, t^{*N})$, implying that the two countries have agreed to tariffs that are efficient given Nash production taxes. The question is, then, whether subsequent to the negotiations the tariffs will remain at the levels $\bar{\tau}$ and $\bar{\tau}^*$ and the production taxes at the levels t^N and t^{*N} under GATT's shallow-integration rules as I have modeled them. If so, then we may conclude that GATT's shallow-integration approach can solve the trade problem, leaving the climate problem unaffected (and presumably to be solved by other means).[6]

Consider first the policy options described in (i) above. Focusing on the home country, it is direct to confirm using (8.2) that, evaluated at the Nash production taxes t^N and t^{*N} and the tariffs $\bar{\tau}$ and $\bar{\tau}^*$,

$$
\frac{dW}{d\tau} + \frac{dW}{d\tau^*} \frac{d\tau^*}{d\tau} \bigg|_{d\bar{p}^w=0} = 0,
$$

implying that the home country can do no better than to select $\bar{\tau}$ in light of the reciprocal response from the foreign country that an increase in its tariff would trigger. And again evaluated at the Nash production

---

6. In saying that the climate problem will be left "unaffected," I simply mean that it will still be the case that carbon taxes are too low, reflecting the presence of an international nonpecuniary externality (a climate problem), with no new (e.g., terms-of-trade manipulation) sources of policy distortions in carbon taxes.

taxes t^N and t^{*N} and the tariffs $\bar{\tau}$ and $\bar{\tau}^*$, it is also straightforward to confirm that

$$\frac{dW}{dt} + \frac{dW}{d\tau^*}\frac{d\tau^*}{dt}\Big|_{d\tilde{p}^w=0} = 0,$$

implying that the home country can do no better than to select t^N in light of the reciprocal response from the foreign country that a decrease in its production tax would trigger. Finally, consider the policy options described in (ii) above. At Nash production taxes t^N and t^{*N} and the tariffs $\bar{\tau}$ and $\bar{\tau}^*$, it follows that

$$\frac{dW}{dt} + \frac{dW}{d\tau}\frac{d\tau}{dt}\Big|_{d\tilde{p}^w=0} = 0,$$

implying that there is no mix of policies that the home country would prefer over $\bar{\tau}$ and t^N that could deliver its negotiated level of market access. Completely analogous statements can be shown to hold for the foreign country using (8.3).

Hence, GATT's shallow-integration approach can solve the trade problem in a world where that problem coexists with the climate problem. And what is left is a climate problem, where carbon taxes are inefficiently low but the inefficiency is due only to an international nonpecuniary externality.

8.2   Carbon Border Adjustments

Suppose that countries are able to find a way to negotiate an enforceable climate accord and implement the increase in production (carbon) taxes that would be needed to move from the Nash production taxes characterized in the second line of (8.5) to the efficient production taxes characterized in the second line of (8.4). Can GATT's shallow approach to integration accommodate the implementation of the climate accord and maintain its solution to the trade problem so that with the climate accord in place, the world then reaches the efficiency frontier?

This is indeed possible, but only if the home-country tariff is allowed to rise with its carbon tax, from the initial level $\bar{\tau}$ defined in (8.7) to the higher level

$$\hat{\tau} = \left[\frac{S^* \times \frac{\eta^{S^*}}{q^*}}{E^* \times \frac{\eta^{E^*}}{\tilde{p}^w}}\right] \times Lc^* + \left[\frac{S \times \frac{\eta^S}{q}}{M \times \frac{\eta^M}{\tilde{p}^w}}\right] \times L^*c, \tag{8.8}$$

and similarly the foreign-country export subsidy is allowed to rise with its carbon tax, from the initial level $\bar{\tau}^*$ defined in (8.7) to the higher level

$$\hat{\tau}^* = -\left[\frac{S \times \frac{\eta^S}{q}}{M \times \frac{\eta^M}{\tilde{p}^w}}\right] \times L^*c - \left[\frac{S^* \times \frac{\eta^{S*}}{q^*}}{E^* \times \frac{\eta^{E*}}{\tilde{p}^w}}\right] \times Lc^*, \qquad (8.9)$$

where all right-hand-side magnitudes in (8.8) and (8.9) are evaluated at the tariffs $\hat{\tau}$ and $\hat{\tau}^*$ and the efficient production taxes t^e and t^{*e}. Notice from (8.8) and (8.9) that $\hat{\tau} + \hat{\tau}^* = 0$. Hence, in combination with the taxes t^e and t^{*e}, these tariff adjustments, which I will refer to as "carbon border adjustments," will allow countries to reach the efficiency frontier as characterized in (8.4).

Assuming that these carbon border adjustments are allowed so that the home country can increase its import tariff from $\bar{\tau}$ to $\hat{\tau}$ and the foreign country can increase its export subsidy from $\bar{\tau}^*$ to $\hat{\tau}^*$, the remaining question is, again, whether the tariffs will then remain at the levels $\hat{\tau}$ and $\hat{\tau}^*$ under GATT's shallow-integration rules as I have modeled them, given that the production taxes are pinned down by the climate accord at the levels t^e and t^{*e}. But it is direct to show that this is indeed the case. Focusing again on the home country, with the magnitudes evaluated at the tariffs $\hat{\tau}$ and $\hat{\tau}^*$ and the efficient production taxes t^e and t^{*e}, it can be checked that

$$\frac{dW}{d\tau} + \frac{dW}{d\tau^*}\frac{d\tau^*}{d\tau}\Big|_{d\tilde{p}^w=0} = 0,$$

implying that the home country can do no better than to select $\hat{\tau}$ in light of the reciprocal response from the foreign country that an increase in its tariff beyond $\hat{\tau}$ would trigger. An analogous statement holds for the foreign country.

The carbon border adjustments that I have characterized above have some interesting properties. They describe an increase in the home-country import tariff that is to occur as the home country raises its carbon tax and an increase in the foreign-country export subsidy that is to occur as the foreign country raises its carbon tax. These carbon border adjustments therefore work to offset competitive effects that the implementation of higher carbon taxes would otherwise create for each country. In this sense, they resonate with the purpose of proposed carbon border adjustments as seen from the perspective of the policy debate—namely as a mechanism for addressing possible trade competitiveness impacts and "carbon leakage" concerns that arise when a country considers implementing more stringent carbon policies and that were highlighted in the passage from Mattoo and Subramanian (2013) that I quoted at the beginning of this chapter.[7]

However, there is also a crucial difference: Unlike the carbon border adjustments typically considered in the policy debate, which envision tariffs that would discriminate across the sources of imports based on measures of the carbon content of those imports (Bordoff 2008; Mattoo and Subramanian 2013; Jensen 2020), the carbon border adjustments described by (8.8) and (8.9)—which imply changes in tariffs relative to $\bar{\tau}$ and $\bar{\tau}^*$ only because the second terms in these expressions are non-zero—do *not* depend on the carbon content of the production of one's trading partner (as captured by c^* from the perspective of the home country and by c from the perspective of the foreign country). This is because these carbon border adjustments are designed to moderate the market access implication of a country's own increase in carbon/production taxes, and to bring to an efficient level the market access that the country provides its trading partner as it raises its carbon tax to the efficient level. And while the market access implication of a country's carbon tax increase does reflect the carbon content of the country's *own* production (because this enters into the determination of the size of the country's carbon tax increase), that implication has nothing to do with the carbon content of production in a country's trading partners.

Indeed, as the second terms in (8.8) and (8.9) indicate, neither the carbon content of a trading partner's production nor, aside from its impact on the world price $\tilde{p}^w$, the level of the trading partner's carbon tax is relevant for the carbon border adjustments that the model would support. In fact, in this light it is easy to see that in a multicountry version of the model, the implied carbon border adjustments would be nondiscriminatory—that is, they would comply with the MFN principle. These properties can help avoid a number of practical problems often associated with the implementation of carbon border adjustments as those border adjustments are typically envisioned in the policy debate; see, for example, the discussion in Brenton and Chemutai (2021, 67–91).

---

7. There is a large empirical literature investigating the trade effects of environmental regulation. See, for example, Cherniwchan and Najjar (2022) for a recent study of the impact of Canadian air quality standards on the export performance of Canadian manufacturing plants.

It is instructive at this point to consider the related discussion of Mattoo and Subramanian (2013, 24). They summarize the current state of the policy disagreements over carbon border adjustments this way:

The question is whether such [carbon border] taxes can be designed in a way that addresses industrial countries' concerns regarding competitiveness while limiting the trade costs for developing countries. What has to be avoided is the imposition of tariffs applied across-the-board on the basis of the carbon content of imports, which would be a "nuclear option" in terms of trade consequences. For example, such an action by the United States and the EU would be the equivalent of imposing a tariff of over 20 percent on China and India, resulting in lost exports of about 20 percent.

Further, they highlight a number of possible solutions, of which their preferred approach involves "across-the-board tariffs and rebates for exporters based on the carbon content in domestic production. These would almost completely offset the adverse effects on U.S. output and exports of energy-intensive manufactures, while limiting declines in China's and India's manufacturing exports to about 2 percent." (Mattoo and Subramanian 2013, 24). The findings that I described above support the approach preferred by Mattoo and Subramanian.

More generally, the discussion above points to an important insight: While the *Nash* tariffs in (8.5) are responsive to the carbon content of a trading partner's production, there is no reason for the *efficient* tariffs as characterized in (8.6) to be based on the carbon content of a trading partner's production, and this is true even in a world where cooperation over climate policy is impossible. The reason is that efficiency only pins down the sum of the tariffs between the home and foreign country, and to achieve the efficient sum of tariffs in (8.6), each country's tariff can be set at the level that reflects the carbon content of its *own* production. This insight also extends to a multicountry version of the model (because in such a world it is the sum of the tariffs along any bilateral trade path that are relevant for efficiency), and it implies that the role for discriminatory tariffs as a response to noncooperative carbon policies is confined to noncooperative trade policy: if international cooperation over tariffs (and export subsidies) is possible, then the existence of a climate problem is not a reason to abandon the MFN principle, even when attempts to cooperate over climate policy have failed.

8.3   Negotiation Linkage

Thus far I have assumed either that there is no cooperation over climate policy or that a stand-alone climate accord is implemented, and I have considered how the GATT/WTO architecture might work in each of those circumstances. I now turn to a different question—the question of linkage between a climate accord and a trade agreement such as the WTO. Maggi (2016) defines three kinds of possible linkage between agreements: enforcement linkage, negotiation linkage, and participation linkage. While each is relevant for consideration in the specific context of trade and climate agreements, I focus here on the possibility of a form of negotiation linkage, where a negotiation over tariff liberalization and carbon taxes is linked through the market access implications of each.

My starting point is the latecomers problem characterized by Bagwell and Staiger (2014) and described in chapter 7. Recall that this problem refers to the asymmetry in the level of market access commitments between the developing/emerging economies, on the one hand, and industrialized countries on the other. This is an asymmetry that has emerged after decades of reciprocal tariff negotiations among industrialized countries, with the developing and emerging economies largely sitting on the sidelines as a result of exemptions from the reciprocity norm that were granted to these countries and codified in special and differential treatment clauses. It is an asymmetry that is at the heart of various diagnoses of the central sticking points at Doha. In essence, industrialized countries want emerging and developing countries to agree to tariff cuts in the WTO Doha Round, but the industrialized countries have few tariff cuts of their own to put on the table in return.

At the same time, a key sticking point in negotiating meaningful climate accords is the strong asymmetry in the positions of emerging and developing countries, on the one hand, and industrialized countries, on the other, regarding the desired response to climate change. Emerging and developing countries want industrialized countries to agree to bear the brunt of the efforts in addressing climate change by, for example, imposing high carbon taxes on their producers, but emerging and developing countries have little leverage to induce industrialized countries to do this (Mattoo and Subramanian 2013). And where industrialized countries are considering carbon taxes on their own, they see new carbon customs duties (carbon border adjustments) as a way to offset the trade competitiveness effects of carbon taxes on their firms and

prevent carbon leakage (Jensen 2020). Moreover, the new carbon customs duties that would accompany the imposition of carbon taxes by
the industrialized countries would likely be imposed on the importation of products that are largely exported by developing and emerging
economies (Carbon Brief 2017).

The point I wish to emphasize is that these two asymmetries, one
regarding the lowering of tariffs and the other regarding the imposition of carbon taxes, have market access implications that are in broad
terms mirror images of each other. And it is these asymmetries that
might be combined into a viable, linked market access negotiation. In
particular, what is suggested by this discussion is the possibility of
combining into a single, reciprocal package of negotiations the market
access consequences of unilateral industrialized country carbon taxes—
without carbon border adjustments—and the unilateral tariff cuts of
emerging/developing economies. In effect, in such negotiations, the
emerging and developing countries would offer reciprocal tariff cuts
in exchange for the market access consequences of carbon taxes offered
by the industrialized countries.

How might this linkage be operationalized? A natural possibility
within the existing GATT/WTO structure, but in the absence of special and differential treatment (SDT), would be to follow a three-step
procedure. In a first step, industrialized countries (and possibly China,
without whom a climate accord would likely fall short) would agree
on an aggressive package of carbon mitigation policies (e.g., carbon
taxes). Then, in a second step, these countries would initiate GATT
Article XXVIII renegotiations with their trading partners and, in the
context of these renegotiations, introduce new MFN carbon customs
duties on top of their existing tariff bindings, calibrated to offset the
trade competitiveness (i.e., market access) effects of their new carbon-
mitigation policies, while offering these new carbon-mitigation policies
as compensation for their carbon customs duties.[8] And finally, in a third

---

8. Paragraph 2 of GATT's Article XXVIII renegotiation clause states:

In such negotiations and agreement, which may include provision for compensatory
adjustment with respect to other products, the contracting parties concerned shall
endeavour to maintain a general level of reciprocal and mutually advantageous concessions not less favourable to trade than that provided for in this Agreement prior to such
negotiations.

The offering of new carbon-mitigation policies that offset the market access consequences
of the new MFN carbon customs duties that I describe in the text would be consistent with
this stipulation.

step, WTO members would engage in a round of tariff negotiations under GATT Article XXVIII bis, with cuts in (and possibly elimination of) the new carbon customs duties of the industrialized countries now on the table being exchanged for reciprocal tariff cuts from emerging and developing countries. When this third step is completed, the entire package of negotiated carbon-mitigation policies and tariff bindings would be implemented. In the end, if the new carbon customs duties were eliminated as a result of the third-step negotiations, the emerging and developing countries would have offered tariff cuts to industrialized countries (and possibly China) in exchange for the reciprocal market access consequences of the carbon-mitigation policies (e.g., carbon taxes) adopted by these countries.[9]

A number of features of this linkage possibility are notable. First, the new carbon customs duties would be *MFN*, because they are designed simply to neutralize the market access effects of a country's new carbon taxes. This is therefore what I would call a case of *indirect* linkage between climate and trade negotiations, because it links the market access consequences of new carbon taxes with the market access consequences of tariff cuts, combining the market access implications of each into a reciprocal package. And in particular, from the WTO's perspective, while this linkage could help to provide the balance across industrialized and emerging/developing countries needed to unlock the Doha Round, it does not introduce issues beyond the market access consequences of policy that are in any event the WTO's central concern.

Second, there is an interesting political economy dimension: Through this linkage, industrialized country export interests might be harnessed to push for carbon taxes, with the knowledge that carbon taxes would be accompanied by carbon customs duties and that reductions in the latter could be offered as bargaining chips to open foreign markets in GATT/WTO negotiating rounds. In making the political environment potentially more favorable to carbon taxes in this way,

---

9. Notice that the carbon border adjustments at issue would play the role of neutralizing the trade effects of carbon taxes, much as border tax adjustments neutralize the trade effects of destination-based value-added taxes (VAT) such as those imposed by the European Union; see Lockwood and Whalley (2010) for a discussion of the connections across these two policy issues. I am then suggesting that industrialized countries could offer to reduce these carbon border adjustments in market access negotiations with emerging and developing economies precisely for the market access/trade implications that the carbon taxes without the border tax adjustments would have.

the linkage could help industrialized countries achieve more aggressive climate commitments.

Third, international commitments on climate policy would gain a potent enforcement mechanism. If an industrialized country (or China) did not follow through on its climate commitments, then from the WTO's perspective the country would be violating its market access commitments, and emerging and developing countries could then seek authorization from the WTO dispute settlement bodies to reciprocally raise their tariffs.[10]

In this way, the market access consequences of carbon taxes would be transformed from a bug into a feature. Instead of responding with carbon border adjustments, industrialized countries could use the market access consequences of carbon-mitigation policies such as carbon taxes as the engine of enforceable negotiated commitments on carbon policies and unfinished Doha Round tariff cuts.

What about carbon leakage? This is a potential concern because under the three-step procedure described above, the new carbon customs duties that are meant to prevent carbon leakage when an industrialized country introduces new carbon-mitigation policies could be bargained away.

One approach to addressing this concern would be to link the reciprocal tariff negotiations described in the third step of the procedure with the transfer of clean technology. For example, Mattoo and Subramanian (2013) propose that an international fund might be set up to finance the transfer of "green" technologies to emerging and developing countries (Brenton and Chemutai 2021 have a related discussion). The new access to industrialized country markets that would arise from the described reciprocal tariff negotiations might be conditioned on the adoption by emerging and developing country exporters of these green technologies. Or the desired technology transfer might be accomplished by foreign direct investment (FDI) from industrialized countries to the emerging and developing countries, with emerging and developing countries agreeing to make liberalizing FDI commitments where needed as part of the third-step negotiations.

Another approach, possibly complementary to the first, would build on the ability of bilateral tariff negotiations to minimize third-party

---

10. Whether such reciprocal responses would be sufficient by themselves to enforce efficient carbon policies is an open question, but at a minimum they could form part of an effective enforcement mechanism for international climate commitments.

trade effects when those negotiations conform to MFN and reciprocity as described in chapter 4. Under this approach, in the third-step market access negotiations, industrialized countries would seek out as bilateral tariff bargaining partners those emerging and developing countries with the cleanest technologies already in place for producing the products whose new carbon customs duties are on the bargaining table, regardless of principal supplier status. As in the chapter 2 discussion of tariff bargaining techniques used by the United States under the 1934 Reciprocal Trade Agreements Act (RTAA), tariff reclassifications might also be made to further guide the grant of industrial-country market access toward clean-technology suppliers, and split concessions could be used to hold in reserve some tariff reductions for later adopters of green technology, incentivizing emerging and developing countries to undertake such investments.

9 Digital Trade

We live in an increasingly digital world. The Internet and digitalization are fundamentally changing the way people, firms, and governments interact, both within and across national borders. Though definitions vary and data is incomplete, economists concur that digital trade has revolutionized the global economy and will continue to do so. In 2018, digitally deliverable services comprised 50 percent of overall global services exports, and estimates place the digital share of global gross domestic product (GDP) between 5 and 16 percent (UNCTAD 2019). The consequences and opportunities posed by the rapid expansion of digital commerce are felt by individual consumers, by small firms and large ones, and by economic superpowers as well as emerging and developing economies (Castro and McQuinn 2015).

In this chapter, I consider the implications of digital trade for the design of the WTO, an institution whose main features were determined while the Internet was in its infancy.[1] Does the importance of digital trade today imply that the WTO's approach to global trade rules is fundamentally out of date?[2]

Certainly, digital trade has made possible new forms of trade protection. The US International Trade Commission (USITC) offers a partial inventory:

---

1. This chapter is based on Staiger (2021), which was written as a background paper on digital trade and trade agreements for the Rotman School of Management of the University of Toronto. The background paper will not be separately published.

2. This is not to say that WTO members have only recently become aware of the disruptive potential of the Internet for global trade rules. Soon after the WTO's creation in 1995, the member governments agreed to convene a "Work Programme on Electronic Commerce" (WTO 1998b), and an initial study of electronic commerce and the role of the WTO was issued in 1998 (Bacchetta et al. 1998). See WTO (2018) for an updated WTO report on digital trade.

Localization requirements, market access limits, data privacy and protection requirements, intellectual property rights infringement, uncertain legal liability rules, censorship, and customs measures in other countries all present obstacles to international digital trade. (USITC 2014, 14)

And in light of these novel forms of trade protection and the ubiquitous nature of digitalization in the global economy, a trade policy paper from the Organization for Economic Cooperation and Development (OECD) argues that countries need to take a more "holistic" approach to market openness as a result of the rise of digital trade, stating:[3]

Today, a simple digital trade transaction rests on a series of trade-related factors that enable or support the transaction. For instance, the ability to order an e-book depends on access to a retailer's website. This in turn depends on the regulatory environment which determines the conditions under which the retailer can establish the webpage as well as on the cost for the consumer of accessing the Internet—a cost which, in turn, is affected by the regulatory environment in the telecommunications sector. The purchase of the e-book will also be affected by other factors, such as the ability to pay electronically and the tariff and nontariff barriers faced by the physical device used to read the e-book.

A barrier on one of these linked transactions will affect the need or the ability to undertake the other transactions. This means that market openness needs to be approached more holistically, taking into consideration the full range of measures that affect the ability to undertake any particular transaction. For instance, Internet access may be a necessary but not sufficient condition for digitally enabled trade in goods to flourish. If logistics services in the receiving (or delivering) country are costly due to service trade restrictions, or if goods are held up at the border by cumbersome procedures, then the benefits of the digital transformation may not materialise. (Casalini, Gonzalez, and Moise 2019, 5)

The WTO has been slow to take up this challenge, and as a result many WTO members have moved away from multilateral efforts to update trade rules for the digital era and are pursuing these goals in deep-integration regional and mega-regional agreements instead (Wu 2017). To what extent these agreements should be seen as a model for the WTO's approach to digital trade is an open question.

In short, with digitalization permeating so deeply into modern life, it is tempting to conclude that the world is now truly "flat," that everything has changed.[4] But for the specific task of designing an effective trade agreement, can we be sure that everything is now different?

---

3. This argument is made widely. See, for example, Ahmed (2019) and Ciuriak (2019).
4. Thomas Friedman's (2005) early pronouncement of the death of distance and that the world is now flat gave rise to critiques by economists (see e.g., Leamer 2007) arguing that in fact distance was alive and well in the trade data (see, e.g., Disdier and Head 2008).

To evaluate the need for a redesign of the WTO in response to the rise of digital trade, I adopt a basic premise from the literature on the economics of trade agreements that I have carried throughout this book: namely, that the design of a trade agreement should reflect its purpose. From this perspective, I ask: Does digital trade change the purpose of a trade agreement? Answering this question clarifies the challenge that digital trade poses for the world trading system and can guide efforts to update the WTO for the digital world.

In this chapter I introduce digital trade into a simple partial equilibrium framework of trade between two countries. For the most part, I focus on trade in goods in this model world economy, but I also describe briefly how the results generalize to a model that features trade in services. To set the stage, I first shut down digital trade and consider the purpose of a trade agreement in a pre-digital world, showing how from the model's perspective, this purpose is reflected in the broad design features of the WTO agreements that govern international trade. This is true for trade in goods as covered by GATT, as I have already indicated in previous chapters, but it is also true for trade in services (Staiger and Sykes 2021) as covered by the General Agreement on Trade in Services (GATS), an agreement best characterized as an effort at deep integration. I then allow for the possibility of digital trade and revisit the purpose of a trade agreement, as implied by the model, to investigate whether the problem for the agreement to solve has changed. It is from this perspective that I evaluate whether the rise of digital trade warrants fundamental changes in the design of the WTO.

I follow the WTO and define digital trade as "the production, distribution, marketing, sale or delivery of goods and services by electronic means."[5] A key question is how to introduce digital trade into a model world economy. Digitalization affects the economy through its impact on transaction costs. Surveying the literature on digital economics, Goldfarb and Tucker (2019, 3) make this observation:

Understanding the effects of digital technology does not require fundamentally new economic theory. However, it requires a different emphasis. Studying digital economics starts with the question of "what is different?" What is easier to do when information is represented by bits rather than atoms? Digital

---

5. I use the term "digital trade" in the same way that the WTO uses the term "electronic commerce" or "e-commerce." The definition of digital trade that I quote in the text is the definition of e-commerce adopted by the WTO (1998b). There are a variety of definitions of digital trade that have been proposed in the literature (see Meltzer 2019), but for my purposes the WTO definition seems appropriate.

technology often means that costs may no longer constrain economic actions. Therefore, digital economics explores how standard economic models change as certain costs fall substantially and perhaps approach zero.

Goldfarb and Tucker emphasize five kinds of costs that can be substantially lowered in the presence of digitalization: (i) search costs, (ii) replication costs, (iii) transportation costs, (iv) tracking costs, and (v) verification costs. They continue:

Search costs are lower in digital environments, enlarging the potential scope and quality of search. Digital goods can be replicated at zero cost, meaning they are often non-rival. The role of geographic distance changes as the cost of transportation for digital goods and information is approximately zero. Digital technologies make it easy to track any one individual's behavior. Last, digital verification can make it easier to certify the reputation and trustworthiness of any one individual, firm, or organization in the digital economy. Each of these cost changes draws on a different set of well-established economic models, primarily search, non-rival goods, transportation cost, price discrimination, and reputation models. (Goldfarb and Tucker 2019, 3–4)

A thorough analysis of the impacts of digital trade on the purpose of trade agreements would build from this taxonomy of cost implications and would consider those impacts in each of a set of economic models that provided appropriate micro-foundations to study the implications of reductions in each kind of cost.[6]

Rather than working with a modeling framework that captures the micro-foundations of how digitalization can affect any of these particular costs, here I take a reduced-form approach and simply assume that digitalization reduces the costs of international trade. In choosing their digital trade policies, governments weigh the trade-cost-reducing impacts that a more open digital environment may bring against any possible nonpecuniary externalities associated with issues of privacy, national security, law enforcement, and the like that may accompany such a policy. Admittedly, this approach misses many of the issues surveyed by Goldfarb and Tucker (2019), especially as these issues relate to the impact of digitalization on replication costs, tracking costs, and verification costs. My intent here is to capture important impacts of digitalization on transportation costs and search costs with this modeling approach; I leave other dimensions of the impacts of digitalization on trade to future research.

---

6. See McCalman (2021) for an early paper that develops an explicit model of search and social media to consider the role of trade agreements in a digital world.

My approach to capturing the impacts of digitalization on trade is similar to that of Freund and Weinhold (2004), who model the impact of the Internet on trade in goods by assuming that it reduces the fixed costs of entering a particular market. It is also in the spirit of the trade literature that interprets the impact that distance has on trade as reflecting search and information frictions (e.g., Allen 2014; Head and Mayer 2014) and that views such frictions as diminished by the Internet and online markets—see, for example, Lendle et al. (2016) for trade in goods, and Blum and Goldfarb (2006) for trade in services.[7]

9.1 What Is Digital Trade?

While a variety of definitions of digital trade have been proposed in the literature, I will make use of the WTO's definition of electronic commerce and define digital trade to mean "the production, distribution, marketing, sale, or delivery of goods and services by electronic means." Before turning to my formal analysis, it is instructive to review briefly some of the issues that arise in the struggle to define and classify digital trade in order to illuminate the nature of the potential challenges that digital trade poses for the WTO and the world trading system.

For example, in describing the electronic commerce that comprises the WTO's definition of digital trade, Bacchetta et al. (1998) distinguish among three stages in electronic transactions, any of which may occur on an arm's-length or within-firm basis: the searching stage, the ordering and payment stage, and the delivery stage. They elaborate on these stages as follows:

The searching stage is where suppliers and consumers interact in the first instance. This stage may or may not lead to an actual transaction. The second stage entails ordering and payment for the good or service, typically through the electronic transmittal of credit card or bank account information. The third stage is delivery. Only those transactions that can be concluded through electronic delivery of digitalized information may be carried through entirely on the Internet. Electronic commerce via the Internet must end at the second stage for purchases which cannot be delivered electronically, including physical

---

7. Blum and Goldfarb (2006) distinguish between "taste-dependent" and "non-taste-dependent" services and show that distance does not reduce demand for non-taste-dependent services that are web-based, consistent with the notion that digitalization has reduced distance-related trade costs for such services to zero. Blum and Goldfarb also find that taste-dependent services continue to exhibit falling demand with distance even when these services are web-based, and they interpret this finding as reflecting regional differences in taste.

goods like flowers or bicycles, and services that can only be supplied if the supplier and consumer are in physical proximity, like haircuts, tourism and construction. It is the expanded scope for the third stage of electronic commerce transactions—that of taking electronic delivery of the purchase—which is perhaps the most notable contribution of Internet technology and the most challenging aspect from a policy perspective. (Bacchetta et al. 1998, 1)

Meltzer (2013) notes the breadth of impact on trade that is implied by the three stages of electronic transactions identified by Bacchetta et al.:

As these three stages demonstrate, the Internet allows for international trade in electronic goods and services and cross-border data flows also have important indirect effects on international trade. For instance, advertising on search engines such as Google and Bing bring together overseas buyers and sellers and is often how consumers learn of the goods and services available in other countries. Advertising is therefore often a necessary precursor to the online transaction that leads to international trade. The ability for researchers in different countries to share data and collaborate can determine whether an international services trade occurs. The Internet and cross-border flow of data is also crucial for other services that support and enable international trade, such as VoIP—internet based communications through sites such as Skype and email. Cross-border data flows are also necessary for the financial transfer to complete the transaction. Meltzer (2013, 11)

The expanded scope for electronic delivery emphasized by Bacchetta et al. (1998) raises several issues of particular concern for the WTO. First, there is the issue of whether the transaction involves a good or a service. This issue arises, for example, when considering a good that is delivered from a foreign source by digital instructions for additive manufacturing ("3D printing") in a domestic location. This issue is consequential because of the different structure and level of market access commitments in GATT and GATS (Staiger 2018).

Second, if the transaction is determined to involve a service, there is the issue of the service's mode of delivery. GATS distinguishes among four modes of trade. "Mode 1" trade involves the cross-border sale of a service from the exporting country to a consumer in the importing country, while "mode 2" involves the consumption of a service in the exporting country by a national of another importing country. "Mode 3" trade involves the establishment of a commercial presence in the importing nation by a foreign service provider. And "mode 4" trade occurs when a foreign supplier not only establishes a commercial presence in the importing nation but also employs foreign nationals in its operations. Because WTO member governments have typically scheduled different levels of market access commitments across the various modes of trade, the assignments of services to these modes is consequential. Digital trade raises new questions about these assignments—for example, should consumers visiting foreign websites to make purchases be viewed as analogous to them traveling abroad physically to make those purchases?

A Taxonomy

For the purposes of the analysis below, I need to partition digital trades into "digital trade in goods" and "digital trade in services." To this end, I will say that trade is "digital" if it involves digital elements in any of the three stages of search, order and payment, or delivery, as described by Bacchetta et al. (1998). And I will define a transaction as involving a "good" ("service") if at the moment of consumption that transaction is a good (service) as traditionally defined in the pre-digital world.[8]

Thus, for my purposes, an Internet search, order, and payment that results in the physical delivery of a book from a foreign publisher would be classified as digital trade in a good. And the cross-border transmission of instructions for 3D printing of a wallet will be classified as digital trade of a good (because it is a wallet at the moment of consumption), while the cross-border purchase of an e-book will be classified as digital trade of a service (because at the moment of consumption the purchaser is not acquiring the book but rather the license to read it). And some transactions, such as the importation of a car with Internet connectivity, may involve digital trade in both a good and a service.

Where it is relevant, I will adopt an analogous approach to identifying modes of supply within services: If a service was classified as mode X in the pre-digital world, then the digital service continues to be classified as mode X. Thus, if in the pre-digital world a domestic citizen would have traveled abroad and taken an in-person foreign cooking class, but in the digital world this person stays at home and enrolls in the cooking class provided virtually from the foreign country over the Internet, I will continue to classify this in the digital world as trade in a mode-2 service, just as it would have been classified in the pre-digital world.

What about truly "new" goods or services that did not exist in the pre-digital world? For the purposes of my taxonomy, these goods and

---

8. That said, it should be noted that the exact boundary between goods and services is nowhere defined in the WTO (see Smith and Woods 2005).

services could be treated like any new good in GATT or new service in GATS—that is, initially placed in the "other" category of the internationally standardized Harmonized System (HS) used by the WTO to classify goods and services.[9]

Importantly, in the analysis to follow I will assume that digitalization does not itself alter the feasibility of imposing a tariff on the trade in question: If a tariff can be imposed on the physical importation of a wallet, then I am assuming it is also feasible to impose the tariff on the imported wallet when it is delivered by the cross-border transmission of instructions for 3D printing.

9.2 What Are the Policies That Affect Digital Trade?

As already noted, I will take a reduced-form approach to modeling the impacts of digitalization on international trade. In particular, in the analysis to follow I will simply assume that digitalization reduces the costs of international trade and that in choosing their digital trade policies, governments weigh the trade-cost-reducing impacts that a more open digital environment may bring against any possible nonpecuniary externalities that may arise with such a policy. But what are these digital policies? There are several kinds of underlying policies that I attempt to capture with my reduced-form modeling approach.

Tariffs

Tariffs are a straightforward policy for restricting trade. In principle, tariffs could constitute a central policy instrument for at least some kinds of digital trade, just as they have for trade in goods historically. But even here the impact of digitalization would be felt, as the small order sizes that the Internet has enabled might necessitate changes in the de minimis values below which customs duties do not apply (see USITC 2013, 5–23). More importantly, WTO members agreed in 1998 to a moratorium on customs duties applied to "electronic transmissions of digital products and services," and this moratorium has been renewed every two years ever since.[10] That said, the issue of what kinds

---

9. For a discussion of possible issues with this approach when it comes to new services, see Bacchetta et al. (1998, 51), and see also WTO (2018, 168–170) for a review of disputes that centered on the legal question of what qualifies as a "new" good or service.

10. The 2019 renewal of the WTO moratorium on customs duties applied to electronic transmissions can be found at https://www.wto.org/english/news_e/news19_e/gc_10dec19_e.htm.

of digital trade this moratorium applies to, and whether the moratorium should be renewed, strengthened to a permanent commitment, or abandoned altogether has been a growing source of contention among WTO members as the importance of digital trade has grown (Azmeh, Foster, and Echavarri 2020). The future role of tariffs as a policy for restricting digital trade is therefore uncertain.

Regulatory Barriers to Digital Trade

The more novel and contentious policies that have an impact on digital trade involve a variety of regulatory issues. There are of course many regulations that have a restrictive impact on international trade and yet serve a legitimate public policy purpose, making the distinction between "protection" and "protectionism" often difficult to draw; the regulatory issues that arise with digital trade are no exception in this regard. But in the digital sphere, many of the regulatory issues are still novel and lie at the center of concerns over highly sensitive questions regarding privacy, law enforcement, and national security, where shared norms of best practice and reasonable behavior are not yet fully developed or broadly accepted. As Aaronson (2018, 3) notes:

Many allegations of digital protectionism are concerns about different approaches to regulating the data flows that underpin the internet within national borders. Although the United States and the EU are trying to create shared rules, the two trade giants have also been the most vociferous in describing other countries' approaches as "protectionist."

Nevertheless, there are some clear regulatory policy areas with respect to digital trade where disciplines in the context of trade agreements are likely to be relevant. Azmeh, Foster, and Echavarri (2020) provide a useful discussion in this regard (see also Meltzer 2013). They offer as illustration three examples of such policies: Internet filtering to block cross-border access to certain websites, data localization, and source-code transfer requirements. As they note:

Access to websites, digital tools, and services located on foreign servers is a prerequisite to access digital goods and services provided by firms, including both digitally delivered products and physically delivered products. As such, engineering the structure of the internet to block such cross-border access is a very effective way of controlling digital trade....

Data localization policy is used to control trade flows and access to foreign digital products. Data localization includes a number of policies that demand that data (or certain categories of data) generated within a state are subject to additional rules, typically rules requiring the storage of data domestically. Such a

policy raises the cost of global firms serving a market by demanding that foreign digital firms build or purchase domestic data storage capacities. Through
such a policy, data localization could strengthen the position of domestic firms
and strengthen local digital ecosystems. . . .
Often as part of security requirements, a number of states adopt policies that
seek to mandate technology transfer through policies such as source code transfer requirements. Such conditions can have major economic implications, as
most companies will consider access to their source code a red line (due to the
risks of losing key intellectual property), leading to this requirement serving
as a market access restriction. Parallel policies are also emerging in regard to
mandating firms to reveal encryption keys and algorithms. This can be a major
issue for companies, as it could lead to blocking market access if they refuse to
comply or to jeopardizing data security and the trust of customers if they do.
(Azmeh, Foster, and Echavarri 2020, 677–678)

The reduced-form approach to modeling the impacts of digitalization on international trade that I introduce below cannot, of course, do
justice to these subtle and complex policy issues, but neither is that
my intent. Instead, motivated by these kinds of digital trade policies
and the issues that they raise, my intent is simply to represent in a
tractable model some of the basic trade-offs that governments must
confront when making their digital policy choices—namely, trade-offs
between the lower trade costs that will be obtained with a more open
digital policy environment and the various non-trade issues that will
arise.

With this in mind, I next develop a benchmark model that can help to
illuminate the purpose of trade agreements in a pre-digital and digital
world. I devote the bulk of this discussion to a model of trade in goods
and consider only briefly the extension of the model to trade in services,
referring the interested reader to Staiger (2021) for a full development
of that extension.

9.3   Digital Trade in Goods

I begin by considering the case of digital trade in goods.[11] I will think
of an open digital policy environment as contributing to lower trade
costs but also possibly generating an externality (e.g., related to privacy
issues or concerns about national security) that may have both local and
cross-border dimensions. I first develop the benchmark model for trade
in goods at a general level that incorporates both the pre-digital world

---

11. The material in this section is a slightly adapted and reinterpreted version of material
in Staiger (2019, sec. 4.1.1).

and the digital world as special cases. I then consider the purpose of a trade agreement in each special case of this benchmark model.

A Benchmark Trade-in-Goods Model

I consider a simple partial equilibrium setting in which a home country imports a competitively produced good from the foreign country, and I let $I \in [0, \infty)$ and $I^* \in [0, \infty)$ denote, respectively, the home and foreign digital ("Internet") policies, with $I = 0$ ($I^* = 0$) corresponding to the absence of a workable Internet in the home (foreign) country and with a higher level of I (I^*) corresponding to a more open digital policy environment in the home (foreign) country. I assume that these policies, which I take to represent the kinds of regulatory barriers to digital trade described in section 9.2, jointly determine the efficiency of trade transactions between the two countries, and in particular that the per-unit (specific) trade cost for exports from foreign to home, ι, can be represented by the function $\iota(I, I^*)$, where $\iota(0, 0)$ is nonprohibitive and with $\iota(I, I^*)$ decreasing and convex in both its arguments and non-negative for all I and I^*.[12] To fix ideas, the good under consideration could be a wallet, and the openness of digital policies in each country could determine the efficacy of digital search including the possibility of targeted ads, the functioning of digital payment systems, and the feasibility of digital delivery through 3D printing.

With the import tariff set by the home government denoted by τ and the export tax set by the foreign government denoted by τ^* (both expressed in specific terms), the arbitrage relationship between the home-country price of this good (p) and the foreign-country price of the good (p^*) that must hold as long as strictly positive trade occurs is given by

$$p = p^* + \iota(I, I^*) + \tau + \tau^*. \tag{9.1}$$

I define the *foreign world price* and the *home world price* by $p^{w*} \equiv p^* + \tau^*$ and $p^w \equiv p - \tau$, respectively. The foreign and home world prices are measures of the foreign- and home-country terms of trade—the foreign terms of trade will improve when p^{w*} rises, and the home terms

---

12. A more realistic assumption might be that the Internet reduces the fixed cost of entering a particular market, as in Freund and Weinhold (2004). Incorporating such an assumption would require the use of a more involved model of (firm-level) trade than the simple (industry-level) model I adopt here, but I suspect that my conclusions would extend to that setting; for example, see Bagwell and Lee (2020), who show that the purpose of a trade agreement is unchanged by the introduction of heterogeneous firms.

of trade will improve when p^w falls—and according to (9.1), they are related by $p^w - p^{w*} = \iota(I, I^*)$. A drop in trade costs ι brings p^w and p^{w*} closer together, and when $\iota = 0$ the home and foreign world prices are equated.

I denote the home and foreign demands for the product under consideration by $D(p)$ and $D^*(p^*)$, and I assume that these demand functions are decreasing in their arguments. For simplicity, I also assume that the product is supplied only by the foreign country and denote foreign supply by the increasing function $S^*(p^*)$.[13] Using the pricing relationship (9.1), and denoting foreign export supply by $E^*(p^*) \equiv S^*(p^*) - D^*(p^*)$ and home import demand by $M(p) \equiv D(p)$, the market clearing condition may be written as

$$M(p^* + \iota(I, I^*) + \tau + \tau^*) = E^*(p^*),$$

yielding the market-clearing foreign price $\tilde{p}^*(\iota(I, I^*) + \tau + \tau^*)$ from which the market-clearing home price and foreign and home world prices also follow:

$$\tilde{p}(\iota(I, I^*) + \tau + \tau^*) \equiv \tilde{p}^*(\iota(I, I^*) + \tau + \tau^*) + \iota(I, I^*) + \tau + \tau^*$$

$$\tilde{p}^{w*}(\iota(I, I^*) + \tau, \tau^*) \equiv \tilde{p}^*(\iota(I, I^*) + \tau + \tau^*) + \tau^*$$

$$\tilde{p}^w(\iota(I, I^*) + \tau^*, \tau) \equiv \tilde{p}(\iota(I, I^*) + \tau + \tau^*) - \tau.$$

Again, as is standard, world prices depend on both τ and τ^*, but home and foreign prices depend only on the sum $\tau + \tau^*$ (and on the digital policies I and I^*).

With the market-clearing price expressions above, the terms-of-trade impacts of policy choices can now be assessed. Regarding the terms-of-trade impacts of trade taxes, direct calculations yield the following (with a prime denoting the derivative of the function with respect to its argument):

$$\frac{\partial \tilde{p}^w}{\partial \tau} = \frac{\partial \tilde{p}^{w*}}{\partial \tau} = \frac{M'}{E^{*\prime} - M'} < 0$$

$$\frac{\partial \tilde{p}^{w*}}{\partial \tau^*} = \frac{\partial \tilde{p}^w}{\partial \tau^*} = \frac{E^{*\prime}}{E^{*\prime} - M'} > 0.$$

As expected, an increase in the home-country tariff improves the home terms of trade and worsens the foreign terms of trade, while an increase

---

13. Here and throughout, I assume that supply curves are unaffected by digital policy, although none of the conclusions I emphasize below depend on this assumption.

in the foreign-country tariff has the opposite effect, improving the foreign terms of trade and worsening the home terms of trade. These are the familiar terms-of-trade effects of tariff intervention that I have featured throughout the book, and they provide the basis for the inefficient prisoner's dilemma situation that, according to the terms-of-trade theory of trade agreements, arises in the absence of a trade agreement.

The terms-of-trade impacts of digital openness (increases in I and I^*) are more novel.[14] The impacts of a more open home-country digital policy are given by

$$\frac{\partial \tilde{p}^w}{\partial \iota} \frac{\partial \iota}{\partial I} = \frac{E^{*\prime}}{E^{*\prime} - M'} \times \frac{\partial \iota}{\partial I} < 0 \tag{9.2}$$

$$\frac{\partial \tilde{p}^{w*}}{\partial \iota} \frac{\partial \iota}{\partial I} = \frac{M'}{E^{*\prime} - M'} \times \frac{\partial \iota}{\partial I} > 0,$$

while for a more open foreign-country digital policy, these impacts are given by

$$\frac{\partial \tilde{p}^{w*}}{\partial \iota} \frac{\partial \iota}{\partial I^*} = \frac{M'}{E^{*\prime} - M'} \times \frac{\partial \iota}{\partial I^*} > 0 \tag{9.3}$$

$$\frac{\partial \tilde{p}^w}{\partial \iota} \frac{\partial \iota}{\partial I^*} = \frac{E^{*\prime}}{E^{*\prime} - M'} \times \frac{\partial \iota}{\partial I^*} < 0.$$

Evidently, an open home-country digital policy improves the home-country terms of trade *while at the same time improving the terms of trade of the foreign country*, and an open foreign-country digital policy works similarly.

This "win-win" prospect for open digital policies makes it tempting to conclude that the terms-of-trade theory cannot explain why countries would need an international agreement to encourage open digital policies at all. But, as I will demonstrate, this is not correct. Intuitively, the key is to note from the derivative expressions in (9.2) and (9.3) that each country's digital openness imparts a positive terms-of-trade externality on the other country, providing a possible reason for *under*-provision of digital openness from an international perspective when countries are guided only by their unilateral interests (i.e., in the absence of an international agreement that covers digital trade policies) and therefore a possible role for a trade agreement that encourages digital openness.

---

14. Staiger (2019) makes the same point about investments in trade facilitation more generally.

I now define the welfare functions for the home and foreign countries. I abstract from political economy/distributional motives, though for reasons analogous to those discussed in chapter 2, the results I report are easily generalized to include such motives. But I allow an open digital environment in a country to generate a nonpecuniary externality, possibly relating to privacy issues or to national security concerns. I assume that this externality takes an "eyesore" form that does not itself affect production and is not internalized by individual consumers and hence does not affect demands, but that detracts in a separable way from aggregate welfare. Moreover, I assume that this externality may have both a local and a cross-border component, with the local component increasing in a country's own digital openness and the cross-border component increasing in the digital openness of one's trading partner. For example, more digital openness in the home country (higher I) might create a digital environment where malicious software could more easily be downloaded to the devices of home-country citizens; this malicious software might (or might not) then negatively affect foreign citizens as well.

Formally, I denote by $c(I)$ and $c^*(I^*)$ the local externality generated in the home and foreign country by the respective levels of digital openness I and I^*, with $c(0) = 0$ and $c^*(0) = 0$ and with c and c^* increasing and convex in their respective arguments; and I let the parameter $\theta \in [0, 1]$ govern the degree of cross-border spillovers so that the externality from the digital policies I and I^* reduces home-country welfare by the amount $[c(I) + \theta c^*(I^*)]$ and reduces foreign-country welfare by the amount $[c^*(I^*) + \theta c(I)]$.

With no home-country production, home welfare is then given by the sum of consumer surplus plus tariff revenue minus the cost of the externality from digital openness. Letting CS denote home-country consumer surplus and using $\tau = p - p^w$, home welfare is given by

$$
\begin{aligned}
W = W(I, &I^*, \tilde{p}(\iota(I, I^*) + \tau + \tau^*), \tilde{p}^w(\iota(I, I^*) + \tau^*, \tau)) \quad (9.4)\\
&\equiv CS(\tilde{p}(\iota(I, I^*) + \tau + \tau^*))\\
&\quad + [\tilde{p}(\iota(I, I^*) + \tau + \tau^*) - \tilde{p}^w(\iota(I, I^*) + \tau^*, \tau)]\\
&\quad \times M(\tilde{p}(\iota(I, I^*) + \tau + \tau^*))\\
&\quad - [c(I) + \theta c^*(I^*)].
\end{aligned}
$$

Accounting for foreign-country production and with PS^* representing the foreign producer surplus, foreign welfare is defined as the sum of consumer and producer surplus plus export tax revenue minus the cost of the externality from digital openness:

$$W^* = W^*(I^*, I, \tilde{p}^*(\iota(I, I^*) + \tau + \tau^*), \tilde{p}^{w*}(\iota(I, I^*) + \tau, \tau^*)) \qquad (9.5)$$
$$\equiv CS^*(\tilde{p}^*(\iota(I, I^*) + \tau + \tau^*)) + PS^*(\tilde{p}^*(\iota(I, I^*) + \tau + \tau^*))$$
$$+ [\tilde{p}^{w*}(\iota(I, I^*) + \tau, \tau^*) - \tilde{p}^*(\iota(I, I^*) + \tau + \tau^*)]$$
$$\times E^*(\tilde{p}^*(\iota(I, I^*) + \tau + \tau^*))$$
$$- [c^*(I^*) + \theta c(I)].$$

Finally, the sum of home and foreign welfare, which I refer to as "world welfare" and denote by W^w, is given by

$$W^w = W^w(I, I^*, \tilde{p}(\iota(I, I^*) + \tau + \tau^*), \tilde{p}^*(\iota(I, I^*) + \tau + \tau^*)) \qquad (9.6)$$
$$\equiv CS(\tilde{p}(\iota(I, I^*) + \tau + \tau^*)) + CS^*(\tilde{p}^*(\iota(I, I^*) + \tau + \tau^*))$$
$$+ PS^*(\tilde{p}^*(\iota(I, I^*) + \tau + \tau^*))$$
$$+ [\tilde{p}(\iota(I, I^*) + \tau + \tau^*) - \tilde{p}^*(\iota(I, I^*) + \tau + \tau^*) - \iota(I, I^*)]$$
$$\times E^*(\tilde{p}^*(\iota(I, I^*) + \tau + \tau^*))$$
$$- [c(I) + \theta c^*(I^*)] - [c^*(I^*) + \theta c(I)].$$

Notice from equations (9.4) through (9.6) that while home and foreign welfare each depend on their respective world prices and hence on the levels of both τ and τ^*, world welfare is independent of world prices—because movements in these prices only serve to redistribute surplus between the home and foreign country—and hence we have the now-familiar property that world welfare depends only on the sum of home and foreign tariffs $\tau + \tau^*$ (in addition to the digital openness levels I and I^*).

The Purpose of GATT in a Pre-Digital World
I will think of the pre-digital world as corresponding to a special case of the benchmark trade-in-goods model described above in which

$$I \equiv 0 \equiv I^* \qquad (9.7)$$

and there is no workable Internet in either country. In this pre-digital world, the benchmark trade-in-goods model is very simple and the purpose of a trade agreement is transparent and familiar from chapter 2. Nevertheless, it is useful to review the steps in determining the purpose of a trade agreement in this specific setting so that a comparison with the digital world can be drawn.

Under (9.7), trade costs are exogenous and given by $\iota(0,0) \equiv \bar{\iota}$, and with no workable Internet anywhere in the world, we also have an absence of digital externalities $c(0) = c^*(0) = 0$. Hence, in the pre-digital world, the only policy choice to be made by each country is its tariff choice, and (9.4) through (9.6) imply that the country and world welfare levels as functions of these policy choices can be expressed in the form $W(\tilde{p}(\bar{\iota} + \tau + \tau^*), \tilde{p}^w(\bar{\iota} + \tau^*, \tau))$, $W^*(\tilde{p}^*(\bar{\iota} + \tau + \tau^*), \tilde{p}^{w*}(\bar{\iota} + \tau, \tau^*))$, and $W^w(\bar{\iota}, \tilde{p}(\bar{\iota} + \tau + \tau^*), \tilde{p}^*(\bar{\iota} + \tau + \tau^*))$.

It is straightforward (and intuitive) to show that there is no efficiency role for tariffs in this setting, and hence

$$\tau^e + \tau^{*e} = 0, \tag{9.8}$$

where a superscript "e" denotes efficient policies. And the Nash policies adopted by the two countries in the absence of a trade agreement, which I denote by τ^N and τ^{*N}, are given by

$$\tau^N = \frac{\tilde{p}^{w*N}}{\eta^{E*N}} \text{ and } \tau^{*N} = \frac{\tilde{p}^{wN}}{\eta^{MN}}, \tag{9.9}$$

with η^{E*N} the elasticity of foreign export supply and η^{MN} the elasticity of home import demand (defined positively) and with $\tilde{p}^{w*N}$ and $\tilde{p}^{wN}$ the world prices, all evaluated at Nash policies. The Nash tariffs in (9.9) represent the usual inverse-trade-elasticity formulas for the Johnson (1953–1954) optimal tariff that applies in a competitive market setting when governments seek to maximize real national incomes with their unilateral tariff choices.

Clearly, then, as a comparison of (9.9) with (9.8) confirms, in the pre-digital world of this benchmark trade-in-goods model, Nash tariffs are too high and Nash trade volumes are too low, and the purpose of a trade agreement is to eliminate the beggar-thy-neighbor incentives that each country has to manipulate the terms of trade with its unilateral tariff choice and thereby to enjoy the mutual benefits from the expanded trade volumes that come from implementation of internationally efficient policies. Moreover, while for simplicity I have adopted here a model setting where governments have no objectives beyond the maximization of real national income and there are no nontariff policy choices to be made in the pre-digital world, I described in chapters 2 and 3 how Bagwell and Staiger (1999, 2001) establish that the purpose of a trade agreement is unchanged in the presence of diverse government policy objectives and when domestic policies are added to the picture, and how these findings can illuminate the logic of GATT's design. I consider next whether these findings hold in a world of digital trade in goods.

The Purpose of GATT in a Digital World

In a world of digital trade in goods, the condition in (9.7) does not hold. According to the benchmark trade-in-goods model, this has two implications. First, the levels of digital openness I and I^* constitute additional policies that have terms-of-trade impacts, and as noted previously, each of these policies generates a win-win outcome for the two countries when it is set at a more open level. Second, greater digital openness generates a (negative) nonpecuniary externality (which may or may not cross borders).

To see what difference all of this makes for the purpose of a trade agreement, as I did when considering the pre-digital world I first characterize efficient policies, then characterize Nash policies, and then compare the efficient and Nash policies to identify the purpose of a trade agreement covering goods trade in a digital world. It is useful to consider two possibilities for the digital world: one where the nonpecuniary externality associated with digital openness is purely local and does not spill over across borders, and the other where this externality has both local and cross-border components.

I consider first the case of a purely local nonpecuniary externality from digital openness. To this end, I now impose the following:

No cross-border nonpecuniary externality: $\theta \equiv 0$,   (assumption 1)

and I note that equations (9.4) through (9.6) imply that the country and world welfare levels in a digital world under assumption 1 can be written in the form

$$W(I, \tilde{p}(\iota(I, I^*) + \tau + \tau^*), \tilde{p}^w(\iota(I, I^*) + \tau^*, \tau))$$
$$W^*(I^*, \tilde{p}^*(\iota(I, I^*) + \tau + \tau^*), \tilde{p}^{w*}(\iota(I, I^*) + \tau, \tau^*))$$
$$W^w(I, I^*, \tilde{p}(\iota(I, I^*) + \tau + \tau^*), \tilde{p}^*(\iota(I, I^*) + \tau + \tau^*)).$$

As before, I define efficient policies as those that maximize world welfare. In the digital world, world welfare depends on the sum of the home and foreign tariffs, $\tau + \tau^*$, and on the degree of home and foreign digital openness, I and I^*. As before, the first-order conditions that define the sum of efficient tariffs, $\partial W^w / \partial[\tau + \tau^*] = 0$, can be simplified to yield

$$[\tau + \tau^*] \times \frac{\partial E^*}{\partial p^*} \frac{\partial \tilde{p}^*}{\partial [\tau + \tau^*]} = 0,$$

which immediately implies

$$\tau^e + \tau^{*e} = 0. \tag{9.10}$$

Again, there is no efficiency role for tariffs, and this is true regardless of the degree of digital openness in each country (and hence regardless of trade costs ι).

Consider next the efficient level of home and foreign digital openness, denoted by I^e and I^{*e}, respectively. The first-order condition that defines I^e implies

$$\{[\tau + \tau^*] \times \frac{\partial E^*}{\partial p^*} \frac{\partial \tilde{p}^*}{\partial [\tau + \tau^*]} - E^*\} \frac{\partial \iota}{\partial I} = c'(I^e),$$

which, evaluated at the efficient tariffs $\tau^e + \tau^{*e}$, simplifies to

$$M^e \times [-\frac{\partial \iota}{\partial I}] = c'(I^e), \tag{9.11}$$

where M^e denotes home import volume evaluated at efficient policies and where in writing (9.11) I have used the market-clearing condition $M = E^*$. In words, the efficient level of home-country digital openness I^e equates the marginal benefit of the last unit of digital opening allowed by the home country (the marginal savings in total trade costs $M^e \cdot [-\frac{\partial \iota}{\partial I}]$) with the marginal cost to the home country owing to the impact of this additional digital opening on the local nonpecuniary externality that is associated with the home country's digital openness ($c'(\cdot)$). The efficient level of digital openness for the foreign country, I^{*e}, is similarly characterized as

$$M^e \times [-\frac{\partial \iota}{\partial I^*}] = c^{*\prime}(I^{*e}). \tag{9.12}$$

Notice from (9.11) and (9.12) that if I and I^* enter symmetrically into the trade cost function $\iota(I, I^*)$, then the efficient digital policies will differ across countries to the extent that the (local) externalities from digital openness differ in the two countries. Hence, the functions $c(\cdot)$ and $c^*(\cdot)$ play a role analogous to the difference across countries in their "preferences" for labor or environmental standards entertained by Bagwell and Staiger (2001b).[15]

---

15. In this regard, my modeling of digital openness therefore resonates with the position of Goldfarb and Trefler (2019), who argue that a country's choice of privacy policy in the context of artificial intelligence technologies raises issues analogous to those associated with the national choice of labor and environmental standards. However, in contrast to

Next, consider the Nash policies adopted by the two countries in the absence of a trade agreement. The first-order conditions for the home country that define its best-response levels of τ and I are given by

$$\frac{\partial W}{\partial \tau} = -M(\tilde{p})\frac{\partial \tilde{p}}{\partial \tau} + \tau \frac{\partial E^*}{\partial p^*}\frac{\partial \tilde{p}^*}{\partial \tau} + M(\tilde{p}) = 0 \qquad (9.13)$$

$$\frac{\partial W}{\partial I} = [-M(\tilde{p})\frac{\partial \tilde{p}}{\partial \iota} + \tau \frac{\partial E^*}{\partial p^*}\frac{\partial \tilde{p}^*}{\partial \iota}]\frac{\partial \iota}{\partial I} - c'(\cdot) = 0.$$

Similarly, the first-order conditions for the foreign country that define its best-response levels of τ^* and I^* are given by

$$\frac{\partial W^*}{\partial \tau^*} = -E^*(\tilde{p}^*)\frac{\partial \tilde{p}^*}{\partial \tau^*} + \tau^* \frac{\partial M}{\partial p}\frac{\partial \tilde{p}}{\partial \tau^*} + E^*(\tilde{p}^*) = 0 \qquad (9.14)$$

$$\frac{\partial W^*}{\partial I^*} = [-E^*(\tilde{p}^*)\frac{\partial \tilde{p}^*}{\partial \iota^*} + \tau^* \frac{\partial M}{\partial p}\frac{\partial \tilde{p}}{\partial \iota^*}]\frac{\partial \iota^*}{\partial I^*} - c^{*\prime}(\cdot) = 0.$$

The Nash policies, which I denote by τ^N, I^N, τ^{*N} and I^{*N}, satisfy the four first-order conditions in (9.13) and (9.14) simultaneously.

Now notice from the pricing relationships above that $\frac{\partial \tilde{p}}{\partial \tau} = \frac{\partial \tilde{p}}{\partial \iota}$ and $\frac{\partial \tilde{p}^*}{\partial \tau} = \frac{\partial \tilde{p}^*}{\partial \iota}$ and that $\frac{\partial \tilde{p}^*}{\partial \tau^*} = \frac{\partial \tilde{p}^*}{\partial \iota^*}$ and $\frac{\partial \tilde{p}}{\partial \tau^*} = \frac{\partial \tilde{p}}{\partial \iota^*}$. Using this information, substituting the top first-order condition in (9.13) into the bottom first-order condition in (9.13), simplifying the top condition in (9.13) further, and performing the analogous steps for the first-order conditions in (9.14), it follows that the Nash tariffs are

$$\tau^N = \frac{\tilde{p}^{w*N}}{\eta^{E*N}} \text{ and } \tau^{*N} = \frac{\tilde{p}^{wN}}{\eta^{MN}}, \qquad (9.15)$$

while the Nash digital policies satisfy

$$M^N \times [-\frac{\partial \iota}{\partial I}] = c'(I^N) \text{ and } M^N \times [-\frac{\partial \iota}{\partial I^*}] = c^{*\prime}(I^{*N}), \qquad (9.16)$$

where, as before, η^{E*N} is the elasticity of foreign export supply and η^{MN} is the elasticity of home import demand (defined positively) and where $\tilde{p}^{w*N}$, $\tilde{p}^{wN}$, and M^N denote their respective previously defined magnitudes, all evaluated at Nash policies. The Nash tariffs in (9.15) again represent the usual Johnson optimal tariff, and the Nash digital openness levels described by (9.16) equate the marginal benefit

---

Goldfarb and Trefler and to Bagwell and Staiger (2001b), I focus here on the impact of digital openness on trade costs.

of further digital openness with its marginal cost, just as described previously in the context of efficient policy choices.

What is the difference between the problem for GATT to solve in the digital world and the problem of insufficient market access that I characterized in the pre-digital world? As in the pre-digital world, Nash tariffs in the digital world are inefficiently high, as a comparison between (9.15) and (9.10) confirms. And in the digital world, the degree of digital openness as reflected in the levels of I and I^* is too low in the Nash equilibrium relative to the efficient level, as can be confirmed from a comparison of (9.16) with (9.11) and (9.12), and from noting that $M^N < M^e$ implies $I^N < I^e$ and $I^{*N} < I^{*e}$.[16]

But notice that *given* the Nash level of trade volume M^N, the expressions in (9.16) that implicitly define I^N and I^{*N} are identical to the expressions in (9.11) and (9.12) that implicitly define I^e and I^{*e}. This is the same structure that Bagwell and Staiger (2001b) exploited to demonstrate that the only problem for a trade agreement to solve is the insufficient-market-access problem, the same problem that I characterized above in the pre-digital world. And it implies that the purpose of a trade agreement is unchanged by the introduction of digital trade in goods. Specifically, in both the pre-digital and digital worlds, the purpose of GATT is to reduce tariffs and thereby expand market access to efficient levels.

If design reflects purpose, then the common purpose of GATT across the pre-digital and digital worlds that I have just described suggests that in principle, there is no reason for the design of GATT to change in the presence of digital trade in goods. To see what this implies for the design of GATT in a digital world, I now want to describe, in detail, how the logic of shallow integration—the same logic that Bagwell and Staiger (2001b) showed would hold when governments can chose both tariffs and domestic standards—continues to apply in the digital world.

A first observation is that an agreement to set tariffs at free trade will not by itself achieve the efficiency frontier, because as is easily shown, such an agreement would induce each country to reduce its digital openness as a second-best means of manipulating its terms of trade once the agreement constrains its tariffs away from such behavior. One approach, then, is for governments to negotiate over both tariffs and their digital policies to ensure that the conditions for efficiency in (9.10) and in (9.11) and (9.12) are met. But, as I have noted,

---

16. This follows from the convexity of $c(\cdot)$ and $c^*(\cdot)$.

this deep-integration approach is not the approach that GATT has traditionally taken. Instead, GATT's shallow-integration approach can in principle work in a digital world as follows.

Beginning from the Nash policies given by (9.15) and (9.16), suppose that governments negotiate over tariffs and agree to a pair of tariffs $\tilde{\tau}$ and $\tilde{\tau}^*$ that satisfy

$$M(\tilde{p}(\iota(I^N, I^{*N}) + \tilde{\tau} + \tilde{\tau}^*)) = M^e. \tag{9.17}$$

According to (9.17), in this first step countries would agree to a pair of tariffs that deliver the efficient level of market access and hence import volume in light of their existing noncooperative digital policies I^N and I^{*N}. Given that the noncooperative digital policies are less open than efficient digital policies, equation (9.17) implies that the tariffs that governments would agree to in their negotiation would be below the efficient free-trade levels.

Then, subsequent to these tariff negotiations, suppose that each government is allowed to set/adjust its digital policy unilaterally, but that governments are subject to a market access preservation rule of the following form: If a government alters its digital policy from the Nash level, it must also adjust its tariff to preserve the market access level implied by its original negotiated tariff commitment. Since policy adjustments by one country that preserve market access also preserve the equilibrium trade volume, policy adjustments for the home government that satisfy the market access preservation rule are defined by

$$\frac{d\tau}{dI}\Big|_{dM=0} = \frac{-\frac{\partial \tilde{p}}{\partial \iota}\frac{\partial \iota}{\partial I}}{\frac{\partial \tilde{p}}{\partial \tau}} > 0, \tag{9.18}$$

with an analogous condition holding for the foreign government. The inequality in (9.18) follows from the signs of price derivatives reported above and implies that the home government must lower (can raise) its tariff if it reduces (increases) its digital openness subsequent to tariff negotiations with the foreign country, and similarly for the foreign government.

Subject to this market access preservation rule, what digital policy will the home government choose? Its unilateral choice will satisfy the first-order condition

$$\frac{\partial W}{\partial I} + \frac{\partial W}{\partial \tau}\frac{d\tau}{dI}\Big|_{dM=0} = 0,$$

which implies

$$[-M^e \frac{\partial \tilde{p}}{\partial \iota} + \tau \frac{\partial E^*}{\partial p^*} \frac{\partial \tilde{p}^*}{\partial \iota}] \frac{\partial \iota}{\partial I} - c'(\cdot) + [-M^e \frac{\partial \tilde{p}}{\partial \tau} + \tau \frac{\partial E^*}{\partial p^*} \frac{\partial \tilde{p}^*}{\partial \tau} + M^e]$$

$$\times \frac{-\frac{\partial \tilde{p}}{\partial \iota} \frac{\partial \iota}{\partial I}}{\frac{\partial \tilde{p}}{\partial \tau}} = 0.$$

But using the pricing relationships reported above, this condition simplifies to

$$M^e \times [-\frac{\partial \iota}{\partial I}] = c'(I^e),$$

which is the condition for the efficient home-country digital policy reported in (9.11).

Hence, with the market access preservation rule preventing the home-country government from manipulating the terms of trade with its choice of digital policy, the home-country government would choose to unilaterally liberalize its digital policy to the efficient level I^e while at the same time raising its tariff from $\tilde{\tau}$ to its efficient level so as to preserve the (efficient) level of market access that was implied by its tariff negotiations. An analogous argument applies to the foreign-country government. Evidently, by this shallow-integration approach, governments can ensure that the conditions for efficiency in (9.10) through (9.12) are met.

At a conceptual level, these arguments imply that, despite the fact that digitalization has indisputably permeated deeply into the modern world, there is no more (or less) reason to take a "holistic" (i.e., deep) approach to liberalization in the digital world than there was in the pre-digital world. At a more practical level, and as I noted more generally in chapter 3, these arguments do not so much mean that no degree of deep integration is necessary in a digital world as they provide a potentially useful guardrail that can help delineate the "depth" that deep trade agreements should go in the digital world: According to these results, just as in the pre-digital world, there is no reason to go deeper in a trade agreement for the world of digital trade in goods than what is required to ensure that property rights over negotiated market access are reasonably secure.

Up until now I have maintained assumption 1 in order to abstract from the possibility that an open digital policy might lead to cross-border nonpecuniary externalities. I now relax assumption 1, and allow the nonpecuniary externalities associated with digital trade to cross borders. This implies that welfare functions are now given by equations (9.4) through (9.6).

Notice that the presence of cross-border nonpecuniary externalities does not alter the Nash policy choices of the two governments, which will still be characterized by (9.15) and (9.16), because with $\theta > 0$ the only difference in a country's welfare function is that its welfare is now reduced directly (for given prices) when its *trading partner's* digital policy is more open, and this is a policy choice that a country has no say in under noncooperative Nash choices. But with $\theta > 0$, the efficient policy choices will now be different than they were under assumption 1. In particular, it is direct to show that while the efficient tariffs are still characterized by (9.10), the efficient levels of digital openness are now characterized by

$$M^e \times [-\frac{\partial \iota}{\partial I}] = [1+\theta] \times c'(I^e) \tag{9.19}$$

for the home-country government and by

$$M^e \times [-\frac{\partial \iota}{\partial I^*}] = [1+\theta] \times c^{*\prime}(I^{*e}) \tag{9.20}$$

for the foreign-country government. As a comparison of (9.19) and (9.20) with (9.11) and (9.12) confirms, efficiency requires a less open digital policy for each country when digital openness imposes cross-border (negative) externalities on trading partners.[17] And this implies that the efficient trade volume is also lower.

What does this mean for the purpose of a trade agreement? As I now demonstrate, when digital trade in goods generates cross-border nonpecuniary externalities, the purpose of a trade agreement is no longer simply to solve the insufficient-market-access problem that I characterized in the pre-digital world. Rather, there are now two problems to solve: the cross-border nonpecuniary externality must be addressed and, conditional on addressing this first problem, the problem of insufficient market access, familiar from the pre-digital world, must also be addressed.

To see that the problem is now more complex, suppose first that countries attempted the same shallow-integration approach that I described previously when assumption 1 held. By negotiating to the appropriate tariffs, governments could position their market access at

---

17. Again, this follows from the convexity of $c(\cdot)$ and $c^*(\cdot)$.

the efficient level appropriate for the case where assumption 1 is violated and $\theta > 0$. The problem is that under the subsequent unilateral policy adjustments subject to the market access preservation rule, governments would choose levels of digital openness I and I^* that satisfied (9.11) and (9.12), not the conditions for efficiency (9.19) and (9.20) that are relevant when $\theta > 0$. This implies that GATT's shallow approach to integration is no longer appropriate for a world of digital trade in goods if that trade generates significant cross-border nonpecuniary externalities.

Notice, though, that even in this case there may be an approach to integration suggested by the discussion above that lies somewhere between shallow integration, on the one hand, and on the other hand, fully deep integration where countries negotiate over all aspects of digital policy that enter into I and I^* in addition to their tariffs. This is because if countries could focus on just those aspects of their digital openness that are generating the cross-border nonpecuniary externalities and address those externalities with limited negotiations, then, from that point forward, we would be back in a world analogous to the world where assumption 1 applies and where achieving the efficiency frontier with GATT's shallow approach to integration is possible.[18] I explore this possibility at the end of this chapter.

9.4 Digital Trade in Services

In Staiger (2021), I extend the model of digital goods trade that I developed in section 9.3 to the case of digital trade in services, and there I perform a parallel analysis for trade in services. I focus on mode-3 services in order to reflect the emphasis of GATS commitments.[19] A useful illustrative example might be trade in construction services. In

---

18. While the existence of a cross-border nonpecuniary externality therefore does change the purpose of a trade agreement, it does so in a way that suggests the possibility of addressing the various problems in separable ways, as I have just described, and in this sense it is very different from the complications raised by "offshoring" and highlighted by Antràs and Staiger (2012a, 2012b), where the nature of the pecuniary externality is itself altered. I return to this point at the end of this chapter and discuss offshoring in detail in chapter 10.

19. For mode-3 services, where a commercial presence in the importing country must be established, it is still the case that restrictive digital policies can raise the cost of trade (as I assumed in section 9.3). For example, data localization requirements can raise the costs of trade by eliminating the option of cloud storage and thereby forcing a mode-3 service provider to invest in costly cybersecurity for its local data. See, for example, the discussion in Goldfarb and Trefler (2019) and the reports listed in

the pre-digital world, a foreign construction company opens a branch office in the home-country market and takes on local road construction projects, thereby providing mode-3 exports of construction services to the home country. In the digital world, all that is still true, but the foreign company advertises its construction services on its foreign website where orders are placed and where electronic payments are also made, and it digitally communicates with the home-country branch office over initial orders and any change orders that arise during the course of construction. The openness of digital policies in each country can impact the functioning of each of these digital tasks.[20]

In the pre-digital world, my model of trade in mode-3 services collapses to that of Staiger and Sykes (2021). Mode-3 services trade has several defining characteristics, including (i) the need for foreign capital to locate in the importing country and establish a commercial presence, (ii) the frequent existence of market failures that offer a legitimate purpose for domestic regulations, and (iii) a lack of readily available tariff-like instruments given that mode-3 trade does not cross national borders. It is also true that the approach to market access liberalization taken by GATS is strikingly at odds with the shallow-integration approach taken by GATT and is instead more aptly described as a deep-integration approach, whereby the negotiated change or removal of domestic regulations and other nontariff barriers to trade in service sectors is seen as the primary method of expanding market access. As Staiger and Sykes note, these observations raise the question: Can the distinctive design of GATS relative to GATT be understood as a reflection of the underlying differences between services trade and goods trade?

Staiger and Sykes (2021) establish that the key feature of mode-3 services trade, which according to the terms-of-trade theory can account for the distinctive design of GATS relative to GATT, is characteristic (iii)—the lack of a readily available tariff-like instrument that can be applied to mode-3 services trade. As they demonstrate, but for this feature, the problem for an agreement on trade in services to solve—and hence, presumably, the design of the agreement—would be identical to that for an agreement on trade in goods. In Staiger (2021), I adopt this "missing tariff instrument" perspective on GATS, and I extend the

---

the Google Public Policy Blog posting at https://publicpolicy.googleblog.com/2015/02/the-impacts-of-data-localization-on.html.

20. There is also the increasing possibility of digitally delivering construction services; see, for example, Lasky (2019) on the construction of homes using 3D printing.

partial equilibrium model of mode-3 services trade put forward by Staiger and Sykes to allow for the possibility of digital trade in services.

The Design of GATS

How can the lack of a tariff instrument for traded (mode 3) services account for the striking difference between GATT and GATS? In short, without a tariff to manipulate its services terms of trade, an importing government will in the Nash equilibrium tend to spread protective distortions widely across the policy instruments that it does wield in the service sector, thereby "contaminating" many of its Nash policies with internationally inefficient terms-of-trade motives. And if this describes the starting point from which governments would have considered the design of a trade-in-services agreement, the strategy of borrowing heavily from the shallow-integration design features of GATT would not seem like an obvious and natural, or even viable, way to proceed, so much so that it seems plausible that this strategy may not have even occurred to GATS negotiators. Rather, facing evident behind-the-border policy distortions spread throughout the domestic service market, a decision to adopt a deep-integration approach to services liberalization seems almost inevitable.

From this perspective, and as Staiger and Sykes (2021) argue in the context of a pre-digital model world economy, the lack of an effective tariff or tariff-equivalent policy instrument for (mode 3) service-sector intervention can go a long way in accounting for the striking differences in the architecture of GATS and GATT.

A GATS Redesign for the Pre-Digital World

Nevertheless, as Staiger and Sykes (2021) demonstrate for the pre-digital world, this does not mean that shallow integration is impossible for services. Rather, it is possible to exploit the elements of the trade-in-goods problem that are shared with the trade-in-services problem to devise a two-step path forward for liberalizing trade in services that has much in common with the shallow-integration approach of GATT.

As Staiger and Sykes (2021) describe, as a first step, governments would agree to a set of blanket rules to apply to services along the lines of the GATT rules that apply to goods—namely, (i) the national treatment (NT) rule, which prohibits domestic regulatory (and tax) policies that discriminate against foreign trade; (ii) the agreement on technical barriers to trade (TBT), which prohibits unnecessarily trade restrictive regulatory choices; and (iii) the non-violation (NV) clause, which protects the value of market access concessions from erosion due to subsequent and unanticipated changes in noncontracted policies. Staiger and Sykes show that, in ruling out discriminatory and unnecessarily trade restrictive regulatory choices, such an agreement would induce governments to unilaterally remove protectionist elements from their regulations in the service sector and divert these elements into a narrow set of fiscal—but not regulatory—measures. And with international policy inefficiencies concentrated in a limited set of instruments, governments could then in a second step use negotiations over these instruments to establish (in concert with the NT, TBT, and NV rules) efficient market access commitments in service sectors, without the need to directly negotiate over a wide range of domestic regulatory measures, much as GATT has used negotiated commitments on tariffs in the goods sector. As Staiger and Sykes argue, this approach to integration of services trade might allow countries to sidestep the difficult sovereignty issues that arise with deep-integration efforts and that may help explain the relative lack of GATS's success to date as compared to GATT (see also Deardorff 2002 for a related proposal).

The Purpose of GATS in a Digital World

As should be clear from the previous discussion, the property of the pre-digital world that Staiger and Sykes (2021) establish and that underpins the possibility of a shallow-integration approach to liberalization in the service sector is this: The problem that a trade-in-services agreement must solve is not so different from the problem that a trade-in-goods agreement must solve, and but for the missing tariff on mode-3 services, the two problems would be identical. In Staiger (2021), I show that this property extends to a digital world, thereby establishing that in the digital world, the possibility of a shallow-integration approach to liberalization in the service sector also exists, just as Staiger and Sykes describe that possibility for the pre-digital world.

Moreover, I show that all of the conclusions reached in section 9.3 for the case of digital trade in goods in the presence of a cross-border nonpecuniary externality from digital openness carry over to the case of digital trade in services as well. In particular, as was the case for digital trade in goods, in the presence of a cross-border nonpecuniary externality from digital openness there are now two problems to solve when talking about digital services trade: The cross-border nonpecuniary externality must be addressed and, conditional on addressing this first problem, the insufficient-market-access problem familiar from the pre-digital world must also be addressed. But, even in this case there may be an approach to integration that lies somewhere between shallow integration, on the one hand, and on the other hand, fully deep integration where countries negotiate over all aspects of digital policy.

9.5 Digital Trade and the Design of the WTO

What does the analysis presented in this chapter mean for the design of the WTO in a world of digital trade? The main message has two parts.

First, if the nonpecuniary externalities associated with open digital policies are purely local, then the purpose of a trade agreement in a digitalized world is to achieve an efficient level of market access, which is the same purpose as in the pre-digital world. And for this purpose, shallow integration can in principle suffice.[21]

Of course, in the analysis above, I have abstracted from a number of challenges that a shallow approach to integration would confront in practice;[22] and in reality, the line between shallow and deep integration is not as stark as my analysis makes it out to be. At a more practical level, therefore, and as I emphasized earlier, the message in this case is not so much that *no* degree of deep integration is necessary in a digital world, but rather that the existing market access orientation of the WTO can provide a potentially useful *guardrail* to delineate the "depth" of integration that trade agreements should contemplate in the digital world. According to the findings above, and just as in the pre-digital world, there is no reason for a trade agreement in the world of digital trade to go deeper than what is required to ensure that property rights over negotiated market access are reasonably secure. The use of such a guardrail could help governments avoid conflicts between globalization and national sovereignty that, according to the analysis presented above, would be unnecessary.[23]

Even in this case, the analysis that I have presented suggests that the rise of digital trade could pose a challenge for the WTO because it

---

21. Interestingly, adopting a very different modeling approach that features monopoly platforms and two-sided markets for platform services and focuses on the particular issue of privacy protection, McCalman (2021) comes to a similar conclusion that shallow integration may suffice for issues related to digital trade.

22. See Staiger and Sykes (2021) for a discussion of a number of these challenges in the context of a shallow-integration approach to the liberalization of trade in services.

23. It should be noted, though, that I am abstracting from certain non-trade issues, such as the right to free speech, that may be particularly salient in this context; see, for example, Meltzer (2013).

has the potential to disrupt the market access implications of existing WTO commitments. For example, while a good delivered as instructions for 3D printing is still a good according to my taxonomy, it may be that as a practical matter, the tariff commitments negotiated in the pre-digital world no longer afford the same protection against imports that they once did; and it may also be that new digital forms of protection become relevant that could undermine existing market access commitments. But, at least in principle, existing WTO rules are well designed to handle these issues because these issues are not new to the digital age. The first of these issues could be handled under the various renegotiation clauses that exist in the WTO, which as I noted in chapter 7 are designed to allow WTO market access commitments to function as liability rules that can be renegotiated without fear of holdup from trading partners.[24] And the second issue can, in principle, be addressed with the existing WTO rules (e.g., NT, TBT, NV) that are designed to handle such issues more broadly.

There is also an interesting further implication of the analysis above when the nonpecuniary externalities associated with open digital policies are purely local: The existing moratorium on tariffs on electronic transmissions might be *complicating* the task of shallow integration in a world of digital trade. This is because, as my analysis demonstrates, it is only when the use of tariffs on digital trade is constrained that nontariff behind-the-border policies become distorted for protectionist terms-of-trade-manipulation purposes. Viewed from this perspective, in the case where the nonpecuniary externalities associated with open digital policies are purely local, the suspension or termination of the moratorium on tariffs on electronic transmissions should have the effect of inducing governments unilaterally to concentrate their protective and internationally inefficient measures on such trade into tariffs, and in inducing such "tariffication" might represent a useful first step toward effective shallow integration in a digital world.

A final pair of observations that apply to this first case are also relevant. First, even if the purpose of a trade agreement does not change with the rise of digital trade, the blurring of the distinction between goods and services that digitalization has caused (and will increasingly cause in the future) presents an important challenge for the WTO in

---

24. In the context of the WTO, renegotiations of market access commitments for services are handled through GATS Article XXI, while for goods they are handled through GATT Article XXVIII.

light of the very different structure of GATT and GATS. This challenge can be reduced if the design features of GATT and GATS are brought closer together, since then the distinction between goods and services becomes less consequential within the WTO legal framework. As I have already described, in principle GATS could be redesigned to be more like GATT. The advent of the digital age may make such a redesign all the more attractive.

At the same time, the analysis in this chapter also suggests a second, related observation: From a functional perspective, a new approach to the classification of goods and services for the digital world might be attractive. Recall that I have adopted a simple taxonomy that partitions digital trade transactions into two groups: digital trade in goods and digital trade in services. To develop this taxonomy I have defined a transaction as involving a good (service) if at the moment of consumption that transaction is a good (service) as traditionally defined. And for the formal analysis I have assumed that digitalization does not itself alter the feasibility of imposing a tariff on the trade in question. My analysis, however, confirms for the digital world what the analysis of Staiger and Sykes (2021) implies for the pre-digital world—namely, that when it comes to the design features of a trade agreement, what functionally distinguishes trade in goods from trade in services is whether or not a tariff can be feasibly applied to that trade. This suggests the attractiveness of adopting an alternative classification system for traded goods and services within the context of the WTO. Simply put, digital or otherwise, traded goods would refer to transactions on which a tariff can feasibly be applied, and these transactions would be covered under GATT; traded services would refer to all other transactions, and these transactions would be governed under GATS.[25] Under this alternative classification, digitalization would change a good into a service, or vice versa, if and only if it altered the feasibility of imposing tariffs on the international transaction.

The second part of the message applies where the nonpecuniary externalities associated with open digital policies cross national borders. In this case the purpose of a trade agreement becomes more

---

25. This alternative classification adopts a functional perspective in the sense that it is based on the answer to the question, "Can a tariff be applied to the transaction?" See Willemyns (2019) for a discussion of alternative functional and other approaches to the classification of services in the WTO. It should also be noted that the alternative classification I describe here would not necessarily conform to the principal of "technological neutrality" that currently applies to GATS commitments (see the WTO Analytical Index Annex 1B at https://www.wto.org/english/res_e/publications_e/ai17_e/gats_art1_jur .pdf).

complex, as there are now two problems to solve: The cross-border non-pecuniary externality must be addressed and, conditional on addressing this first problem, the insufficient-market-access problem familiar from the pre-digital world must also be addressed. But I also emphasized a further point: Even in this case, there may be an approach to integration for goods and services trade in a digital world that lies somewhere between GATT's shallow integration approach on the one hand, and on the other hand fully deep integration, where countries negotiate over all aspects of digital policy. This is because if countries could jointly focus on just those aspects of their digital openness that are generating the cross–border nonpecuniary externalities and address those externalities with limited negotiations, then, from that point forward, we would be back in a world where there are no (unaddressed) cross-border nonpecuniary externalities and where only local nonpecuniary externalities remain. And that is a world where achieving the efficiency frontier with GATT's shallow approach to integration is possible.

To illustrate this point, I now briefly describe a middle ground between shallow and deep integration in the context of the "data de-correlation" scheme proposed by Acemoglu et al. (forthcoming). They consider a situation in which users of a digital platform value privacy to varying degrees and impose negative externalities on each other when they share their personal data with the platform, provided that their data is correlated with other users so that the platform also learns something about other users through this correlation. In such a situation, individual-level data is underpriced and the market economy generates too much data. As Acemoglu et al. describe it, data de-correlation represents one possible solution to address this problem. De-correlation is a scheme for mediating (through a trusted third party) data transactions in a way that reduces their correlation with the data of other users—and in particular the correlation between the data of a user who is not sharing data with the data of others who have shared their data—and thereby mitigates these externality-induced privacy concerns.[26]

In the context of the present discussion, we could think of WTO member governments agreeing to a limited form of this proposal, tailored to address just the correlation with the data of other *international*

---

26. As Acemoglu et al. (forthcoming) discuss, the de-correlation scheme that they propose is different from procedures that anonymize data, because the latter hides information about the user who is sharing their own data while the former only hides information about others who are correlated with this user.

users—and hence addressing just the cross-border nonpecuniary externality associated with these digital privacy issues—and leaving the handling of the correlation of users' data *within* national borders to the discretion of each national government. In this way, users of the digital platform would retain private property rights over their own cross-border data flows and thereby avoid the associated cross-border nonpecuniary externality that would otherwise arise, and such property rights might be protected within the WTO Agreement on Trade-Related Aspects of Intellectual Property Rights (TRIPS). Whether or not users retained such rights over their own within-country data flows would be a decision for each national government to make.

Finally, it should be emphasized that I have taken a reduced-form approach to modeling the impact of digitalization on the world economy and, in so doing, have abstracted from many important features of digital trade and digital policies. If modeled, a number of these features would introduce potentially important departures from the simple competitive industry environment that I have adopted for my formal analysis, and it is possible that such departures could alter my findings. The terms-of-trade theory of trade agreements has been shown to yield robust findings across a wide range of market structures, and I suspect that my findings here will prove fairly robust as well. Still, it is important to move beyond the reduced-form approach I have adopted and investigate the impacts of digitalization on the purpose of a trade agreement in models of digital trade that include appropriate micro-foundations. In this regard, Antràs and Staiger (2012a, 2012b) have shown that the terms-of-trade theory does not extend to "offshoring" settings where domestic and foreign buyers exchange specialized inputs whose prices are determined by bilateral bargaining and are not disciplined by industry-wide market-clearing conditions.[27] In chapter 10, I discuss the challenge that offshoring that exhibits this characteristic may pose for the WTO. But to the extent that digital trade, and especially digital trade in services along a global value chain, is also thought to exhibit this characteristic, an important potential caveat to the results I have derived here should be kept in mind.

---

27. Further qualifications to the case for shallow integration arise in the setting analyzed by Grossman, McCalman, and Staiger (2021). I discuss their findings in detail in chapter 11. See also Bagwell, Bown, and Staiger (2016) for a review of other modeling frameworks where the shallow-integration results of the terms-of-trade theory need not hold.

10   The Rise of Offshoring and Global Value Chains

The rise of offshoring—the sourcing of intermediate inputs from foreign suppliers—and the creation of global value chains (GVCs) in production has been a defining feature of globalization over the past three decades. This is illustrated in figure 10.1, which shows the GVC share of global trade holding steady at around 40 percent through the 1970s and 1980s, and then rising sharply in the 1990s to a peak on the eve of the 2008 financial crisis before leveling off at around 50 percent.

Does offshoring create new problems of global policy cooperation whose solutions require international agreements with novel features? In this chapter, I discuss the answer to this question as provided by Antràs and Staiger (2012a, 2012b). They show that if offshoring can be seen as changing the nature of the dominant form of international price determination, from a process governed by a standard market-clearing mechanism to one that is described by a collection of bilateral bargains between specialized foreign suppliers and their domestic buyers, then the rise in offshoring will have changed the nature of the dominant international policy externality, and it will as a consequence create the need for fundamental changes in the WTO's approach to trade liberalization. In particular, Antràs and Staiger argue that the rise of offshoring may make it increasingly difficult for governments to rely on the traditional concepts and rules of the GATT and the WTO—such as market access, reciprocity and nondiscrimination—that have underpinned the GATT/WTO shallow-integration approach as I have described that approach in previous chapters. I focus now on the potential implications of offshoring for the choice between shallow and deep integration.

To illustrate the findings of Antràs and Staiger (2012a, 2012b), I consider a model that features trade in an "offshored" input, the building block of GVCs. To make the key points emphasized by Antràs

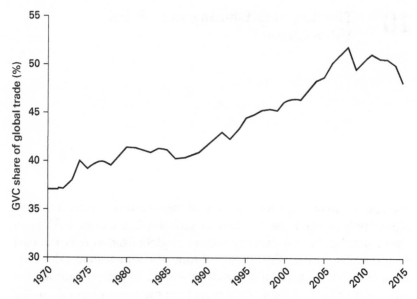

Figure 10.1
The rise of global value chains. *Source*: Reproduced from World Bank (2020, fig. 2).

and Staiger, I present two versions of this offshoring model. In a first version, the input is standardized and its price is determined by an international market-clearing condition. In this version I confirm that the purpose of a trade agreement is unchanged by the introduction of offshoring and that the logical basis of a shallow approach to integration remains intact, and hence that offshoring per se poses no challenge to the GATT/WTO design. In a second version of the offshoring model, I assume that the input is specialized and that its price is determined by bilateral bargaining between buyer and seller. It is in this version of the offshoring model that the difficulty that a shallow approach to integration would face becomes apparent. I then offer an assessment of the implications of these findings for the treatment of behind-the-border policies in trade agreements when offshoring is present and for the efficacy of the GATT/WTO shallow approach to integration in an offshoring world.[1]

---

1. As Antràs and Staiger (2012b) emphasize, the key feature of the economy needed for results of the kind I describe below is that international prices are determined by bilateral bargaining, and the rise of offshoring is one plausible way in which this method of price determination may have become increasingly prominent in recent decades. Also, in the model dicussed here I follow Antràs and Staiger and abstract from international factor

10.1   GVCs and Deep Integration

I consider a very stylized two-country partial equilibrium setting to illustrate the key points developed by Antràs and Staiger (2012a, 2012b). A final good y is consumed only in the home country, which is also the only country that can produce it. Home-country demand for good y is given by the downward-sloping demand curve $D(p_y)$, where p_y is the price of good y faced by domestic consumers.

There are two technologies available in the home country for production of good y. One technology is linear in the numeraire, and I assume that units of y have been chosen so that one unit of the numeraire produces one unit of good y. This technology is available to any producer in the home country that would like to use it, ensuring that there is a "competitive fringe" of infinitely elastic supply of good y at a home-country consumer price of 1. Provided that supply from the home-country competitive fringe is strictly positive, which I will assume to be the case, the home-country consumer price of good y is then pinned down at 1, and home-country demand for good y is fixed at $D(1)$.

The other technology is owned by a single home-country firm and requires an input x that is produced only in the foreign country: This is the "offshoring" technology, which I represent with the increasing and concave function $f_y(x)$. I consider two cases for the good-y offshoring technology and for the structure of the foreign x-producing industry that is implied. In a first case, I assume that the offshoring technology requires a standardized input, and that the input can be sourced from any firm in a competitive foreign x-producing industry. In this case, the price at which the input is exchanged between the single offshoring home firm and the competitive foreign exporting industry is determined by a standard international market-clearing condition. In a second case, I assume that the input x required by the offshoring home firm is highly specialized and must be sourced from a single specialized foreign supplier. In this case, the price at which the input is exchanged between the single offshoring home firm and the single foreign supplier is then determined by bilateral bargaining between the parties.

In terms of policy instruments, I assume that the foreign-country government is passive, but the home-country government has two tax

ownership and the presence of multinational firms; see also Blanchard (2010) and the discussion in Bagwell and Staiger (2016, 497–499).

instruments.[2] First, the home-country government has a production tax t_y (defined in specific terms, negative if a subsidy) at its disposal that it can impose on the good-y production of the home-country offshoring firm, leaving the production of the competitive fringe untaxed. And second, the home-country government has a good-x import tariff τ_x (defined in specific terms, negative if a subsidy) at its disposal, imply-ing that the relationship between the home-country price of x, p_x and the foreign country price of x, p_x^* is given by $p_x = p_x^* + \tau_x$. With the for-eign government assumed passive in this industry, the foreign price p_x^* is also the "world" (untaxed) price of x and hence the terms of trade between the two countries.

International Input Price Determined by Market Clearing

I begin with the case where the input x is standardized and produced by a competitive foreign industry of suppliers. I represent the foreign industry supply curve of the input x by the upward-sloping func-tion $S_x^*(p_x^*)$. In this case, the price at which the input x is exchanged between the single offshoring home firm and the competitive foreign industry of input suppliers is determined by a standard international market-clearing condition. Specifically, and denoting as D_x^m the off-shoring home firm's derived demand for the input x, the international x-market-clearing condition is given by

$$S_x^*(p_x^*) = D_x^m \tag{10.1}$$

and defines the market-clearing world price of x as a function of D_x^m,

$$\tilde{p}_x^* = S_x^{*-1}(D_x^m) \equiv \overset{(+)}{\tilde{p}_x^*}(D_x^m). \tag{10.2}$$

As is intuitive, (10.2) implies that a higher derived demand D_x^m for the input x leads to a higher world price of x and, through the pric-ing relationship $p_x = p_x^* + \tau_x$, leads also to a higher input price paid by the offshoring home firm, reflecting its monopsony power on world markets.

Given that the offshoring home firm is a price taker in its output mar-ket and receives $1 - t_y$ for each unit of y that it produces, the problem it faces is simple: Its only decision is how much x to import from the for-eign country in order to optimally exploit its monopsony power. Facing

---

2. Antràs and Staiger (2012a, 2012b) consider the case where both home and foreign countries are policy active.

the tariff on imported inputs τ_x, the offshoring home firm's derived demand for x solves

$$\max_{D_x^m} \pi \equiv (1 - t_y) \times f_y(D_x^m) - (\tilde{p}_x^*(D_x^m) + \tau_x) \times D_x^m.$$

The first-order condition equates marginal revenue to marginal cost and implies

$$D_x^m = D_x^m(\overset{(-)}{\tau_x}, \overset{(-)}{t_y})$$

(10.3)

and hence, using (10.2),

$$\tilde{p}_x^* = \tilde{p}_x^*(D_x^m(\overset{(-)}{\tau_x}, \overset{(-)}{t_y})) \equiv \tilde{p}_x^*(\overset{(-)}{\tau_x}, \overset{(-)}{t_y}).$$

(10.4)

Again, as is intuitive, according to (10.4) the world price of the input x is decreasing in the home tariff on imported inputs τ_x and decreasing as well in the home production tax on its offshoring firm t_y, because both of these taxes reduce the derived demand for imported inputs.

I can now define welfare for the home and foreign countries. I begin with home-country welfare. To this end, I first use (10.3) and (10.4) to define the optimized profits of the offshoring home firm as a function of the taxes it faces:

$$\pi(\tau_x, t_y) \equiv (1 - t_y) \times f_y(D_x^m(\tau_x, t_y)) - (\tilde{p}_x^*(\tau_x, t_y) + \tau_x) \times D_x^m(\tau_x, t_y).$$

Home-country welfare then consists of the sum of consumer surplus, $CS(1)$, which is fixed, the profits of the offshoring home firm, $\pi(\tau_x, t_y)$, and net tax revenues, or

$$W = CS(1) + \pi(\tau_x, t_y) + \tau_x \times D_x^m(\tau_x, t_y) + t_y \times f_y(D_x^m(\tau_x, t_y))$$

(10.5)

$$= CS(1) + f_y(D_x^m(\tau_x, t_y)) - \tilde{p}_x^*(\tau_x, t_y) \times D_x^m(\tau_x, t_y) \equiv W(\tau_x, t_y).$$

Foreign-country welfare is composed only of the producer surplus of foreign producers of the input x, which is defined by

$$PS_x^* = \int_0^{\tilde{p}_x^*(\tau_x, t_y)} S_x^*(p_x^*) dp_x^* \equiv PS_x^*(\tau_x, t_y).$$

Foreign-country welfare is then defined as

$$W^* = PS_x^*(\tau_x, t_y) \equiv W^*(\tau_x, t_y).$$

(10.6)

I am now ready to characterize efficient and noncooperative (Nash) policies in a world of offshoring, but where international prices continue to be determined by international market-clearing conditions (i.e., where $\tilde{p}_x^*$ is determined by (10.1)).[3] As usual, I will define efficient policies as those that maximize "world" welfare (i.e., the sum of home and foreign welfare) $W^w \equiv W + W^*$. The two first-order conditions that must hold at the efficient choices of τ_x and t_y are

$$\frac{\partial[W(\tau_x, t_y) + W^*(\tau_x, t_y)]}{\partial \tau_x} = 0 \qquad (10.7)$$

$$\frac{\partial[W(\tau_x, t_y) + W^*(\tau_x, t_y)]}{\partial t_y} = 0.$$

The two first-order conditions that must hold at the Nash choices of τ_x and t_y are

$$\frac{\partial W(\tau_x, t_y)}{\partial \tau_x} = 0 \qquad (10.8)$$

$$\frac{\partial W(\tau_x, t_y)}{\partial t_y} = 0.$$

Using the expressions for $W(\tau_x, t_y)$ and $W^*(\tau_x, t_y)$ in (10.5) and (10.6), respectively, it is straightforward to establish that the efficiency conditions in (10.7) imply that the efficient policies, which I denote by τ_x^e and t_y^e, satisfy

$$\frac{\tilde{p}_x^*(\tau_x^e, t_y^e)}{f_y'(D_x^m(\tau_x^e, t_y^e))} = 1. \qquad (10.9)$$

The condition in (10.9) has an intuitive interpretation. The expression on the left-hand side is the marginal cost of the last unit of y produced by the offshoring home firm, where the cost of the input x is valued at the world price $\tilde{p}_x^*(\tau_x^e, t_y^e)$. And the right-hand side is simply the consumer price of y in the home country (which is fixed at 1). Hence, (10.9) says that for efficiency, τ_x and t_y must be set to correct the monopsony distortion of the home offshoring firm, so that it imports the input x to the point where its marginal cost of y production valued at world prices equals the consumer price of y. In the simple model of offshoring that

---

3. Here and throughout this chapter I will refer to the noncooperative choices as "Nash" policies, even though I have assumed that the foreign government is passive, which implies that these policies are simply the unilateral noncooperative choices of the home government.

I have constructed, by design the policies τ_x and t_y do not impact consumer decisions; they are both instruments that only affect the producer margin, and hence any combination of τ_x and t_y that satisfies (10.9) is efficient.

To evaluate the efficiency properties of the Nash policy choices characterized in (10.8), I first rewrite the efficiency conditions of (10.7) in the equivalent form

$$\frac{\partial[W(\tau_x, t_y) + W^*(\tau_x, t_y)]}{\partial \tau_x} = 0 \tag{10.10}$$

$$\frac{\partial[W(\tau_x, t_y) + W^*(\tau_x, t_y)]}{\partial t_y} + \frac{\partial[W(\tau_x, t_y) + W^*(\tau_x, t_y)]}{\partial \tau_x} \frac{d\tau_x}{dt_y}\Big|_{dD_x^m=0} = 0,$$

where $\frac{d\tau_x}{dt_y}\big|_{dD_x^m=0}$ denotes the change in τ_x which, when accompanied by a small increase in t_y, will hold the import volume $D_x^m(\tau_x, t_y)$ fixed. The efficiency conditions in (10.10) are equivalent to those in (10.7), because the novel second term in the second line of (10.10) is zero at efficient policies by the first line of (10.10). But notice from (10.4)—which follows from the international market-clearing condition (10.1)—that changes to τ_x and t_y that hold $D_x^m(\tau_x, t_y)$ fixed also hold fixed $\tilde{p}_x^*(\tau_x, t_y)$, and hence by (10.6) they hold fixed $W^*(\tau_x, t_y)$. That is,

$$\frac{\partial W^*(\tau_x, t_y)}{\partial t_y} + \frac{\partial W^*(\tau_x, t_y)}{\partial \tau_x} \frac{d\tau_x}{dt_y}\Big|_{dD_x^m=0} = 0, \tag{10.11}$$

allowing me in turn to write (10.10) equivalently as

$$\frac{\partial[W(\tau_x, t_y) + W^*(\tau_x, t_y)]}{\partial \tau_x} = 0 \tag{10.12}$$

$$\frac{\partial W(\tau_x, t_y)}{\partial t_y} + \frac{\partial W(\tau_x, t_y)}{\partial \tau_x} \frac{d\tau_x}{dt_y}\Big|_{dD_x^m=0} = 0.$$

The efficiency conditions in (10.12) are analogous to those derived by Bagwell and Staiger (2001b) for the case of tariffs and domestic standards in a competitive general equilibrium setting, as I described those conditions in chapter 3, and they have an analogous interpretation. The bottom condition in (10.12) can be viewed as the "domestic" efficiency condition, as it ensures that the domestic mix of policies that delivers a given trade volume is chosen efficiently. And the top condition in (10.12) can then be viewed as the "international" efficiency condition that ensures that the volume of trade is also efficient.

It can now be seen from a comparison of the Nash conditions in (10.8) that Nash policies violate the international efficiency condition in the top line of (10.12) with tariffs that are too high, but Nash policies satisfy the domestic efficiency condition in the bottom line of (10.12).[4] The nature of the Nash inefficiency is therefore familiar from earlier chapters: there is one problem for a trade agreement to solve, and that is the problem of insufficient market access.

Hence, offshoring per se does not alter the purpose of a trade agreement, at least not when offshoring involves standardized inputs and international prices continue to be determined by market-clearing conditions.[5] And as I noted in chapter 3, it is the structure of the market access problem that needs to be solved as reflected here in (10.8) and (10.12) that facilitates the possibility of shallow integration—a focus on negotiated tariff liberalization, with "market access preservation rules" to prevent the reemergence of terms-of-trade manipulation through the introduction of new distortions in behind-the-border measures—as an efficient solution. I next ask whether this conclusion survives when offshoring involves a specialized input and international prices are determined by bilateral bargaining.

International Input Price Determined by Bilateral Bargaining
I now assume that the input x required by the home offshoring firm is highly specialized and cannot be sourced from a competitive industry of foreign suppliers. I focus on a single foreign producer of x, where the input x is exchanged between the offshoring home firm and this single foreign input supplier at a price that is determined by bilateral bargaining between the parties.

More specifically, I follow Antràs and Staiger (2012a, 2012b) and adopt an incomplete contracts setting where, to make a sale to the offshoring home firm, the foreign supplier must first invest in production and then (symmetric Nash) bargain over the price—the *international* price—at which it sells its produced inputs to the home firm. I take the

---

4. More specifically, conditions (10.8) and (10.12) imply that the Nash tariff is too high given the Nash production tax. This can be seen by noting that, with τ_x^N and t_y^N denoting Nash taxes, the top line of (10.8) implies $\frac{\partial W(\tau_x^N, t_y^N)}{\partial \tau_x} = 0$, and therefore at Nash taxes the top line of (10.12) is violated with $\frac{\partial [W(\tau_x^N, t_y^N) + W^*(\tau_x^N, t_y^N)]}{\partial \tau_x} = \frac{\partial W^*(\tau_x^N, t_y^N)}{\partial \tau_x} < 0$, implying that the Nash tariff is too high given the Nash production tax.

5. If this were not the case, the terms-of-trade theory would face a serious limitation, since input trade itself is not new. What is new is the highly specialized nature of that trade.

input to be specialized for use by the offshoring home firm and worthless if not sold to this firm, and I assume that the offshoring home firm has no alternative source of input supply: Hence the outside option of both the offshoring home firm and its foreign supplier is zero. I also now assume that the unit cost of foreign production is a constant c^*. The decisions of the offshoring home firm and its foreign supplier imply an import quantity M_x that then determines the level of y produced by the offshoring home firm according to the production function $f_y(M_x)$. As should come as no surprise, in this setting there is a holdup problem that leads to undersupply of the input because the foreign input supplier is unable to capture all the surplus from its marginal supply decision, and an efficiency role for tax/tariff intervention arises as a result. The question is how non-cooperative policy choices diverge from these efficient choices.

The structure of the bilateral buyer-seller relationship can be formalized in a three-stage game. I assume that all government policies are fixed in advance of the start of this game, which is then captured in the following sequence of events:

Stage 1. The foreign supplier decides on the amount M_x to be produced (at marginal cost of c^*).

Stage 2. The foreign supplier and the home offshoring firm (symmetric Nash) bargain over the price at which the input will change hands. Failure to reach agreement leaves both partners with their zero outside option.

Stage 3. The home offshoring firm imports the quantity M_x from the foreign supplier, payments agreed in stage 2 are settled, and the home offshoring firm produces $f_y(M_x)$ units of good y and sells its y production to domestic consumers at the consumer price of 1 (with the tariff τ_x and production tax t_y collected at the time of importation and production, respectively).

Consider the subgame perfect equilibrium of this three-stage game. First, if the offshoring home firm and its foreign supplier reach agreement in stage 2, the home firm can produce $f_y(M_x)$ units of good y for sale in the home-country market and make net-of-tax/tariff revenues in the amount of $[(1 - t_y) \times f_y(M_x) - \tau_x M_x]$, whereas disagreement in stage 2 results in both parties receiving their outside option of zero. Hence, given the quantity of inputs M_x, it follows that in the symmetric Nash bargain of stage 2, the offshoring home firm and the foreign supplier split the bargaining surplus and each receives $\frac{1}{2}[(1-t_y) \times f_y(M_x) - \tau_x M_x]$. For the home offshoring firm, its share of the bargaining surplus is also its profits, and I record these profits (conditional on M_x) for future reference:

$$\Pi(M_x, \tau_x, t_y) = \frac{1}{2}[(1-t_y) \times f_y(M_x) - \tau_x M_x], \qquad (10.13)$$

where I have used an upper-case Π to distinguish the offshoring home firm's profit function here from its profit function π defined in the previous version of the offshoring model that I presented above.

Now consider the foreign supplier's output choice in stage 1. Recalling that the unit cost of production for the foreign supplier is c^*, the foreign supplier chooses M_x to maximize its profits, which are given by

$$\Pi^*(M_x, \tau_x, t_y) = \frac{1}{2}[(1-t_y) \times f_y(M_x) - \tau_x M_x] - c^* M_x. \qquad (10.14)$$

Using (10.14), the level of M_x chosen by the foreign supplier in stage 1 is then implicitly defined by the first-order condition

$$\frac{1}{2}(1-t_y) \times f_y'(M_x) - \left(\frac{\tau_x}{2} + c^*\right) = 0, \qquad (10.15)$$

where the first term in (10.15) is the foreign supplier's share of the marginal revenue from producing another unit of x and the second term is the foreign supplier's share of the marginal (delivered) cost.

With the first-order condition in (10.15) implicitly defining the foreign input supplier's stage-1 choice $M_x(\tau_x, t_y)$, (10.13) and (10.14) can then be used to define home- and foreign-firm profits as a function of the tariff/tax policies only, $\Pi(\tau_x, t_y)$ and $\Pi^*(\tau_x, t_y)$, according to

$$\Pi(\tau_x, t_y) \equiv \frac{1}{2}[(1-t_y) \times f_y(M_x(\tau_x, t_y)) - \tau_x M_x(\tau_x, t_y)]$$

$$\Pi^*(\tau_x, t_y) \equiv \frac{1}{2}[(1-t_y) \times f_y(M_x(\tau_x, t_y)) - \tau_x M_x(\tau_x, t_y)] - c^* M_x(\tau_x, t_y).$$

And with this, home- and foreign-country welfare may be defined respectively as

$$W = CS(1) + \Pi(\tau_x, t_y) + \tau_x \times M_x(\tau_x, t_y) + t_y \times f_y(M_x(\tau_x, t_y)) \qquad (10.16)$$

$$= CS(1) + \frac{1}{2}[(1+t_y) \times f_y(M_x(\tau_x, t_y)) + \tau_x \times M_x(\tau_x, t_y)] \equiv W(\tau_x, t_y)$$

and

$$W^* = \Pi^*(\tau_x, t_y) \equiv W^*(\tau_x, t_y). \tag{10.17}$$

The efficient and Nash tax/tariff policies again must satisfy the first-order conditions specified in (10.7) and (10.8), respectively, the same first-order conditions that applied in the previous version of the offshoring model, where offshoring involved standardized inputs and international prices were determined by market-clearing conditions. For ease of reference, I reproduce these conditions here. The two first-order conditions that must hold at the efficient choices of τ_x and t_y are

$$\frac{\partial[W(\tau_x, t_y) + W^*(\tau_x, t_y)]}{\partial \tau_x} = 0 \tag{10.18}$$

$$\frac{\partial[W(\tau_x, t_y) + W^*(\tau_x, t_y)]}{\partial t_y} = 0,$$

and the first-order conditions that must hold at the Nash choices of τ_x and t_y are

$$\frac{\partial W(\tau_x, t_y)}{\partial \tau_x} = 0 \tag{10.19}$$

$$\frac{\partial W(\tau_x, t_y)}{\partial t_y} = 0,$$

where these sets of first-order conditions are now evaluated with the home-country and foreign-country welfare functions given in (10.16) and (10.17), respectively. It is straightforward to show that the efficiency conditions in (10.18) describe tariff/tax intervention that encourages the production of the input x and corrects the undersupply created by the holdup problem. But with these welfare functions, the difference between the Nash and efficient policies is now more complex than was the case in the previous version of the offshoring model.

To show this, I proceed as before and first rewrite the efficiency conditions of (10.18) in the equivalent form

$$\frac{\partial[W(\tau_x, t_y) + W^*(\tau_x, t_y)]}{\partial \tau_x} = 0 \tag{10.20}$$

$$\frac{\partial[W(\tau_x, t_y) + W^*(\tau_x, t_y)]}{\partial t_y} + \frac{\partial[W(\tau_x, t_y) + W^*(\tau_x, t_y)]}{\partial \tau_x} \frac{d\tau_x}{dt_y}\bigg|_{dM_x=0} = 0,$$

where $\frac{d\tau_x}{dt_y}|_{dM_x=0}$ denotes the change in τ_x which, when accompanied by a small increase in t_y, will hold the import volume $M_x(\tau_x, t_y)$ fixed. But recall that, rather than an international market-clearing condition, in this version of the offshoring model it is the first-order condition in (10.15) that defines $M_x(\tau_x, t_y)$. And using (10.15), it follows that $\frac{d\tau_x}{dt_y}|_{dM_x=0} = -f_y'(M_x)$, which implies by (10.17) that

$$\frac{\partial W^*(\tau_x, t_y)}{\partial t_y} + \frac{\partial W^*(\tau_x, t_y)}{\partial \tau_x} \frac{d\tau_x}{dt_y}|_{dM_x=0} = -\frac{M_x}{2}[\frac{f_y(M_x)}{M_x} - f_y'(M_x)].$$

This in turn allows me to rewrite the efficiency conditions in (10.20) as

$$\frac{\partial[W(\tau_x, t_y) + W^*(\tau_x, t_y)]}{\partial \tau_x} = 0 \tag{10.21}$$

$$\frac{\partial W(\tau_x, t_y)}{\partial t_y} + \frac{\partial W(\tau_x, t_y)}{\partial \tau_x} \frac{d\tau_x}{dt_y}|_{dM_x=0} = \frac{M_x}{2}[\frac{f_y(M_x)}{M_x} - f_y'(M_x)],$$

where the term on the right-hand side of the bottom line of (10.21) is positive given the concavity of $f_y(M_x)$.

It is now easy to see from a comparison of the Nash conditions in (10.19) that Nash policies violate the international efficiency condition in the top line of (10.21), with tariffs that are too high, just as I showed was the case in the previous version of the offshoring model, where offshoring involved standardized inputs and international prices were determined by market-clearing conditions. But now the Nash policies also violate the *domestic* efficiency condition in the bottom line of (10.12), with production taxes that are too high.

More specifically, the top lines of conditions (10.19) and (10.21) imply that the Nash tariff is too high given the Nash production tax: Evaluated at the Nash policies, the left-hand side of the top line of (10.21) (which is negative) is less than the right-hand side (zero). Similarly, the bottom lines of conditions (10.19) and (10.21) imply that the Nash production tax is too high given the Nash tariff: Evaluated at the Nash policies, the left-hand side of the bottom line of (10.21) (which is zero) is less than the right-hand side (which is positive). The nature of the Nash inefficiency is therefore different from that described in the previous version of the offshoring model. When international prices are determined by bilateral bargaining rather than a market-clearing condition, there is an insufficient market access problem associated with tariffs that are too high, but there is also now an additional inefficiency that involves the setting of behind-the-border measures.[6]

This difference has important implications for the efficacy of shallow integration in such a world. An immediate implication is that behind-the-border measures will be distorted in the Nash equilibrium, and so the logic of shallow integration, with its focus on negotiated tariff liberalization combined with market access preservation rules to prevent the reemergence of terms-of-trade manipulation through the introduction of new distortions in behind-the-border measures, no longer provides a coherent path to internationally efficient policies. Moreover, a market access preservation rule cannot stop terms-of-trade manipulation in this setting, because the nature of the international policy externalities has changed.

To show this last point, I now consider the equilibrium world (untaxed) price at which the input x is exchanged between the foreign input supplier and the home offshoring firm, which I denote by $\hat{p}_x^*$. This is simply the total revenue received by the foreign supplier divided by the quantity of inputs that are exchanged, or

$$\hat{p}_x^* \equiv \frac{1}{2}[(1-t_y) \times \frac{f_y(M_x)}{M_x} - \tau_x].$$ (10.22)

Using the definition of the world price of inputs $\hat{p}_x^*$ in (10.22), which is also the terms of trade between the home and foreign country, it follows that

$$\frac{\partial \hat{p}_x^*}{\partial t_y} + \frac{\partial \hat{p}_x^*}{\partial \tau_x}\frac{d\tau_x}{dt_y}\Big|_{dM_x=0} = -\frac{1}{2}[\frac{f_y(M_x)}{M_x} - f_y'(M_x)] < 0.$$ (10.23)

As (10.23) confirms, the home country can reduce $\hat{p}_x^*$ and improve its terms-of-trade by raising its production tax t_y even as it lowers its tariff τ_x to preserve the equilibrium import volume $M_x(\tau_x, t_y)$. Evidently, even subject to a market access preservation rule that had the

---

6. In fact, Antràs and Staiger (2012a) establish formally that, despite the difference that I have emphasized in the text, when political economy motivations are absent (as is the case in the simple model I have developed here), the problem for a trade agreement to solve in the presence of offshoring can still be given a terms-of-trade interpretation, even when inputs are specialized and international prices are determined by bilateral bargaining. However, they also show that this interpretation no longer applies once political economy motives are introduced, and they show that in any case shallow integration can no longer be used to reach the international efficiency frontier when offshoring takes this form, as I next confirm.

effect of preventing changes in behind-the-border measures that altered the volume of trade, the home country can still engage in terms-of-trade manipulation when offshoring involves a specialized input and international prices are determined by bilateral bargaining.[7]

10.2   What the Rise of GVCs Means for the Design of Trade Agreements

If the rise of offshoring is indeed changing the nature of international price determination and the implied international policy externalities in the way I have described, then GATT/WTO rules will be relatively poorly suited for liberalizing tariffs on the customized inputs that form the bulk of GVC trade, and we might expect to observe that WTO members are less successful in negotiating tariff cuts for this kind of trade. Figure 10.2 provides some suggestive evidence in this regard.

For a sample of 16 countries that joined the WTO after its creation in 1995, figure 10.2 shows that negotiated tariff cuts were greater in sectors with low levels of input customization than they were in sectors with high levels of input customization, suggesting that countries have more difficulty liberalizing trade through WTO negotiations in sectors where customized inputs are especially prevalent. While only suggestive, this evidence points to the possibility that the rise of offshoring may indeed have altered (deepened) the kinds of rules needed to help countries address their international policy inefficiencies.

Further suggestive evidence is provided from another angle. As Antràs and Staiger (2012a) observe, if offshoring is causing a problem for the WTO, then WTO member governments whose countries experience a rise in the importance of offshoring might seek alternative agreements with the countries in their GVCs as a way to achieve the deep integration that WTO commitments in their current form could not adequately provide. Laget et al. (2019) provide evidence of this; see also Orefice and Rocha (2014). Focusing on the depth of preferential trade agreements (PTAs) that WTO members negotiate under the GATT

---

7. Antràs and Staiger (2012a) consider several interpretations of a market access preservation rule, including the one I consider here that amounts to preserving trade volume and also a more expansive one that amounts to preserving both the trade volume and the world price. As they demonstrate, while the former would allow too much policy flexibility, the latter allows too little, and neither would allow shallow integration to achieve the efficiency frontier in this setting.

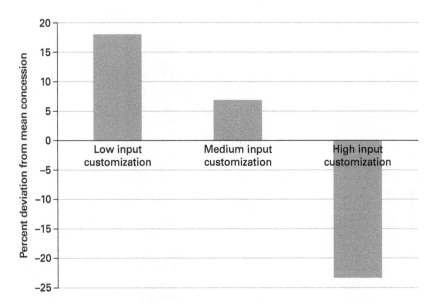

Figure 10.2
Source: Reproduced from Antràs and Staiger (2012a, fig. 1).

Article XXIV exception to the MFN clause, they find that the deepest PTAs were negotiated among countries with the greatest GVC-related trade. Figure 10.3 depicts this relationship.

Moreover, in their econometric analysis, which employs a structural gravity model to estimate the relationship between cross-border production linkages and the depth of PTAs, Laget et al. (2019) find that there is a positive impact of deep trade agreements on GVC integration, and that this impact is driven by trade in inputs rather than in final goods and services. This is again suggestive of the possibility that countries might seek deep trade commitments that the WTO framework cannot provide in order to facilitate the trade in specialized inputs that dominate GVCs.

It is possible, then, that the rise of offshoring has introduced into the world trading system a novel form of international policy externality, at least among countries trading specialized inputs along a common GVC, and in doing so it has made the shallow-integration approach of the GATT/WTO no longer well designed to solve the fundamental trade agreement problem for these countries. If this is so, then deeper forms of integration will be required for these countries to achieve internationally efficient policies, and a stark trade-off between sovereignty and globalization may be unavoidable.

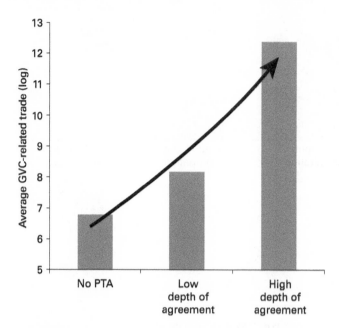

Figure 10.3
Source: Based on the results of Laget et al. (2019) and reproduced from the 2020 *World Development Report* (World Bank, 2020, fig. 9.9).

But as I noted, the evidence that I have reviewed above is only suggestive of this possibility, and I am unaware of direct empirical evidence on what the findings of Antràs and Staiger (2012a, 2012b) indicate is the crucial question—namely, whether the recent rise in off-shoring has changed the nature of the dominant form of international price determination. And so it is also possible that the rise of offshoring has *not* changed the nature of the international policy externality (or has changed the nature of the policy externalities only temporarily, as offshoring itself may have peaked or possibly even be more of a transitory phenomenon). In light of these unknowns, building on the GATT/WTO foundation, rather than abandoning it, in an attempt to address those issues that arise with offshoring while preserving the beneficial features of the GATT/WTO architecture for addressing tra-ditional international policy externalities, seems like the best course of action, at least until there is more direct empirical evidence that can be brought to bear on this question.

Where, specifically, does this leave us? As this discussion suggests, there is likely no easy answer for addressing the novel challenges that are posed by the rise of offshoring, and there is still much that is unknown about these challenges. But as I will discuss further in chapter 13, a reasonable approach may be to encourage plurilateral agreements within the WTO framework that achieve deeper integration among willing countries but that do not contain preferential discriminatory tariff commitments as is the case with PTAs.[8]

---

8. As Bagwell and Staiger (1999, 2002) have shown, and as further indicated by the discussion in chapters 4 and 5, the existence of preferential agreements involving discriminatory tariff commitments present their own problems for the effectiveness of the GATT/WTO architecture.

11 The Push toward Regulatory Convergence

In his 2015 Jan Tumlir Lecture, former WTO director general Pascal Lamy emphasized the growing importance of a particular form of international externality, different from market access issues and arising instead from regulatory heterogeneity across countries. Lamy argued that the focus of trade negotiations will increasingly be about achieving cost savings through harmonization, or at least convergence, in regulatory measures that are designed to protect consumers—regulations that Lamy characterized as motivated by "precaution." And he drew the following distinction between "old" and "new" trade agreements:

What trade media tell us is that today's trade theater is about two big shows, TPP [the Trans Pacific Partnership] and TTIP [the Transatlantic Trade and Investment Partnership]. What they do not tell you is that TPP is in many ways the last show of the old world of trade, and that TTIP is the first show of the new world of trade. TPP is mostly, though not only, about classical protection related market access issues, which is why it will be concluded soon, likely with modest results. TTIP is mostly, though not only, about precaution relating to regulatory convergence. . . . Because precaution is, at the end of the day, risk-related and thus value-related, it is much more politically sensitive because it makes legitimacy harder to build. (Lamy 2015)

In effect, according to Lamy (2015, 2016), with traditional trade barriers now reduced to low levels, the protectionist motive for insulating producers from foreign competition is being replaced by the precautionary motive for regulation designed to protect consumers' health, safety, and values. As a result, according to Lamy, trade agreements are becoming less about eliminating protective barriers and more about reducing differences between regulatory policies that have legitimate aims, in pursuit of the cost savings that such regulatory harmonization implies. Yet Sykes (1999a, 1999b) points to a possible downside of regulatory harmonization, observing that international differences in incomes, cultures, risk preferences, and tastes generally justify some degree of regulatory heterogeneity, even if the added costs of satisfying a multitude of rules are also recognized. This raises the question of the appropriate balance between the reduction of regulatory differences across countries to lower the costs of serving multiple markets and the preservation of regulatory differences across countries to reflect their heterogeneous tastes. And it raises the question of what role, if any, a trade agreement might play in helping countries achieve this balance, and how the agreement should be designed to serve that role.

I have discussed the treatment of regulations in trade agreements in earlier chapters in the context of the terms-of-trade theory, but the terms-of-trade theory cannot take us very far in answering the questions I have just posed, because according to that theory, harmonizing regulations would be desirable only to the extent that it is needed to secure the property rights over negotiated market access, not as an end it itself. In this chapter, I discuss the findings of Grossman, McCalman, and Staiger (2021), who propose a modeling framework that can provide answers to these questions.

In their model, traditional market access/terms-of-trade manipulation concerns are put to the side, so that the distinct issues associated with regulatory harmonization as raised by Lamy (2015, 2016) and Sykes (1999a, 1999b) can be explored. Specifically, in the model that Grossman, McCalman, and Staiger develop, firms design products to appeal to local consumer tastes, which differ across countries, as Sykes emphasizes. But the firms' fixed costs increase with the differences between versions of their products destined for different markets, and hence there are potential cost savings from regulatory harmonization, as emphasized by Lamy.

Grossman, McCalman, and Staiger distinguish between two settings: one setting, where there are no externalities associated with the consumption of products with different attributes (e.g., chicken that has or has not been subject to chlorine wash), and the other setting where such consumption externalities are present but do not cross national borders (e.g., the safety features of cars on the road).[1] In the first setting, where consumption externalities are absent, they show that firms'

---

1. As a general matter, the role for international agreements to handle nonpecuniary externalities that do cross national borders is already well understood. In chapters 8 and 9, I have discussed how such externalities might arise naturally in the specific context of atmospheric carbon and digital trade, respectively, and how the design of trade agreements might be adjusted in the presence of these externalities.

profit-maximizing choices of product attributes are globally optimal, but national governments have unilateral incentives to invoke regulatory protectionism, not for purposes of terms-of-trade manipulation but rather to induce firm "delocation"—the entry of firms in the home market at the cost of firm exit abroad—as in Venables (1987) and Ossa (2011). An efficient trade agreement will, of course, require commitments that prevent such opportunistic behavior, but in this first setting Grossman, McCalman, and Staiger show that shallow integration is still possible: A rule requiring mutual recognition of standards can be used to achieve efficiency with shallow integration, though one that requires only national treatment, as in the WTO, falls short. By contrast, they show that in the second setting, where product attributes confer local consumption externalities, a deeper approach to integration will be required to achieve efficiency, because in this instance an efficient trade agreement must coordinate the fine details of countries' regulatory policies.[2]

To sketch the model put forward by Grossman, McCalman, and Staiger and describe their findings, it is convenient to present the model as they develop it, first in the absence of consumption externalities and then extended to include such externalities. I conclude the chapter with a discussion of what their findings mean for the design of the WTO.

11.1 A Model of Regulatory Heterogeneity and Firm Delocation

To explore the trade-offs associated with regulatory harmonization that are suggested by the considerations in Lamy (2015, 2016) and Sykes (1999a, 1999b), Grossman, McCalman, and Staiger extend the model of trade in differentiated products from Venables (1987) to allow for a second dimension of differentiation for each brand. It is along this second dimension of differentiation that countries are assumed to have "collective preferences," the term used by Lamy (2016) to refer to valuations that reflect countries' idiosyncratic local conditions, incomes, and cultures. And it is when a firm caters to each country's collective preferences with multiple versions of a brand—either by its own

---

2. Grossman, McCalman, and Staiger refer to "new" versus "old" trade agreements rather than "deep" versus "shallow," in order to connect with Lamy's (2015, 2016) terminology and to reflect the particular focus on regulatory heterogeneity that their paper adopts. In describing their work here, I maintain the terminology of deep versus shallow agreements that I have used throughout the book.

profit-maximizing calculations or in order to conform to distinct regulatory standards in each market—that its fixed cost of serving multiple
markets is assumed to rise.

In particular, representing the utility of the N^J identical consumers
in country $J \in \{H, F\}$ with the quasi-linear utility function

$$U^J = 1 + C_Y^J + \log\left(C_D^J\right) , \quad J \in \{H, F\}, \tag{11.1}$$

where C_Y^J is per-capita consumption of a homogeneous good Y in
country J and C_D^J is a sub-utility index for per-capita consumption
of differentiated products, Grossman, McCalman, and Staiger assume
that the goods in the bundle C_D^J bear two distinct characteristics. One
characteristic makes each brand unique and ensures that every pair of
brands is a constant-elasticity-of-substitution (CES) substitute, with an
elasticity of substitution greater than one so that consumers prefer variety. The other characteristic of a brand determines the local evaluation
of the version of the brand sold in each country. This second characteristic is captured with the parameter a_i^J, which positions the variant
of brand i sold in country J along some finite segment of the real line,
$[a_{\min}, a_{\max}]$. With c_i^J denoting the representative individual's consumption of brand i in country J, Grossman, McCalman, and Staiger assume
that the sub-utility index C_D^J then takes the form

$$C_D^J = \left\{ \sum_{i \in \Theta^J} A\left(a_i^J, \gamma^J\right) \left(c_i^J\right)^\beta \right\}^{\frac{1}{\beta}} , \quad J \in \{H, F\}, \tag{11.2}$$

with $A\left(a_i^J, \gamma^J\right) > 0$ for all $a \in [a_{\min}, a_{\max}]$, $\gamma^H > \gamma^F$ and $\beta \in (0, 1)$, and
where Θ^J represents the set of brands available in country J. The func-
tion $A\left(a_i^J, \gamma^J\right)$ is assumed to be log-supermodular with $A_{aa}\left(a_i^J, \gamma^J\right) <$
0 for all a_i^J and γ^J. According to the formulation in (11.2), $A_i^J \equiv$
$A\left(a_i^J, \gamma^J\right)$ acts as a "demand shifter," where γ^J is a parameter describing the local economic or social conditions in country J that are relevant
for evaluation of the good. And as Grossman, McCalman, and Staiger
describe, this formulation is general enough to be consistent with
both horizontal and vertical differentiation of the different versions of
brand i.

Maximizing the utility in (11.1) subject to a budget constraint gives
the per-capita demand for brand i in country J, which, with good Y

designated as the numeraire, is given by

$$c_i^J = \left(A_i^J\right)^{\sigma} \left(p_i^J\right)^{-\sigma} \left(P^J\right)^{\sigma-1}, J \in \{H, F\},$$ (11.3)

where p_i^J is the price of brand i in country J and where P^J is the price index associated with (11.2), which takes the form

$$P^J \equiv \left[\sum_{i \in \Theta^J} \left(A_i^J\right)^{\sigma} \left(p_i^J\right)^{1-\sigma}\right]^{-\frac{1}{\sigma-1}}, J \in \{H, F\},$$ (11.4)

with $\sigma = 1/(1-\beta)$ the elasticity of substitution between every pair of brands. The aggregate demand for brand i by the N^J identical consumers in country J is $N^J c_i^J$, and the indirect utility of the representative consumer is

$$V\left(P^J, I^J\right) = I^J - \log P^J, \quad J \in \{H, F\},$$ (11.5)

where I^J is per-capita disposable income in country J.

Turning to supply, Grossman, McCalman, and Staiger assume that the numeraire good Y is always produced in both countries and freely traded between them, with a technology that turns one unit of labor into one unit of numeraire and hence fixes the common wage rate across countries at one. The differentiated product industry, by contrast, has a free-entry monopolistic competition structure. To enter this industry, a firm pays a fixed cost in units of labor that depends on its design choices for the versions of its brand that it offers in each market, according to the function $F_i \equiv F(|a_i^H - a_i^F|)$ with $F(0) > 0$, $F'(\cdot) > 0$ and $F''(\cdot) \geq 0$. Hence, firms in the differentiated product industry face lower fixed costs of serving multiple markets when they sell versions of their brand across these markets that are closer together in the relevant characteristic space, consistent with the possibility of cost savings that could come from regulatory harmonization. Once the fixed costs have been paid, a firm faces constant marginal costs. In particular, a firm i producing a version of its brand with characteristic a_i uses $\lambda(a_i)$ units of labor per unit of output, with $\lambda'(a_i) \geq 0$; in the case of horizontal differentiation across the brand versions, $\lambda'(a_i) \equiv 0$ so that all versions cost the same to produce, while with vertical differentiation $\lambda'(a_i) > 0$ so that higher quality costs more.[3]

---

3. Grossman, McCalman, and Staiger also impose some additional structure on the marginal cost function to ensure that second-order conditions hold.

As in Venables (1987), firms face both iceberg transport costs $(1 + v$ units must be shipped for delivery of one unit) and ad valorem trade taxes (with τ^J denoting the tax/subsidy imposed on imports by country J and e_J denoting the tax/subsidy on goods exiting country J's ports).[4] The variable trade costs faced by a firm located in country J are then summarized by ι_J where

$$\iota_J = 1 + v + e_J + \tau^K$$

and where I will adopt the convention that K refers to the country that is "not J." Each government J is also assumed to have at its disposal an ad valorem consumption subsidy, s^J, that it can use to address the monopoly-markup distortion in the differentiated product sector that is known to arise in settings such as this (Helpman and Krugman 1989, 137–145). Hence, if firm i located in country J sets a (common) factory-gate price q_i, then consumers in country J pay $p_i^J = (1 - s^J)q_i$ per unit for this product while consumers in country K pay $p_i^K = (1 - s^K)\iota_J q_i$.

For any given product characteristics, Grossman, McCalman, and Staiger show that profit-maximizing firms in the differentiated product sector will adopt familiar markup pricing behavior, which in this particular setting leads to the f.o.b. price for the version of brand i produced in country J and destined for country J' of

$$q_{iJ}^{J'} = \frac{\sigma}{\sigma - 1} \lambda \left(a_{iJ}^{J'} \right), J = H, F \text{ and } J' = H, F. \tag{11.6}$$

The consumer price of a typical local brand in country J is then

$$p_J^J = \left(1 - s^J \right) q_J^J, J = H, F, \tag{11.7}$$

while the consumer price of an imported brand in country J is

$$p_K^J = \left(1 - s^J \right) \iota_K q_K^J, J = H, F. \tag{11.8}$$

Finally, defining the "world" price of the exports from country J, p_J^w, as the offshore price after export taxes have been collected but before transport costs, import tariffs, and consumption subsidies have been imposed, it follows that $p_J^w \equiv (1 + e_J) q_J^K$. Notice that world prices

---

4. In what follows I adopt the convention that country superscripts refer to the destination country and thus to variables or parameters related to demand, whereas country subscripts refer to the source country and thus to variables or parameters related to supply. I will sometimes apply both a subscript and a superscript to distinguish a good that is produced in one country and exported to the other.

are independent of any horizontal characteristics of the differentiated products because the marginal cost function $\lambda(\cdot)$ is constant across horizontally differentiated versions and hence q_j^K is a constant according to (11.6). And in the case of vertical characteristics, equation (11.6) implies that world prices will rise one-for-one with the costs of the characteristics embodied in a brand supplied to a market, and hence the cost of vertical standards are completely passed through to consumers in the importing country.

For these reasons, in this model governments cannot use their regulatory policies (or their consumption subsidies or import tariffs, since world prices are independent of these) to manipulate world prices. This allows Grossman, McCalman, and Staiger to ignore market access/terms-of-trade manipulation concerns associated with the choice of standards and to focus instead on the delocation motives for standard setting that are novel in this setting.[5]

I now turn to the firm's choice of product design for the versions of its brand that it will sell in each market. Firms may be constrained in this choice by government regulations of course, but for now I consider the choices a firm would make if it had free rein over these choices. Firm i located in country J chooses a_{iJ}^J and a_{iJ}^K so as to maximize its overall profits taking the price index in each country as given and pricing its own brand according to (11.6). Its profits are given by

$$\pi_{iJ} = [q_{iJ}^J - \lambda(a_{iJ}^J)]N^J c_{iJ}^J + [q_{iJ}^K - \lambda(a_{iJ}^K)](1+v)N^K c_{iJ}^K - F\left(\left|a_{iJ}^J - a_{iJ}^K\right|\right),$$

which using (11.3) and (11.6) through (11.8) can be written as

$$\pi_{iJ} = \sigma^{-\sigma}(\sigma-1)^{\sigma-1} \times \left[N^J \left(1 - s^J\right)^{-\sigma} A^J \left(a_{iJ}^J\right)^\sigma \lambda \left(a_{iJ}^J\right)^{1-\sigma} \left(P^J\right)^{\sigma-1} \right.$$

$$\left. + (1+v) N^K \left(1 - s^K\right)^{-\sigma} \iota_J^{-\sigma} A^K \left(a_{iJ}^K\right)^\sigma \lambda \left(a_{iJ}^K\right)^{1-\sigma} \left(P^K\right)^{\sigma-1} \right]$$

$$- F\left(\left|a_{iJ}^J - a_{iJ}^K\right|\right). \tag{11.9}$$

---

5. Bagwell and Staiger (2015) have shown in the Venables (1987) model that the delocation incentive with regard to trade taxes can be given a terms-of-trade interpretation, but only as long as governments have at their disposal a complete set of trade tax instruments (and in particular export tax/subsidies). As will become clear below, the thought experiment considered by Grossman, McCalman, and Staiger is to suppose that trade taxes have been constrained by an existing trade agreement and to then ask whether the regulatory choices of governments must also be constrained to achieve an efficient level of regulatory harmonization, along the lines articulated by Lamy (2015, 2016).

If it were maximizing its operating profits alone, firm i could ignore the last term in (11.9), and this would allow it to choose a^J_{ij} and a^K_{ij} so as to best serve each market separately, yielding $a^H_{ij} = \hat{a}^H$ and $a^F_{ij} = \hat{a}^F$, where $\hat{a}^J \equiv \arg\max_a A^J(a)^\sigma \lambda(a)^{1-\sigma}$, and implying by the log-supermodularity of A and for $\gamma^H > \gamma^F$ that $\hat{a}^H > \hat{a}^F$. As Grossman, McCalman, and Staiger observe, $\hat{a}^J$ also happens to be the "ideal version" in the eyes of consumers in country J, considering both the direct effect on utility and the indirect effect on prices.[6] But in light of the fixed costs captured in the last term in (11.9), firms will not deliver the ideal version to any market when they have free rein over their choice of product characteristics. This is because a small reduction in a^H_{ij} below $\hat{a}^H$, which is the ideal level for country-H consumers, would generate only a second-order loss in operating profits for firm i but a first-order savings in design costs, and the same would happen for a small increase in a^F_{ij} above $\hat{a}^F$. Reflecting this logic, the unregulated firm i maximizes its profits by choosing versions of its brand that satisfy $\hat{a}^H > a^H_{ij} > a^F_{ij} > \hat{a}^F$. With all firms in a country making the same design choices and earning the same profits according to (11.9), I now drop the firm-i subscripts and denote by $\tilde{a}^H_J$ and $\tilde{a}^F_J$ the optimal, unregulated characteristic of a brand that is offered for sale in the home and foreign markets, respectively, and produced in country J.

Whatever the regulatory regime, free entry will ensure that in equilibrium, π_J is nonpositive for each J when evaluated at the equilibrium price indexes, and these free-entry conditions determine the equilibrium number of brands, n_J, produced in each country J. If each country produces a strictly positive number of brands in equilibrium, then the pair of zero-profit conditions $\pi_H = 0 = \pi_F$ must hold; otherwise, for some J, $n_J = 0$ and $\pi_J \leq 0$. Grossman, McCalman, and Staiger establish three properties that must hold in the "unregulated equilibrium" where governments place no constraints on the choices of characteristics, provided that trade taxes and consumption subsidies are such that $\iota_H > 1$ and $\iota_F > 1$.

First, the profit-maximizing choices of product characteristics are such that $\hat{a}^H > \tilde{a}^H_H > \tilde{a}^H_F$ and $\tilde{a}^F_H > \tilde{a}^F_F > \hat{a}^F$. Intuitively, while no firm

---

6. If the versions of the brand are horizontally differentiated, then we have $\lambda'(a_i) \equiv 0$, and the ideal version will simply maximize the demand shifter. With vertical differentiation, $\lambda'(a_i) > 0$ and the ideal reflects not only the local taste for higher quality, but also the recognition that quality comes at a cost.

delivers the ideal version of its brand to any market ($\hat{a}^H > \tilde{a}_H^H$ and $\tilde{a}_F^F > \hat{a}^F$), when $\iota_H > 1$ and $\iota_F > 1$, each firm makes a relatively greater share of its sales in its local market, so it is firms located in country H that have the relatively greater incentive to cater to country-H consumers ($\tilde{a}_H^H > \tilde{a}_F^H$), while it is firms located in country F that have the relatively greater incentive to cater to country-F consumers ($\tilde{a}_H^F > \tilde{a}_F^F$).

Second, beginning at the optimal unregulated product characteristics, a small increase in any product characteristic $a_J^{J'}$ induces exit by firms located in country H ($dn_H / da_J^{J'} < 0$) and entry by firms located in country F ($dn_F / da_J^{J'} > 0$) for all $J \in \{H, F\}$ and $J' \in \{H, F\}$. To see why, consider the case where $J' = H$. Starting from the optimal unregulated product characteristics, a small increase in a_J^H has no first-order effect on profits at the initial price indexes, but for fixed n_H and n_F it will reduce the country-H price index P^H directly because a_J^H moves in the direction of the country-H ideal version $\hat{a}^H$. This leads to negative profits for all firms, but given the relative dependence of the firms located in country H on country-H sales, it hurts the firms located in country H more than it hurts firms located in country F, and the only way to bring back zero profits for all firms is for firms located in country H to exit while firms located in country F enter. A similar intuition holds for the case where $J' = F$.

And third, beginning at the optimal unregulated product characteristics, a small change in any product characteristic $a_J^{J'}$ has no first-order effect on the home price index ($dP^H / da_J^{J'} = 0$) or on the foreign price index ($dP^F / da_J^{J'} = 0$), for $J \in \{H, F\}$ and $J' \in \{H, F\}$. In other words, the changes in n_H and n_F described above that are induced by a small change in $a_J^{J'}$ are such that the price indexes P^H and P^F are left unchanged. This is because, starting from the optimal unregulated product characteristics, a small change in $a_J^{J'}$ has no first-order effect on profits anywhere at the initial price indexes, and so the zero-profit conditions will be maintained if entry and exit is such that the price indexes P^H and P^F remain unchanged.

How is welfare measured in this model? In (11.5) the indirect utility of the representative consumer in country J is defined by $V(P^J, I^J) = I^J - \log P^J$; now it remains to define I^J, the per-capita disposable income in country J. But as the free-entry conditions ensure that equilibrium profits are zero everywhere, the per-capita disposable income in country J is simply the sum of country J's per-capita labor income, which is constant and given by L^J/N^J, and per-capita net tax revenue, R^J, which Grossman, McCalman, and Staiger show is given by

$$R^J = \frac{\sigma}{\sigma-1}\left(\tau^J N^J n_K \lambda_K^J c_K^J + e_J N^K n_J \lambda_J^K c_J^K\right) - N^J \frac{s^J}{1-s^J},$$

where $\lambda_J^{J'} \equiv \lambda\left(a_J^{J'}\right)$ and where I have omitted the functional dependence of the equilibrium numbers of firms and the consumption levels on the tax rates and the product characteristics induced by the regulatory regime.

This allows aggregate national welfare in country J, Ω^J, to be written as

$$\Omega^J = L^J + \frac{\sigma}{\sigma-1}\left(\tau^J N^J n_K \lambda_K^J c_K^J + e_J N^K n_J \lambda_J^K c_J^K\right) - N^J \frac{s^J}{1-s^J} - N^J \log P^J.$$

(11.10)

And world welfare, $\Omega \equiv \Omega^H + \Omega^F$, can then be written as

$$\Omega = \sum_J L^J + \sum_J z^J N^J n_K \frac{\sigma}{\sigma-1}\lambda_K^J c_K^J - \sum_J N^J \log P^J - \sum_J N^J \frac{s^J}{1-s^J},$$

(11.11)

where $z^J \equiv \tau^J + e_K$ is the net trade tax on goods exported from K to J. As usual, since the prices of imported goods in J do not depend separately on τ^J and e_K but only on the net trade tax, z^J, it follows that the consumption levels c_K^J and the price index P^J also depend only on z^J, as do the profit-maximizing characteristics in any regulatory regime and the equilibrium numbers of brands. And this implies the by-now-familiar property that global welfare depends on the choices of z^H and z^F and not on the particular combination of import tariff and export tax that are used to achieve these net taxes.

11.2 Mutual Recognition When Consumption Externalities Are Absent

In the setting I have described, where consumption externalities are absent, Grossman, McCalman, and Staiger show that firms' profit-maximizing choices of product attributes are globally optimal, but national governments have unilateral incentives to invoke regulatory protectionism to induce firm delocation as in Venables (1987) and Ossa

(2011). But they also show that shallow integration is still possible: If tariffs are negotiated to efficient levels, and if consumption subsidies must conform to national treatment and hence must be offered by a country on a nondiscriminatory basis for the consumption of all differentiated products regardless of origin, then a rule requiring mutual recognition of standards can be used to achieve efficiency with a shallow form of integration, though shallow integration that relies only on national treatment would fall short.

To explain these results, I consider first the efficiency of firms' profit-maximizing choices of product attributes in the unregulated equilibrium and the unilateral incentive governments have to delocate foreign firms with regulatory protectionism. This can be understood with the help of figure 11.1. To construct this figure, I set net tariffs and consumption subsidies at their efficient levels $z^{He} = 0 = z^{Fe}$ and $s^{He} = 1/\sigma = s^{Fe}$, respectively, where as before a superscript "e" denotes an efficient magnitude, and I position product attributes at the profit-maximizing levels that firms would choose in an unregulated equilibrium when net tariffs and consumption subsidies are set in this way. That there is an efficiency role for a consumption subsidy in each country and that it is inversely related to the elasticity of substitution between pairs of brands is not surprising, because it is well known that such a subsidy can correct the monopoly-markup distortion in the differentiated product sector of each country that arises in settings such as this. The absence of an efficiency role for tariff intervention should also come as no surprise. But notice from (11.11) that with tax/subsidies set in this efficient fashion, world welfare is then given by

$$\Omega = \sum_J L^J - \sum_J N^J \log P^J - \sum_J N^J \frac{1}{\sigma - 1} \tag{11.12}$$

and depends only on P^H and P^F. Therefore, figure 11.1, with N^H $(P^H)^{\sigma-1}$ and $N^F (P^F)^{\sigma-1}$ on the axes, has all the information needed to assess world welfare and hence the efficiency properties of a given set of product attributes.

The combinations of $N^H (P^H)^{\sigma-1}$ and $N^F (P^F)^{\sigma-1}$ that are consistent with zero profits for home firms are given by the downward-sloping line labeled $\pi_H = 0$, while the combinations of $N^H (P^H)^{\sigma-1}$ and $N^F (P^F)^{\sigma-1}$ that are consistent with zero profits for foreign firms are given by the downward-sloping line labeled $\pi_F = 0$. That these lines are downward sloping reflects the fact that a lower price index in one

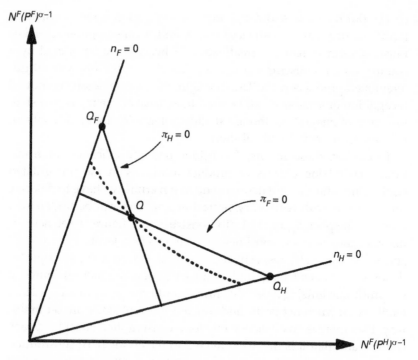

Figure 11.1
The unilateral incentive for regulatory protectionism. *Source*: Reproduced from Grossman, McCalman, and Staiger (2021, figure 1).

market makes that market more competitive and reduces firm profits there, and for a firm to maintain zero profits, this must be offset by a higher price index in the other market. And as drawn, the $\pi_H = 0$ line must be steeper than the $\pi_F = 0$ line, reflecting the relative importance of the local market for firms of each country that comes from positive trade impediments.

Figure 11.1 also depicts the combinations of $N^H \left(P^H \right)^{\sigma-1}$ and $N^F \left(P^F \right)^{\sigma-1}$ that are consistent with $n_H > 0$ and $n_F > 0$—namely, the combinations that lie inside the cone defined by the rays from the origin labeled $n_H = 0$ and $n_F = 0$. These rays can be derived from the expressions for P^F and P^H, and they depict the combinations of $N^H \left(P^H \right)^{\sigma-1}$ and $N^F \left(P^F \right)^{\sigma-1}$ for which the world's production of differentiated products would be concentrated in one country or the other—country H along the ray labeled $n_F = 0$ and country F along the ray labeled $n_H = 0$. For combinations of $N^H \left(P^H \right)^{\sigma-1}$ and $N^F \left(P^F \right)^{\sigma-1}$

inside the cone, both countries have an active differentiated product sector, and in that case, equilibrium requires $\pi_H = 0$ and $\pi_F = 0$. Such an equilibrium is depicted in figure 11.1 by the point labeled Q, where the two zero-profit lines intersect. This implies that the unregulated equilibrium has active producers in the differentiated-product sectors of both countries.[7]

Finally, figure 11.1 depicts the iso-world-welfare curve passing through the unregulated equilibrium point Q, as implied by equation (11.12). This curve is globally convex, and when Q falls inside the cone defined by $n_H = 0$ and $n_F = 0$, its slope lies between the slope of the $\pi_H = 0$ line and that of the $\pi_F = 0$ line. World welfare is increasing for lower iso-world-welfare curves that lie closer to the origin.

To see that firms' profit-maximizing choices of product attributes are globally optimal when coupled with zero net trade taxes and markup-offsetting consumption subsidies, recall that beginning at the optimal unregulated product characteristics, a small change in any product characteristic $a_J^{J'}$ has no first-order effect on the home price index $(dP^H/da_J^{J'} = 0)$ or on the foreign price index $(dP^F/da_J^{J'} = 0)$ for $J \in \{H, F\}$ and $J' \in \{H, F\}$. But by (11.12), this means that when trade taxes and consumption subsidies are set at their efficient levels and beginning at the optimal unregulated product characteristics, the first-order conditions for maximizing Ω are satisfied at Q; and Grossman, McCalman, and Staiger show that the second-order conditions are globally met at Q as well.

The upshot is that if net tariffs are set to their efficient level of zero, and if consumption subsidies are set at their markup-offsetting levels, then the unregulated profit-maximizing firm choices of product attributes will deliver the world to the efficiency frontier. What kind of a trade agreement can deliver this outcome? Grossman, McCalman, and Staiger show that the agreement will have to constrain tariffs to efficient levels, consistent with the earlier findings of Venables (1987), Ossa (2011), and Bagwell and Staiger (2015). They also show that the level of consumption subsidies need not be constrained by an agreement, as long as the agreement specifies that these subsidies satisfy national treatment and are therefore offered by a country on a nondiscriminatory basis for the consumption of all differentiated products regardless

7. I will restrict my discussion here to nonspecialized equilibria of this kind, but Grossman, McCalman, and Staiger discuss the full set of equilibrium possibilities.

of origin.[8] In terms of figure 11.1, this property reflects the fact that a nondiscriminatory deviation from the efficient consumption subsidy level initiated by one country will shift both the $\pi_H = 0$ line and the $\pi_F = 0$ line in a way that leaves the price index of the other country—and hence the welfare of the other country—unchanged; and with the consumption subsidy initially positioned at the efficient level, the first country cannot benefit from this deviation if the welfare of the second country does not fall.

How should product standards be handled in a trade agreement? Figure 11.1 makes clear that they cannot simply be left out of the agreement. Consider, for example, the incentives that country H has to impose product regulations if it has free rein to do so, noting that any regulation that requires firms to adopt a discretely different product characteristic than their profit-maximizing choice will reduce their profits. If country H were to regulate its own firms' offerings in the local market by requiring that a_H^H differ discretely from the profit-maximizing choice $\tilde{a}_H^H$, then the $\pi_H = 0$ line in figure 11.1 would shift out, leading to a rise in P^H (once the firm entry and exit needed to restore zero profits for all firms had occurred) and therefore to a fall in country-H welfare. A similar result would occur if country H were to regulate a_H^F, the product attribute that its firms chose for sales in the foreign market. Clearly, country H therefore has no incentive to regulate its own firms. But, if country H were to regulate the offerings of foreign firms in its local market by requiring that a_F^H differ discretely from the profit-maximizing choice $\tilde{a}_F^H$, then the $\pi_F = 0$ line in figure 11.1 would shift to the right, leading to a rise in P^F but a *fall* in P^H once the firm entry and exit needed to restore zero profits for all firms had occurred, and therefore to a rise in country-H welfare at the expense of the welfare of country F. In effect, by regulating foreign firms in its market, a country can diminish the profits of foreign firms and cause the exit of firms in the foreign country, triggering entry of firms in the home country as a result of the reduction in world wide competition. The resulting "firm delocation" is beneficial to the country that acquires more local firms, owing to the savings on trade costs that is implied.[9]

---

8. This property also reflects the fact that, as I mentioned earlier, in the model of Grossman, McCalman, and Staiger consumption subsidies cannot be used to manipulate the terms of trade.

9. As Grossman, McCalman, and Staiger observe, in addition to the firm delocation incentive there is also a "product suitability" effect that helps drive the incentive to

Grossman, McCalman, and Staiger show that, if left unchecked, these incentives would lead countries to impose extreme product standards on their imported products that, in the Nash equilibrium of a noncooperative standard-setting game, would result in product standards that imply inefficiently high design costs for firms attempting to serve multiple markets. By implication, a trade agreement that led countries from this starting point to the efficiency frontier would therefore indeed result in regulatory convergence, consistent with the views expressed by Lamy (2015, 2016), if by that term what is meant is an agreement that calls for changes in product standards across countries that reduce firms' total design costs. The remaining question is how to design an agreement that would achieve the needed convergence in product standards and deliver countries to the efficiency frontier. Is there anything short of deep integration (i.e., negotiating directly over product standards) that would do the trick?

It might be thought that an extension of the national treatment rule that would apply not only to consumption subsidies but also to product standards (as is true of the national treatment requirement in the GATT/WTO) might be sufficient to prevent the kind of regulatory protectionism that I have just described and, in so doing, allow governments to reach the efficiency frontier with a shallow approach to integration. But Grossman, McCalman, and Staiger show that, while better than nothing, reliance on the national treatment rule would fall short in this regard. As they note, there are two problems with such an approach.

First, if the national treatment rule were interpreted as requiring that the same product standard applied to local firms in a market must also apply to the sales of foreign firms in that market, then efficiency could not be achieved because the efficient product characteristics in a given market are different for local and foreign firms, with efficiency dictating that the product attributes of the former should be closer to the local ideal than those of the latter. Suppose, then, that the national treatment rule is interpreted more broadly and allows governments to announce a *set* of permissible standards, requiring only that all firms selling in a given market must be confronted with the same set of standards to choose from in that market. This leads to the second problem:

---

deviate from efficient standards in their model. However, as they note in their online appendix, the product suitability motive may or may not be operative on the margin in the Nash equilibrium, but the delocation motive always is operative, which is why I emphasize that motive in the text.

As Grossman, McCalman, and Staiger demonstrate, if firms selling to a market were offered a common set of standards from which to choose, all firms would choose the standard meant to apply to local firms in that market (and hence the less-distortionary standard), and therefore welfare can be no higher than what is achievable under a single standard for each country, which we already know cannot achieve efficiency.

As it turns out, what *would* allow a shallow-integration approach to work in this setting is a so-called mutual recognition clause of the sort included, for example, in the customs treaty of the European Union. Under this clause, each country agrees to respect the legitimacy of the other's regulatory aims, and any product that meets the standards in an exporting country is therefore considered acceptable for sale in the importing country as well. Under mutual recognition, then, exporting firms have a choice of whether to meet the standards in the destination market or those in their own country. As Grossman, McCalman, and Staiger demonstrate, a rule requiring mutual recognition of standards can be used to achieve efficiency with shallow integration in this setting.

To see this, suppose that, as above, countries negotiate tariffs to efficient levels and require that consumption subsidies satisfy national treatment, but now also include in the agreement a mutual recognition clause for product standards. Subsequent to the agreement, countries are then allowed to set their consumption subsidies and choose their product standards unilaterally as they see fit, subject to these rules. As before, with tariffs constrained to efficient levels and $z^{He} = 0 = z^{Fe}$, neither country will have any incentive to deviate from adopting an efficient consumption subsidy, with the result that the two governments will also implement the efficient consumption subsidies $s^{He} = 1/\sigma = s^{Fe}$.

But now, in the ensuing standard-setting game with mutual recognition, each government maintains a degree of control over the standards under which its own firms must operate, since its firms can always choose to operate everywhere under the standards that the government sets. In particular, as long as governments are allowed to choose multiple acceptable standards (or a range of acceptable standards), then in the Nash equilibrium of this standard-setting game, each government will choose as permissible standards for its market the (pair of) standards that would maximize the profits of its representative national firm, because by mutual recognition its firms can then produce to (their choice among) these standards in each of the markets that they serve.

In terms of figure 11.1, these choices are optimal for each government because they allow each government to position the zero-profit line applicable to its firms—the only zero-profit line that it has control over in the presence of the mutual recognition clause—at its lowest level possible.

Evidently, under national treatment for taxes and mutual recognition for product standards and with tariff negotiations alone, a trade agreement can achieve the degree of regulatory harmonization needed to replicate the unregulated equilibrium. And in this way, governments can in principle still arrive at the efficiency frontier with a shallow approach to integration—though an approach that relies on mutual recognition of product standards and therefore differs in important ways from current GATT/WTO practice—despite the presence of the kinds of international externalities that can arise with regulatory heterogeneity as Lamy (2015, 2016) emphasized and that may nonetheless be justified by cross-country differences in collective preferences as noted by Sykes (1999a, 1999b).[10]

11.3 Deep Integration in the Presence of Consumption Externalities

The findings of Grossman, McCalman, and Staiger lend support to the efficacy of a form of shallow integration even when a degree of regulatory harmonization is desirable, but these findings are derived under the assumption that there are no externalities associated with consumption—an assumption that underpins the property of the model that, given free rein, firms would choose the "right" product attributes. A remaining question is whether the support for shallow integration provided by these findings extends to a setting where consumption externalities are present.

As Grossman, McCalman, and Staiger observe, introducing consumption externalities into the model will naturally introduce scope

---

10. Grossman, McCalman, and Staiger observe that the mutual recognition clause of the European Union includes a stipulation that the clause can be invoked by an exporter only if a similar good is "lawfully marketed" in its local market. If this term is interpreted as a minimum sales requirement, then the stipulation would interfere with the efficiency properties of mutual recognition, according to the arguments I have outlined. However, as Grossman, McCalman, and Staiger point out, the legal interpretation of this stipulation is unclear, and so the extent of the inefficiency that it creates according to their findings is also unclear.

for efficiency-enhancing product standards. For example, an individual's utility might be a function not only of how close the products that the person consumes are to an idealized version but also how close the products consumed by this person's fellow nationals come to this ideal. This is an externality associated with consumption that the sub-utility index c_D^J defined in (11.2) does not allow, but it is the kind of externality that might arise in the context of safety features that are embodied in the cars on the road in a given country, or when a product's health or environmental impact on a country depend on the country's collective choices. In a setting where such externalities are present, an efficiency-enhancing role for product standards naturally arises. The question, then, is whether in this setting the shallow approach to integration, or something like it, could continue to deliver governments to the efficiency frontier.

To capture these kinds of externalities, Grossman, McCalman, and Staiger introduce the following extended version of the sub-utility index defined in (11.2):

$$c_D^J = \left\{ \sum_{i \in \Theta^J} \left\{ A^{*J} + \xi \left[A^J \left(a_i^J \right) - A^{*J} \right] \right\} \left(c_i^J \right)^\beta \right.$$

$$\left. + (1 - \xi) \left[A^J \left(a_i^J \right) - A^{*J} \right] \left(c_{i\mu}^J \right)^\beta \right\}^{\frac{1}{\beta}}, \quad 0 < \xi < 1, J = \{H, F\}.$$

$$(11.13)$$

In (11.13), $A^{*J} \equiv \max_{a_i^J \in [a_{\min}, a_{\max}]} A^J \left(a_i^J \right)$ is the demand shifter associated with the "idealized product type"—that is, the most appealing version of brand i to consumers in country J, regardless of price—and $c_{i\mu}^J$ denotes mean country-J consumption, while the parameter ξ measures (inversely) the extent of the consumption externality. When $\xi \to 1$, the expression for c_D^J in (11.13) converges to the original expression in (11.2), where consumers care only about the characteristics of brand i that they consume themselves and suffer a loss in utility to the extent that the version they themselves consume differs from their idealized product type. But when $\xi \to 0$, consumers care only negligibly about the particular types of goods that they purchase for themselves and almost entirely about the types of goods consumed in their country in the aggregate. In this case, the externality is extreme, as the consumer benefits the same from buying any version of a brand i, but loses utility when others in the country make purchases that are far from the consumer's idealized product type. Indeed, when $\xi \to 0$, the use-value to an individual is the same for all feasible versions of a brand, and so consumers ignore its negative attributes entirely when expressing their market demands.

Notice that, according to (11.13), the negative externality disappears when $a_i^J = a^{*J} \equiv \arg\max_a A^J(a)$ and the product attributes offered to country J coincide with country J's idealized product types. This allows Grossman, McCalman, and Staiger to abstract from spillovers that arise from consumption *per se*, and which give rise to the usual arguments for Pigouvian taxes, and focus instead on those associated with product type and that might motivate product standards.

Moreover, note that when $c_i^J = c_{i\mu}^J$ (as must be true in equilibrium with identical consumers in each country), the aggregate C_D^J is independent of ξ: That is, according to (11.13), as the parameter ξ drops from a value of 1, the equilibrium valuation that the representative consumer in country J places on deviations of the product attribute from a^{*J} is held constant while the fraction of this valuation that is attributable to the consumption of others is increased. This implies that the size of ξ does not affect the globally optimal product characteristics, consumption per brand, or numbers of home and foreign firms, which I have already described above for the case of $\xi = 1$ and which evidently apply also for any $\xi \in (0,1)$. For future reference, I now denote the globally optimal product attributes for goods produced in country J and sold in country J', which as I have just noted are simply the efficient product attributes for the case of $\xi = 1$ as characterized above, by $a_J^{J'e}$.

The upshot is that I now need only describe how the market equilibrium in the absence of corrective policies differs from the social optimum when $\xi < 1$, and then describe the set of policy interventions that will induce the social optimum. Armed with these results, I can then investigate the kind of trade agreement that would be capable of implementing those policy interventions and thereby deliver countries to the efficiency frontier in the presence of consumption externalities.

According to (11.13), each individual in country J now perceives the demand shifter $A_i^J \equiv (1 - \xi) A^{*J} + \xi A\left(a_i^J, \gamma^J\right)$ when calculating their optimal purchases of brand i. This continues to generate the per-capita demands in (11.3), where the price index for differentiated products P^J continues to be computed as in (11.4). However, P^J—which I now refer to as the "*brand-level* price index"—no longer is the same as the price index that guides the allocation of spending to differentiated products, nor is it the price index that enters the indirect utility function in (11.5). Rather, as Grossman, McCalman, and Staiger show, in the presence of consumption externalities, the indirect utility function is now given by

$$V\left(\mathcal{P}^J, I^J\right) = I^J - \log \mathcal{P}^J, \quad J \in \{H, F\},$$

where

$$\mathcal{P}^J = \left[\frac{\sum_{i \in \Theta^J} \left(A_i^J\right)^\sigma \left(p_i^J\right)^{1-\sigma}}{\sum_{i \in \Theta^J} \left(\frac{\mathcal{A}_i^J}{A_i^J}\right) \left(A_i^J\right)^\sigma \left(p_i^J\right)^{1-\sigma}} \right]^{\frac{\sigma}{\sigma-1}} P^J \qquad (11.14)$$

and $\mathcal{A}_i^J \equiv A\left(a_i^J, \gamma^J\right)$ is the demand shifter that accounts for the externalities.

I will follow Grossman, McCalman, and Staiger and refer to $\mathcal{P}^J$ as the *"industry-level* price index." When $\xi = 1$ we have $A_i^J = \mathcal{A}_i^J$, and it then follows from (11.14) that $\mathcal{P}^J = P^J$ and the industry-level and brand-level price indexes coincide. But the presence of consumption externalities ($\xi < 1$) implies that $A_i^J > \mathcal{A}_i^J$ and therefore, by (11.14), that $\mathcal{P}^J > P^J$: The industry-level price index that determines aggregate spending on differentiated products as a group is greater than the brand-level price index that guides individual consumption choices at the variety level. This implies that each consumer spends less on the bundle of differentiated goods as a whole than the consumer would facing the same prices but with no externalities, reflecting the fact that the negative externalities reduce consumer enthusiasm for this bundle. At the same time, the externality causes a *relative* distortion of consumption across brands, away from varieties whose characteristics are closer to a^{*J} and toward those whose characteristics are relatively far from a^{*J}. In other words, individuals over consume inferior goods when they ignore the externalities that their consumption choices confer on others.

As Grossman, McCalman, and Staiger demonstrate, these additional consumption distortions imply that there are new roles for trade policy and consumption tax policy in the presence of consumption externalities. In particular, global efficiency now requires $z^H > 0$ and $s^H > 1/\sigma$. Further, it requires $z^F > 0$ and $s^F > 1/\sigma$ if versions of a brand are horizontally differentiated but $z^F < 0$ and $s^F < 1/\sigma$ if versions of a brand are vertically differentiated.

Intuitively, and recalling that the efficient product attributes $a_J^{J'e}$ are the same as those in the absence of consumption externalities and therefore satisfy $a^{*H} > a_H^{He} > a_F^{He}$ in the market of country H, the goal of efficient tax policy intervention is to confront country-H consumers with prices that lead them to shift consumption toward locally produced brands and away from imports, owing to the greater (negative) externality associated with the consumption of imports implied by $a^{*H} > a_H^{He} > a_F^{He}$. A positive net import tariff ($z^H > 0$) can achieve this goal when it is combined with a country-H consumption subsidy greater than the level needed to offset the monopoly-markup distortion ($s^H > 1/\sigma$): The larger subsidy generates extra demand for local brands, while the combined consumption subsidy and net trade tax discourage consumption of imported brands. If brands are horizontally differentiated, analogous arguments applied to country F explain why efficiency also requires $z^F > 0$ and $s^F > 1/\sigma$; and if brands are vertically differentiated, then the negative externality is strictly decreasing in the characteristic that measures product quality, and it is the consumption of local brands in country F with their lower quality that confer the greater negative externalities and must be discouraged, which can be accomplished with $z^F < 0$ and $s^F < 1/\sigma$.

What about the regulation of product characteristics? Recall that in the absence of consumption externalities, no regulation of product characteristics is needed because the characteristics that firms would choose to maximize their profits coincide with the efficient characteristics. But as I have noted, when $\zeta < 1$ and consumption externalities are present, consumers are insufficiently sensitive to the negative attributes of a product that deviates from the idealized type when expressing their market demands. And so, if given free rein to respond to market demands, firms in both countries will insufficiently differentiate the local and export versions of their brands compared to what is globally efficient. Regulation is therefore now needed to ensure efficient product designs, with the optimal standards inducing firms to design products closer to the idealized product type in each destination market compared to their profit-maximizing choices.

Having described the set of policy interventions that induce the social optimum, I now want to consider the kind of trade agreement that would be capable of implementing these policy interventions and thereby capable of delivering countries to the efficiency frontier in the presence of consumption externalities. A first observation is immediate: Shallow integration based on mutual recognition cannot implement efficient product standards in the presence of consumption externalities.[11] This much is clear, once it is recalled that in the absence of consumption externalities, a mutual recognition clause works because it allows governments to provide their own firms with the ability to choose profit-maximizing product standards in all markets— which in the absence of consumption externalities are, after all, the efficient product attributes—and both governments and their firms have incentive to make these efficient selections. But as I have noted, when consumption externalities are present the product characteristics chosen by profit-maximizing firms are inefficient; in fact, as Grossman, McCalman, and Staiger observe, neither firms nor their governments would have incentive to select efficient product standards under mutual recognition in this case. Hence, the logic of mutual recognition as a rule for implementing efficient product standards breaks down when consumption externalities are present.

Is there an alternative approach to shallow integration with respect to product standards that could work in this setting? As I have reviewed in previous chapters, the non-violation clause, at least in principle, has been shown to be a versatile tool for facilitating shallow integration in many settings when other rules are insufficient to do the job, providing governments with a last-resort "market access preservation rule." But as Grossman, McCalman, and Staiger observe, reliance on the non-violation clause for this purpose, even in a potentially modified version, appears especially challenging in the current setting.

To see why, recall that the core feature of the non-violation clause is that in its presence, country K is insulated from the effects of any unilateral behind-the-border policy adjustments that country J might consider once an agreement on border measures has been signed between K and J—a feature that naturally leads country J to make such policy choices efficiently. As I have described in previous chapters, according to the terms-of-trade theory of trade agreements, this insulation is accomplished with a non-violation clause that is built around a simple concept of market access and where the terms of trade are preserved under any post-agreement behind-the-border policy adjustments made by country J that are consistent with this clause. For a non-violation clause to work in the present setting, then, the allowable unilateral policy adjustments of country J must, under the non-violation clause, preserve the welfare of country K, $V\left(\mathcal{P}^K, I^K\right)$.

---

11. Costinot (2008) reports an analogous finding, though in a very different setting.

There are two challenges in specifying a workable non-violation clause in this setting. A first challenge arises whenever product standards are under consideration and relates to the fact that, unlike standards for workplace safety that impact the costs of domestic production or fiscal interventions such as tariffs and subsidies, product standards alter the nature of the goods to which the standards apply, and this complicates the interpretation of market access: Should it be concluded that market access is preserved as long as sales volume at the original exporter price would not be altered, even when foreign exporters are required to meet a new and higher product standard and, as a consequence, now face higher costs? Staiger and Sykes (2011, 2021) show in the context of the terms-of-trade theory that the non-violation clause can be applied to the case of product standards without further modification if market access is defined with reference to the exporter price of the "raw" unregulated product. But in the present setting, where it is regulatory heterogeneity across markets that raises costs and the fixed costs of market entry are affected by this heterogeneity, making reference to the exporter price of an unregulated product no longer does the job. In this case, it is not clear what alternative modifications to the non-violation clause would suffice.

A second challenge is due specifically to the presence of consumption externalities. If a non-violation clause is to succeed in the present setting at allowing country J to consider only those unilateral policy adjustments that would preserve the welfare of country K, then the clause will have to be sensitive to more than just market magnitudes. In particular, to ensure that $V\left(\mathcal{P}^{K}, I^{K}\right)$ is not altered by country J's behind-the-border policy adjustments, the non-violation clause must be sensitive to country K's *industry-level* price index $\mathcal{P}^{K}$, a sensitivity that, as (11.14) confirms, requires knowledge beyond the market magnitudes that determine the *brand-level* price index P^{K} and extends to detailed information about the consumption externalities in country K. In effect, while the consumption externalities themselves do not cross national borders by assumption, it is nevertheless the case that the choices of product attributes made by country-J firms will interact with the consumption externalities in country K, independent of the market magnitudes induced by these choices. Accordingly, this second challenge is in some sense more fundamental than the first, because it means that in the present setting a rule that ensures the preservation of market access—however defined—will not be enough to facilitate shallow integration.

11.4   The Push for Regulatory Convergence and the Design of the WTO

The findings of Grossman, McCalman, and Staiger (2021) reviewed above have several implications for the design of the WTO in a world where preferences are heterogeneous across countries and firms face higher costs when they tailor brand attributes to local tastes. Where consumption externalities exist and product standards have a clear role to play in addressing these externalities, the implications for the design of the WTO are most profound. In this case, and even when these externalities do not cross national borders, the WTO's shallow approach to integration is ill-equipped to orchestrate the degree of regulatory convergence that would be required to eliminate the inefficiencies associated with the unilateral choices of such standards. According to these findings, an efficient trade agreement must instead coordinate the fine details of such standards.

Where the existence of consumption externalities cannot be established, however, these findings suggest that less-fundamental changes to WTO design may be needed. Here, the finding that national treatment by itself would not be sufficient to allow countries to implement efficient product standards with shallow integration is not so different from the findings of Staiger and Sykes (2011, 2021), who report a similar result in the context of the terms-of-trade theory but argue that national treatment, when combined with a non-violation clause as a last-resort method of preventing terms-of-trade manipulation, can nevertheless lead to effective shallow integration. While in the present context the non-violation clause faces significant challenges when consumption externalities are present, these challenges are likely to be more manageable when externalities are absent and the second challenge enumerated above is not operative; in this case, a modified non-violation clause might arguably be combined with national treatment to facilitate efficient shallow integration, along the lines that Staiger and Sykes have suggested. Still, the findings reviewed above indicate that mutual recognition could be a particularly effective rule in this setting for achieving efficient product standards with shallow integration, suggesting that such an approach might be an attractive alternative for the WTO to consider.

Finally, it should be emphasized that product standards per se are not the issue here, nor is the issue simply the presence of externalities that can motivate the use of product standards. After all, as I noted in chapter 3, Staiger and Sykes (2011, 2021) have shown that the broad features of the GATT/WTO shallow approach to integration are well suited to allowing countries to achieve efficient product standards in the context of the terms-of-trade theory, and their results apply whether or not (local) externalities exist that can provide an efficiency rationale for such standards. Rather, it is in a world where preferences are heterogeneous across countries and firms face higher costs when they tailor their product attributes to local tastes, in combination with the presence of consumption externalities the size of which are determined by those product attributes, that the most serious potential problems of a shallow-integration approach to product standards have been shown by Grossman, McCalman, and Staiger to arise.

Taken together, these findings suggest that countries might negotiate selectively over product standards where externality problems are sufficiently severe and then rely on some combination of national treatment and the non-violation clause plus mutual recognition, perhaps with exceptions to mutual recognition allowed if the existence of harmful externalities can be proved, to achieve efficient policies for standards that were not directly negotiated.[12] I will return to discuss this possibility further in chapter 13.

---

12. In essence, such exceptions to mutual recognition amount to a "rebuttable presumption" that regulatory requirements imposed by the host country on a foreign provider will violate the mutual recognition clause, mirroring the design of the European Union's mutual recognition clause (Ortino 2007, 312).

III The Future of the Rules-Based Multilateral Trading System

To wrap up, I cover briefly in chapter 12 three topics that have been omitted up until now: the clash of sovereignty and globalization, the decline of US hegemonic power and its implications for the world trading system, and the WTO's role in preparing for the next pandemic. In chapter 13, I distill the findings from all the previous chapters and broadly outline the functioning of a world trading system for the twenty-first century. Finally, chapter 14 presents some brief conclusions.

12   The Elephants in the Room

No single book can cover all of the important issues that have been raised by globalization over the past several decades and with which the world trading system of the twenty-first century must contend. But omitted from the coverage of previous chapters are several issues that deserve special mention. In this chapter, I touch briefly on these "elephants in the room."

12.1   The Clash of Sovereignty and Globalization

The conflict between openness and national sovereignty is at the forefront of contemporary debate over globalization. This conflict has been growing since the early 1990s, but it was not always present. During much of the GATT era, any hint of such a conflict would have been resolved in favor of the preservation of national sovereignty. For example, writing about the approach taken by the drafters of GATT to issue areas relating to behind-the-border measures, Hudec (1990, 24) provides a window into the subservient status of trade agreements relative to issues of national sovereignty at the time, observing that "governments would never have agreed to circumscribe their freedom in all these other areas for the sake of a mere tariff agreement."

Of course, the evolution toward deep-integration agreements, described in chapter 1 and revisited in various chapters throughout the book, makes Hudec's observation now appear quaint. Indeed, this evolution, taking place in regional and mega-regional negotiations around the world and to a lesser extent in the transition from GATT to the WTO, has in large part been the focus of those who feel that the sovereignty of their national governments has been eroded by globalization. But has globalization really come at the cost of national sovereignty? And what exactly is meant by sovereignty, anyway? An answer to this second question must logically precede an answer to the first. And scholars who have thought deeply about the meaning of sovereignty don't always answer the first question in the affirmative. For example, on the particular question of whether the GATT/WTO violates traditional notions of national sovereignty, Rabkin (1998, 85–86) takes the position that it does not, stating:[1]

> Probably the single most effective and consequential international program of the postwar era has been the mutual reduction of trade barriers under the General Agreement on Tariffs and Trade, initiated in 1947. Reasonable questions may be raised about certain aspects of the World Trade Organization, established in 1995 to help administer GATT norms. But, fundamentally, the trading system is quite compatible with traditional notions of sovereignty. It was developed on the foundations of much older sorts of international agreement, which would have been quite recognizable to the Framers of the Constitution.

More broadly, what are the sovereign rights of nations, and to what extent do these rights stand in the way of achieving internationally efficient outcomes? Here I briefly describe the findings of Bagwell and Staiger (2018b), who propose answers to these questions and employ those answers to evaluate the design features of the GATT/WTO with respect to the issues of national sovereignty.

As Bagwell and Staiger observe, defining sovereignty is not a simple task, especially if the goal is to capture elements that feature prominently in the common usage of the term. This difficulty stems in part from the fact that the international political economy literature where sovereignty has been most discussed is not always clear about the precise meaning of the term and, when clear, does not always adopt a uniform meaning. Krasner (1999) employs a taxonomy to represent four distinct ways in which the term "sovereignty" has been commonly used in this literature: *domestic sovereignty*, which refers to the organization and effectiveness of political authority within the state; *international legal sovereignty*, which refers to the mutual recognition of states; *interdependence sovereignty*, which refers to the scope of activities over which states can effectively exercise control; and *Westphalian sovereignty*, which maintains as its central premise the rule of nonintervention in the internal affairs of other states.

The definition of sovereignty proposed by Bagwell and Staiger builds from the Westphalian norm of nonintervention in the internal

---

1. See also Rodrik (2020), who articulates a similar view for GATT but less so for the WTO.

affairs of other states. To formalize this norm, the terms "noninter-vention" and "internal affairs" must be defined. Bagwell and Staiger argue that three key features of Westphalian sovereignty can be ascertained from a review of the international political economy literature and that these features can serve as a guide to an acceptable definition of sovereignty. First, commitments that result from voluntary international agreements do not *necessarily* violate Westphalian sovereignty. Second, international commitments over policies that concern "sufficiently domestic" affairs (i.e., internal affairs) *do* violate Westphalian sovereignty. And third, international commitments that *distort or derange* the normal operation of domestic institutions also violate Westphalian sovereignty. Bagwell and Staiger argue that these three features should be reflected in a definition of sovereignty that is meant to capture the Westphalian norm in the context of voluntary international agreements.

To construct a definition of sovereignty that can reflect these features, Bagwell and Staiger propose a formal definition of internal affairs that augments the Westphalian emphasis on authority over the determination of institutions and policies and adds to this an emphasis on authority and control over the determination of outcomes and therefore payoffs as well, all evaluated from the perspective of the Nash policy equilibrium of a given model world. This defines the domain of a country's sovereign rights, from which encroachment by international agreements can then be assessed. In effect, the definition of internal affairs proposed by Bagwell and Staiger combines elements of authority with elements of control/effectiveness and, in so doing, delivers a notion of sovereignty that exhibits traditional features of Westphalian sovereignty (the maintenance of authority over institutions and policies), interdependence sovereignty (the maintenance of effective control over cross-border activities), and domestic sovereignty (the maintenance of authority and effective control over activities within the territory).

The characterization of a country's internal affairs that results according to this definition depends on the nature of interdependence across countries, which is in turn defined by the "externality" variables of the model world that capture how one country's policy choices affect the welfare of other countries. And as the nature of interdependence changes, so too will the scope of a country's internal affairs and hence the domain of its sovereign rights. This property resonates with the views of Jackson (2003), who argues for the need to update the traditional Westphalian concept of sovereignty.[2]

Of particular relevance when applied to trade agreements is what this property means for the internal affairs of large versus small countries. Countries that are small in world markets, and that therefore have no impact on world prices when they make their unilateral policy choices, enjoy a greater degree of policy independence—and hence, according to Bagwell and Staiger's definition, possess a wider set of policies that qualify as their internal affairs and therefore a wider domain of sovereign rights—than countries that are large in world markets and therefore impact world prices, facing the implied additional degree of interdependence when making their unilateral policy choices. I return to this property below.

In any case, with a definition of internal affairs in hand, the broad approach taken by Bagwell and Staiger to evaluate the design features of the GATT/WTO with respect to issues of national sovereignty can now be described as follows. In a first step, the normal operation of a country's domestic institutions in the domain of its internal affairs is characterized. This amounts to a consideration of the way in which the preferences of the country's citizens would be translated into choices over the policy instruments that lie in the domain of its internal affairs if those choices were made in the absence of any international agreement. And then, in a second step, an international agreement is said to violate the sovereignty of a member state—that is, one state has intervened in the internal affairs of another state as a result of the international agreement—whenever the international agreement leads the government of a country to make external commitments over matters that (i) concern the country's internal affairs or (ii) alter (and therefore distort/derange) the normal operations of

---

2. Jackson (2003) proposes an updated concept of Westphalian sovereignty that he terms "sovereignty-modern" and that is meant to be more consistent with international efficiency and the need for international policy coordination in the modern world. The formal definition of sovereignty that Bagwell and Staiger propose achieves some of what Jackson has in mind, because according to their definition the domain of sovereignty will evolve as the nature of international interdependence evolves. But unlike Jackson, Bagwell and Staiger do not tailor their definition of sovereignty on a case-by-case basis to be in harmony with international efficiency. Instead, they evaluate formally the circumstances when a trade-off between maintaining national sovereignty according to their definition and achieving international efficiency can be avoided, and they also consider when this trade-off will necessarily arise.

the country's domestic institutions within the domain of its internal affairs.[3]

Adopting the perspective of the terms-of-trade theory of trade agreements and therefore working in a setting where the externality variable is the world price p^w, Bagwell and Staiger demonstrate that market access commitments—defined as a policy commitment to conditions of competition between domestic producers and foreign exporters (see chapter 3, note 2) and therefore as a commitment to a specific level of import volume when foreign exporters price at p^w—fall outside the domain of a large country's internal affairs, while the particular policies employed to deliver a level of market access are the country's internal affairs. As such, Bagwell and Staiger are able to conclude that international agreements that entail market access commitments for large countries do not by themselves violate national sovereignty. What *would* violate a country's sovereignty according to this perspective are commitments to the details of the policies that the country will employ to deliver its market access commitments, or commitments that distort the normal operation of the country's institutions relevant for the determination of these policies.

In short, for environments where the terms-of-trade theory applies, the formalization of national sovereignty developed by Bagwell and Staiger implies that shallow-integration commitments do not violate a country's sovereignty as long as those commitments are interpreted as commitments to a level of market access. But deep-integration commitments that pin down the details of the country's relevant policies on market access or distort the normal operation of the domestic institutions that determine those policies would violate the country's sovereignty.

Armed with this conclusion, and exploiting the implications of the terms-of-trade theory regarding the nature of the inefficiency that a trade agreement must solve (as described in chapter 2), it is then a short step to the further conclusion that, in a world of two large countries, a market access agreement between them can achieve the international efficiency frontier without violating the sovereignty of either country. Moreover, when a multicountry world economy is considered where

---

3. So as not to necessarily tie all of my statements about sovereignty in this book to the particular formalization of that term that is put forward by Bagwell and Staiger (2018b) and described here, in earlier chapters whenever I have used the term sovereignty I mean it in an informal sense along the lines consistent with common usage of the term.

all countries are large in world markets, Bagwell and Staiger demonstrate that a commitment to nondiscriminatory tariffs as implied by MFN treatment would not violate any country's sovereignty either. Intuitively, for large countries, discriminatory tariffs make possible certain market access choices that would be impossible under MFN; but as already noted, market access choices are not the internal affairs of a large country, and so restrictions can be placed on these choices through voluntary international agreement without violating national sovereignty.

This last point is important because, as Bagwell and Staiger demonstrate, it allows them to conclude that if some (but not all) countries are large, then achieving international efficiency and preserving national sovereignty are mutually consistent goals of an international agreement *if and only if* the agreement is limited to MFN market access commitments. In particular, they find that "politically optimal" market access agreements (i.e., market access agreements that implement the politically optimal policies as defined in chapter 2) that are also nondiscriminatory and therefore conform to MFN provide the unique path to achieving international efficiency while preserving national sovereignty in this setting. To see why, recall that small countries enjoy a greater degree of policy independence and thus a wider domain of sovereign rights than large countries. In fact, Bagwell and Staiger show that market access choices fall into the domain of internal affairs for small countries, implying that in any international agreement that does not violate their sovereignty, small countries must be left unconstrained to choose their best-response policies and implied market access levels. This requirement is consistent with international efficiency according to the terms-of-trade theory, but as Bagwell and Staiger show, only when all tariffs are nondiscriminatory and the MFN politically optimal tariffs are implemented.

Taken together, these findings have potentially important implications for the design of the GATT/WTO and its ability to facilitate globalization while respecting the sovereignty of its member governments. As I have described in previous chapters, the GATT/WTO has from its inception been concerned most fundamentally with nondiscriminatory market access commitments, and it has traditionally sought to anchor these commitments with negotiations over border measures (e.g., tariffs) that are "multilateralized" through the MFN requirement and secured by a set of GATT articles that serve as "market access preservation rules." The findings described above suggest that this tradition could be a winning combination for achieving international policy efficiency while preserving national sovereignty, at least in environments where the terms-of-trade theory applies.

But this tradition is being eroded on two fronts. First, the prevalence of discriminatory trade agreements has increased dramatically in recent decades, diminishing adherence to the MFN principle as a practical matter in the global economy. And second, increasingly trade agreements are becoming a forum for the negotiation of international commitments on a host of behind-the-border policies. As I have suggested in previous chapters, to some extent these developments may be the result of changes in the nature of the problems that trade agreements are being asked to solve, away from the problem identified by the terms-of-trade theory and toward novel forms of international externalities. Whatever the drivers of these developments, the findings described here convey a clear message: The further the WTO and the world trading system that it governs depart from a reliance on agreements that take the form of nondiscriminatory market access commitments, the more likely it will be that these agreements pose a threat (and possibly, an avoidable one) to the sovereignty of the member countries.

Finally, I have omitted from my discussion of sovereignty those issues that are associated with the operation of the WTO Dispute Settlement Body, but of course those issues have also become critical in the globalization debate, especially in recent years as the United States has taken actions that have led to the breakdown of the appeals process at the WTO. At issue here is the appropriate level of "activism" for the WTO court. For example, after describing the WTO Appellate Body's (AB) interpretation of the term "public body," which had the effect of limiting the scope for using WTO rules to respond to the competitive distortions associated with China's state-owned enterprises, Matthes (2021, 18) describes the issue this way:

> From this viewpoint, the AB acted as a normal court in interpreting rules and established a new meaning pertaining to WTO law. However, the US holds the opinion that the AB is not a usual court but should stick very closely to WTO law.

In essence, the debate is about whether to stick with the WTO legal system, possibly circumscribed in various ways to rein in the mandate of panel and appellate body judges, or rather to return to something less formal and closer to the original GATT legal system. And while the tactics used by the United States in the context of this debate have been very disruptive to the operations of the WTO, what is at stake in this debate—namely, the appropriate level of court activism—does not pose an existential threat to the WTO in the way that the tensions between international efficiency and national sovereignty that I have highlighted here do.[4]

12.2 The Declining Hegemon

In chapter 5, I described how the Trump tariffs might be interpreted as a crude attempt by the then president's administration to implement its vision of the global trading system. In particular, as I observed in chapter 5, Mattoo and Staiger (2020) argue that these actions amount to a US-led effort to repeal the rules-based trading system and replace it with a power-based system where countries are free to bargain in a way that is not constrained by a particular set of agreed-on rules of behavior. And as Mattoo and Staiger note, while the Trump administration accelerated a move away from the rules-based trading system and toward a power-based approach, it was not the first US administration to move in this direction.[5] In this section I elaborate further on Mattoo and Staiger's explanation for why this might be happening now.

Mattoo and Staiger begin from the observation that the rules-based system of the GATT/WTO has two main potential advantages over a power-based approach to tariff bargaining. First, the rules of the GATT/WTO can simplify the tariff bargaining problem and make it manageable, and this can help countries negotiate to more efficient policies. Chapters 4 and 5 have reviewed evidence consistent with this position, and in principle all countries could share in the implied efficiency gains generated by a rules-based system. Second, these rules tend to mitigate the power of the most powerful countries (in chapter 5 I discussed some evidence in support of this position as well) and in so doing can encourage the participation of weaker countries in the global trading system—countries that might otherwise be vulnerable to exploitation by the stronger countries and choose to opt out altogether.

---

4. See also the discussion of Maggi and Staiger (2011) in chapter 6, where some of the issues associated with court activism are covered.
5. Evidence of power-based bargaining could be seen in the strategy used by the major players in the GATT Uruguay Round to deal with "holdout" countries in creating the WTO—namely, withdrawing from GATT and acceding to the newly formed WTO (see Posner and Sykes 2014).

It is on this second potential advantage of a rules-based trading system that Mattoo and Staiger focus their attention. In essence, they argue that the rules-based trading system may be in peril because the dominant position of the United States in the world economy has eroded, which has implications for the rules-based system's ability to generate participation benefits of a magnitude that would justify continued US submission to the rules.

That commitment to a rules-based system could generate participation benefits that are sufficiently large to justify a powerful country's submission to those rules is illustrated in a stylistic way for a two-country world in figure 12.1, which builds on McLaren (1997) and is adapted from Bagwell and Staiger (1999). In this figure, the welfare of the domestic country, W, is plotted on the vertical axis and the welfare of the foreign country, W^*, is plotted on the horizontal axis. The dashed frontier depicted in the figure represents the combinations of domestic and foreign welfare levels achievable under efficient tariff bargaining. The welfare levels at the origin of the figure, labeled $N_{ex\text{-}post}$, represent the "disagreement point" for the two countries: These are the welfare

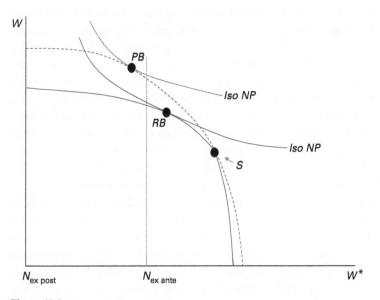

Figure 12.1
The participation benefits of a rules-based system. W = welfare of the domestic country, W^* = welfare of the foreign country, NP = Nash product, RB = rules-based bargaining outcome, PB = power-based bargaining outcome, S = politically optimal outcome. *Source*: Adapted from Bagwell and Staiger (1999, fig. 5B).

levels that the domestic and foreign country would achieve if their tariff bargaining broke down. And the point on the frontier labeled PB is the outcome of the power-based bargain, assuming that both the domestic and the foreign country participate in the bargain and that this bargain can be represented as a Nash bargain that reaches the highest iso-Nash-Product contour (the dashed iso-Nash-Product contour labeled in the figure as *Iso NP*) consistent with the dashed frontier. As depicted, at the point PB, both countries achieve higher welfare than their disagreement welfare levels at $N_{ex\text{-}post}$, indicating that each country does better under the agreement summarized by the point PB than it would do by walking away from the deal.

But these disagreement welfare levels may not be the relevant welfare levels for assessing whether the decision to *participate* in the bargain is worthwhile. This is because the act of showing up at the bargaining table to participate in the bargain may itself imply incurring some sunk costs, economic or political, which cannot then be recouped should the bargaining break down, and which are therefore netted out from the welfare levels at $N_{ex\text{-}post}$. Under the assumption that the foreign country is the weaker, smaller country of the two and that it experiences such sunk costs when it agrees to participate in a tariff bargain with the larger, more powerful domestic country (perhaps because its exporters will sink investments into serving the large domestic-country market once it is known that the two countries have agreed to bargain), the disagreement point relevant for the participation decision—which excludes the sunk costs that would be incurred by showing up—is labeled in figure 12.1 as $N_{ex\ ante}$. The figure depicts the case where, under power-based bargaining, the foreign country does worse than if it had not shown up to the bargaining table; hence, anticipating this, it will choose not to participate in such a bargain and the two countries will be stuck at their (ex ante) disagreement welfare levels.

This is where the commitment to a rules-based system could benefit all countries, including the most powerful countries. Here I illustrate the impact of committing to the reciprocity rule as it arises in the context of GATT Article XXVIII renegotiation. Recall from the discussion in chapter 4 that if a powerful country pushes for better-than-reciprocal terms in an efficient bargain, its trading partner can subsequently renegotiate subject to reciprocity, introducing inefficiencies in the bargaining outcome that are borne by the powerful country and serve to penalize it for exercising its power in the bargain. The implications of this are illustrated in figure 12.1 by the solid welfare frontier, which lies everywhere inside the dashed frontier except at the point marked S, where each country has set its tariffs at the levels it would have chosen if it were a small country, and therefore where no country is exerting bargaining power to push the deal in its favor.[6] The Nash bargain in the presence of this reciprocity-constrained frontier would then deliver the rules-based bargaining outcome labeled RB in figure 12.1, which marks the highest iso-Nash-Product contour (the solid iso-Nash-Product contour labeled in the figure as $Iso\ NP$) consistent with the solid frontier. As illustrated in figure 12.1, the rules-based bargaining outcome RB penalizes the powerful domestic country and favors the weaker foreign country relative to the power-based bargaining outcome PB; but for the powerful domestic country this is no loss, since it could not get the foreign country to participate in power-based bargaining in any event. And relative to their ex ante disagreement welfare levels, both countries now do better under the rules-based bargaining outcome RB.

The discussion here suggests that the most powerful countries may benefit from a rules-based multilateral trading system precisely because they *are* so powerful. This may help explain why the United States was, along with the United Kingdom, the champion of the rules-based system at its creation in 1947 with the birth of GATT. But it is not hard to see from figure 12.1 that, if the domestic country were the more powerful of the two but not so dominantly more powerful as I have illustrated in the figure, the foreign country could well choose to participate in trade bargaining even under a power-based system. And in that case, the more powerful domestic country would prefer to escape from the rules and pursue power-based trade bargaining with the now-participating foreign country (assuming that the efficiency benefits of rules-based bargaining noted above were not large enough to carry the day on their own).

This suggests the possibility that, with the rise of the large emerging and developing economies and the decline in hegemonic status that the United States has experienced in recent decades, its enthusiasm for the rules-based system it helped to create could wane: Being far less dominant in the global economy than it was in 1947, the United States is no longer in need of a set of international rules to help it commit not to exploit other countries in trade bargaining so that they feel comfortable engaging in the global economy. And if the declining hegemonic position of the United States is indeed a primary cause of the challenges

---

6. This point corresponds to the political optimum as defined in chapter 2.

now facing the rules-based multilateral trading system, to repair that system the world may have to wait for the rise of another hegemon. It is this possibility that Mattoo and Staiger describe, and which is illustrated in stylistic fashion in figure 12.2.

With the passage of time measured from left to right on the horizontal axis, figure 12.2 depicts in a schematic way a hypothetical evolution in the world trading system, from a rules-based system to a power-based system and back again. This evolution is driven by an exogenous process in which one country, referred to as "the US," experiences an erosion over time in its position of hegemony atop the world economy, while a second country, referred to as "China," ascends to this position of hegemony. For simplicity, countries are assumed to be myopic, and the choice between a rules-based and a power-based trading system in any period is assumed to be determined by the more powerful country in that period, who decides whether it will subject itself to rules for the period under consideration.[7] The thick solid lines in figure 12.2 depict the equilibrium payoffs of each country under the equilibrium regime choice in each period, and as depicted, the periods can be separated into four phases that reflect these equilibrium regime choices.

In the US hegemony phase, the United States chooses to tie its hands in a rules-based regime. This is because during this phase, the weak country (China) can credibly threaten not to bargain with the United States in the absence of rules, and hence the United States must rely on rules to induce China's participation, much like the situation illustrated in figure 12.1. This feature is reflected in figure 12.2 by the fact that in the US hegemony phase, the payoff to China under power-based bargaining (dashed upward-sloping thick line), while above China's ex post once-the-bargaining-has-begun Nash payoff (dotted upward-sloping thin line), is below its ex ante Nash payoff (solid upward-sloping thin line)—that is, it is below the payoff China could expect if it simply stayed away from the bargaining table and never let the bargaining process get off the ground. And so the payoffs for the two countries under a power-based regime would be their (ex ante) Nash payoffs (solid downward-sloping thin line for the United States, solid upward-sloping thin line for China) which, reflecting the

---

7. As Mattoo and Staiger note, the assumption that the relatively more powerful country determines the regime can be formalized in a two-stage game: in stage 1, the more powerful country decides whether or not to commit to rules for bargaining, and then in stage 2, the more powerful country invites the weaker country to bargain, an invitation that the weaker country can either accept or reject.

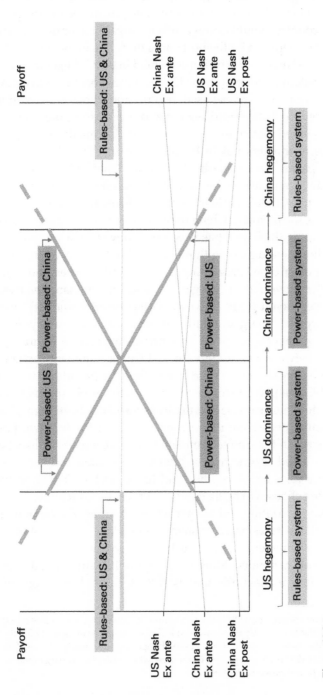

Figure 12.2
Hegemonic transition of the world trading system. *Source:* Reproduced from Mattoo and Staiger (2020, fig. 2).

positive-sum gains from bargaining and the assumption that these gains are split evenly in the rules-based bargain, are below the payoffs that each country would receive when bargaining under the rules-based regime, depicted by the horizontal thick line in the figure. Hence the rules-based regime will be implemented in the US hegemony phase.

In the US dominance phase, the United States does better in a power-based regime than a rules-based regime and chooses to withdraw support from the rules-based regime and escape from the constraints of the rules-based system that it once created. During this phase, China would like to threaten not to bargain with the United States in the absence of rules, but unlike in the US hegemony phase, this threat is not credible, and hence the United States does not need to rely on rules to induce China's participation. This is because in the US dominance phase, the payoff to China under power-based bargaining (solid upward-sloping thick line) has now risen above China's ex ante Nash payoff (solid upward-sloping thin line), and so China is willing to participate in power-based bargaining with the United States; and initially, at the border between the US hegemony and US dominance phases, the United States payoff (solid downward-sloping thick line) captures all the gains from the bargain relative to the ex ante Nash payoffs. The power-based payoffs of the two countries converge in figure 12.2 at the border between US dominance and China dominance where the two countries are equally powerful, and then the payoffs of the United States and China play mirror-image roles as the world moves through the China dominance phase and finally to the China hegemony phase.[8] The remaining phases are then mirror images of the first two phases just described. In the China dominance phase, China now does better in a power-based regime than a rules-based regime and chooses not to support a rules-based regime. And finally, in the China hegemony phase, China chooses to tie its hands in a rules-based regime.

According to Mattoo and Staiger's interpretation, the erosion of US support for the rules-based system is not likely to be a short-term temporary phenomenon that will be reversed now that the Trump administration has ended. Moreover, if figure 12.2 embodies the correct diagnosis, it is a diagnosis that is full of irony. The design of the

---

8. That the power-based payoffs of the two countries converge to their rules-based payoffs at the border between US dominance and China dominance in figure 12.2 reflects an assumption that power-based and rules-based bargaining are equally efficient. See Mattoo and Staiger (2020) for a depiction of the case where rules-based bargaining is more efficient than power-based bargaining.

rules-based multilateral trading system has proved effective in solving an important and still-relevant problem, yet the system will inevitably collapse. While there may be nothing fundamentally wrong with the existing rules-based system, there are certainly important improvements in the design of the rules that could be made, yet such improvements will likely do nothing to save the system. And while China is seen by many as a source of some of the greatest challenges for the rules-based trading system of the twenty-first century, if this diagnosis is correct, it may be that the rise of China is the world's best hope for the return of a viable rules-based multilateral trading system.

12.3   The WTO's Role in Preparing for the Next Pandemic

The COVID-19 pandemic that began in the winter of 2020 has shaken the entire world, and the world trading system has certainly not been spared. The challenges created for the WTO by this pandemic are many and varied, though they are not new: Public health researchers and economists have been concerned for some time that the growing interdependence engendered by globalization carries increasing risks of disease transmission across countries, and there have been calls for the WTO to address this concern (see Mackey and Liang 2012; Hoekman 2020). But the COVID-19 pandemic has brought these risks into sharp focus, laying bare for the world trading system a number of serious and interrelated challenges that have the potential to erupt during pandemics, ranging from supply chain disruption to issues relating to erratic vaccine distribution and associated patent rights to the imposition of export restrictions on personal protective equipment (PPE).

What is the WTO's role in meeting these challenges, and in helping countries prepare for the next pandemic? The World Health Organization (WHO) is the institution tasked with addressing international health issues, and the appropriate role for issue linkage between the WTO and the WHO as well as other international agencies must be a central concern in any comprehensive answer to this question.[9] Here I focus on a narrow slice of this question: Can WTO rules be effective in preventing governments from imposing export restrictions during a pandemic? And relatedly, what is the appropriate balance for the

---

9. On the role that the WHO and other international agencies can play in prevention, preparedness, and response to pandemics, see National Research Council (2016 chap. 4).

WTO between that goal and the goal of encouraging trade-related public health measures that would reduce the probability of a pandemic in
the first place?

I examine these questions through the lens of the enforcement constraints with which a trade agreement such as the GATT/WTO must
contend (see Dam 1970; Bagwell and Staiger 2002, chap. 6). In particular, because there is no world jail where national leaders can be thrown
if they violate GATT/WTO commitments, meaningful commitments in
the GATT/WTO, like meaningful commitments in any international
trade agreement, must be self-enforcing so that the member governments see it in their self-interest to follow through on commitments.
Adopting a modeling approach to self-enforcing trade agreements similar to Bagwell and Staiger (1990) and highlighting the basic incentive
constraint that a self-enforcing agreement must obey, I argue that there
are good reasons to expect export restraints to move closer to noncooperative levels during a pandemic, reflecting the fact that during a
pandemic, efforts to maintain fully cooperative export policy will be
especially fraught. Further, when the possibility of encouraging policy
commitments that could reduce the probability of a pandemic is also
considered, looking to a trade agreement as a forum for blunting the
use of export restraints during a pandemic can be counter productive.

These points can be formalized with the aid of a simple model. To
keep the analysis focused, I consider a two-country partial equilibrium
"endowment-economy" world, where the home country is endowed
with a fixed amount of good y and the foreign country is endowed
with a fixed amount of good x, and where x and y might be thought
of as two different forms of PPE (or possibly one form of PPE and a
vaccine, but I will use the term PPE as shorthand). Aside from their
endowment structure, I will assume that the two countries are otherwise identical in every way, and therefore the home country will import
x and export y while the foreign country imports y and exports x. For
simplicity, I focus on the use of tax instruments to restrict trade rather
than quotas, though the qualitative nature of the conclusions I emphasize below do not depend on this.[10] And I abstract from import tariffs
and focus instead on the use of export taxes, with the home-country
tax on exports of good y denoted by τ_y and the foreign-country tax

10. The modeling framework of Bagwell and Staiger (1990) on which I build can handle
both tariffs and quotas, and as they demonstrate, the qualitative predictions of the model
are robust to the choice of policy instrument.

on exports of good x denoted by τ_x^*. The simplification of endowment economies means that an export tax is equivalent to a subsidy to local consumption of the export good. This simplification allows me to focus on export taxes while abstracting from the production distortions that would otherwise arise with their use.

In each period, there is a chance that a new virus will be introduced into the human population and lead to a pandemic. If a pandemic occurs in a period, I assume that it lasts for the period and then exogenously ends. Hence, governments can do nothing to impact the duration of a pandemic if it occurs. But I assume that governments can impact the chance that a pandemic occurs in the first place.

In particular, at the beginning of each period, the home and foreign countries have an opportunity to invest in public health measures I and I^* for the period and incur costs $c(I)$ and $c(I^*)$, respectively. These investments determine the probability that a new virus jumps from the animal to the human population and leads to a pandemic in the period, which I summarize with the reduced-form pandemic probability function $\rho(I, I^*)$, with $\rho(I, I^*) \in (0, 1)$ for all I and I^*. I assume that $c(\cdot)$ is increasing and convex in its argument, and I assume that $\rho(I, I^*)$ is decreasing and concave in each of its arguments. Therefore, the probability that a pandemic occurs in any period, $\rho(I, I^*)$, is jointly determined by the public health investments made by the two countries in that period and falls as those investments rise. These investments are a stand-in for public health measures designed to prevent a virus of animal origin from jumping to the human population or for standards and regulations that could help stop a new virus of animal origin that has jumped to the human population from taking hold in the population sufficiently to become a pandemic. Of course, in reality, these same kinds of investments might impact the duration of a pandemic, not just the chance that a pandemic occurs in the first place; but by assuming that the probability of a pandemic in any period is endogenous while the duration of a pandemic if it occurs is exogenous, I keep the model simple and focused on the main points.[11]

---

11. Such measures are covered under the WTO Agreement on Technical Barriers to Trade (TBT) and the Agreement on the Application of Sanitary and Phytosanitary Measures (SPS). For a discussion in the context of COVID-19 of public health measures that are aimed at preventing a virus of animal origin from jumping to the human population, see WTO (2020a). For a discussion of standards and regulations that could help prevent a new virus of animal origin that has jumped to the human population from taking hold in the population sufficiently to become a pandemic, see WTO (2020b). See Burris, Anderson,

In a period where the pandemic occurs, the home country suffers a welfare loss equal to $C(D_x, D_y)$, where C is the pandemic loss function assumed to be positive, decreasing, and convex in both of its arguments, and where D_x and D_y are the home-country consumption levels of good x and y, respectively, that correspond to points on downward-sloping demand curves. I have in mind that the welfare cost of a pandemic to the home country is diminished when its consumption of either form of PPE is increased during the pandemic, but that these benefits are (local) externalities when viewed by the individual consumer in the home country (and hence enter into the function $C(D_x, D_y)$ rather than into home-country consumer surplus). Similarly, for the foreign country, I assume that in a period where the pandemic occurs it suffers a welfare loss equal to $C(D_x^*, D_y^*)$ with D_x^* and D_y^* the foreign-country consumption levels of good x and y, respectively. I will sometimes refer to a period where the pandemic occurs as the "pandemic state" of the world and to the no-pandemic state as "normal times."

Consider now the welfare measures for the two countries. At the time that the export taxes τ_y and τ_x^* for the period are chosen, public health investments for the period are a bygone, and the state of the world (pandemic or no pandemic) for the period is known. In normal times, home and foreign welfare for the period are given by the usual economic surplus measures

$$\omega = \sum_{i \in \{x,y\}} CS_i(\bar{\tau}_y, \bar{\tau}_x^*) + PS_y(\bar{\tau}_y) + TR_y(\bar{\tau}_y) \equiv \omega(\bar{\tau}_y, \bar{\tau}_x^*) \tag{12.1}$$

$$\omega^* = \sum_{i \in \{x,y\}} CS_i^*(\bar{\tau}_y, \bar{\tau}_x^*) + PS_x^*(\bar{\tau}_x^*) + TR_x^*(\bar{\tau}_x^*) \equiv \omega^*(\bar{\tau}_y, \bar{\tau}_x^*),$$

with world welfare then given by

$$\omega^w(\bar{\tau}_y, \bar{\tau}_x^*) \equiv \omega(\bar{\tau}_y, \bar{\tau}_x^*) + \omega^*(\bar{\tau}_y, \bar{\tau}_x^*), \tag{12.2}$$

where CS_i is home-country consumer surplus associated with good $i \in \{x, y\}$ and PS_y and TR_y are, respectively, home-country producer surplus and trade tax revenue, and where CS_i^*, PS_x^* and TR_x^* are similarly defined for the foreign country, and where I use $\bar{\tau}_y$ and $\bar{\tau}_x^*$ to denote the home and foreign export taxes that are applied in normal times. In the pandemic state, home and foreign welfare for the period are given by economic surplus minus the welfare loss from the pandemic,

---

and Wagenaar (2021) on the importance of appropriate laws and regulations for effective pandemic control more generally.

$$\omega_{PAN} = \sum_{i\in\{x,y\}} CS_i(\hat{t}_y, \hat{t}_x^*) + PS_y(\hat{t}_y) + TR_y(\hat{t}_y) - C(D_x(\hat{t}_x^*), D_y(\hat{t}_y))$$

$$\equiv \omega_{PAN}(\hat{t}_y, \hat{t}_x^*) \tag{12.3}$$

$$\omega_{PAN}^* = \sum_{i\in\{x,y\}} CS_i^*(\hat{t}_y, \hat{t}_x^*) + PS_x^*(\hat{t}_x^*) + TR_x^*(\hat{t}_x^*) - C(D_x^*(\hat{t}_x^*), D_y^*(\hat{t}_y))$$

$$\equiv \omega_{PAN}^*(\hat{t}_y, \hat{t}_x^*),$$

with world welfare in the pandemic state then given by

$$\omega_{PAN}^w(\hat{t}_y, \hat{t}_x^*) \equiv \omega_{PAN}(\hat{t}_y, \hat{t}_x^*) + \omega_{PAN}^*(\hat{t}_y, \hat{t}_x^*) \tag{12.4}$$

$$= \sum_{i\in\{x,y\}} CS_i(\hat{t}_y, \hat{t}_x^*) + PS_y(\hat{t}_y) + TR_y(\hat{t}_y)$$

$$+ \sum_{i\in\{x,y\}} CS_i^*(\hat{t}_y, \hat{t}_x^*) + PS_x^*(\hat{t}_x^*) + TR_x^*(\hat{t}_x^*)$$

$$- [C(D_x(\hat{t}_x^*), D_y(\hat{t}_y)) + C(D_x^*(\hat{t}_x^*), D_y^*(\hat{t}_y))],$$

where $\hat{t}_y$ and $\hat{t}_x^*$ are the home and foreign export taxes applied during a pandemic.

Unlike export taxes, at the time that the public health investment levels I and I^* are chosen in each period the state of the world for the period has not yet been determined, and so what is relevant for the choice of investment levels is ex ante expected welfare. Each country's ex ante expected welfare for the period is given by its expected economic surplus minus its expected loss from a pandemic, or

$$W = [1 - \rho(I, I^*)] \times \left\{ \sum_{i\in\{x,y\}} CS_i(\bar{t}_y, \bar{t}_x^*) + PS_y(\bar{t}_y) + TR_y(\bar{t}_y) - c(I) \right\}$$

$$+ \rho(I, I^*) \times \left\{ \sum_{i\in\{x,y\}} CS_i(\hat{t}_y, \hat{t}_x^*) + PS_y(\hat{t}_y) + TR_y(\hat{t}_y) - c(I) \right.$$

$$\left. - C(D_x(\hat{t}_x^*), D_y(\hat{t}_y)) \right\} \equiv W(\bar{t}_y, \bar{t}_x^*, \hat{t}_y, \hat{t}_x^*, I, I^*) \tag{12.5}$$

for the home country and

$$W^* = [1 - \rho(I, I^*)] \times \left\{ \sum_{i\in\{x,y\}} CS_i^*(\bar{t}_y, \bar{t}_x^*) + PS_x^*(\bar{t}_x^*) + TR_x^*(\bar{t}_x^*) - c(I^*) \right\}$$

$$+ \rho(I, I^*) \times \left\{ \sum_{i\in\{x,y\}} CS_i^*(\hat{t}_y, \hat{t}_x^*) + PS_x^*(\hat{t}_x^*) + TR_x^*(\hat{t}_x^*) - c(I^*) \right.$$

$$\left. - C(D_x^*(\hat{t}_x^*), D_y^*(\hat{t}_y)) \right\} \equiv W^*(\bar{t}_y, \bar{t}_x^*, \hat{t}_y, \hat{t}_x^*, I, I^*) \tag{12.6}$$

for the foreign country. Ex ante world welfare is given by

$$W^w(\bar{\tau}_y, \bar{\tau}_x^*, \hat{\tau}_y, \hat{\tau}_x^*, I, I^*) \equiv W(\bar{\tau}_y, \bar{\tau}_x^*, \hat{\tau}_y, \hat{\tau}_x^*, I, I^*) + W^*(\bar{\tau}_y, \bar{\tau}_x^*, \hat{\tau}_y, \hat{\tau}_x^*, I, I^*)$$

$$= [1 - \rho(I, I^*)] \times \{ \sum_{i \in \{x,y\}} CS_i(\bar{\tau}_y, \bar{\tau}_x^*) + PS_y(\bar{\tau}_y) + TR_y(\bar{\tau}_y)$$

$$+ \sum_{i \in \{x,y\}} CS_i^*(\bar{\tau}_y, \bar{\tau}_x^*) + PS_x^*(\bar{\tau}_x^*) + TR_x^*(\bar{\tau}_x^*) - [c(I) + c(I^*)] \}$$

$$+ \rho(I, I^*) \times \{ \sum_{i \in \{x,y\}} CS_i(\hat{\tau}_y, \hat{\tau}_x^*) + PS_y(\hat{\tau}_y) + TR_y(\hat{\tau}_y)$$

$$+ \sum_{i \in \{x,y\}} CS_i^*(\hat{\tau}_y, \hat{\tau}_x^*) + PS_x^*(\hat{\tau}_x^*) + TR_x^*(\hat{\tau}_x^*) - [c(I) + c(I^*)]$$

$$- [C(D_x^*(\hat{\tau}_x^*), D_y^*(\hat{\tau}_y)) + C(D_x^*(\hat{\tau}_x^*), D_y^*(\hat{\tau}_y))] \}. \tag{12.7}$$

To characterize efficient (i.e., ex ante world welfare maximizing) policy choices in this setting, I first consider the choice of export taxes conditional on each state of the world and then the choice of (ex ante) investment policies. In normal times, as expected, there is no efficiency role for trade tax intervention, and hence the efficient export taxes that maximize the expression for ω^w in (12.2) are given by $\bar{\tau}_y^e = 0 = \bar{\tau}_x^{*e}$. In the pandemic state, the first-order conditions associated with (12.4) that maximize ω^w_{PAN} reduce to

$$\frac{\partial \omega^w_{PAN}}{\partial \hat{\tau}_y} = - \left[\frac{\partial C(D_x, D_y)}{\partial D_y} \frac{\partial D_y}{\partial \hat{\tau}_y} + \frac{\partial C(D_x^*, D_y^*)}{\partial D_y^*} \frac{\partial D_y^*}{\partial \hat{\tau}_y} \right] = 0 \tag{12.8}$$

$$\frac{\partial \omega^w_{PAN}}{\partial \hat{\tau}_x^*} = - \left[\frac{\partial C(D_x, D_y)}{\partial D_x} \frac{\partial D_x}{\partial \hat{\tau}_x^*} + \frac{\partial C(D_x^*, D_y^*)}{\partial D_x^*} \frac{\partial D_x^*}{\partial \hat{\tau}_x^*} \right] = 0,$$

which given the convexity of C and the cross-country symmetry assumptions I have imposed imply that, again, $\hat{\tau}_y^e = 0 = \hat{\tau}_x^{*e}$ and there is no efficiency role for trade tax intervention. Intuitively, in the pandemic state, there is no role for trade taxes for the purpose of maximizing worldwide economic surplus because cross-country symmetry ensures that under free trade, the supply (endowment) of each form of PPE in the world will be allocated equally across countries, and therefore allocated so as to minimize the worldwide cost of the pandemic ($C(D_x, D_y) + C(D_x^*, D_y^*)$).

Now consider the efficient choice of public health investments I^e and I^{*e}. These are the choices of I and I^* that maximize the ex ante world welfare W^w defined in (12.7) when W^w is evaluated at the efficient export taxes (i.e., free trade in all states). The associated first-order conditions imply that I^e and I^{*e} must satisfy

$$\frac{\partial W^w}{\partial I} = -\frac{\partial \rho(I, I^*)}{\partial I} \times [C(D_x^e, D_y^e) + C(D_x^{*e}, D_y^{*e})] - c'(I) = 0$$

$$\tag{12.9}$$

$$\frac{\partial W^w}{\partial I^*} = -\frac{\partial \rho(I, I^*)}{\partial I^*} \times [C(D_x^e, D_y^e) + C(D_x^{*e}, D_y^{*e})] - c'(I^*) = 0,$$

where I use the superscript "e" to denote a magnitude that is evaluated at the efficient export taxes. As (12.9) indicates, the efficient choice of public health investment in each country, I^e and I^{*e}, equates the marginal benefit of a small increase in investment in terms of reduced expected worldwide welfare loss from a pandemic in the period to the marginal cost of the investment.

What are the noncooperative policies in this setting? The noncooperative (Nash) export tax choices in normal times, which I denote by $\bar{\tau}_y^N$ and $\bar{\tau}_x^{*N}$, are defined by the first-order conditions

$$\frac{\partial \omega}{\partial \bar{\tau}_y} = \frac{\partial [CS_i(\bar{\tau}_y, \bar{\tau}_x^*) + PS_y(\bar{\tau}_y) + TR_y(\bar{\tau}_y)]}{\partial \bar{\tau}_y} = 0 \tag{12.10}$$

$$\frac{\partial \omega^*}{\partial \bar{\tau}_x^*} = \frac{\partial [CS_i^*(\bar{\tau}_y, \bar{\tau}_x^*) + PS_x^*(\bar{\tau}_x^*) + TR_x^*(\bar{\tau}_x^*)]}{\partial \bar{\tau}_x^*} = 0.$$

The first-order conditions in (12.10) describe the export taxes that each country would choose to maximize its own economic surplus, and these export taxes amount to the usual Johnson (1953–1954) optimal tariffs. By contrast, the noncooperative export tax choices in the pandemic state, which I denote by $\hat{\tau}_y^N$ and $\hat{\tau}_x^{*N}$, are defined by the first-order conditions

$$\frac{\partial \omega_{PAN}}{\partial \hat{\tau}_y} = \frac{\partial [CS_y(\hat{\tau}_y, \hat{\tau}_x^*) + PS_y(\hat{\tau}_y) + TR_y(\hat{\tau}_y)]}{\partial \hat{\tau}_y}$$

$$- \frac{\partial C(D_x, D_y)}{\partial D_y} \frac{\partial D_y(\hat{\tau}_y)}{\partial \tau_y} = 0 \tag{12.11}$$

$$\frac{\partial \omega_{PAN}^*}{\partial \hat{\tau}_x^*} = \frac{\partial [CS_i^*(\hat{\tau}_y, \hat{\tau}_x^*) + PS_x^*(\hat{\tau}_x^*) + TR_x^*(\hat{\tau}_x^*)]}{\partial \hat{\tau}_x^*}$$

$$- \frac{\partial C(D_x^*, D_y^*)}{\partial D_x^*} \frac{\partial D_x^*(\hat{\tau}_x^*)}{\partial \hat{\tau}_x^*} = 0.$$

In each expression of (12.11), the second term on the right-hand side is a product of two terms: a negative term by the properties of the pandemic loss function, and a positive term given downward-sloping demand and the impact of export taxes on local prices.

As a comparison of (12.10) and (12.11) makes clear, in a pandemic state the same optimal tariff incentives are at work as those that define the non-cooperative export taxes in normal times, but in the pandemic state there is also something more: Each country has an incentive to use its export tax to keep more PPE for its own citizens, in order to reduce the welfare losses experienced by its citizens during the pandemic. The two incentives reinforce each other and push toward higher export taxes, ensuring that $\hat{t}_y^N > \bar{\tau}_y^N$ and $\hat{t}_x^{*N} > \bar{\tau}_x^{*N}$. But the optimal tariff incentives that prevent the export tax from becoming prohibitive in normal times can be swamped in the pandemic state by the incentive to hoard PPE, leading a country to adopt prohibitive export taxes in the pandemic state if this latter incentive is strong enough. Whether this occurs or not will depend on the properties of the pandemic loss function C, and in particular on the magnitude of $\frac{\partial C(D_x, D_y)}{\partial D_y}$ and $\frac{\partial C(D_x^*, D_y^*)}{\partial D_x^*}$, reflecting the degree to which this loss function is sensitive to the amount of PPE its citizens consume.

Finally, the Nash public health investment levels I^N and I^{*N} are defined by the first-order conditions

$$\frac{\partial W}{\partial I} = -\frac{\partial \rho(I, I^*)}{\partial I} \times C(D_x^N, D_y^N) - c'(I) = 0 \tag{12.12}$$

$$\frac{\partial W^*}{\partial I^*} = -\frac{\partial \rho(I, I^*)}{\partial I^*} \times C(D_x^{*N}, D_y^{*N})) - c'(I^*) = 0,$$

where I use the superscript "N" to denote a magnitude that is evaluated at the noncooperative trade taxes for the relevant state, which in the context of (12.12) is the pandemic state. As is intuitive, (12.12) implies that, unlike the efficient investment levels defined by (12.9), the noncooperative levels of investments in public health only take into account the benefits experienced by the country making the investment and are therefore too low relative to efficient levels, as each country ignores the beneficial impact of its investment on its trading partner.

Given the unilateral incentives that each country has to make inefficient public health investment and export tax choices, can efficient choices be sustained in a self-enforcing agreement in this setting? The answer is "yes," but only if the future cost borne by a country that deviates from efficient policy choices is large enough to outweigh the one-time gain that it can achieve from the deviation. This describes the basic incentive constraint that a self-enforcing agreement must obey.

To see whether efficient choices can be sustained in a self-enforcing agreement in this setting, it is necessary to consider in some detail the incentive constraints that are implied by the self-enforcement requirement. To this end, I will assume that policy deviations from the agreement are only observed by the other party at the end of the period. Moreover, for simplicity, I will follow Bagwell and Staiger (1990) and assume that any deviation from the policies that the countries agree to will be met by infinite Nash reversion beginning in the next period. These assumptions ensure that if a country were to deviate in a period from its agreed public health investment level, it would deviate in that period also with respect to its agreed export tax level, regardless of which state of the world prevails (because once it deviates from the agreed investment level in a period, it will trigger the punishment beginning next period no matter what export tax it chooses for the period, so it might as well choose its unilaterally optimal export tax). This feature is special, but it helps to illustrate in stark terms the more general points that I highlight below, and it reduces the taxonomy of deviation and punishment possibilities that I would otherwise need to consider.

What is the future cost borne by a country that deviates from the policy choices specified in the agreement? When viewed from a period in which a government is considering deviating, the cost to the country of the infinite Nash reversion that would follow this deviation beginning in the next period is the discounted difference between its expected future welfare under the cooperative policies dictated by the agreement and its expected future welfare under the Nash policies. Assuming for the moment that the agreement calls for efficient public health investments and export tax levels, the per-period cost to the home country of forgoing the agreement and reverting to Nash is then

$$Y^e \equiv W(\bar{\tau}_y^e, \bar{\tau}_x^{*e}, \hat{\tau}_y^e, \hat{\tau}_x^{*e}, I^e, I^{*e}) - W(\bar{\tau}_y^N, \bar{\tau}_x^{*N}, \hat{\tau}_y^N, \hat{\tau}_x^{*N}, I^N, I^{*N}) > 0,$$

where W is defined by (12.5). And discounting the infinite stream of per-period costs with the discount factor $\delta \in (0,1)$, back to the current period where the deviation is under consideration, yields the future cost borne by the home country if it deviates in the current period from the efficient policy choices specified in the agreement,

$$\frac{\delta}{1-\delta} Y^e. \tag{12.13}$$

In light of the cross-country symmetry of the model, (12.13) also gives the future cost borne by the foreign country if it deviates from the policy choices specified in the agreement. Importantly, as (12.13) reflects, regardless of whether the current period where the deviation is under consideration corresponds to a pandemic or to normal times, the future cost borne by a country that deviates from the policy choices specified in the agreement always looks the same.[12]

What is the one-time gain that a country can achieve from deviating? Focusing again on the home country, there are three relevant possibilities for a deviation from the efficient policies called for in the agreement. The home country could deviate from its agreed public health investment level, which it would have to do before the state of the world for the period is determined; then, as noted above, it would deviate as well from its agreed export tax regardless of which state of the world obtains in that period. Alternatively, the home country could make the agreed public health investment and then deviate from the agreed export tax only if a pandemic occurs, or only during normal times.

Consider the last option first—that is, the home country invests in public health as prescribed under the agreement and then deviates from the agreed export tax $\bar{\tau}_y^e$ (free trade) if times turn out to be normal (there is no pandemic for the period). In this case the one-period gain from deviating to $\bar{\tau}_y^N$ when times are normal is given by $\omega(\bar{\tau}_y^N, \bar{\tau}_x^{*e}) - \omega(\bar{\tau}_y^e, \bar{\tau}_x^{*e})$, where ω is defined by (12.1), implying that this deviation is not profitable for the home country and $\bar{\tau}_y^e$ can be part of a self-enforcing agreement if and only if

$$[\omega(\bar{\tau}_y^N, \bar{\tau}_x^{*e}) - \omega(\bar{\tau}_y^e, \bar{\tau}_x^{*e})] \leq \frac{\delta}{1-\delta} Y^e. \tag{12.14}$$

The inequality in (12.14) is the incentive constraint associated with the home-country choice of $\bar{\tau}_y$, with an analogous incentive constraint applying to the foreign-country choice of $\bar{\tau}_x^*$. As (12.1) confirms, the left-hand side of (12.14) reflects the usual incentive to manipulate the

---

12. This property reflects the i.i.d. nature of the pandemic shock as I have modeled it, a feature that is also shared by the shocks studied by Bagwell and Staiger (1990). See Bagwell and Staiger (2003) for an analysis of self-enforcing trade agreements in the presence of persistent shocks.

terms of trade with an export tax, and if the one-period gain from such opportunistic behavior is not too large and/or the discount factor δ is large enough, the inequality in (12.14) will be met, the home country will see it in its own self-interest to follow through on its export-tax commitment, and the efficient home-country export tax $\bar{\tau}_y^e$ will be sustainable as part of a self-enforcing agreement, with an identical statement holding for $\bar{\tau}_x^{*e}$.

Next, suppose that the home country invests in public health as prescribed under the agreement and then deviates from the agreed export tax $\hat{\tau}_y^e$ (free trade) if there is a pandemic. In this case, the one-period gain from deviating to $\hat{\tau}_y^N$ if the pandemic arrives is given by $\omega_{PAN}(\hat{\tau}_y^N, \hat{\tau}_x^{*e}) - \omega_{PAN}(\hat{\tau}_y^e, \hat{\tau}_x^{*e})$, where ω is defined by (12.3), implying that this deviation is not profitable for the home country and $\hat{\tau}_y^e$ is sustainable as part of a self-enforcing agreement if and only if

$$[\omega_{PAN}(\hat{\tau}_y^N, \hat{\tau}_x^{*e}) - \omega_{PAN}(\hat{\tau}_y^e, \hat{\tau}_x^{*e})] \leq \frac{\delta}{1-\delta} Y^e. \tag{12.15}$$

The inequality in (12.15) is the incentive constraint associated with the home-country choice of $\hat{\tau}_y$, with an analogous incentive constraint applying to the foreign-country choice of $\hat{\tau}_x^*$. Notice, though, that with $\bar{\tau}_y^e = 0 = \hat{\tau}_y^e$ and $\bar{\tau}_x^{*e} = 0 = \hat{\tau}_x^{*e}$, and hence with free trade the efficient export tax in both normal times and during a pandemic, we have by (12.1) and (12.3) that

$$\omega_{PAN}(\hat{\tau}_y^e, \hat{\tau}_x^{*e}) = \omega_{PAN}(\bar{\tau}_y^e, \bar{\tau}_x^{*e})$$

$$= \omega(\bar{\tau}_y^e, \bar{\tau}_x^{*e}) - C(D_x(\bar{\tau}_x^{*e}), D_y(\bar{\tau}_y^e)),$$

while with $\hat{\tau}_y^N > \bar{\tau}_y^N$ we must also have

$$\omega_{PAN}(\hat{\tau}_y^N, \hat{\tau}_x^{*e}) = \omega_{PAN}(\hat{\tau}_y^N, \bar{\tau}_x^{*e})$$

$$> \omega_{PAN}(\bar{\tau}_y^N, \bar{\tau}_x^{*e})$$

$$= \omega(\bar{\tau}_y^N, \bar{\tau}_x^{*e}) - C(D_x(\bar{\tau}_x^{*e}), D_y(\bar{\tau}_y^N)),$$

and it then follows that

$$[\omega_{PAN}(\hat{\tau}_y^N, \hat{\tau}_x^{*e}) - \omega_{PAN}(\hat{\tau}_y^e, \hat{\tau}_x^{*e})] > [\omega(\bar{\tau}_y^N, \bar{\tau}_x^{*e}) - \omega(\bar{\tau}_y^e, \bar{\tau}_x^{*e})]$$

$$+ [C(D_x(\bar{\tau}_x^{*e}), D_y(\bar{\tau}_y^e)) - C(D_x(\bar{\tau}_x^{*e}), D_y(\bar{\tau}_y^N))]$$

$$> [\omega(\bar{\tau}_y^N, \bar{\tau}_x^{*e}) - \omega(\bar{\tau}_y^e, \bar{\tau}_x^{*e})]. \tag{12.16}$$

Therefore, while the right-hand sides of the incentive constraints in (12.15) and (12.14) are the same, (12.16) indicates that the left-hand side of the incentive constraint that applies during a pandemic, (12.15), must be bigger than the left-hand side of the incentive constraint that applies during normal times, (12.14), implying that in a self-enforcing agreement it will be harder to sustain efficient export taxes during a pandemic than in normal times. For example, if the discount factor δ is such that the incentive constraint on $\bar{\tau}_y$ described by (12.14) holds with equality, then (12.16) indicates that the incentive constraint on $\hat{\tau}_y$ described by (12.15) must be violated. Intuitively, this reflects two key ingredients. First, the noncooperative export tax $\bar{\tau}_y^N$ is higher than the efficient level $\bar{\tau}_y^e$ even in normal times, due to the unilateral incentive to manipulate the terms of trade. And second, even if it deviated only to $\bar{\tau}_y^N$ during a pandemic, the one-time gain from this deviation for the home country would rise during the pandemic, because in addition to enjoying the same terms-of-trade gains that the home country would enjoy in normal times, in a pandemic the home country would also enjoy the PPE-hoarding gains that come from the higher-than-efficient export tax; deviating to the optimal deviation-export-tax level $\hat{\tau}_y^N$ that applies during a pandemic can only further increase this one-time gain.

This does not mean that cooperation over export restrictions must break down during a pandemic. As Bagwell and Staiger (1990) show, countries can *manage* the incentive to defect from an agreement by adjusting the trade policies that they agree to implement under the agreement toward the non-cooperative levels, thereby preventing the incentive constraints from ever being violated and keeping the agreement intact, even as it is buffeted by various external shocks. In the present context, that would mean building in to the agreement the flexibility to allow export taxes to rise somewhat during pandemics, in an implicit acknowledgment that the agreement must be self-enforcing and that the implied incentive constraints on export restrictions are especially demanding in a pandemic.[13] Indeed, this provides one interpretation of the "escape" provisions included in GATT that have become the main avenue through which countries

---

13. Such an adjustment in the agreed policies reduces the one-time gain from deviation, but it also reduces the per-period benefits from maintaining the agreement. As Bagwell and Staiger (1990) show, in their model the former effect is larger than the latter so that an adjustment of this kind can always be found that brings the incentive constraint into compliance. The same property can be shown to hold in the present setting.

have imposed export restrictions during the COVID-19 pandemic.[14] Note, however, that unless the discount factor is sufficiently high so that incentive constraints never bind at the efficient policies, this does mean that some efficiency will by necessity be sacrificed during a pandemic. Further, depending on the properties of the pandemic loss function C, it is possible that the "most-cooperative" agreement (i.e., the agreement that implements the policies closest to the efficient policies while not violating any incentive constraints) would by necessity permit export taxes during a pandemic that are almost as high as the noncooperative levels.

Finally, consider the first deviation possibility listed above—namely, the home country deviates from its agreed public health investment level, which it would have to do before the state of the world for the period is determined, and then it deviates as well from its agreed export tax regardless of which state of the world obtains in that period. In this case, and continuing to suppose for the moment that the agreement calls for efficient public health investments and export tax levels, the incentive constraint becomes

$$[W(\bar{\tau}_y^N, \bar{\tau}_x^{*e}, \hat{\tau}_y^N, \hat{\tau}_x^{*e}, I^{BR}, I^{*e}) - W(\bar{\tau}_y^e, \bar{\tau}_x^{*e}, \hat{\tau}_y^e, \hat{\tau}_x^{*e}, I^e, I^{*e})] \leq \frac{\delta}{1-\delta} Y^e,$$

(12.17)

where W is defined by (12.5) and where I^{BR} denotes the home country's optimal unilateral best-response choice of public health investment given that the foreign country invests the efficient amount I^{*e}.[15] The inequality in (12.17) is the incentive constraint associated with the home-country choice of I, with an analogous incentive constraint applying to the foreign-country choice of I^*. As (12.17) together with (12.5) indicate, whether or not efficient public health investments, can be part of a self-enforcing agreement will depend on the elasticity of

---

14. See Sykes (2020) and Congressional Research Service (2021). For example, though GATT Article XI provides for the general elimination of quantitative restrictions on trade, including limitations on exports, it exempts "export prohibitions or restrictions temporarily applied to prevent or relieve critical shortages of foodstuffs or other products essential to the exporting contracting party." And GATT Article XX carves out from GATT/WTO commitments more generally any measures "necessary to protect human, animal, or plant life or health," as long as nondiscrimination is upheld and such measures are not merely "disguised restriction[s] on international trade."

15. I did not need to introduce a separate notation for best-response export taxes in addition to Nash export taxes because given the absence of import tariffs and the separability of the x and y sectors, the Nash and best-response export taxes are one and the same.

pandemic risk mitigation with respect to public health investments, as reflected in $\rho(I, I^*)$ and the properties of the investment cost function $c(\cdot)$, as well as on the magnitude of the discount factor δ.

Something more interesting can be said, however, once it is recalled that the incentive constraints for $\bar{\tau}_y$ and $\hat{\tau}_y$ will also have to be met in any self-enforcing agreement. In particular, suppose that at the most-cooperative export taxes the incentive constraints for $\bar{\tau}_y$ and $\hat{\tau}_y$ hold with equality. Then, denoting the most-cooperative home-country export taxes as $\bar{\tau}_y^c$ and $\hat{\tau}_y^c$, we would have

$$[\omega(\bar{\tau}_y^N, \bar{\tau}_x^{*c}) - \omega(\bar{\tau}_y^c, \bar{\tau}_x^{*c})] = \frac{\delta}{1-\delta} Y^c \qquad (12.18)$$

$$[\omega_{PAN}(\hat{\tau}_y^N, \hat{\tau}_x^{*c}) - \omega_{PAN}(\hat{\tau}_y^c, \hat{\tau}_x^{*c})] = \frac{\delta}{1-\delta} Y^c,$$

where Y^c is defined by

$$Y^c \equiv W(\bar{\tau}_y^c, \bar{\tau}_x^{*c}, \hat{\tau}_y^c, \hat{\tau}_x^{*c}, I^c, I^{*c}) - W(\bar{\tau}_y^N, \bar{\tau}_x^{*N}, \hat{\tau}_y^N, \hat{\tau}_x^{*N}, I^N, I^{*N}) > 0,$$

with I^c satisfying the incentive constraint

$$[W(\bar{\tau}_y^N, \bar{\tau}_x^{*c}, \hat{\tau}_y^N, \hat{\tau}_x^{*c}, I^{BR}, I^{*c}) - W(\bar{\tau}_y^c, \bar{\tau}_x^{*c}, \hat{\tau}_y^c, \hat{\tau}_x^{*c}, I^c, I^{*c})] \leq \frac{\delta}{1-\delta} Y^c.$$

$$(12.19)$$

In (12.19), I^{BR} is the home country's best-response choice of public health investment given that the foreign country invests the amount I^{*c}, and I^c is uniquely defined by (12.19) when this incentive constraint is binding and therefore holds with equality; $\bar{\tau}_x^{*c}$, $\hat{\tau}_x^{*c}$ and I^{*c} are similarly defined for the foreign country.

But now recall that defection from I^c will be accompanied by a defection from the cooperative export tax which, by (12.18), would by itself yield a one-time gain equal to $\frac{\delta}{1-\delta} Y^c$, regardless of whether the world ends up in normal times for the period—and therefore the top line of (12.18) applies—or in a pandemic, in which case the bottom line of (12.18) applies. Hence there can be no additional gain for the home country in deviating from I^c if the incentive constraint (12.19) is to hold. In other words, if the agreement achieves the most-cooperative export taxes and leaves no slack in those incentive constraints, then it must implement the noncooperative Nash levels of public health investment.[16]

---

16. This follows from my assumption that policy deviations from the agreement are only observed by the other party at the end of the period.

It is intuitive and easy to establish that the optimal (ex ante world welfare maximizing) agreement in this setting would never allocate all enforcement power to cooperation only on export taxes in the way I have just described.[17] The upshot is that an optimal self-enforcing agreement that faces constraints on enforcement power, and that for this reason cannot implement the fully efficient policies, will leave some slack in the export tax incentive constraints in order to allow countries to cooperate at least to some degree on their choices of public health investments. This provides an additional reason why looking to a trade agreement as a forum for blunting the use of export taxes during a pandemic can be counter productive, and it suggests that the WTO might better allocate its scarce enforcement power toward helping countries cooperate over measures that could reduce the probability of pandemics in the first place, perhaps partnering with the WHO in this effort.

Notice, too, that the difficulties in cooperating over export restraints during a pandemic have potentially important ramifications for the organization of supply chains related to the production of vaccines, PPE, and other products and materials whose demand is likely to surge during a pandemic. If the incentive to hoard during a pandemic cannot be controlled by international agreements, countries would be wise to acknowledge this and organize their supply chains accordingly. Put differently, while I have not attempted to model it here, the efficient organization of supply chains for pandemic-related products and materials is itself likely to be affected in important ways by the enforcement-constraint limitations that governments face when attempting to cooperate over export restraints during a pandemic.

---

17. In fact, in a setting that features terms-of-trade externalities and both trade and behind-the-border policies, Ederington (2001) shows that scarce enforcement power would be allocated first to nontariff instruments to secure their efficient setting and only then used to reduce trade taxes toward efficient levels as the incentive constraint allows. The setting I consider here includes as well international (nonpecuniary) externalities through the pandemic probability function $\rho(I, I^*)$ that extend beyond the terms-of-trade externality, so Ederington's result does not apply. But it nonetheless points in the same direction—namely, that in a setting with multiple policy instruments that can generate international externalities, an optimal self-enforcing agreement would never allocate all enforcement power to cooperation only on export taxes.

13 A World Trading System for the Twenty-First Century

The WTO faces challenges on many fronts. The shallow approach to integration pioneered by GATT seems to have fallen out of favor in recent decades, and the world trading system is increasingly dominated by deep-integration initiatives with a focus on the trade effects of regulations and other behind-the-border measures and a push toward regulatory convergence. Meanwhile, China's entry into the WTO has challenged an approach to globalization that was designed fundamentally with market economies in mind, even while developing economies have long felt that it is the industrialized countries that have mostly gained from GATT/WTO-sponsored market access liberalization. And within many countries there has been a strong backlash more recently against globalization itself, from those who have not shared in the gains from globalization and from others who feel that globalization has eroded the sovereignty of their national governments. These challenges have arisen against the backdrop of a dramatic increase in the economic importance of developing and emerging economies and changes in the nature of trade brought about by offshoring and global value chains and by digitalization and a rise in the importance of trade in services. And beyond these direct challenges, the increasing urgency of addressing climate change has raised questions about the role that the WTO should play in this effort.

In light of these developments, do we need a new global trade order for the twenty-first century? In the preceding chapters, I have argued that meeting globalization's challenges in the twenty-first century will require a nuanced response capable of addressing multilateralism's current shortcomings. And to succeed, we need a correct diagnosis of those shortcomings. I have argued that for such a diagnosis, it is imperative to understand why GATT worked, the economic environment it is best suited for, and whether the changes in the economic environment that have occurred in recent decades imply the need for changes in the design of the GATT/WTO, or possibly a new approach to trade agreements altogether, or rather simply better use of the agreements already in place.

Why did GATT work? In part I of this book, I review a body of economics research that, in a surprisingly wide set of economic environments, consistently identifies the central purpose of trade agreements as providing governments with an escape from what amounts formally to a terms-of-trade-driven prisoner's dilemma. And I have shown how this research, which I have referred to collectively as the terms-of-trade theory of trade agreements, supports the position that the broad design features of the GATT/WTO appear well suited to serve this purpose. Hence, in those economic environments for which these findings apply, the design features of the GATT/WTO can be understood to reflect a sound economic logic; and to the extent that the economic environment of the GATT era did not depart in important ways from those environments, it is GATT's design features that can therefore account for its success.

On this basis, I have argued for the legitimacy of the GATT/WTO as the constitution of the world trading system for the twentieth century. It appears well designed to solve a problem for member governments which, if not the only problem for a trade agreement to solve, was arguably at least the central problem of the GATT era. I have acknowledged that my argument adopts a state-centered view of legitimacy, and that a complete case for the legitimacy of the GATT/WTO would extend to a people-centered perspective as well; but I have maintained that it is the state-centered view of legitimacy that is relevant for the central international task of designing a constitution for the world trading system.

From this understanding of GATT's success, do the changes in the economic environment that have occurred in recent decades imply the need for changes in the design of the GATT/WTO? I have argued in part II of this book that the legitimacy of the GATT/WTO can be seen to transcend many of the current challenges that it faces, because those challenges do not stem from changes in the economic environment that would alter the central purpose of a trade agreement from that identified by the terms-of-trade theory. This is not to say that meeting those challenges will require no response from the WTO. While in some cases better use of the existing GATT/WTO structure may suffice, in other cases reforms of the WTO seem warranted in order to better position the WTO to meet those challenges—reforms that would not necessarily be viewed as minor by the member governments. Still, a key message of the findings presented in part II is that to meet those challenges, fundamental departures from the GATT/WTO approach seem unnecessary and are, arguably, unlikely to lead to better outcomes. Part II also presents research that raises the possibility that some recent changes in the economic environment may indeed have altered the purpose of trade agreements. To meet the challenges that arise under these possibilities, more fundamental changes in the approach of the WTO may be required.

Gathering these insights together, in this chapter I synthesize and summarize in broad terms what an effective world trading system for the twenty-first century might look like. To develop this synthesis, it is useful to begin by putting aside the issues raised by offshoring (chapter 10) and the push toward regulatory convergence (chapter 11) and to focus initially on the challenges described in the first three chapters of part II. These challenges stem from the rise of the large emerging economies, including China (chapter 7); efforts to address global climate change and the positive role that the WTO might play in addressing this issue (chapter 8); and the implications of digital trade, considering trade in both goods and services (chapter 9). For each of these challenges, I have suggested that the basic logic of GATT's design still applies so that fundamental departures from the GATT/WTO approach are unnecessary. However, to better meet these challenges, there are a number of reforms to the WTO suggested by my analysis that seem warranted, which I summarize below.

To put the logic of these reforms in a broader context, I first note two cross-cutting themes that emerge from the body of economics research I reviewed in Part I. A first theme is this: Trade agreements that lack deep-integration provisions are not necessarily "weak" agreements; by the same token, those trade agreements that contain the most developed deep-integration provisions should not necessarily be seen as the "gold standard." Indeed, in light of the discussion of globalization and national sovereignty in chapter 12, it might be concluded that where the terms-of-trade theory is applicable the opposite may be closer to the truth, as shallow-integration agreements hold out the possibility that countries could reach the international efficiency frontier without sacrificing national sovereignty.

More broadly, as I have emphasized in various places throughout the book, at a practical level the message of the terms-of-trade theory is not so much that *no* degree of deep integration is necessary to reach the efficiency frontier, but rather that the market access orientation of the GATT/WTO can provide a potentially useful *guardrail* to delineate the depth of integration that governments should be willing to contemplate in their agreements in order to reach the efficiency frontier. According to the terms-of-trade theory, there is no reason for a trade agreement to go deeper than what is required to ensure that property rights over negotiated market access are reasonably secure. Such a guardrail can help governments avoid conflicts between globalization and national sovereignty that, according to the terms-of-trade theory and in particular the discussion in chapter 12, would be unnecessary. Viewed from this perspective, the fact that the GATT/WTO lags behind various regional initiatives to deepen the negotiated commitments of their member governments may be a virtue of the WTO rather than a shortcoming. A better understanding of this may help to serve as a break on the rising dominance of preferential trade agreements relative to the WTO in the global trading system.

A second cross-cutting theme can also be gleaned from the research I reviewed in Part I. To a first order, when it comes to trade agreements, the primary task of national governments during the GATT era was to dismantle the excessively high trade barriers of the large industrialized countries and to move the world from a starting point far away from the international efficiency frontier to a position on the frontier. By the end of the twentieth century much, though not all, of this task had been completed. For the twenty-first century, it could be argued that the primary task for the WTO has shifted away from helping governments traverse *to* the efficiency frontier and toward providing them with the flexibility they need to remain *on* the frontier in the face of various shocks to the world trading system, including the rise of China and the large emerging economies, the digitalization of trade, and the rising threat of climate change. For this era, the capabilities of countries to rebalance and renegotiate their commitments within the GATT/WTO framework is likely to become paramount to the WTO's success. In principle, the GATT/WTO is as well equipped for this second task as the GATT proved to be for the first task, but some WTO reforms may be warranted so that member governments can exercise these features more effectively.

With these cross-cutting themes serving as a backdrop, I now consider what a world trading system for the twenty-first century might look like, putting aside for the moment the issues raised by offshoring and the push toward regulatory convergence. In effect, to meet the remaining challenges that I have described in part II, there is no need for fundamental changes to the logic of the GATT/WTO. But a number of reforms are suggested by the findings reviewed in those chapters that could help the WTO more effectively meet these challenges, and there are also ways that WTO members might be encouraged to use existing WTO features more effectively in the context of these challenges.

For starters, it is clear that the world trading system of the twenty-first century cannot be effective if it does not find a way to accommodate China's unique economic system. But, as noted in chapter 7, at issue here is ultimately the task of rebalancing market access commitments to restore a reciprocal balance between rights and obligations for China and its trading partners. In principle, there is no inconsistency between China's economic system and the GATT/WTO shallow-integration approach. That is, the challenge for the WTO posed by China is not to find the capacity to evolve beyond its essential focus on market access in order to successfully accommodate China, nor is it to find a way to convince China to adopt market reforms. Rather, the challenge for the WTO is to find a way for China to make additional policy commitments, tailored to compensate for the nonmarket elements of its economy, that can serve the role of preserving the market access implied by its tariff bindings, essentially comparable to the role that GATT articles play for market-oriented economies. And I have argued in chapter 7 that the non-violation claim, possibly augmented with some adjustments to usual practices in acknowledgment of the extraordinary circumstances surrounding the challenge for the WTO posed by China, is particularly well suited to meet this challenge.

Once the reciprocal balance between China's market access rights and obligations in the WTO has been restored, many of the remaining challenges faced by the world trading system amount to finding ways for countries to reconsider and reorient the levels of their reciprocal market access commitments, possibly through a sequence of renegotiations and negotiations, and possibly facilitated by a number of reforms, all of which might best be orchestrated in the context of a renewed multilateral round of negotiations. As described in chapter 7, for the reconsideration of the level of market access commitments that some industrialized countries may desire, GATT Article XXVIII renegotiations in the context of a multilateral round would be relatively straightforward, given the liability-rule structure of the market access commitments that would be the focus of these renegotiations. Furthermore, to address the latecomers problem, in principle a sequence of GATT Article XXVIII renegotiations between industrialized countries followed by Article XXVIII bis negotiations between industrialized and developing/emerging countries in a multilateral round could suffice. An important WTO reform that could in principle help countries address the latecomers problem would be to revisit the special and differential treatment clause and to consider formally terminating this clause at least as it applies to the market access concessions of the large emerging and developing countries.

Similar statements apply to the issues faced by the WTO in accommodating and possibly playing a constructive role in efforts to address climate change. As described in chapter 8, the implementation of carbon border adjustments that might accompany a country's carbon taxes and that took the form of new MFN tariffs could be accomplished in the context of GATT Article XXVIII renegotiations, and the possibility of reducing these new tariffs in the context of a multilateral round of market access negotiations could be handled in Article XXVIII bis negotiations between industrialized and developing/emerging countries. Here, possible reforms of WTO rules might include provisions that are explicit about the form and function of allowable carbon border adjustments, along the lines of what I have described in chapter 8, to clarify permissible behavior in anticipation that such adjustments might become commonplace going forward.

As I have described in chapter 9, the challenges to the WTO posed by the rise of digital trade may also introduce new reasons for negotiation and renegotiation of market access commitments. For digital goods trade, the issues are relatively straightforward, provided that any nonpecuniary externalities associated with open digital policies are purely local: It may be that as a practical matter, the tariff commitments negotiated in the pre-digital world no longer afford the same degree of trade protection against imports of that good that they once did; and it may also be that new digital forms of protection become relevant, which could undermine existing market access commitments. The first of these issues could in principle be addressed in the context of Article XXVIII renegotiations, while the second issue could in principle be addressed with the existing WTO rules that are designed to address the erosion of market access commitments with behind-the-border policies more generally.

For digital services trade, analogous issues arise, but there are a number of substantial reforms, covered in chapter 9, that would bring

GATS more in line with the shallow approach to integration taken by GATT and that could facilitate further market access negotiations in services. These reforms might be sensible also in the absence of digital trade, but they are made even more attractive by the blurring of the distinction between goods and services that the rise of digital trade is causing.

Where nonpecuniary externalities associated with open digital policies cross national borders, the relevant digital policies must be the subject of direct negotiations by the impacted governments, just as with any nonpecuniary international externality. But as chapter 9 confirms, conditional on these nonpecuniary international externalities being addressed, achieving the efficiency frontier with GATT's shallow approach to integration for all other policies is possible, and so the issues remain as described just above.

I now turn to the issues raised by offshoring and the push toward regulatory convergence, as discussed in chapters 10 and 11, respectively. Here, more fundamental changes in the approach of the WTO may be required.

Consider first the issues raised by offshoring. It is possible that the rise of offshoring has introduced into the world trading system a novel form of international policy externality, at least among countries trading specialized inputs along a common global value chain, and in doing so it has made the shallow-integration approach of the GATT/WTO no longer suitable for solving the fundamental trade agreement problem for these countries. If this is so, then deeper forms of integration will be required for these countries to achieve internationally efficient policies, and a stark trade-off between sovereignty and globalization may be unavoidable.[1] But as I noted in chapter 10, it is also possible that the rise of offshoring has *not* changed the nature of the international policy externality, because to date the available evidence on this point is only indirect and suggestive and there is no empirical evidence on the crucial question—namely, whether the rise in offshoring has changed the nature of the dominant form of international price determination.

In light of these unknowns and until there is more direct empirical evidence on the nature of the changes wrought by the rise of offshoring,

---

1. Here I am again using sovereignty in the informal sense that I have used it everywhere in the book except for chapter 12. An open question is whether efficiency could be reached in the offshoring models of Antràs and Staiger (2012a, 2012b), or the version of their model that I have developed in chapter 10, without violating a country's sovereignty as that notion is formalized in Bagwell and Staiger (2018b) and described in chapter 12.

a conservative approach to advocating changes in the world trading system in response to offshoring seems appropriate—an approach
that builds on the GATT/WTO foundation and so continues to be
well suited for addressing traditional international policy externalities
while responding to those issues that are introduced by offshoring with
bespoke arrangements as warranted. A reasonable approach might be
to embrace plurilateral agreements within the WTO framework (provided for in WTO Article II.3) as a safety valve for achieving deeper
integration among countries that strongly desire to pursue such agreements. The benefits of plurilateral agreements for this purpose—as
opposed to preferential trade agreements of the kind allowed under
GATT Article XXIV and currently the vehicle of choice—have been discussed in the literature (Hoekman and Mavroidis 2015; Hoekman and
Sabel 2020), and they are likely to provide a route toward deeper integration for willing countries that is less disruptive to the fundamental
principles of the GATT/WTO than other routes.

A potential impediment to this approach is that the WTO requires
plurilateral agreements to be approved by a consensus of WTO members, including those who do not intend to joint the plurilateral. This
raises the possibility that some countries with no intention of join-
ing the plurilateral and with no direct interest in it might nevertheless
hold up its approval to gain leverage in other unrelated negotiations.
A possible reform of the WTO might involve relaxing in some way
the consensus requirement for the formation of plurilateral agreements
in the WTO; for the outlines of one such proposal, see Hoekman and
Mavroidis (2015). But even without this reform, relying on plurilaterals that can achieve consensus to serve as an outlet for the desires of
countries that wish to pursue deeper-integration agreements may be
an attractive option for the world trading system as a response to offshoring, given that the conservative approach that I have argued for in
this case would indicate that erring on the side of caution and adopting
a criterion for such agreements that is too stringent is arguably better
than adopting a criterion for such agreements that is too permissive.

With regard to the question of regulatory convergence discussed in
chapter 11, it is useful to distinguish cases where product standards
have a clear role in addressing an important consumption externality from cases where the existence of such consumption externalities
cannot be established. In the former case, and even when the externality does not cross national borders, direct negotiations over the
fine details of the relevant product standards will be warranted, but

only if, in addition, preferences for the products are heterogeneous across countries and firms face higher costs when they tailor their product attributes to local tastes. The fact that these are relatively special circumstances suggests that in the former case and where such circumstances arise, countries could address the issue with deep-integration initiatives that involve negotiating selectively over the relevant standards, possibly with plurilaterals again serving as the most attractive vehicle for accommodating these commitments.

For all other circumstances, a shallow approach to integration with regard to product standards would suffice. Here, some combination of national treatment, other elaborations on nondiscrimination rules, and the non-violation clause, combined in some circumstances with a rebuttable presumption of mutual recognition, would in principle allow countries to achieve efficient policies for standards that were not directly negotiated. The introduction of mutual recognition, even in limited circumstances (i.e., where preferences for the products are heterogeneous across countries and firms face higher costs when they tailor their product attributes to local tastes), would be novel in the context of the WTO, yet it is a reform worth considering according to the findings that I have reviewed in chapter 11.

Finally, looming over all of this is the possibility that neither the rise in offshoring nor the conditions that have led to the turn toward regulatory convergence are in fact a root cause of concern for the WTO. Instead, for the reasons discussed in chapter 12, it may be that without US leadership, the rules-based multilateral trading system is simply heading into a period of decline and, as Erianger (2018) puts it in his review of Kagan (2018), "returning the world to its natural state—a dark jungle of competing interests, clashing nationalism, tribalism and self-interest." But even if this apocalyptic diagnosis does capture the main cause of the rules-based trading system's ills, there is great value in attempting to support, preserve, and improve the existing global trade order until such time as a new hegemon arrives and the rules-based system can again thrive. As I have described in previous chapters, the fundamental design of the rules-based multilateral trading system has proved effective in solving an important and, by this diagnosis still central problem, and it should not be allowed to wither away. By this diagnosis, the shallow-integration approach of the GATT/WTO is well designed to solve the fundamental trade agreement problem. As such, a stark trade-off between sovereignty and globalization may be avoidable, but only if the WTO is supported and its approach

strengthened. Could China be the next hegemon that the WTO is looking for? At present, to many this may seem unlikely, but along the lines
sketched out in chapter 12, as its dominance grows, China may see that
it is in its interest to more fully commit to making these rules work.
Until that time, even according to this apocalyptic diagnosis, the WTO
deserves broad support as the legitimate constitution of the global trade
order.

14   Conclusion

I have argued in this book that the best hope for creating an effective world trading system for the twenty-first century is to build on the foundations of the world trading system of the twentieth century. I have constructed this argument in two steps: first, by developing an understanding of why GATT worked and the economic environment it is best suited for, and second, by evaluating according to this understanding whether the changes in the economic environment that have occurred in recent decades imply the need for changes in the design of GATT and the WTO. I have argued that the terms-of-trade theory of trade agreements offers a compelling framework for understanding the success of GATT in the twentieth century, and that according to this understanding, the logic of GATT's design features transcend many, though not all, of the current challenges faced by the WTO.

It is from this perspective that one could say, as I wrote in the introduction, that the best advice for designing a world trading system for the twenty-first century may not be "Move fast and break things," but rather "Keep calm and carry on." With this advice I am not claiming that reforms to the world trading system are not needed or that all is well at the WTO. But I am claiming that the architecture of the GATT/WTO—and the GATT, in particular—is well suited to guide the design of the world trading system of the twenty-first century.

Even if the logic of my argument is accepted, there is still the question: How could the designers of GATT have gotten it so right? Two observations can help to answer this question. First, the designers of GATT did not build GATT from scratch. Rather, as I described in chapter 2, GATT was modeled on the US Reciprocal Trade Agreements Act, whose design in turn benefited from decades of experimentation with various trade agreement designs both in the United States and Europe. So the designers of GATT were very much standing on the shoulders of those before them, and they were beneficiaries of a trial-and-error learning process that had been going on for decades.

A second observation may also help explain how the designers of GATT could have gotten it so right. GATT was born in the aftermath of World War II, when the world economy was in a period of deep crisis and some of the best economic minds of the day, including James Meade and John Maynard Keynes, were recruited to help in its design. Meade was a member of the British delegation to the London and Geneva conferences in 1946 and 1947, which produced the charter for the International Trade Organization and GATT, and along with Keynes, Meade was widely regarded as a central figure in these conferences (Penrose 1953, 89–90). And so economics clearly held a position of prominence in shaping the design decisions that led to GATT, arguably far more than would have been the case if GATT had been designed under less exceptional circumstances.[1]

Of course, this begs the question of whether these economists emphasized the terms-of-trade externality associated with commercial policy that lies at the heart of the terms-of-trade theory of trade agreements and, if they did, whether they viewed GATT as a forum for addressing these terms-of-trade externalities. But as Bagwell and Staiger (2016) have observed, a report commissioned by GATT and written by a panel of experts composed of Roberto de Oliveira Campos, Gottfried Haberler, James Meade, and Jan Tinbergen (commonly referred to as the Haberler Report) suggests an affirmative answer to this question.

Addressing the topic of commercial policy in the 1950s and the agricultural protectionism of industrialized countries during that period, the Haberler Report does indeed emphasize terms-of-trade externalities, expressed in a multicountry setting along the lines that I have sketched in chapter 4:

The problem of the interests of different primary producing countries outside industrialized Western Europe and North America is ... not only a question which of the other countries would gain by a moderation of agricultural protectionism in these two great industrialized regions; there are undoubtedly cases

---

1. It has long been observed that periods of crisis can create favorable conditions for the creation of institutions to solve otherwise intractable problems. See, for example, Langan-Riekhof, Avanni, and Janetti (2017).

in which an increase in agricultural protectionism in these two regions, while it would be to the disadvantage of some of the unindustrialized countries, would actually be to the advantage of others.... An increased stimulus to the production of wheat in any of the countries of North America or of Western Europe by increasing the exportable surplus of North America and decreasing the import requirements of Western Europe would depress the world market for wheat. This might mean that a country like India or Japan would obtain cheaper imports of wheat (either because of a fall in the world price or because of a development of special sales or gifts for the disposal of surplus wheat by the United States), but a country like Australia or the Argentine which competed in the world export market for wheat would be damaged....

In general, if one considers any particular agricultural product, a protective stimulus to its production in any one country by increasing supplies relatively to the demand for that product will tend to depress the world market for that product. This will damage the interests of other countries which are exporters of the product on the world market. But it will be to the national interest of countries which import the product from the world market. Whether the initial protective stimulus confers a net benefit or a net damage to all other countries concerned depends, therefore, upon whether the country giving the protective stimulus to its own production is an exporter or an importer of the product; if it is an exporter it is conferring a benefit on the world by giving its supplies away at a cheap price; if it is an importer it is damaging the rest of the world by refusing to take their supplies.

This general principle can be applied to a single country or to a whole region. It is because Western Europe and North America in combination are net *importers* of agricultural produce that we reach the general conclusion that a reduction of agricultural protectionism in these areas will on balance benefit the rest of the world. (GATT 1958, 93–94, original emphasis, footnotes omitted)

Here, when describing the impacts of agricultural protectionism in the industrialized world on various countries in the rest of the world, the report's references to "depress the world market," "fall in the world price," gains for other importing countries from "cheaper imports," and losses for countries which "competed in the world export market" reflect a simple terms-of-trade logic.

Moreover, the Haberler Report's references to the protective policies of "any of the countries of North America or of Western Europe," "any one country," and "a single country" suggest that the report's authors accepted the notion that a single country's protective choices could have world price impacts; indeed, the general principle for signing the international externalities associated with commercial policy intervention stated by the report in the quoted passage above is couched in terms of "the country giving the protective stimulus." Hence, in these paragraphs, the authors appear to be describing the terms-of-trade externality that is at the heart of the terms-of-trade theory of trade agreements.

And it also appears that the authors of the Haberler Report viewed GATT as a forum for addressing these terms-of-trade commercial policy externalities, as the report makes recommendations that are based on these terms-of-trade externality patterns. For example, the following recommendation, taken from the report's executive summary, reflects the application of the international externality signing principle as articulated in the quoted excerpt above:

Since in North America and Western Europe as a whole net imports of agricultural products represent the relatively narrow margin by which their large domestic consumption exceeds their large, but not quite so large, domestic production, a relatively small restraint on domestic production or stimulus to domestic consumption could lead to a large percentage increase in their net imports. For this reason much could be achieved by some moderate change in the direction of the agricultural policies of the highly industrialized countries. (GATT 1958, 9)

It is therefore accurate to say that GATT was forged with the benefit of a substantial amount of knowledge, accumulated through prior experience, about what worked and what did not work, and at a moment in history where the best economists of the day were able to exert a remarkable level of influence over its design. This unique set of circumstances may go a long way toward explaining how the designers of GATT got it so right.

More speculatively, this may also help to account for the fact that, with the creation of the WTO, a number of features were added to the basic architecture of GATT that are less clearly supported by economic arguments.[2] The Uruguay Round negotiations that gave birth to the WTO in 1995 did not correspond to a period of crisis for the world economy in the way that GATT's creation in 1947 did, and it is perhaps in part for this reason that industry lobbies appear to have had a much bigger role in driving the design of the WTO than was true of

---

2. For example, Sykes (2003) offers a critique of the design and legal interpretations of the elaborations on GATT Article XIX embodied in the WTO Safeguard Agreement. Bagwell and Staiger (2006), too, have argued that the WTO Agreement on Subsidies and Countervailing Measures may have marked a step backward relative to GATT's treatment of subsidies (see also Sykes 2005). And a number of economists have questioned the wisdom of including TRIPS in the WTO and its particular design (see, for example, Deardorff 1990).

GATT.[3] Whether or not the world economy is entering a crisis phase akin to that which gave rise to GATT, there is reason to hope that with an economist now at the helm of the WTO, economics may again be elevated to a position of prominence in the design decisions for the world trading system of the twenty-first century.

---

3. See, for example, the account in Gad (2003) of the influence of the pharmaceutical lobbies on the TRIPS negotiations, among others.

References

Aaronson, Susan A. 2018. "What Are We Talking about When We Talk about Digital Protectionism?" *World Trade Review* (August): 1–37.

Acemoglu, Daron, Ali Makhdoumi, Azarakhsh Malekian, and Asu Ozdaglar. Forthcoming. "Too Much Data: Prices and Inefficiencies in Data Markets." *American Economic Journal: Microeconomics.*

Ahmed, Usman. 2019. "The Importance of Cross-Border Regulatory Cooperation in an Era of Digital Trade." *World Trade Review* 18(S1): s99–s120.

Allen, Treb. 2014. "Information Frictions in Trade." *Econometrica* 82(6): 2041–2083.

Amiti, Mary, Stephen J. Redding, and David E. Weinstein. 2019. "The Impact of the 2018 Tariffs on Prices and Welfare." *Journal of Economic Perspectives* 33(4): 187–210.

Amiti, Mary, Stephen J. Redding, and David E. Weinstein. 2020. "Who's Paying for the US Tariffs? A Longer-Term Perspective." *American Economic Review Papers and Proceedings* 110: 541–546.

Antràs, Pol, and Robert W. Staiger. 2012a. "Offshoring and the Role of Trade Agreements," *American Economic Review* 102(7): 3140–3183.

Antràs, Pol, and Robert W. Staiger. 2012b. "Trade Agreements and the Nature of Price Determination." *American Economic Review Papers and Proceedings* 102(3): 470–476.

Autor, David H., David Dorn, and Gordon H. Hanson. 2013. "The China Syndrome: Local Labor Market Effects of Import Competition in the United States." *American Economic Review* 103(6): 2121–2168.

Azmeh, Shamel, Christopher Foster, and Jaime Echavarri. 2020. "The International Trade Regime and the Quest for Free Digital Trade." *International Studies Review: Analytical Essay* 22: 671–692.

Bacchetta, Marc, Patrick Low, Aaditya Mattoo, Ludger Schuknecht, Hannu Wagner, and Madelon Wehrens. 1998. *Electronic Commerce and the Role of the WTO.* Geneva: World Trade Organization Special Studies 2.

Bagwell, Kyle, Chad Bown, and Robert W. Staiger. 2016. "Is the WTO Passe?" *Journal of Economic Literature* 54(4): 1125–1231.

Bagwell, Kyle, and Seung Hoon Lee. 2018. "Trade Policy under Monopolistic Competition with Heterogeneous Firms and Quasi-Linear CES Preferences." Unpublished manuscript.

Bagwell, Kyle, and Seung Hoon Lee. 2020. "Trade Policy under Monopolistic Competition with Firm Selection." *Journal of International Economics* 127.

Bagwell, Kyle, and Robert W. Staiger. 1990. "A Theory of Managed Trade." *American Economic Review* 80(4): 779–795.

Bagwell, Kyle, and Robert W. Staiger. 1999. "An Economic Theory of GATT." *American Economic Review* 89(1): 215–248.

Bagwell, Kyle, and Robert W. Staiger. 2001a. "Reciprocity, Non-discrimination and Preferential Agreements in the Multilateral Trading System." *European Journal of Political Economy* 17(2): 281–325.

Bagwell, Kyle, and Robert W. Staiger. 2001b. "Domestic Policies, National Sovereignty, and International Economic Institutions." *Quarterly Journal of Economics* 116: 519–562.

Bagwell, Kyle, and Robert W. Staiger. 2002. *The Economics of the World Trading System.* Cambridge, MA: MIT Press.

Bagwell, Kyle, and Robert W. Staiger. 2003. "Protection and the Business Cycle." *The B.E. (Berkeley Electronic) Journal of Economic Analysis & Policy* 3(1): 1–45.

Bagwell, Kyle, and Robert W. Staiger. 2005. " 'Multilateral Trade Negotiations, Bilateral Opportunism and the Rules of GATT/WTO.' " *Journal of International Economics* 67 (2): 268–294.

Bagwell, Kyle, and Robert W. Staiger. 2006. "Will International Rules on Subsidies Disrupt the World Trading System?" *American Economic Review* 96(3): 877–895.

Bagwell, Kyle, and Robert W. Staiger. 2010a. "The World Trade Organization: Theory and Practice." *Annual Reviews of Economics* 2: 223–256.

Bagwell, Kyle, and Robert W. Staiger. 2010b. "Backward Stealing and Forward Manipulation in the WTO." *Journal of International Economics* 82(1): 49–62.

Bagwell, Kyle, and Robert W. Staiger. 2011. "What Do Trade Negotiators Negotiate About? Empirical Evidence from the World Trade Organization." *American Economic Review* 101(4): 1238–1273.

Bagwell, Kyle, and Robert W. Staiger. 2012a. "Profit Shifting and Trade Agreements in Imperfectly Competitive Markets." *International Economic Review* 53(4): 1067–1104.

Bagwell, Kyle, and Robert W. Staiger. 2012b. "The Economics of Trade Agreements in the Linear Cournot Delocation Model." *Journal of International Economics* 88(1): 32–46.

Bagwell, Kyle, and Robert W. Staiger. 2014. "Can the Doha Round Be a Development Round? Setting a Place at the Table." In *Globalization in an Age of Crisis: Multilateral Economic Cooperation in the Twenty-First Century*, edited by Robert C Feenstra and Alan M Taylor. Chicago: University of Chicago Press.

Bagwell, Kyle, and Robert W. Staiger. 2015. "Delocation and Trade Agreements in Imperfectly Competitive Markets." *Research in Economics* 69: 132–156.

Bagwell, Kyle, and Robert W. Staiger. 2016. "The Design of Trade Agreements." In *Handbook of Commercial Policy*, vol. 1A, edited by Kyle Bagwell and Robert W. Staiger. Amsterdam: Elsevier.

Bagwell, Kyle, and Robert W. Staiger. 2018a. "Multilateral Trade Bargaining and Dominant Strategies." *International Economic Review* 59(4): 1785–1824.

Bagwell, Kyle, and Robert W. Staiger. 2018b. "National Sovereignty in an Interdependent World." In *World Trade Evolution: Growth, Productivity and Employment*, edited by Lili Yan Ing and Miaojie Yu. London: Routledge.

Bagwell, Kyle, Robert W. Staiger, and Ali Yurukoglu. 2018. "'Nash-in-Nash' Tariff Bargaining with and without MFN." Mimeo, May.

Bagwell, Kyle, Robert W. Staiger, and Ali Yurukoglu. 2020a. "Multilateral Trade Bargaining: A First Look at the GATT Bargaining Records." *American Economic Journal: Applied* 12(3): 72–105.

Bagwell, Kyle, Robert W. Staiger, and Ali Yurukoglu. 2020b. "'Nash-in-Nash' Tariff Bargaining." *Journal of International Economics* 122 (January).

Bagwell, Kyle, Robert W. Staiger, and Ali Yurukoglu. 2021. "Quantitative Analysis of Multiparty Tariff Negotiations." *Econometrica* 89(4): 1595–1631.

Battigalli, Pierpaolo, and Giovanni Maggi. 2002. "Rigidity, Discretion, and the Costs of Writing Contracts." *American Economic Review* 92(4): 798–817.

Beckett, Grace L. 1941. *The Reciprocal Trade Agreements Program.* New York: Columbia University Press.

Beitz, Charles. 1979. "Bounded Morality: Justice and the State in World Politics." *International Organization* 33: 405–424.

Beshkar, Mostafa, and Eric W. Bond. 2017. "Cap and Escape in Trade Agreements." *American Economic Journal: Microeconomics* 9(4): 171–202.

Beshkar, Mostafa, Eric W. Bond, and Youngwoo Rho. 2015. "Tariff Binding and Overhang: Theory and Evidence." *Journal of International Economics* 97(1): 1–13.

Bhagwati, Jagdish N., and V. K. Ramaswami. 1963. "Domestic Distortions, Tariffs and the Theory of the Optimum Subsidy." *Journal of Political Economy* 71(1): 44–50.

Blanchard, Emily J. 2010. "Reevaluating the Role of Trade Agreements: Does Investment Globalization Make the WTO Obsolete?" *Journal of International Economics* 82(1): 63–72.

Blum, Bernardo S., and Avi Goldfarb. 2006. "Does the Internet Defy the Law of Gravity?" *Journal of International Economics* 70: 384–405.

Bordoff, Jason E. 2008. "International Trade Law and the Economics of Climate Policy: Evaluating the Legality and Effectiveness of Proposals to Address Competitiveness and Leakage Concerns." Chap. 2 in *Brookings Trade Forum 2008/2009, Climate Change, Trade, and Competitiveness: Is a Collision Inevitable?* 35–68. Washington, DC: Brookings Institution Press.

Borjas, George J., and Valerie A. Ramey. 1995. "Foreign Competition, Market Power, and Wage Inequality." *Quarterly Journal of Economics* 110(4): 1075–1110.

Bourguignon, Francois. 2019. "Inequality, Globalization, and Technical Change in Advanced Countries: A Brief Synopsis." In *Meeting Globalization's Challenges*, edited by Luis Catao, Maurice Obstfeld, and Christine Lagarde, 94–110. Princeton, NJ: Princeton University Press.

Bown, Chad P. 2021. "The US–China Trade War and Phase One Agreement." *Journal of Policy Modeling* 43(4): 805–843.

Bown, Chad P., and Meredith A. Crowley. 2013. "Self-Enforcing Trade Agreements: Evidence from Time-Varying Trade Policy." *American Economic Review* 103(2): 1071–1090.

Bown, Chad P., and Meredith A. Crowley. 2016. "The Empirical Landscape of Trade Policy." In *Handbook of Commercial Policy*, vol. 1A, edited by Kyle Bagwell and Robert W. Staiger. Amsterdam: Elsevier.

Bown, Chad, and Jennifer A. Hillman. 2019. "WTO'ing a Resolution to the China Subsidy Problem." PIIE Working Paper No. 19–17.

Brenton, Paul, and Vicky Chemutai. 2021. *The Trade and Climate Change Nexus: The Urgency and Opportunities for Developing Countries*. Washington, DC: World Bank Group.

Broda, Christian, Nuno Limão, and David E. Weinstein. 2008. "Optimal Tariffs and Market Power: The Evidence." *American Economic Review* 98(5): 2032–2065.

Buchanan, Allen. 2003. *Justice, Legitimacy and Self-Determination*. Oxford: Oxford University Press.

Buchanan, Allen, and Robert O. Keohane. 2006. "The Legitimacy of Global Governance Institutions." *Ethics and International Affairs* 20(4): 405–437.

Burris, Scott, Evan D. Anderson, and Alexander C. Wagenaar. 2021. "The 'Legal Epidemiology' of Pandemic Control." *New England Journal of Medicine* 384 (May 27): 1973–1975.

Calabresi, Guido, and A. Douglas Melamed. 1972. "Property Rules, Liability Rules, and Inalienability: One View of the Cathedral." *Harvard Law Review* 85(6): 1089–1128.

Caliendo, Lorenzo, and Fernando Parro. 2015. "Estimates of the Trade and Welfare Effects of NAFTA." *Review of Economic Studies* 82 (1): 1–44.

Campolmi, Alessia, Harald Fadinger, and Chiata Forlati. 2014. "Trade Policy: Home Market Effect versus Terms-of-Trade Externality." *Journal of International Economics* 93: 92–107.

Campolmi, Alessia, Harald Fadinger, and Chiata Forlati. 2020. "Trade and Domestic Policies in Models with Monopolistic Competition." http://fadinger.vwl.uni-mannheim.de/Research_files/CFF_2018_1004.pdf.

Carbon Brief. 2017. "Mapped: The World's Largest CO2 Importers and Exporters." July 5. https://www.carbonbrief.org/mapped-worlds-largest-co2-importers-exporters.

Casalini, F., J. Lopez Gonzalez, and E. Moise. 2019. "Approaches to Market Openness in the Digital Age,"*OECD Trade Policy Papers* 219. http://dx.doi.org/10.1787/818a7498-en.

Castro, Daniel, and Alan McQuinn. 2015. "Cross-Border Data Flows Enable Growth in All Industries." Information Technology and Innovation Foundation, February. http://www2.itif.org/2015-cross-border-data-flows.pdf.

Cavallo, Alberto, Gita Gopinath, Brent Neiman, and Jenny Tang. 2021. "Tariff Pass-Through at the Border and at the Store: Evidence from US Trade Policy." *American Economic Review: Insights* 3(1): 19–34.

Charnovitz, Steve. 2014. "Green Subsidies and the WTO." Robert Schuman Centre for Advanced Studies Research Paper No. RSCAS 2014/93.

Cherniwchan, Jevan, and Nouri Najjar. 2022. "Do Environmental Regulations Affect the Decision to Export?" *American Economic Journal: Economic Policy* 14(2): 125–160.

Ciuriak, Dan. 2019. "World Trade Organization 2.0: Reforming Multilateral Trade Rules for the Digital Age." Policy Brief No. 152, Centre for International Governance Innovation, July.

Congressional Research Service. 2021. "Export Restrictions in Response to the COVID-19 Pandemic." *In Focus*, April 23.

Copeland, Brian R. 1990. "Strategic Interaction among Nations: Negotiable and Non-negotiable Trade Barriers." *Canadian Journal of Economics,* 23(1): 84–108.

Corden, Warner Max. 1974. *Trade Policy and Economic Welfare.* Oxford: Clarendon Press.

Costinot, Arnaud. 2008. "A Comparative Institutional Analysis of Agreements on Product Standards." *Journal of International Economics* 75: 197–213.

Costinot, Arnaud, Dave Donaldson, and Ivana Komunjer. 2011. "What Goods Do Countries Trade? A Quantitative Exploration of Ricardo's Ideas." *Review of Economic Studies* 79 (2): 581–608.

Costinot, Arnaud, Andres Rodriguez-Clare, and Ivan Werning. 2016. "Micro to Macro: Optimal Trade Policy with Firm Heterogeneity." NBER Working Paper No. 21989.

Costinot, Arnaud, Andres Rodriguez-Clare, and Ivan Werning. 2020. "Micro to Macro: Optimal Trade Policy with Firm Heterogeneity." *Econometrica* 88(6): 2739–2776.

Culbert J. 1987. "War-Time Anglo-American Talks and the Making of GATT." *World Economy* 10:381–407.

Curzon, Gerard. 1965. *Multilateral Commercial Diplomacy: The General Agreement on Tariffs and Trade and Its Impact on National Commercial Policies and Techniques.* London: Michael Joseph.

Dam, Kenneth W. 1970. *The GATT: Law and International Economic Organization.* Chicago: University of Chicago Press.

Deardorff, Alan V. 1990. "Should Patent Protection Be Extended to All Developing Countries?" *The World Economy* 13(4): 497–508.

Deardorff, Alan V. 2002. "Tariffication in Services." In *Issues and Options for U.S.-Japan Trade Policies,* edited by Robert M. Stern. Ann Arbor: University of Michigan Press.

Disdier, Anne-Celia, and Keith Head. 2008. "The Puzzling Persistence of the Distance Effect on Bilateral Trade." *Review of Economics and Statistics* 90(1): 37–48.

Douglass, Andrew Ian. 1972. "East-West Trade: The Accession of Poland to the GATT," *Stanford Law Review* 24(4): 748–764.

Drazen, Allan, and Nuno Limo. 2008. "A Bargaining Theory of Inefficient Redistribution Policies." *International Economic Review* 49(2): 621–657.

Eaton, Jonathan, and Samuel Kortum. 2002. "Technology, Geography, and Trade." *Econometrica* 70(5): 1741–1779.

Ederington, Josh. 2001. "International Coordination of Trade and Domestic Policies." *American Economic Review* 91(5): 1580–1593.

Erlanger, Steven. 2018. "Is the World Becoming a Jungle Again? Should Americans Care?" *New York Times*, September 22.

European Commission. 2013. "Guidance Document: The Concept of 'Lawfully Marketed' in the Mutual Recognition Regulation (EC) No 764/2008." Commission Working Document, August 16.

European Commission. 2016. "Elements for a New EU Strategy on China." Joint Communication to the European Parliament and the Council, Brussels, June 22.

European Parliament. 2018. "Mutual Recognition of Goods Lawfully Marketed in Another Member State." Briefing: Initial Appraisal of a European Commission Impact Assessment, March.

Fajgelbaum, Pablo, Pinelopi K. Goldberg, Patrick J. Kennedy, and Amit K. Khandelwal. 2020. "The Return to Protectionism." *Quarterly Journal of Economics* 135(1): 1–55.

Flaaen, Aaron, Ali Hortacsu, and Felix Tintelnot. 2020. "The Production Relocation and Price Effects of US Trade Policy: The Case of Washing Machines." *American Economic Review* 110(7): 2103–2127.

Fontagne, Lionel, Julien Gourdon, and Sebastien Jean. 2013. Transatlantic Trade: Whither Partnership, Which Economic Consequences?" CEPII Policy Brief No. 1, September.

Franck, Thomas. 1990. *The Power of Legitimacy Among Nations*. New York: Oxford University Press.

Freund, Caroline L., and Diana Weinhold. 2004. "The Effect of the Internet on International Trade." *Journal of International Economics* 62: 171–189.

Friedman, Thomas L. 2005. *The World Is Flat: A Brief History of the Twenty-First Century*. New York: Farrar, Straus and Giroux.

Gad, Mohamad O. 2003. "Impact of Multinational Enterprises on Multilateral Rule Making: The Pharmaceutical Industry and the TRIPS Uruguay Round Negotiations." *Law and Business Review of the Americas* 9(4): 667–697.

GATT. 1958. *Trends in International Trade: A Report by a Panel of Experts*. Geneva: General Agreement on Tariffs and Trade.

Goldfarb, Avi, and Daniel Trefler. 2019. "Artificial Intelligence and International Trade." In *The Economics of Artificial Intelligence: An Agenda*, edited by Ajay Agrawal, Joshua Gans, and Avi Goldfarb, 463–492. Cambridge, MA: National Bureau of Economic Analysis.

Goldfarb, Avi, and Catherine Tucker. 2019. "Digital Economics." *Journal of Economic Literature* 57(1): 3–43.

Grossman, Gene M. 2016. "The Purpose of Trade Agreements." In *Handbook of Commercial Policy*, vol. 1A, edited by Kyle Bagwell and Robert W. Staiger. Amsterdam: Elsevier.

Grossman, Gene M., and Elhanan Helpman. 1994. "Protection for Sale." *American Economic Review* 84 (September): 833–850.

Grossman, Gene M., Phillip McCalman, and Robert W. Staiger. 2021. "The 'New' Economics of Trade Agreements: From Trade Liberalization to Regulatory Convergence?" *Econometrica* 89(1): 215–249.

Haus, Leah. 1991. "The East European Countries and GATT: The Role of Realism, Mercantilism, and Regime Theory in Explaining East-West Trade Negotiations." *International Organization* 45(2): 163–182.

Head, Keith, and Thierry Mayer. 2014. "Gravity Equations: Workhorse, Toolkit, and Cookbook." In *Handbook of International Economics*, vol. 4, edited by Kenneth Rogoff, Elhanan Helpman, and Gita Gopinath, 131–195. Amsterdam: Elsevier.

Helpman, Elhanan, and Paul R. Krugman. 1989. *Trade Policy and Market Structure*. Cambridge: MIT Press.

Hillman, Jennifer. 2018. "The Best Way to Address China's Unfair Policies and Practices Is through a Big, Bold Multilateral Case at the WTO," *Testimony before the U.S.-China Economic and Review Security Commission Hearing on U.S. Tools to Address Chinese Market Distortions*, Friday June 8, Dirksen Senate Office Building, Washington, DC.

Hoda, Anwarul. 2001. *Tariff Negotiations and Renegotiations under the GATT and the WTO: Procedures and Practices*. Cambridge: WTO and Cambridge University Press.

Hoekman, Bernard. 2020. "WTO Reform Priorities Post–COVID-19." *East Asian Economic Review* 24(4): 337–348.

Hoekman, Bernard, and Michel Kostecki. 1995. *The Political Economy of the World Trading System: From GATT to WTO*. Oxford: Oxford University Press.

Hoekman, Bernard, and Petros C. Mavroidis. 2015. "Embracing Diversity: Plurilateral Agreements and the Trading System." *World Trade Review* 14(1): 101–116.

Hoekman, Bernard, and Charles Sabel. 2020. "Open Plurilateral Agreements, Global Spillovers and the Multilateral Trading System." Bertelsmann Stiftung Working Paper, March 25.

Hofmann, Claudia, Alberto Osnago, and Michele Ruta. 2017. "Horizontal Depth: A New Database on the Content of Preferential Trade Agreements." World Bank Policy Research Working Paper 7981, February.

Horn, Henrik, Giovanni Maggi, and Robert W. Staiger. 2010. "Trade Agreements as Endogenously Incomplete Contracts." *American Economic Review* 100(1): 394–419.

Horn, Henrik, and Asher Wolinski. 1988. "Bilateral Monopolies and Incentives for Merger," *RAND Journal of Economics* 19(3): 408–419.

Horn, Henrik, and Asher Wolinski. 1988. "Bilateral Monopolies and Incentives for Merger," *RAND Journal of Economics* 19(3): 408–419.

Hudec, Robert E. 1990. *The GATT Legal System and World Trade Diplomacy*. 2nd ed. New York: Praeger Publisher.

IMF. 2017. *World Economic Outlook: October*. Washington, DC: International Monetary Fund.

Interim Commission for the ITO. 1949. *The Attack on Trade Barriers: A Progress Report on the Operation of the General Agreement on Tariffs and Trade*. Geneva: ICITO. https://docs.wto.org/gattdocs/q/GG/SPEC/61-300.pdf.

Jackson, John H. 1969. *World Trade and the Law of GATT*. New York: Bobbs-Merrill.

Jackson, John H. 1997. *The World Trading System*. 2nd ed. Cambridge MA: MIT Press.

Jackson, John H. 2003. "Sovereignty-Modern: A New Approach to an Outdated Concept." *American Journal of International Law* 97:782–802.

Jawara, Fatoumata, and Aileen Kwa. 2003. *Behind the Scenes at the WTO: the Real World of International Trade Negotiations*. London: Zed Books.

Jensen, Michael Friis. 2020. *How Could Trade Measures Being Considered to Mitigate Climate Change Effect LDC exports?* Washington, DC: World Bank Group.

Johnson, Harry G. 1953–1954. "Optimum Tariffs and Retaliation." *Review of Economic Studies* 21(2): 142–153.

Johnston, George A. 1970. *The International Labour Organization: Its Work for Social and Economic Progress*. London: Europa Publications.

Kagan, Robert. 2018. *The Jungle Grows Back: America and Our Imperiled World*. New York: Alfred A. Knopf.

Keohane, Robert O. 1986. "Reciprocity in International Relations." *International Organization* 40(1): 1–27.

Kim, Sung Eun, and Yotam Margalit. 2021. "Tariffs as Electoral Weapons: The Political Geography of the US–China Trade War." *International Organization* 75 (Winter): 1–38.

Kletzer, Lori G. 2019. "Trade and Labor Market Adjustment: The Costs of Trade-Related Job Loss in the United States and Policy Responses." In *Meeting Globalization's Challenges*, edited by Luis Catao, Maurice Obstfeld, and Christine Lagarde, 167–178. Princeton, NJ: Princeton University Press.

Kostecki, Maciej. 1974. "Hungary and GATT." *Journal of World Trade Law* 8: 401–419.

Krasner, Stephen D. 1999. *Sovereignty: Organized Hypocrisy*. Princeton, NJ: Princeton University Press.

Krugman, Paul R. 2019. "Globalization: What Did We Miss?" In *Meeting Globalization's Challenges*, edited by Luis Catao, Maurice Obstfeld, and Christine Lagarde, 113–120. Princeton, NJ: Princeton University Press.

Laget, Edith, Alberto Osnago, Nadia Rocha, and Michele Ruta. 2019. "Deep Trade Agreements and Global Value Chains." Robert Schuman Centre for Advanced Studies Research Paper No. RSCAS 2019/86, October 1.

Lamy, Pascal. 2015. "The New World of Trade." *Jan Tumlir Lecture*. https://pascallamy.eu /2015/03/09/colloque-le-bien-commun-futur-paradigme-de-la-gouvernance-de-mers/.

Lamy, Pascal. 2016. "The Changing Landscape of International Trade." *The Frank D. Graham Lecture*. https://pascallamyeu.files.wordpress.com/2017/02/2016-04-07-lamy -princeton-graham-lecture-final.pdf.

Langan-Riekhof, Maria, Arex B. Avanni, and Adrienne Janetti. 2017. "Sometimes the World Needs a Crisis: Turning Challenges into Opportunities." Brookings Institution, April 10.

Lardy, Nicholas R. 2001. "Issues in China's WTO Accession." Brookings Institution Testimony, May 9.

Lasky, Julie. 2019. "A 3D Print-Out You Could Call Home." *New York Times*, November 8.

Lawrence, Robert Z. 2003. *Crimes and Punishments? Retaliation under the WTO.* Washington, DC: Institute for International Economics.

Leamer, Edward E. 2007. "A Flat World, a Level Playing Field, a Small World After All, or None of the Above? A Review of Thomas Friedman's *The World Is Flat.*" *Journal of Economic Literature* 45(1): 83–126.

Lendle, Andreas, Marcelo Olarreaga, Simon Schropp, and Pierre-Louis Vézina. 2016. "There Goes Gravity: eBay and the Death of Distance." *The Economic Journal* 126: 406–441.

Limão, Nuno, and Patricia Tovar. 2011. "Policy Choice: Theory and Evidence from Commitment via International Trade Agreements." *Journal of International Economics* 85(2): 186–205.

Lockwood, Ben, and John Whalley. 2010. "Carbon-Motivated Border Tax Adjustments: Old Wine in Green Bottles?" *The World Economy* 33(6): 810–819.

Ludema, Rodney D., and Anna Maria Mayda. 2013. "Do Terms-of-Trade Effects Matter for Trade Agreements? Theory and Evidence from WTO Countries." *Quarterly Journal of Economics* 128(4): 1837–1893.

Mackey, Tim K., and Bryan A. Liang. 2012. "Lessons from SARS and H1N1/A: Employing a WHO–WTO forum to Promote Optimal Economic–Public Health Pandemic Response." *Journal of Public Health Policy* 33(1): 119–130.

Maggi, Giovanni. 1999. "The Role of Multilateral Institutions in International Trade Cooperation." *American Economic Review* 89(1): 190–214.

Maggi, Giovanni. 2016. "Issue Linkage." In *Handbook of Commercial Policy*, vol. 1B, edited by Kyle Bagwell and Robert W. Staiger. Amsterdam: Elsevier.

Maggi, Giovanni, and Ralph Ossa. 2020. "Are Trade Agreements Good for You?" NBER Working Paper No. 27252.

Maggi, Giovanni, and Robert W. Staiger. 2011. "The Role of Dispute Settlement Procedures in International Trade Agreements." *Quarterly Journal of Economics* 126(1): 475–515.

Maggi, Giovanni, and Robert W. Staiger. 2015. "The Optimal Design of Trade Agreements in the Presence of Renegotiation." *American Economic Journal: Microeconomics* 7(1): 109–143.

Maggi, Giovanni, and Robert W. Staiger. 2018. "Trade Disputes and Settlement." *International Economic Review* 59(1): 19–50.

Martill, Benjamin, and Uta Staiger. 2018. "Cultures of Negotiations: Explaining Britain's Hard Bargaining in the Brexit Negotiations." Dahrendorf Forum IV, Working Paper No. 04, September 14.

Matthes, Jurgen. 2021. "How to Unlock the WTO Blockage and Why China Holds the Key." *CESifo Forum* 22(2): 17–21.

Mattoo, Aaditya, and Robert W. Staiger. 2020. "Trade Wars: What Do They Mean? Why Are They Happening Now? What Are the Costs?" *Economic Policy* 35(103): 561–584.

Mattoo, Aaditya, and Arvind Subramanian. 2013. *Greenprint: A New Approach to Cooperation on Climate Change.* Washington, DC: Center for Global Development.

Mayer, Wolfgang. 1981. "Theoretical Considerations on Negotiated Tariff Adjustments." *Oxford Economic Papers* 33:135–153.

McCalman, Phillip. 2021. "e-Globalization and Trade Agreements." University of Melbourne. Mimeo, May.

McLaren, John. 1997. "Size, Sunk Costs, and Judge Bowker's Objection to Free Trade." *American Economic Review* 87(3): 400–420.

Meade, James Edward. 1942. *A Proposal for an International Commercial Union*. E.C.(S)(42) 19. British Library of Political and Economic Science, London, July 28.

Meltzer, Joshua P. 2013. "The Internet, Cross-Border Data Flows and International Trade." *Issues in Technology Innovation* 22 (February).

Meltzer, Joshua P. 2019. "Governing Digital Trade." *World Trade Review* 18(S1): s23–s48.

National Research Council. 2016. *The Neglected Dimension of Global Security: A Framework to Counter Infectious Disease Crises*. Washington, DC: The National Academies Press. https://doi.org/10.17226/21891.

Nicita, Alessandro, Marcelo Olarreaga, and Peri Silva. 2018. "Cooperation in WTO's Tariff Waters?" *Journal of Political Economy* 126(3): 1302–1338.

Nordhaus, William. 2015. "Climate Clubs: Overcoming Free-Riding in International Climate Policy." *American Economic Review* 105(4): 1339–1370.

Orefice, Gianluca, and Nadia Rocha. 2014. "Deep Integration and Production Networks: An Empirical Analysis." *The World Economy* 37(1): 106–136.

Ortino, Matteo. 2007. "The Role and Functioning of Mutual Recognition in the European Market of Financial Services." *International and Comparative Law Quarterly* 56:309–338.

Ossa, Ralph. 2011. "A 'New Trade' Theory of GATT/WTO Negotiations." *Journal of Political Economy* 119:122–152.

Ossa, Ralph. 2014. "Trade Wars and Trade Talks with Data." *American Economic Review* 104(12): 4104–4146.

Pauwelyn, Joost. 2008. *Optimal Protection of International Law: Navigating between European Absolutism and American Volunteerism*. Cambridge: Cambridge University Press.

Penrose, Ernest F. 1953. *Economic Planning for the Peace*. Princeton, NJ: Princeton University Press.

Peter, Fabienne. 2017. "Political Legitimacy." In *The Stanford Encyclopedia of Philosophy* (Summer), edited by Edward N. Zalta. https://plato.stanford.edu/archives/sum2017/entries/legitimacy/.

Petersmann, Ernst-Ulrich. 1997. *The GATT/WTO Dispute Settlement System: International Law, International Organization and Dispute Settlement*. London: Kluwer Law International.

Posner, Eric A., and Alan O. Sykes. 2014. "Voting Rules in International Organizations." *Chicago Journal of International Law* 15: 195–228.

Rabkin, Jeremy. 1998. *Why Sovereignty Matters*. Washington, DC: AEI Press.

Rhodes, Carolyn. 1993. *Reciprocity, U.S. Trade Policy, and the GATT Regime*. Ithaca, NY: Cornell University Press.

Rodrik, Dani. 1987. "Policy Targeting with Endogenous Distortions: Theory of Optimum Subsidy Revisited." *Quarterly Journal of Economics* 102(4): 903–911.

Rodrik, Dani. 2020. "Putting Global Governance in Its Place." *The World Bank Research Observer* 35(1): 1–18.

Rosegrant, Susan. 2006. "Standing Up for Steel." In *Case Studies in US Trade Negotiations, Volume 2: Resolving Disputes*, edited by Charan Devereaux, Robert Lawrence, and Michael Watkins, 193–233. Washington, DC: Institute for International Economics.

Samuelson, Paul A. 1954. "The Theory of Public Expenditure." *Review of Economics and Statistics* 36(4): 386–389.

Schwartz, Warren F., and Alan O. Sykes. 2002. "The Economic Structure of Renegotiation and Dispute Resolution in the World Trade Organization." *Journal of Legal Studies* 31(1): S179–204.

Smith, Fiona, and Lorna Woods. 2005. "A Distinction without a Difference: Exploring the Boundary between Goods and Services in the World Trade Organization and the European Union." *Yearbook of European Law* 24(1): 463–510.

Staiger, Robert W. 2018. "On the Implications of Digital Technologies for the Multilateral Trading System." In *WTO World Trade Report*, Opinion Piece, 150. Geneva: World Trade Organization.

Staiger, Robert W. 2019. "Non-Tariff Measures and the WTO." In *The WTO and Economic Development*, edited by Ben Zissimos. Cambridge, MA: MIT Press.

Staiger, Robert W. 2021. "Does Digital Trade Change the Purpose of a Trade Agreement?" NBER Working Paper No. 29578, December.

Staiger, Robert W., and Alan O. Sykes. 2011. "International Trade, National Treatment, and Domestic Regulation." *Journal of Legal Studies* 40(1): 149–203.

Staiger, Robert W., and Alan O. Sykes. 2013. "Non-Violations." *Journal of International Economic Law* 16 (4): 741–775.

Staiger, Robert W., and Alan O. Sykes. 2017. "How Important Can the Non-Violation Clause Be for the GATT/WTO?" *American Economic Journal: Microeconomics* 9(2): 149–187.

Staiger, Robert W., and Alan O. Sykes. 2021. "The Economic Structure of Trade-in-Services Agreements." *Journal of Political Economy* 129(4): 1287–1317.

Staiger, Robert W., and Guido Tabellini. 1987. "Discretionary Trade Policy and Excessive Protection." *American Economic Review* 77(December): 823–837.

Sykes, Alan O. 1999a. "The (Limited) Role of Regulatory Harmonization in International Goods and Services Markets." *Journal of International Economic Law* 2:49–70.

Sykes, Alan O. 1999b. "Regulatory Protectionism and the Law of International Trade." *University of Chicago Law Review* 66:1–46.

Sykes, Alan O. 2000. "Regulatory Competition or Regulatory Harmonization? A Silly Question?" *Journal of International Economic Law* 3:257–264.

Sykes, Alan O. 2003. "The Safeguard Mess: A Critique of WTO Jurisprudence." *World Trade Review* 2(3): 261–295.

Sykes, Alan O. 2005. "Subsidies and Countervailing Measures." In *The World Trade Organization: Legal, Economic and Political Analysis*, edited by Patrick F. J. Macrory, Arthur E. Appleton, and Michael G. Plummer, 83–108., New York: Springer Science and Business Media.

Sykes, Alan O. 2020. "Short Supply Restrictions and International Trade: Economic Lessons from the Pandemic," *American Journal of International Law* 114(4): 647–656.

Tasca H. J. 1938. *The Reciprocal Trade Policy of the United States: A Study in Trade Philosophy.* Philadelphia: University of Pennsylvania Press.

The Economist. 2011. "Dead Man Talking: Ten Years of Trade Talks Have Sharpened Divisions, Not Smoothed Them." *The Economist*, April 28.

UNCTAD. 2019. *Digital Economy Report 2019.* Geneva: United Nations Conference on Trade and Development. https://unctad.org/system/files/official-document/der2019_en.pdf.

US Council of the International Chamber of Commerce. 1955. *The Organization for Trade Cooperation and the New G.A.T.T: A Statement of the Committee on Commercial Policy.* New York: The Chamber.

USITC. 2013. "Digital Trade in the U.S. and Global Economies, Part 1." Investigation No. 332-531, USITC Publication 4415, July.

USITC. 2014. "Digital Trade in the U.S. and Global Economies, Part 2." Investigation No. 332-540, USITC Publication 4485, August.

USTR. 2021. *2020 Report to Congress on China's WTO Compliance.* Washington, DC: Office of the United States Trade Representative.

Venables, Anthony. 1987. "Trade and Trade Policy with Differentiated Products: A Chamberlinian-Ricardian Model." *Economic Journal* 97:700–717.

Wallace, Benjamin B. 1933. "Tariff Bargaining." *Foreign Affairs* 1933:621–633.

Wallace-Wells, David. 2019. *The Uninhabitable Earth: Life after Warming.* New York: Tim Duggan Books.

Webster, Timothy. 2014. "Paper Compliance: How China Implements WTO Decisions." *Michigan Journal of International Law* 35(3): 525–578.

Weitzman, Martin L. 2014. "Can Negotiating a Uniform Carbon Price Help to Internalize the Global Warming Externality?" *Journal of the Association of Environmental and Resource Economists* 1(1/2): 29–49.

Willemyns, Ines. 2019. "GATS Classification of Digital Services: Does 'the Cloud' Have a Silver Lining?" *Journal of World Trade* 53(1): 59–82.

World Bank. 2020. "Trading for Development in the Age of Global Value Chains." *World Development Report.* Washington, DC: World Bank Group.

World Trade Organization. 1998a. *Japan: Measures Affecting Consumer Photographic Film and Paper.* WT/DS44, adopted April 22, para. 10.36.

World Trade Organization. 1998b. *Work Programme on Electronic Commerce.* Geneva: World Trade Organization.

World Trade Organization. 2001. *Accession of the People's Republic of China: Decision of 10 November 2001*. WT/L/432, November 23.

World Trade Organization. 2007. *World Trade Report. Six Decades of Multilateral Trade Cooperation: What Have We Learnt?* Geneva: World Trade Organization.

World Trade Organization. 2018. *World Trade Report—The Future of World Trade: How Digital Technologies Are Transforming Global Commerce.* Geneva: World Trade Organization.

World Trade Organization. 2020a. "Future Resilience to Diseases of Animal Origin: The Role of Trade," November 3. Geneva.

World Trade Organization. 2020b. "Standards, Regulations and COVID-19: What Actions Taken by WTO Members?" Information Note, December 4. Geneva.

WTO—see World Trade Organization.

Wu, Mark. 2016. "The 'China, Inc.' Challenge to Global Trade Governance." *Harvard International Law Journal* 57(2): 261–324.

Wu, Mark. 2017. "Digital Trade-Related Provisions in Regional Trade Agreements: Existing Models and Lessons for the Multilateral Trade System." RTA Exchange Overview Paper, Inter-American Development Bank, International Centre for Trade and Sustainable Development, November.

Zhou, Weihuan. 2019. *China's Implementation of the Rulings of the World Trade Organization*, London: Hart Publishing.

Zhou, Weihuan, and Mandy Meng Fang. 2021. "Subsidizing Technology Competition: China's Evolving Practices and International Trade Regulation in the Post-Pandemic Era." *Washington International Law Journal* 30(3).

Index